INTERNATIONAL ECONOMICS AND INTERNATIONAL ECONOMIC POLICY: A READER

Contributors

Anne O. Krueger
Bruce Scott
C. Fred Bergsten
Charles Collyns
Clemens F. J. Boonekamp
Dorothy Christelow
Frances Stewart
George C. Ceorgiou
George N. Hatsopoulos,
Jacob Frenkel
Jahangir Amuzegar
Jane Sneddon Little
Jeffrey Sachs
Joan E. Spero
John Zysman
Lawrence H. Summers
Martin Feldstein
Milton Friedman
Paul R. Krugman
Philip King
Raymond Vernon
Richard S. Weinert
Robert A. Mundell
Robert H. Girling
Stephen S. Cohen
Steven Dunaway
T. N. Srinivasan
The Economist
Willem H. Buiter
William R. Cline

INTERNATIONAL ECONOMICS AND INTERNATIONAL ECONOMIC POLICY:

A Reader

Philip King

San Francisco State University

McGraw-Hill Publishing Company
New York   St. Louis   San Francisco   Auckland   Bogotá   Caracas
Hamburg   Lisbon   London   Madrid   Mexico   Milan   Montreal
New Delhi   Oklahoma City   Paris   San Juan   São Paulo
Singapore   Sydney   Tokyo   Toronto

INTERNATIONAL ECONOMICS AND
INTERNATIONAL ECONOMIC POLICY: A Reader

2 3 4 5 6 7 8 9 0 DOCDOC   9 4 3 2 1 0

ISBN 0-07-034641-0

Desktop publishing by Jennifer Delyth Clough, Dryad Graphics.
The editor was Scott D. Stratford; the production supervisor was Phil
Galea.
The cover was designed by Amy E. Becker.
R. R. Donnelley & Sons Compay was printer and binder.

Library of Congress Cataloging-in-Publication Data

International economics and international economic
    policy.
    Includes bibliographical references.
    1. International trade.   2. International finance.
I. King, Philip, (date).
HF1379.I57   1990   382'.3   89-14534
ISBN 0-07-034641-0

Contents

III

Trade Policies and Developing Countries

IV

Economic Integration among Developed Countries

V

The Multinational Corporation and World Trade

VI

OPEC

VII

International Monetary Reform: is the Current System Working?

VIII

The IMF: Pro and Con

IX

Macro and Micro Adjustments after the Fall of the Dollar

X

The Debt Crisis: Diagnoses and Prescriptions

XI

Recent Developments in the Eurodollar Market

Acknowledgments

Preface

Not long ago, international trade and finance was considered an arcane subject which was confined to a tiny corner of the field of economics. Today, it is difficult to discuss any aspect of economic theory or policy, from macroeconomics to antitrust, without considering international markets. The reason for this trend is not hard to determine. The late eighties have been a time of great upheaval and uncertainty in the world economy. Even a casual observer of the events of the past few years cannot help but be struck by the significance of recent events such as the fall of the dollar, the debt crisis, the world stock market crash, and the enormous U.S. trade deficit. All of these events reflect the growing interdependence of the world economy as well as a breakdown of the clear guidelines established at Bretton Woods just after World War II.

The uncertainty surrounding international trade and international financial markets has brought about increasing interest in the subject from both inside and outside of academia. Economists have responded to the great demand for more analysis of the international economy with a steadily increasing supply of articles and books intended for people who do not necessarily have Ph.D.'s in the field.

This reader is designed to present a number of the most important of these articles between the covers of a single book. In putting together this reader I had several criteria in mind. First, each article had to be on a topic of key interest given the situation in today's international economy. Second, I searched for articles which were well written and interesting. I wanted articles with a clear theoretical framework and clear policy prescriptions spelled-out in terms which someone with a literacy in economics could understand. As it turned out, I found that the best articles were often those written by leaders in the field in such journals as: *Foreign Policy, Finance and Development* and *Foreign Affairs*. My third criterion was that all major sides of any particular debate be presented, preferably by their main proponents. Last of all, I wanted articles which discussed the institutions within which the policy debate occurs. (Too often in economics, academics discuss theories without relating them to the institutional framework within which they must be applied.)

These readings are designed to accompany an upper level undergraduate course or a masters/MBA level course in international economics, international business or international relations, though anyone with an interest in learning more about contemporary international economic issues should find all of these readings stimulating. I have collected these articles and presented them by topic, with a brief introduction to each section.

The increase in interest in international economics among college and MBA students in the last ten years has been phenomenal and I hope that this reader will satisfy their demands to go beyond the text book level analysis of international trade and finance and enter the real world of policy and decision making.

Philip King

I

FREE TRADE VERSUS PROTECTIONISM

For over forty years, much of the world's trade has been conducted under the rules of GATT, the General Agreement on Tariffs and Trade. GATT is an agreement under which participating countries agree to lower their trade barriers, in particular, their tariff barriers. When GATT was created, however, many loopholes in the agreement were left which allow countries which formally follow GATT to create substantial trade barriers. This section examines many of the types of trade barriers which exist in the world today. Many of these arrangements are referred to as nontariff barriers (NTB's) since they involve trade restrictions other than tariffs.

The first article below, "The cost of trade restraints" presents an analysis of one particular trade barrier: import quotas on Japanese automobiles sold in the United States. The article concludes that these quotas increased the price of automobiles substantially in the U.S.. In 1984, they estimate that the average price of a car was $600 higher than it would have been without the quotas; if one also examines the effect on quality, the authors conclude that the cost is over $1000 per car. The study also concludes that Japanese automobile producers have benefited from import quotas by several billion dollars.

The second article, "Voluntary Export Restraints," by Clemens Boonekamp, examines one of the most common import barriers Voluntary Export Restraints (VERs); Boonekamp argues that VERs represent a convenient loophole in GATT since they are essentially informal agreements between two countries. The article also points out that exporting countries may benefit from VER's since they collect the rents resulting from the higher prices. The selection by William Cline examines the history of the multifibre agreement, an agreement among many nations to restrict production of textiles by Asian and other textile exporting countries. Cline also examines the cost of these types of restraints.

Another important trade issue of the 80's was the enormous trade deficit run by the US and the corresponding trade surplus of Japan. The increasing awareness of Japan's economic power and its enormous trade surplus have lead to calls for protectionism in the US. There is growing concern that it is losing out as a major economic power and that the Japanese are ascending. Many have argued that Japan is not following the international rules of the game, formalized in GATT. Instead, the argument goes, the Japanese are running an essentially mercantilist policy, exporting as much as they can and importing as little as possible. Several bills proposed before the US Congress call for the retaliation against unfair trade by countries, like Japan, which run huge trade surpluses against the US.

Are the Japanese running a free trade policy or a protectionist policy? In terms of its formal barriers, the Japanese are no worse, possibly slightly better, than the US (except for agriculture which is mostly exempt from GATT). Many have argued that the most significant barriers to trade in Japan are implicit barriers which cannot be easily detected by economists. The fourth article, "Japan's intangible barriers to trade in manufactures" contends that while Japan has relatively few formal trade restrictions such as tariffs or quotas many of its other policies do in fact create significant trade barriers. The article focuses on three areas where substantial barriers occur: product standards, the distribution system, and favorable government procurement. The paper concludes that elimination of these barriers would increase Japan's imports by 7%, much of this being in the telecommunications industry, the computer industry, and industrial machinery.

The final selection, "Countertrade offsets, barter and buybacks," by Cohen and Zysman, points out that up to 25% of world trade is conducted under some form of modified barter arrangement as opposed to a market form of exchange. Cohen and Zysman describe the different type of arrangements and give examples.

1

The Cost of Trade Restraints. The Case of Japanese Automobile Exports to the United States

Charles Collyns and Steven Dunaway

In early 1981, the Japanese authorities imposed restraints on exports of automobiles to the United States in order to pre-empt more restrictive measures advocated by the U.S. automobile industry. Export restraints have been maintained since that time, although the quantitative limits were relaxed substantially in March 1985. Since the imposition of the restraints, the domestic share of sales has risen appreciably, reversing the previous downward trend. At the same time, new car prices have risen almost twice as rapidly as consumer prices in general. This paper assesses the degree to which developments in automobile sales and prices were affected by export quotas during the period 1981-84, when restraints were at their tightest. These estimates are used to assess the impact of the restraints on net revenues of the domestic automobile industry and foreign producers and to measure the costs to purchasers.

In theory, the restraints on Japanese automobile exports would be expected to affect prices, sales, and types of cars purchased in the United States. Under the export quotas, individual Japanese producers are constrained in the number of cars they can export to the United States. To maximize profits subject to this constraint, Japanese producers have an incentive to raise the prices they charge for given models. The action would reduce competitive pressures on U.S. producers and non-Japanese exporters and prompt them to raise their prices in turn, although probably by less than the increase in Japanese prices. Faced with higher prices on most models, U.S. purchasers may be expected to buy fewer new automobiles. Nevertheless, sales of domestic cars and imports of non-Japanese automobiles may increase as purchasers shift away from relatively more expensive Japanese cars.

In addition to these effects, the restraints on Japanese automobile exports may have had a significant impact on the average quality of cars purchased in the United States. To maximize the profits derived from each unit sale, Japanese producers are likely to shift the mix of cars exported to the United States toward larger or more luxurious models that can be sold at higher prices. Producers may also be expected to install more "optional" equipment in each unit. These actions would tend to raise the average quality of imported Japanese automobiles and to reduce the extent to which the quotas would curtail real expenditures on such cars.[1] The average transactions price of Japanese automobiles sold in the United States would tend to increase, reflecting the higher average quality of each unit. The average quality of domestic cars may also rise if Japanese automobiles are relatively closer substitutes for higher-quality rather than for lower-quality domestic automobiles.

The technique used in this paper to quantify the effects of the Japanese export restraints is to compare actual outcomes during the quota period with outcomes predicted by a small model of the U.S. automobile sector estimated over the period preceding the imposition of the restraints. The central assumption underlying this approach is that the Japanese export restraints were the dominant factor excluded from the model that affected the auto market during the quota period.

A major difference between the present study and other recent attempts to assess the impact of the Japanese export restraints[2] is that the model developed in this paper directly allows for the effects of the quotas on the average quality of automobiles purchased. The estimated effect of the the restraints on the average transactions price of new cars is divided between pure changes in price and changes in price associated with variations in the mix of automobiles being sold. The ability to distinguish between pure price effects and quality effects makes it possible to assess the welfare costs and income transfers resulting from the imposition of the export restraints.

RECENT DEVELOPMENTS IN THE U.S. AUTOMOBILE SECTOR

In the late 1970s, the U.S. automobile industry was faced with severe difficulties as sales dwindled and foreign imports took up an increasing share of the market. Japanese imports increased particularly rapidly, accounting for over 21 percent of total U.S. sales in 1980 compared with less that 10 percent five years earlier. Net income of U.S. producers shifted from a profit of $4.9 billion in 1978 to a loss of $4.2 billion in 1980, while production and employment were curtailed sharply. In June 1980, the industry filed a petition for import relief under the escape clause, on the grounds that both automobiles and trucks were being imported in such quantities as to damage the domestic industry.   The U.S. International Trade Commission ruled that, while increased imports were a contributing factor, the "substantial" causes of the industry's difficulties were a general decline in the demand for automobiles and a switch by consumers toward more fuel-efficient vehicles.   The Commission recommended that no restrictive action be taken.

Despite the Commission's decision, pressures for protection of the U.S. automobile industry remained intense and led to legislation being introduced in the Congress to restrict Japanese imports of passenger cars. In May 1981, the Japanese Government responded by announcing measures to restrain exports of automobiles to the United States for two years. These restraints limited Japanese exports to the United States to 1.68 million units in the year ended March 1982, about 8 percent below their 1980 level. Within this total, individual Japanese producers were allotted export quotas based on their market share prior to the imposition of the restraints. In the second year of the restraints, shipments were to be held at the first-year level, with a provision for an increase if there was a rise in domestic U.S. automobile sales; in the event, this increment did not materialize. Total sales in the United States continued to decline in 1981 and 1982, reflecting the general weakness of the U.S. economy and high interest rates. At the same time, the Japanese share of the U.S. market increased further, albeit at a much slower rate than in previous years.

In 1983 and 1984, demand for automobiles picked up sharply, reflecting a substantial decline in interest rates and the strengthening of economic activity in the United States. Domestic producers increased production in line with growing sales, and were able to achieve record profits after several years of weak earnings. The restraints on Japanese car exports were extended for third and fourth years; the ceiling was held fixed in the third year and raised 10 percent in the fourth year to 1.85 million units.[3] Sales of Japanese automobiles remained roughly unchanged in this period, and the market share of imports from Japan declined significantly, dropping to 18 1/4 percent in 1984.

In early 1985, the U.S. authorities judged that the domestic automobile industry had been able to adjust to import competition and announced that they would not ask Japan to extend the restraints. Nevertheless, the Japanese Government decided to extend the restraints for two additional years through March 1987. In this period, the ceiling was raised by 24 percent to 2.3 million units a year, while the export shares allotted to individual producers were reallocated to increase the shares of producers that previously had received relatively small shares. In early 1987, the export restraints were extended for a further year without an increase in the export ceiling.

The record levels of net income achieved in 1983 and 1984 by U.S. automakers were earned on sales volumes similar to those in 1980, when the automobile industry incurred unprecedented losses. In part, this turnaround reflected efforts made by the industry to control production and inventory costs. Capital spending by the industry was exceptionally high during 1979-81, although it dropped somewhat in 1982-84; much of this investment was directed toward raising labor productivity as well as improving product quality. In conjunction with this investment, employment was cut back sharply while increases in hourly compensation were moderated by union wage concessions in 1981-82. As a result of these measures, the rate of increase in unit labor costs fell substantially, and was well below that in the nonfarm business sector as a whole during 1981-84.

Despite improvements in the cost performance of the U.S. automobile sector, the gap between production costs in the United States and Japan did not appear to narrow significantly. Hourly compensation of automobile production workers in Japan (expressed in terms of U.S. dollars) rose at a somewhat slower rate than hourly compensation in the U.S. industry during 1981-84, although there is some evidence that productivity may have improved somewhat more rapidly in the United States than in Japan. The Japanese cost advantage in producing a subcompact model in 1984 was estimated to be $1,500-2,500, roughly the same as in 1980.[4]

A dramatic feature of the period 1981-84 was the rapid increase in automobile prices, which far exceeded the rate of consumer price inflation. The average transactions price of new passenger cars jumped by 17 $1/2$ percent in 1981 alone and increased by 49 percent during 1981-84 as a whole; the consumer price index for all items (CPI) rose by only

26 percent over the period. Much of the increase in automobile prices during this period apparently reflected an upgrading in the average quality of cars sold. The new-car component of the CPI, which is adjusted for quality changes in an attempt to isolate pure changes in price,[5] rose by only 18 percent during 1981-84. The 31 percentage point difference between the rate of increase in average transactions prices and the CPI for new automobiles during this period would imply an unusually large change in average car quality. By way of comparison, during 1975-79 average transactions prices increased by only 1 $1/2$ percentage points a year faster than the new-car component of the CPI.

A significant portion of the apparent upgrading in the quality of cars purchased during 1981-84 resulted from compliance with federal safety and emission regulations. It has been estimated that compliance with such regulations may have raised production costs by about $700 a unit during the period, which would imply an increase in transactions prices of about 10 percent (Crandall, 1984). The remaining increase in quality would be accounted for by such factors as a shift in the mix of purchases toward larger vehicles and increased installation of factory — or dealer — installed options. In this regard, there was a shift in the composition of sales away from compact and subcompact models toward intermediate and larger models during 1981-84.

Transactions prices of imported automobiles have generally increased more rapidly than those of domestic cars; import prices rose by 61 percent from 1980 to 1984 while domestic prices rose by 45 percent. In part, the rapid growth in import prices resulted from a substantial change in the composition of European imports away from small automobiles, reflecting a shift toward U.S. production by a major manufacturer and the declining popularity of several models.[6] The prices of Japanese automobile imports into the United States also increased considerably after the imposition of quotas, although at a lesser pace than non-Japanese imports. Data available from the U.S. Department of Commerce suggest that transactions prices of Japanese automobiles increased by 38 percent from 1980 to 1984.[7] Part of the rise in transactions prices of Japanese cars would be accounted for by an increase in the average quality of cars sold. In this regard, there was a marked shift in the mix of sales toward medium — and high-priced models[8] and a significant rise in both factory — and dealer-installed options.   However, substantial increases in list prices on standard models and in dealer markups also took place.

WELFARE COSTS OF JAPANESE EXPORT RESTRAINTS

The estimates of the effects of the Japanese export restraints on prices, sales, and imports can be used to quantify the overall costs imposed by these restraints on automobile purchasers in the United States and the associated benefits to domestic and foreign producers.

COSTS TO PURCHASERS

The implications for the welfare of domestic purchasers stemming from the pure price increase induced by the quotas are illustrated in the accompanying figure.[9] The line DD relates the demand for real expenditures on automobiles to the CPI for new cars. Pa and Qa are the actual values of the CPI for new cars and total real expenditures on new cars; Pa and Qp are the values predicted for these variables in the absence of the restraints; Qus is the actual value of real expenditures on domestic new automobiles. The welfare cost to domestic purchasers arising from the effect of the export restraints on prices is then represented by the sum of the areas A, B and C. Areas A and B represent transfers from purchasers to the domestic industry and foreign producers, respectively, arising from the pure increase in prices, while area C represents a deadweight loss.

The export restraints are estimated to have raised the level of the CPI for new cars throughout 1981-84. This index was 6 percent higher in 1984 than it would have been otherwise, implying that the average price of a standard passenger model was raised by $617. On the basis of these figures, domestic purchasers of automobiles were more than $6 $1/2$ billion worse off in 1984 owing to higher prices, with a deadweight loss of $130 million. Over the four-year period 1981-84, the export restraints cost domestic purchasers $16 $3/4$ billion, with a deadweight loss of $280 million.

These estimates of the welfare loss to purchasers reflect only the pure price effects of the export restraints. In addition, purchasers would be worse off to the extent that the quotas restricted the effective range of choice available to them. It was estimated above that the export restraints may have led suppliers to sell large models with more optional equipment, and that this effect may have raised the transactions price of the average automobile sold by over $1,000 in 1984. On this basis, purchasers spent an extra $10 $3/4$ billion on increasing quality in 1984 and $25 billion during the quota period.

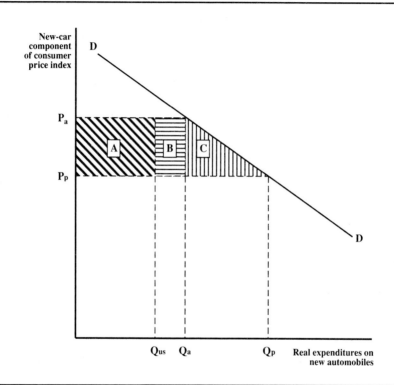

The welfare cost of this additional spending on quality would depend on the degree to which purchasers were willing to substitute quality for quantity. This elasticity of substitution has not been estimated; however, the additional welfare cost to purchasers owing to reduced choice may have been substantial.

BENEFITS TO DOMESTIC INDUSTRY

Estimates of the transfer from purchasers to the domestic industry (and foreign producers) depend on the assumption made concerning the distribution of the pure price effects of the export restraints. Under the assumption that the quotas led to equivalent pure price effects on domestic and imported cars, the U.S. automobile sector is estimated to have gained $5 billion in 1984 and almost $12 $1/4$ billion over 1981-84; this transfer from automobile purchasers is represented by area *A* in the figure. Under the alternative assumption, according to which pure price increases for domestic automobiles are estimated to have been less than those for imports, the income transfer to domestic producers was $1 $1/4$ billion in 1984 and $6 billion over 1981-84.[10]

BENEFITS TO FOREIGN PRODUCERS

Foreign producers benefited from the pure price effects of the export restraints by over $1 $1/2$ billion in 1984 and by almost 4 $1/2$ billion in 1981-84, assuming that the pure price effects of the quotas were the same for imported and domestic automobiles. Under this assumption, Japanese producers are estimated to have received an income transfer of $1 billion in 1984 and $2 $3/4$ billion over the 1981-84 period. Making the alternative assumption of equal quality effects, foreign producers are estimated to have received a transfer of nearly $5 $1/2$ billion in 1984 and a total of $10 $1/2$ billion over 1981-84, of which Japanese producers received $5 $1/4$ billion in 1984 and $9 $3/4$ billion in 1981-84.

It should be noted that these aggregate numbers are likely to obscure considerable divergences in the effects of the quotas on individual Japanese producers. Real expenditures on imports are likely to have been adversely affected for all Japanese companies, while the gain in profit owing to the pure price effects of the quotas would mainly accrue to those with established market shares prior to 1981, since they were able to obtain the bulk of the export rights to the United States.

CONCLUSIONS

According to the analysis presented in this paper, the restraints on exports of Japanese automobiles to the United States have had substantial effects on sales and prices. The precise quantitative estimates provided need to be treated with caution, given the difficulties inherent in modeling the U.S. automobile sector, but they do provide a broad indication of the magnitude of these effects. Concerning prices, the results suggest that the average transactions price for new automobiles would have increased by 27 percent during the period 1981-84 in the absence of the quotas, compared with an actual increase of nearly 50 percent. These higher prices resulted from a combination of a pure price increase and a shift in the composition of sales toward larger units with more factory or dealer-installed optional equipment. As a result of the quotas, real expenditures on new cars during 1981-84 were reduced by more that 3 percent and sales by 4 million units, while the value of expenditures on new cars was raised by $5 $1/4$ billion, as increases in average transactions prices more than offset the effects of the restraints on volumes sold. The restraints bolstered the domestic industry's market share and raised real expenditures on domestic models by 2-4 percent and the value of such expenditures by over $17 $3/4$ billion during 1981-84. At the same time, expenditures on Japanese automobiles were 23-29 percent lower in real terms and nearly $15 billion lower in value terms.

The rise in car prices (adjusted to exclude price increases owing to changes in the quality of automobiles purchased) induced by the export restraints is estimated to have cost purchasers $16 $3/4$ billion during the period 1981-84. Of this increase in purchasers' costs, $6-12 billion represented a transfer to the U.S. automobile industry. The remaining $5-11 billion is accounted for by a transfer to foreign producers and a deadweight loss to purchasers, and can be considered to be a measure of the loss to the domestic economy as a whole stemming from the restraints on Japanese exports. The net loss may in fact have been larger if account is taken of the loss in welfare stemming from the reduced choice facing purchasers, reflected in the significant increase in the average quality of automobiles purchased during the period.

The 2-4 percent increase in real expenditures on domestic automobiles induced by the quotas during 1981-84 is estimated to have boosted employment in the U.S. automobile sector by 40,000-75,000 man-years. These figures imply that the net cost to the economy of each job created by the quotas was about $110,000 to $145,000.

Notes

1   See Rodriguez (1979) for a formal treatment of the effects of quotas on the quality of imports.
2   See, for example, Wharton Econometric Forecasting Associates (1983); Crandall (1984); and United States (1985).
3   Sales of Japanese cars in the United States exceeded the export quota level as inventories were run down.
4   For further information on comparative cost and productivity movements in the U.S. and Japanese industries, see United States (1984).
5   The CPI for new passenger cars is a fixed-weight price index that is adjusted for changes in standard equipment mandated by federal government regulations or made at the manufacturer's discretion by using data for the production costs of such equipment changes.
6   Direct information on the extent to which the rise in transactions prices of automobile imports reflected a rise in average quality is not available; the CPI for new passenger cars is not broken down between domestic and imported automobiles.
7   This figure may be somewhat low given that the unit value index of passenger cars imported from Japan rose by 55 percent during the same period. It might be expected that transactions prices of Japanese cars would rise more rapidly than import unit values during the quota period, as the latter statistic would not include any effect of the quotas on dealer markups or dealer-installed options. An overstatement of the average transactions price in 1980 and 1981, related to problems in estimating dealer premiums for discounts from list prices, may help to explain the slower rise in transactions prices than import unit values in 1981 and 1982.
8   The share of subcompact models in total sales of Japanese cars declined from 67 percent in 1980 to 48 percent in 1984. During the same period, the share of compact models in sales of Japanese cars increased from 21 percent to 33 percent, and the share of luxury models rose from 12 percent to 18 percent (United States, 1985).
9   As drawn, the figure is based on the assumption that the pure price effects of the quotas on domestic and imported cars are the same.
10 Estimates presented here are based on the assumption that the automobile industry achieves constant returns to scale in production. If the industry in fact achieves increasing returns to scale, then the benefits to producers would be somewhat higher than the figures presented here.

2

Voluntary Export Restraints

Clemens F. J. Boonekamp

Successive rounds of multilateral trade negotiations under the aegis of the General Agreement on Tariffs and Trade (GATT) have progressively reduced the importance of tariffs as barriers to trade. This, however, has not been matched by a corresponding liberalization of international trade. Since the early 1970s, with the relatively slow rates of growth and the rise in surplus capacity in many countries, protectionist pressures have steadily built up, especially in industrialized countries whose international competitiveness in traditional industries has declined, in particular vis-à-vis Japan and the newly industrializing countries of Asia. As a result, nontariff barriers have become more prevalent, to the point that they currently rival, if not exceed, tariffs as impediments to trade.

Voluntary export restraints (VERs) are now a common form of nontariff barrier, having grown in number and spread, in recent years, from textiles, clothing, steel, and agriculture to automobiles, electronic products, and machine tools. This article discusses the basic elements of VERs, why they are employed, and their economic consequences.

WHAT ARE VERS?

A VER is a measure by which the government or an industry in the importing country arranges with the government or the competing industry in the exporting country for a restriction on the volume of the latter's exports of one or more products. By this definition, the term VER is a generic reference for all bilaterally agreed measures to restrain exports. Strictly speaking, however, a VER is an action unilaterally taken and administered by the exporting country and is "voluntary" in the sense that the country has a formal right to eliminate or modify it. Usually a VER arises because of pressure from an importing country; it can then be thought of as "voluntary" only in the sense that the exporting country may prefer it to alternative trade barriers that the importing country might use. Further, in a noncompetitive, especially oligopolistic, industry exporting firms might find it to their advantage to negotiate a VER, which is then truly "voluntary."

A VER that consists of a government-to-government agreement is normally referred to as an orderly marketing arrangement and often specifies export management rules, consultation rights, and the monitoring of trade flows. In some countries, notably the United States, orderly marketing arrangements are legally distinct from a VER as strictly defined. Agreements which involve industry participation are often referred to as voluntary restraint arrangements. The distinction between these forms of VER is largely legal and terminological and has little bearing on the economic impact of VERs.

A typical VER limits the supply of exports, by commodity type, by country, and by volume. GATT Articles, which are concerned with governmental actions affecting trade, prohibit export restraints under normal circumstances; when permitted, they must be nondiscriminatory and applied only through duties, taxes, and charges. However, the involvement of governments in VERs is not always clear. Also, VERs do not always have firm market-sharing provisions; they may, for example, be in the form of an export forecast and thus become cautionary in nature. For these reasons, VERs fall into a "grey area" in that there can be doubt as to their illegality under GATT. Further, parties to a VER are unlikely to request a finding under the GATT's dispute settlement procedures — they have never done so — while third parties can often appear to benefit from a VER and may therefore be reluctant to initiate dispute procedures. Finally, signatories to the Code on Subsidies and Countervailing Duties Code that resulted from the Tokyo Round of trade negotiations seem to have acquired legal powers to negotiate VERs. It is in these respects that the decision of the GATT Council of Representatives in 1987 to establish a dispute panel to examine the Japan-U.S. semiconductor agreement is important.

WHY ARE VERS INTRODUCED?

Broadly speaking, restrictive trade measures are taken usually for two purposes: to protect or improve the balance of payments situation, and to provide relief for industries adversely affected by foreign competition, in principle allowing them time to undertake the adjustments necessary to regain external competitiveness. VERs are employed for this latter purpose and, compared to other forms of protectionism, offer several advantages from the viewpoint of the protecting country.

Under GATT rules, safeguard provisions exist for the temporary, emergency protection of domestic industries injured by import competition. Such safeguard actions, however, involve negotiating compensation with the countries affected by the measures. These negotiations can be difficult and may not succeed. In that case, the protecting country risks retaliation by the exporting country. In either case — compensation or retaliation — the exports of the country taking the safeguard action my suffer. VERs, on the other hand, have built-in compensation in the form of rents (i.e., higher earnings arising out of the scarcity of a product). This makes acceptance by the exporting source more likely and retaliation less probable.

The importing country, in negotiating a VER, tends to avoid the frequently lengthy, public, and often multilateral, debate that invariably precedes other forms of protectionism, such as increasing tariffs or imposing quotas. In such a debate, the cost of the protective measure is likely to become more clearly recognized, making the action politically expensive and risky. A VER then has the advantage that, as an action taken by a foreign source, a domestic legislative struggle may be avoided; it often can be negotiated quickly without its costs becoming obvious. Further, in the context of exports which are, or are suspected of being, subsidized, the domestic authorities can bypass the often expensive and time-consuming process of a countervailing-duty investigation by coming to a VER agreement with the exporter. Finally, it can be argued that a VER, by addressing the source of the problem, that is the one or few low-cost suppliers disrupting the domestic industry, obviates the need for wider action that could harm third countries, as would be the case with a nondiscriminatory import quota of equivalent import-reducing effect (see below). For any of these reasons domestic policy makers often prefer a VER to alternative measures; it offers relatively quick, politically inexpensive assistance to an industry threatened by import competition.

A VER can also be attractive to the exporting country. As indicated above, it offers rents which, at least in the short run, are windfall gains to the extent that demand in the rest of the world is elastic so that terms of trade losses are minimal or zero. This can be important relative to alternative trade barriers that the importing country might take; tariff revenues, for example, accrue to the government that levies them. Also, VERs can serve to assure the exporter of market access to the importing country, terminate the uncertainty inherent in a countervailing-duty investigation, and provide the exporting government with an element of control over its domestic industry. These factors suggest that when faced with the probability of protection by the importing country, particularly if it is an important market for other products, the exporter might agree readily to a VER.

PREVALENCE OF VERS

Quantitative export restraints first seem to have appeared in 1935 when Japan was induced to limit its textile exports to the United States. However, only in the past decade or so have they come into widespread use. The accompanying table lists almost 100 major, known VERs. The actual number may well be greater as there are reported to be various undisclosed industry-to-industry and government-to-industry arrangements. Of the known number of VERs, 55 restrict exports to the European Community or its individual member states, and 32 restrain exports to the United States. In general, VERs have been introduced to protect industries in OECD markets where certain developing countries, East European countries, or Japan have become serious competitors. Indeed, the exports of these countries are restrained by about 80 VERs.

The above numbers do not include the Multi-Fibre Arrangement (MFA), which together with its predecessor, the Long-Term Arrangement on Cotton Textiles (1962-72), has been the model for VERs. The MFA is a negotiated, multilateral departure from GATT based on the principle that industrial countries, which are the main importers of textiles, require special protection against "market disruption" by lower-cost, normally developing-country, exports. Under its aegis a multiplicity of bilateral export restraint agreements have been concluded, covering approximately 50 percent of trade in textiles and clothing. In addition, as the table notes, there are 11 known VERs in this sector outside the scope of the MFA. As a result a considerable portion of world trade in textiles and clothing is managed, and thus not subject to the normal forces of international trade.

Table 1

Prevalence of VERs

Major known VERs (excluding the MFA)[1]		Restrained exporters (by number of arrangements)[2]	Protected markets (by number of arrangements)[2]
Total:	99	Japan (24), Korea (14), Brazil (4); ODCs (21); OICs (20); E. Eur. (16)	EC (55)[3]; USA (32); (Canada, Japan, Norway (12)
Steel	39	EC (4); OICs (12); DCs (12); E. Eur. (11)	USA (25); EC (14)
Agricultural products	17	DCs (6); E. Eur. (5)	EC (16); Canada (1)
Automobiles and transport equipment	13	Japan (11); Korea (2)	EC (9); USA (1); OICs (3)
Textiles and clothing	11	Korea (2); ODCs (9)	USA (4); EC (3); OICs (4)
Electronic products	7	Japan (6); Korea (1)	EC (6); USA (1)
Footwear	5	Korea (3); Japan (1); Taiwan (1)	EC (2); OICs (3)
Machine tools	3	Japan (3)	EC (2); USA (1)
Other	4	Korea (3); ICs (1)	EC (3); Norway (1)

Sources: GATT Secretariat, and M. Kostecki, "Export Restraint Arrangements," *World Economy*, forthcoming.

[1] VERs known to be in place in late 1986.

[2] EC is the European Community; E. Eur. is East Europe; ODCs are other developing countries; OICs are other industrialized countries; DCs are developing countries; ICs are industrialized countries. The term "other" in ODC and OIC refers to countries other than those identified in the particular classification (e.g., OICs under "footwear" refer to all industrial countries other than EC).

[3] Including 2 arrangements.

Apart from textiles and clothing, steel is the product category most heavily affected by VERs. Since the first restraint in this sector was negotiated in 1968 between the United States and several European and Japanese exporters, about a quarter of the total trade in steel has come under VERs, affecting exports from nearly all the major third country suppliers to the United States and the European Community, as well as exports from the European Community to the United States. Exports of agricultural products are also restrained by VERs, principally from the more efficient producers, such as Australia and Argentina, to the

European Community. In automobiles and transport equipment, as well as in electronic products and machine tools, Japanese exporters limit their sales to both the European Community and the United States, while in footwear a number of OECD markets are protected by VERs with Korean exporters.

According to one calculation, in 1984 some 10 percent of total world trade, and 12 percent of non-fuel trade, was covered by VERs ("Export Restraint Arrangements" by M. Kostecki, *World Economy*, forthcoming). This study also estimated that in the same year approximately 38 percent of Japanese exports to the European Community and 32 percent of Japanese exports to the United States were covered by VERs. Other commentators estimate that in 1983 about 11 percent of world trade in developing countries' manufactured goods was restrained by VERs. Further, the percentages appear to have risen rapidly in the early 1980s. By one estimate the share of exports of the newly industrialized countries of Asia and Japan affected by VERs rose from some 15 percent in 1980 to about 32 percent in 1983.

THE ECONOMICS OF VERS

In general, the effect of VERs is to reduce the level of imports and thus increase the price of the product in question in the importing country. This will happen as the normally low-cost, but now restricted, foreign suppliers raise their export prices to capture the rents created by the VER. The higher price will normally encourage an increase in domestic output of the product.

However, even if the VER is set at the free trade level of imports, in an oligopolistic industry prices can rise because a VER fundamentally changes the nature of competition in the affected industry. Given that the exporting industry (or country) administers the VER, producers in the protecting country become "price leaders" relative to those in the exporting country: any increase in the price by domestic producers must result in an appropriate rise in the price of the imported substitute if the VER is to be observed. In these circumstances the profits of both the domestic and foreign firms increase. Consumers, will, of course, lose. Producers in the exporting country can be expected to agree willingly to a proposed VER, particularly since it can increase their share of the importing country's market, if the demand for the domestic product is more responsive to changes in the price of the home product than to changes in the price of the imported substitute. The VER then protects domestic producers, by raising their profits, but does not protect domestic production.

These results become less tenable the larger the number of firms in the industry. First, it becomes more difficult to persuade all domestic firms to be part of the price-leadership role; some may prefer to increase market share by price competition. Second, if not all foreign firms are covered by a VER, they, too, may seek a larger market share. Thus the larger the number of firms in the industry, the more likely that the VER will need to be set at an import-reducing level if the domestic price is to rise and encourage higher local production levels. However, the oligopolistic example does point to the important conclusion that, regardless of the number of firms in the industry, a VER provides an incentive of collusion between firms to change the nature of competition. This creates vested interests in both the importing and exporting country. A VER may encourage, therefore, what anti-monopoly legislation is meant to forestall.

Price rises due to VERs can be substantial. In a recent study of the impact of the VER on Japan's automobile exports to the United States ("The Cost of Trade Restraints" by Charles Collyns and Steven Dunaway, IMF *Staff Papers*, March 1987) it was estimated that the average price of a car sold in the United States in 1984 was about $1,650, or 17 percent, higher than it would have been in the absence of the VER. Of this estimated increase about $1,030 reflected improvements in quality. Exporters under a volume constraint have an incentive to upgrade the quality of their product on the restricted market in order to maximize profit per unit sold. Unrestricted foreign suppliers and domestic producers are likely to follow suit if their products are relatively close substitutes for the improved, export-restrained, product. In the above study the pure price effect was some $620 per car in 1984; this cost U.S. consumers a total of $6.6 billion.

VERs can distort trade and production in a number of ways. First, in the importing country the market share of exporters not subject to VERs can increase. The price of the product subject to the VER in the importing country is likely to exceed the world price; the latter may in fact fall, particularly if the importing country's market is large and the VER well enforced. In these circumstances, non-restrained suppliers may divert exports to the protected market, thus distorting the pattern of trade. At the time of the 1977 orderly marketing arrangement for color television sets between Japan and the United States, Japan accounted for some 90 percent of U.S. imports of such sets. Two years later Japan's share had fallen to about 50 percent, while that of the Republic of Korea and Taiwan, Province of China had grown significantly. Subsequently the OMA was extended to Korea and Taiwan.

Second, there may be an incentive for new firms in both the importing and other countries to enter the affected industry, making investments that might not have been efficient at the free trade level of imports. Third, the existing VER-affected firms in the exporting country may seek to circumvent their constraints by exporting via third countries. Finally, foreign suppliers may take to exporting, or increasing exports of, close substitutes for the VER-protected products to the importing market.

If VERs spread so as to cover imports of a product from all sources, the VER-system then resembles an import quota. The process, however, is quite different. A quota is normally applied on a global basis; it is nondiscriminatory, usually being allocated either on a "first-come, first-served" basis or by quota-shares in accord with the previous pattern of import shares. VERs are bilaterally negotiated, normally with one or a few suppliers. They are discriminatory, therefore, with export volumes depending on negotiation strength. They can bias the pattern of trade of the VER-covered product to the importing country against the more efficient exporters and may create investment signals for producers in third countries that could turn out to be wrong. As such, VERs can lead to larger efficiency losses than a globally applied quota of equivalent import-reducing volume.

As already indicated, VERs can — and have — spread from country to country and from product to product. In this respect their demonstration effect can be important. Moreover, as previously noted, a VER tends to lower the world price of the product, increasing demand in third countries, which might be satisfied by imports of the product. This effect could be reinforced to the extent that the VER-covered exporters are able to use their rents from the protected market to win market share in nonprotected countries. These factors may help to persuade third countries, especially those that manufacture the product in question, also to negotiate VERs. Eventually, as in textiles, clothing, and steel, a VER network could effectively result in a globally managed market-sharing arrangement.

VERs tend to create rents, which can be substantial, for foreign producers. The OECD has estimated that the annual transfer from OECD countries to exporters of textiles and clothing in the newly industrialized countries of Asia is at least $2 billion under MFA bilateral export restraint arrangements. In the above-noted study of the VER on Japan's auto exports to the United States, it was calculated that Japanese exporters, on pure price effects alone, "earned" rents of $1 billion in 1984; the total transfer to foreign suppliers was $1.67 billion, indicating that third-country exporters not restrained by the VER may have benefited from it. M. Kostecki, using a VER tariff-equivalent method, has estimated that the rent transfers resulting from VERs worldwide in 1984 could have been as much as $27 billion.

Trade policy makers are not unaware of the effects discussed above, in particular of efficiency losses in the allocation of resources. This is one reason why VERs are generally negotiated to have a relatively short lifespan. Nevertheless, VERs can be a tempting form of protection. Once they are in place, vested interests may work against their removal.

DO VERS WORK?

The answer to this question depends on whether a VER serves its purpose of safeguarding employment and promoting adjustment in the protected sector, and, if so, at what price. These aims might not be consistent with each other. Modernization to regain competitiveness often entails switching to a more capital-intensive mode of production. Similarly, if a VER implies a political constraint to retain employment, adjustment by the industry might be delayed. This might happen in any event as the VER, akin to other forms of protectionism, reduces competitive pressures and makes it easier to continue production with outdated and inefficient technology. The industry then retains low-quality staff, displacing potentially higher-skilled employees who could make a greater contribution to raising real incomes.

More generally, by raising domestic profits VERs can make resources available for adjustment. This appears to have happened in the U.S. automobile industry and in certain parts of the textile and steel industries in both the European Community and the United States. However, in these sectors the VER protection has also afforded the exporters an opportunity to upgrade the quality of their products. The domestic industries thus face increased competition in precisely those areas where they might otherwise have had a comparative advantage.

A recent GATT report shows that VERs have not prevented a loss of employment in the textile, clothing, and steel industries in the protecting countries. In the period 1973-84, employment in the steel sectors of the European Community and the United States declined by 42 percent and 54 percent, respectively; in textiles and clothing the declines were 46 percent and 43 percent, respectively, in the European Community, and 22 percent and 18 percent, respectively, in the United States. Modernization, gains in productivity, and changes in macroeconomic conditions dominated the employment situation in these sectors, as they did in the U.S. automobile industry where employment fell by some 250,000 jobs in the early 1980s. It is possible, however, that employment in these sectors would have fallen further in the absence of protective measures. Thus, by one estimate between 40,000-75,000 jobs were saved in the U.S. automobile industry during 1981-84 as a result of the VER on Japan's car exports to the United States. Similarly it has been calculated that a 50 percent relaxation in the VERs protecting the Swedish clothing industry would reduce clothing employment in Sweden by about 6 percent.

Job maintenance by VERs can be very costly. Estimates for 1984 indicate that the annual cost, as a result of higher prices, to U.S. consumers under VERs on textiles and clothing amounted to $50,000 and $39,000, respectively, per position saved, as compared with annual average textile and clothing wages of $13,400 and $10,500 respectively. The OECD has calculated that each job protected under the orderly marketing arrangement on Japan's color television exports to the United States cost about $60,000 per year.

REGULATING VERS

The prevalence of VERs and their inherent drawbacks, especially their tendency to spread and fragment the trading system into a series of market-sharing arrangements dominated by the major trading nations, has led some commentators to suggest that they should be regulated and their use be subjected to strict conditions and multilateral surveillance. This would encourage greater adherence to internationally agreed trade rules. These observers also note that GATT already sanctions certain departures from the principle of nondiscrimination as, for example, in its provisions for customs unions and free trade areas. Others suggest that the principle of nondiscrimination is too vital to be further weakened by giving VERs official approval. Nondiscrimination in economic terms means that a given level of protection for domestic producers can be achieved at minimum cost to domestic consumers and the rest of the world. It also protects the interests of smaller trading nations and helps to ensure the access of new entrants to the international market place. Its role in GATT rules lends transparency and predictability to international trade relations and to domestic decision making. In this view, VERs would be controlled by a firmer commitment by trading nations to nondiscrimination in the formulation and practice of their trade policies.

This issue is on the agenda of the recently launched Uruguay Round of multilateral trade negotiations, especially in the context of GATT's safeguard provisions. The decisions of the negotiators could have an important effect on the future of the international trading system and by implication on the growth and employment prospects of its member countries.

3

The Evolution of Protection in Textiles and Apparel

William R. Cline

Textiles and apparel are the most systematically and comprehensively protected sectors in the world today. The unique degree of their protection dates from at least the late 1950s, when new restrictive regimes began to emerge even as overall protection of manufactures was beginning to decline through successive postwar tariff negotiations. Multilateral coordination of protection in the sectors began in the early 1960s for cotton textile products. A decade later, major trading nations expanded coverage to man-made fiber products under the Multi-Fiber Arrangement (MFA). First negotiated in 1974 and renewed in 1977 and again in 1981, the MFA most recently acquired an additional five-year term under a renewal agreement reached in July of 1986.

In many ways the most important feature of the special regime for textiles and apparel protection is its seeming permanence. In other sectors, protection has come and gone (and in cases, come again). Color television sets, footwear and automobiles are examples of sectors that have experienced U.S. protection in recent years but are currently free from overt barriers (except for a truly voluntary restraint on Japanese autos). Steel protection has also fluctuated, and currently appears to be in a phase of tightening of restrictions.

With continuous restrictive regimes since the early 1960s, the textile and apparel sectors are preeminent in durability of import protection. An important reason for this durability is the persistent view that in the absence of international regimes (the MFA), protection in the United States and abroad could be even more severe.

THE SHORT AND LONG TERM ARRANGEMENTS ON COTTON
   TEXTILES

After World War I, British textiles still dominated the industry
internationally, but through protection the United States had already
become a major producer in the late nineteenth century. The U.S. Tariff
Acts of 1922 and 1930 established unusually high tariffs for the industry
under the prevailing view that it was of special importance and could
not survive without protection. Thus, in 1930 the average U.S. tariff on
cotton goods was 46 percent and on woolen goods 60 percent, compared
with 35 percent for metal manufactures and 31 percent for chemicals. [1]

During the Great Depression, textile trade fell sharply even as
competition from Japan rose. The United Kingdom applied imperial
preferences in response, while other nations began the widespread use of
quotas. By the late 1930s a major portion of Japan's textile exports was
subject to quantitative restrictions as well as high tariffs internationally.
For its part, in 1936 the United States induced Japan to enter a
"gentlemen's agreement" restricting exports — a precursor of the most
widespread form of quantitative restrictions today, the voluntary export
restraint. [2]

By the 1950s, the remaining welter of restrictions from the 1930s
began to yield to postwar negotiations for U.S.-European trade, but
restraints on Japan, Eastern Europe, and the developing countries
continued or tightened. When Japan applied for membership in the
General Agreement on Tariffs and Trade (GATT) in 1955, many member
countries chose to continue restricting imports from the country under
Article XXXV adopted for that purpose. Although the United States did
not invoke this article, the Eisenhower administration did propose in
1955 that Japan voluntarily limit its exports of selected cotton textiles.
Section 204 of the Agricultural Act of 1956 authorized the President to
negotiate limitations of textile exports from other countries, and in the
same year Japan adopted a five-year limitation to begin in 1957. [3]

What followed inaugurated a cycle that has plagued textile
protection ever since: the spillover of imports from controlled to
uncontrolled areas. Under self-restraint, Japan's share of U.S. imports of
cotton textiles fell from 63 percent in 1958 to 26 percent in 1960, while the
share of Hong Kong rose from 14 percent to 28 percent; imports also
surged from several other countries. Moreover, U.S. agricultural policy
aggravated import competition for a decade after the 1956 act, by forcing

domestic textile mills to purchase cotton at an artificially high support price while foreign producers could buy exported U.S. cotton at a lower price. [4]

Led by U.S. negotiators, GATT discussions in 1959 and 1960 developed the concept of "market disruption," defined as instances of sharp import increases associated with low import prices not attributable to dumping or foreign subsidies. In November 1960 GATT adopted the Decision on the Avoidance of Market Disruption. This concept made important changes going beyond the existing Article XIX safeguard mechanism. It provided that restrictions could be applied even if actual injury had not taken place, and against individual countries responsible for the import surge rather than on a most-favored-nation basis. It also established the presence of a price differential between imports and comparable domestic goods as a basis for determining the need for restriction. In adopting the Short Term Arrangement (STA) in 1961 the GATT applied the concept of market disruption, and it remained a cornerstone of textile and apparel protection thereafter in the Long Term Arrangement (LTA), and then the MFA. Although the original Decision adopting the concept in 1960 did not intend to limit it to textiles and apparel, GATT has not spread its application to other sectors. [5]

MULTI-FIBER ARRANGEMENT

Import growth persisted despite the LTA. Thus, at 1982 prices U.S. imports of textiles rose from $1.02 billion in 1961 to $2.4 billion in 1972, while imports of apparel rose form $648 million to $3.5 billion, for an average annual growth rate of 11.5 percent for the two sectors combined. Import growth was focused in textiles and apparel of man-made fibers not covered under the cotton textile arrangement. Thus, from 1960 to 1970 U.S. imports of man-made fiber textiles rose from 31 million pounds to 329 million pounds. [6] By the late 1960s and early 1970s an increasingly overvalued dollar aggravated import pressure.

The potential of the Multi-Fiber Arrangement for tighter protection became more apparent in its renewal in 1977. While the United States had been the principal protagonist in the mechanisms' creation, by the late 1970s Europe was leading the drive for increasing its restrictiveness. European markets were under considerable pressure, as total imports of textiles and apparel rose from $14.8 billion in 1973 to

$22.0 billion in 1976 (an increase of 49 percent). U.S. imports rose nearly as much in proportionate terms (40 percent, from $3.7 billion to $5.3 billion) but from a much smaller base. Much of the rise in European imports was in intraregional trade associated with further development of specialization within the European Community, but the pace of increased imports from nonoil developing countries was also rapid: from $1.9 billion in 1973 to $3.9 billion in 1976 (an increase of 106 percent), compared with an increase in the United States from $2.1 billion to $3.6 billion (by 75 percent). [7]

MFA COVERAGE

By the early 1980s, the formation and successive renewals of the MFA had established it as a comprehensive mechanism for the control of international trade in textiles and apparel. There are currently 43 signatories to the MFA, representing 54 countries. [8] The United States has bilateral agreements with 34 countries under the MFA, and some 80 percent of U.S. textile and apparel imports from developing countries are limited by quotas under these agreements. [9] The EC has maintained bilaterally negotiated restrictions on imports from some 25 countries, along with unilateral restraints on Taiwan and some Eastern European countries. [10]

There are notable exceptions to MFA country coverage. Although eight major industrial countries are members (United States, Canada, Japan, EC, Austria, Finland, Sweden, Switzerland), two — Australia and New Zealand — are not. And despite their membership, Japan and Switzerland do not maintain quotas under bilateral agreements as permitted by the MFA. On the exporting side, Taiwan and East European countries are not members, and the People's Republic of China joined only in 1984.

Nonmembership does not of course exempt Taiwan and Eastern Europe from quantitative restrictions, whether bilaterally negotiated (U.S.) or unilateral (EC). Conversely, by far the largest bloc of textile and apparel trade that takes place unfettered is among the industrial countries themselves, whether members of the MFA or not. The exception is Japan as a supplier country; it remains subject to MFA restrictions on a number of textile and apparel categories, in considerable part because of the historical context in which it was the principal source of import pressure in the 1930s and again in the 1950s.

There are other areas of textile trade unencumbered by quantitative restrictions. They have included EC preferential treatment to Mediterranean basin countries, which are granted access free of quantitative restraints or, since 1978, with far fewer restricted categories than for imports from other developing countries and Eastern Europe. The EC has also avoided restrictions on imports from the 66 African, Caribbean, and Pacific countries of the Lomé Convention. Offshore processing enjoys duty-free entry for imports corresponding to intermediate inputs originally obtained from the importing country. U.S. practice accords no special quota treatment to offshore processing, however, and while in some bilateral agreements the EC identifies quotas for these imports separately, it is unclear whether their special status increases the total volume of quotas from levels that would otherwise be permitted.

Table 1 presents a broad decomposition of world trade in textiles and apparel by coverage of nontariff trade restraints. As indicated, approximately 43 percent of world trade in textiles and 35 percent of total trade in apparel are free from nontariff restraints: the trade among the industrial countries themselves, with the exception of their imports from Japan. Coverage under MFA restraints is shown in the second portion of the table. Broadly, the MFA restrains trade from Japan and the developing countries into the industrial countries. The volume of these flows amounts to 3 percent and 11 percent, respectively, of world textile trade, and 1.4 percent and 38.5 percent of world apparel trade. The remainder of world trade in the sectors is generally subject to other quantitative restraints, unilaterally or through bilateral agreements. Essentially this remaining bloc of non-MFA, but restricted, trade encompasses industrial country imports from the Eastern area countries, and imports of developing countries and Eastern area countries from all sources.

The estimates of Table 1 are only approximate. They treat all industrial country imports from Japan and the developing countries as controlled under the MFA, whereas in fact there are numerous combinations of supplier countries and product categories that are not constrained by quotas. Nonetheless, because the MFA framework

Table 1

Shares of World Trade in Textiles and Apparel subject to MFA and other Restraints
Percentage

Importing area	Supplying area	Textiles	Apparel	Total
1. Free of restraints				
Industrial countries	Industrial countries except Japan	42.8	35.1	39.2
2. MFA restraints				
Industrial countries	Japan	3.0	35.1	39.2
	Developing countries	11.0	38.5	23.9
	Subtotal	14.0	39.9	26.2
3. Bilateral or national restraints				
Industrial countries	Eastern area	3.6	5.0	4.3
Developing countries	All sources	30.8	12.8	22.4
Eastern area	All sources	8.7	7.2	8.0
Subtotal, restrained	(2 + 3)	57.1	64.9	60.8
Total		100.0	100.0	100.0
Memorandum: value (billion dollars)		53.5	46.0	99.5

Source: GATT, *International Trade 1984/85*, table A39; OECD, *Trade by Commodities*, series C, vol. 2, 1984

provides for potential protection for virtually this entire subset of suppliers, the estimate here is useful for policy purposes. The table also does not distinguish the imports of Australia and New Zealand (approximately $2 billion in 1984, of which most was from non-OECD sources) from imports into other industrial countries, although for these two markets the controls should be grouped under other restraints rather than the MFA. In addition, there is some overstatement of the flow of trade under other restraints by treating all developing country and Eastern bloc imports in this category. Thus, Hong Kong has sizable restraint-free imports. Nonetheless, the table provides an approximate gauge of the division of world trade into restraint-free, MFA, and other-restraint groupings.

These estimates indicate that the MFA covers approximately one-fourth of world trade in textiles and apparel. However, the coverage is much higher for apparel (40 percent) than for textiles (14 percent), reflecting the larger role of developing-country suppliers in apparel than in textiles. The estimates also bring out other important patterns. First, there is probably a larger share of world trade restrained by national and other non-MFA restrictions than by the MFA. Second, the developing countries account for an impressive share of world imports: 30.8 percent of textiles and 12.8 percent even in apparel. This large market, especially in textiles, should serve both as a base for developing-country negotiating power on one hand, and as a significant target for industrial country efforts toward multilateral trade liberalization on the other. Third, although the MFA itself is much more heavily oriented toward protection against apparel than against textiles (because it restrains more in apparel than textiles), if other bilateral and national restraints are taken into account the share of world trade subject to such protection is close to 60 percent for both categories of products.

Notes

1   F. W. Taussig, as cited in Donald B. Keesing and Martin Wolf, Textile Quotas Against Developing Countries (London: Trade Policy Research Center, 1980), p. 11.
2   General Agreement on Tariffs and Trade (GATT), Textiles and Clothing in the World Economy (Geneva: GATT, 1984), pp. 62-63.
3   Ibid, p. 64; United Nations Conference on Trade and Development, Programme of Cooperation among Developing Countries, Exporters of Textiles and Clothing, Manual for Textile Negotiators, vol. 1 (Geneva: UNCTAD, 1983), p. 8.
4   Keesing and Wolf, Textile Quotas, pp. 14-15.
5   GATT, Textiles and Clothing, pp. 5, 65.
6   Davidson, Feigenoff, and Ghadar, International Competition, p. 34.
7   GATT, International Trade 1976/77 (Geneva: GATT, 1977), tables A and D.
8   GATT, "Extension of Multifibre Arrangement Agreed," Press Release 1390. 5 August 1986.
9   Jim Berger, "US Textiles and Apparel: Is Protection a Solution?" Policy Focus No. 6 (Washington: Overseas Development Council, 1985), p. 7.
10   Gerard Curzon et al., MFA Forever? p. 7.

4

Japan's Intangible Barriers to Trade in Manufactures

Dorothy Christelow

Mounting U.S. trade deficits over the past three years have greatly intensified political and economic pressures for trade protectionism. These pressures have subsided somewhat following the recent decline in the dollar but will most likely continue to be strong over the near-term. Japan has born the brunt of the criticism because our bilateral trade deficit — the largest with any country — has been growing very rapidly and now accounts for about one-third of our total trade deficit. While Japan's tariffs and quotas, at least on manufactured products, are recognized as being similar to or lower than most industrial countries, many suspect that what are sometimes called "intangible" barriers to imports contribute to Japan's trade surplus.

Intangible barriers are mainly systems and regulations applying both to domestic and foreign producers which, by accident or design, work to the special disadvantage of imports. In Japan those barriers provoking the most foreign complaints have been product standards and testing procedures, the wholesale and resale distribution systems, and government procurement. Intangible trade barriers are found in many countries and have attracted increasing international criticism as tariffs and quotas have gradually been negotiated downward. In fact, reductions of some barriers were included in the Tokyo Round of multilateral trade agreements that became effective in 1980. As a signatory, Japan has adopted a series of measures designed to substantially reduce its intangible barriers. Because the changes are being phased in gradually between 1983 and 1988, and because the trade response will take time, the results will emerge slowly.

This article briefly describes the nature of intangible barriers to imports of manufactures, the products principally affected, the liberalization moves already made and those planned for 1986-88, and systemic changes that could also ease entry of foreign products. Finally, it offers rough estimates of the long-run trade consequences of greatly reducing those barriers.

We find that these intangible barriers have probably been important for a significant number of products. These include computers, sophisticated telecommunications equipment, and other industrial machinery for which several industrial countries compete strongly with Japan. It is also true of chemicals and some other products for which Japan is at a comparative disadvantage. We estimate, very roughly, that other things being equal, reduction of intangible trade barriers, as defined here, for affected products to the level prevailing in the United States and the European community (EC), could ultimately raise Japan's imports by as much as 7 percent, or about $9 billion from the 1983 level. However, because only partial barrier removal can be expected, the actual increase in imports over the next five to ten years would be smaller. About half of any gain would accrue to U.S. exports to Japan. [1]

JAPAN'S IMPORT POLICY IN PERSPECTIVE

Japan's markets are sometimes perceived as relatively closed to foreigners. But as far as tariffs and quantitative restrictions are concerned, this is certainly not true. In the early postwar years, Japan imposed high tariffs and stringent quotas to allow war-ravaged industries to rebuild and to protect infant industries such as automobiles as well as the relatively inefficient agriculture sector. However, as basic industries like steel regained their footing and the automobile and consumer electronics industries became strong competitors in world markets, Japan joined with other nations in mutual reduction of tariffs and quotas on imports of manufactures. Before the latest round of tariff reductions in 1980, Japan's trade-weighted average tariff on manufactured goods was around 10 percent, nearly identical to the EC average and slightly higher than that of the United States. [2] When the Tokyo Round cuts are fully implemented, which in Japan's case had already occurred, Japan's average tariff on manufactures, at 2.9 percent, will be one and one-half to four percentage points lower than the also low averages for the other industrial countries. [3]

In the area of quantitative restrictions, Japan maintains 22 quotas on imports of agricultural products, rivaling the EC in the protectionist thrust of its trade policy. But for manufactures, its use of restrictions is more limited: there are quotas only on leather products and coal briquettes. And Japan is a member, along with the United States and the EC countries, in the multi-fiber agreement which limits exports of textile products from developing countries to industrial countries. However, unlike the United States, Canada, and the EC countries, Japan has not requested that its trading partners impose other "voluntary" restraints on their exports to Japan.

While quantitative restrictions apply to a limited range of Japan's imports of manufactures, the scope of intangible barriers is broader. Foreign countries have complained that restrictive product standards and related inspection and certification procedures, the wholesale and retail distribution systems, and government procurement procedures make Japanese markets for many manufactured products difficult to penetrate. These barriers have included clear and specific elements of discrimination against imports. But beyond this, some have limited market access to all newcomers, domestic and foreign, and this may have also served to restrict imports. Pressures on the Japanese government to eliminate these intangible barriers to imports have mounted sharply as the country's trade surplus has widened. The following three sections will describe these intangible barriers, the Japanese government's moves to reduce them, and systemic changes working in the same direction.

PRODUCT STANDARDS

Product standards are frequently mentioned as Japan's most important intangible barrier to trade. Established by the central government to cover most domestic and imported manufactures, standards are of two kinds. First, there are awards for excellence. The Japanese Industrial Standards Committee awards the "JIS" mark to products made in factories where production methods and quality controls meet committee standards. Similarly, the Minister of Agriculture, Forestry, and Fisheries awards the "JAS" mark (Japanese Agricultural Standards) to processed foods and forestry products from factories meeting its standards. The standards underlying the JIS and JAS marks are so rigorous that many small- and medium-sized firms do not apply for them. But the marks greatly increase product saleability and in many cases have become mandatory for sales to public bodies. Second, most products must meet *required* minimum standards. These are set by various government departments, with the advice of industry committees, and are designed to protect the health and safety of consumers and to assure overall product quality.

For foods and pharmaceuticals, where health and safety are involved, the Japanese and U.S. approaches to setting required minimum standards are generally similar. But for other products, Japanese standards-setting is more concentrated in the central government and more comprehensive. In the United States, standards-setting is often left to local governments (e.g., local plumbing and wiring ordinances) or trade associations (e.g., standards for electrical appliances). There is also great reliance in the United States on competition and consumer response, rather than elaborate standards requirements, to assure quality — and perhaps stronger industry resistance to central government standards-setting.

Until recently, the Japanese system of standards overtly discriminated against foreign suppliers. This was recognized in an official report of 1981, [4] and the barriers were described in some detail in a 1980 report of an unofficial group drawn from United States and Japanese business firms and government agencies. [5] The major discriminatory features identified were the following:

- The coveted JIS and JAS marks were not available to foreigners.
- Exporters to Japan were not members of the advisory standards-setting committees and had no direct channels for making their views known to the authorities since they were required to work through Japanese importers.
- The standards themselves were often "non-transparent" - i.e., vaguely worded, hard to understand, and frequently not published in a readily available source.
- Testing requirements were more burdensome and expensive for imports than for domestically produced products. Japanese producers could choose among three methods of meeting standards: "type approval", based on factory inspection and product testing; "lot inspection", i.e., testing samples from each lot; or individual inspection of each product. For the large producer, "type approval" is usually the cost-efficient choice. But until 1983, exporters to Japan could not use this method. Instead they were required to pass "lot

inspection" or even individual inspection, and to work through a Japanese agent. [6]

Foreign exporters claiming to have been unfavorably affected by one or more of these restrictions have included foreign suppliers of plywood products, pharmaceuticals, agricultural chemicals, cosmetics, forest products, automobiles, electrical appliances, telecommunications equipment, and some types of industrial machinery.

These discriminatory features did not conform to the standards agreement under the General Agreement of Tariffs and Trade (GATT) that became effective in 1980. That agreement specified that standards should avoid unnecessary obstacles to trade, be transparent, conform to international standards where appropriate, and provide "national" treatment to foreign suppliers (i.e., treat foreign suppliers the same as domestic suppliers). Although Japan initiated limited moves toward compliance in 1980, major efforts began only in 1983. At that time 16 statutes were amended in order to provide national treatment for foreign suppliers. Following the 1980-83 changes, foreigners were permitted to apply for the JIS and JAS plant approval marks, to elect the "type approval" route to meeting required standards, to become members of advisory committees, and to present their views directly to official standards-setting bodies.

Despite these changes, product standards remained a major irritant in Japan's trade relations. As foreign and domestic suppliers became subject to the same requirements, foreign pressures for change shifted to the standards themselves. Complaints were focused on the complexity of Japanese standards and their dissimilarity to international standards (where such existed), or to those in the supplier's own country. Objections were also raised to Japanese government inspection of factories outside Japan, and to the need for product testing in Japan rather than by approved foreign certification agencies. These aspects of Japanese standards requirements did not always violate national treatment precepts. However, they may have put a greater financial burden on foreign entrants to Japanese markets than they did on Japanese producers. If so, they may have discouraged imports of products for which foreign producers had a comparative advantage.

The Japanese authorities had made a start at addressing these complaints in 1983. But in 1985, spurred by a widening trade surplus and mounting tension with trading partners, they initiated a new broad-scale program scheduled to take effect gradually between 1985 and 1988. To meet the criticism that the standards were unnecessarily complicated, some standards were eliminated altogether and many others were to be simplified. Instead of requiring Japanese inspection of foreign factories, Japan decided to accept approved foreign tests for many products and permit self-certification by suppliers of numerous products. The government also agreed to step up its study of international standards and to consult with other interested countries and international standards- setting bodies. For a few products, Japan also agreed to accept a few international standards in 1985 and 1986. (Details of the 1985 program are given in the appendix.) Since many aspects of the 1985 program remained to be spelled out, official U.S.-Japan trade groups continued to meet, hammering out specifics acceptable to both sides.

THE DISTRIBUTION SYSTEM AS A BARRIER TO IMPORTS

As with product standards, the Japanese distribution system has presented two types of barriers to imports: clear discrimination against imports in a few areas, and more pervasive systemic barriers to new entrants, foreign or domestic. Both sorts of barriers are crumbling — the discriminatory ones at the insistence of foreign suppliers and the systemic ones as part of a slow evolution.

The outstanding case of deliberate discrimination against imports, *per se,* in the distribution system has been that practiced by the government-owned Japan Tobacco and Salt Public Corporation (JTS). In addition to monopolizing the purchase of raw materials and the manufacture of tobacco and salt products, JTS controlled the *distribution* of tobacco products until 1985. By limiting the number of retailers permitted to sell foreign cigarettes and restricting advertising expenditures, it limited imports to about 2 percent of total sales. In April 1985, JTS was "privatized," becoming Japan Tobacco (JT), a "special corporation" under government jurisdiction. [7] In response to political pressure from Japanese tobacco growers, it will continue to monopolize purchases of tobacco and the manufacture of cigarettes and other tobacco products. But it has relinquished its control over the *distribution* of tobacco products and will allow foreign cigarettes and other tobacco manufactures to compete freely by allowing them unlimited access to wholesale and retail distribution channels.

A wider-spread problem for foreign suppliers of many consumer goods has been the barrier to new entry, domestic or foreign, created by exclusive dealer arrangements. Such arrangements thrived in the highly fragmented distribution system of the early postwar years but are losing importance as the distribution system changes.

In the early postwar period, the small store was predominant in Japanese retailing. In 1960, for example, nearly 50 percent of all retail sales were made in establishments of one to four employees and only 13 percent in stores with 50 or more employees. Linking manufacturers to retailers was a network of national, regional, and local wholesalers, which also tended to be small. Producers of manufactured consumer goods easily dominated this fragmented distribution system, either by direct ownership of some wholesalers or by exclusive dealer arrangements. Wholesalers in turn often made exclusive agreements with retailers. Given their small size, most retailers had little ability or incentive to resist such arrangements.

However, changes in the Japanese economy gradually forced changes in the size of the distribution unit. As the ownership of automobiles and refrigerators, rare in the 1950s and early 1960s, become common later in the 1960s and after, the need for small retail stores close to home diminished. At the same time, increasing competition in labor markets in the 1960s increased the need for larger, more labor-efficient distribution units. The government contributed to the shift to larger distribution units by making low-interest loans to wholesalers and retailers for relocating and modernizing. By the mid-1970s, only 34 percent of all retail sales were made in establishments with one to four employees and sales of stores with 50 or more employees had risen to 21 percent of the total. The scale of wholesalers increased correspondingly. [8]

Since the mid-1970s, however, the trend toward larger retailers and wholesalers has slowed. At least part of the explanation lies in changing government policy. As the growth of employment opportunities in manufacturing diminished, government policy shifted from fostering more efficient operations to protecting the small retailer and employment in retailing by limiting the size of retailers. A 1974 law required Ministry of International Trade and Industry approval for construction of any retail store of 1,500 square meters or more (3,000 square meters in ten large cities). Since then, several prefectures have enacted even more stringent regulations.

However, changes in the scale of retailing that had occurred before the mid-1970s and the continued increase in the proportion of mid-sized retailers were enough to loosen the grip of exclusive dealer arrangements in some areas. Many large retailers, especially in consumer electronics, have gone into high-volume discount sales, bypassing wholesalers altogether and dealing directly with a number of competing manufacturers. [9] Wholesalers, fighting for their existence, are also beginning to avoid exclusive marketing agreements and are offering a wide variety of products. [10]

Developments of this sort should ease entry of all new market participants, including foreign suppliers. However, these trends seem to be strongest in consumer electronics, where few if any foreign suppliers are competitive. In retail areas where imports should be competitive, some distribution difficulties persist. A recent government survey of distribution markups of domestic and imported products found that for whiskeys, candies, edible oils, men's overcoats, and footwear, markups on imports were double those on domestic products. [11] Even after allowing for the inclusion of tariffs in the markup on imports, the discrepancy between markups for imports and those for domestic products remained large. The difference in markups suggests the presence of exclusive distribution arrangements. The resulting high price for imports has probably limited the sale of imported products.

GOVERNMENT PROCUREMENT

In Japan as in other industrial countries, government procurement has favored domestic producers. To reduce this discrimination, the Tokyo Round included an agreement on government procurement, which Japan and most other industrial countries accepted. This requires that foreigners be permitted to bid on government contracts valued at SDR 150,000 (about $165,000-U.S.) or more, and that bidding procedures be "transparent."

Interest in the Japanese government's procurement of industrial products has been focused on Nippon Telephone and Telegraph (NTT) which has purchased annually about $2-3 billion of telecommunications equipment in recent years. Following the Tokyo Round agreement and a special bilateral agreement with the United States in 1981, NTT opened its procurement to foreign bidders. The modest rise in its foreign purchases that followed proved disappointing to foreign suppliers. Judging from complaints registered with GATT in 1983, Japan was especially remiss in its reliance on single tendering, but was also criticized for short bid deadlines, short delivery times, maximum price specifications, and complex qualification requirements. Somewhat similar criticisms were made of other countries as well. [12]

In its market-opening package of 1985, Japan attempted to meet these complaints. It promised to review single tendering (acknowledging that this method should be used only exceptionally), to increase bid times (from 30 to 40 days) and to simplify qualification procedures. It also expanded the number of government agencies and corporations which would open their procurement to foreign bidding. However, there are still important omissions such as the National Space Development Agency, the sole government purchaser for communications satellites.

In the meantime, however, the opportunities for marketing sophisticated telecommunications equipment and computers have shifted to the private sector. This shift is partly because NTT was "privatized" [13] in 1985, thus moving a major purchaser of computers and sophisticated telecommunications equipment from the public to the private sector. But it is also because the telecommunications industry has been transformed by breaking the NTT monopoly over telecommunications and permitting the entry of foreigners.

In Japan the telecommunications industry is now divided into two branches: common carriers and services known as Value-Added Networks (VANs), The latter include data processing, computer linkages, teleconferencing, and videotex. Foreign firms may hold no more that one-third interest in common carriers but are permitted 100 percent ownership of VANs. A number of large U.S. firms have entered or are about to enter the VANs area, alone or with Japanese partners including NTT. Since VANs were slow to develop in the period of the NTT monopoly, experienced foreign firms may have at least a temporary technological advantage.

Both common carriers and VANs (domestic and foreign) constitute a rapidly expanding market for sophisticated telecommunications equipment, computers, and software. NTT has pledged to conform to the procurement policies to which it had been committed as a government corporation under the GATT agreement on government procurement. Further, since private firms, including NTT, are not permitted to buy foreign communications satellites, a market for the U.S. product has been opened. In view of the importance of standards for computers and software in the competitive and rapidly growing telecommunications market, a U.S.-Japan committee was organized to negotiate the development of standards. As a result, standards and standards procedures originally proposed by Japan have been simplified. [14] Manufacturer-generated test data will be accepted and standards will be limited to insuring that the equipment does not harm the Japanese telecommunications network. [15] Bilateral negotiations with the United States covering these and other points were successfully concluded in January 1986.

TRADE CONSEQUENCES OF ELIMINATING INTANGIBLE BARRIERS TO IMPORTS

Now that Japan's intangible barriers to imports of manufactures are falling, the natural question is how much of an increase in imports of manufactures can be expected as a result. We start with a very rough estimate of the maximum increase in Japan's imports of specified manufactured products that could ultimately come from reducing intangible barriers to the levels prevailing in the United States and the EC countries. These estimates are based on the presumption that, in the absence of trade barriers or subsidies to domestic output (or with uniform low trade barriers and subsidies across countries), countries with roughly similar comparative advantage in producing a given product will have similar propensities to import it. [16] These propensities are measured as the ratio of imports to GNP. We approximate comparative advantage in each product group by the ratio of the country's share in *supplying* world imports of all products. [17] A ratio significantly higher than one denotes comparative advantage.

Table 1 provides a rough snapshot indicator of the comparative advantage of Japan, the United States, and the EC in 1983 for those products affected by Japan's intangible trade barriers described in the preceding sections. [18]

Table 1

Comparative Advantage Indicators [a] for Japan, the United States, and the European Community
Selected industrial products groups

Products grouped according to Japan's comparative advantages relative to the United States and the European Community	Japan	United States	European Community
Much stronger			
Consumer electronics	5.6	0.6	0.4
Road vehicles	3.9	1.3	1.2
Roughly similar or somewhat weaker			
Office and data processing machinery	2.9	3.0	0.8
Electrical machinery not elsewhere specified	1.9	1.5	1.3
General industry machinery	1.4	1.7	2.2
Professional, scientific, and control instruments	1.2	3.0	1.5
Much weaker			
Chemicals	.5	1.7	2.2
Pharmaceuticals	0.5	1.7	2.2
Essential oils and cosmetics	0.2	1.4	3.0
Fertilizers	b	1.2	0.8
Cork and wood products	0.2	0.6	0.5
Clothing	0.2	0.1	0.9
Beverages	0.1	0.2	4.4
Tobacco and manufactures	b	2.6	0.4

[a] Ratio of share in OECD imports of given product group to share in OECD imports of all products. Based on data for 1983 as published in OECD, *Foreign Trade by Commodities, Volume II, Imports*. Intra-European Community trade has been excluded form the OECD imports total and the European Community share.
[b] Less than 0.05

For consumer electronic and road vehicles, it is clear that Japan has an overwhelming comparative advantage relative to the United States and the EC. For office machinery (including computers), the comparative advantages of Japan and the United States are quite similar. For electrical machinery, a product group which includes both sophisticated telecommunications equipment and consumer electrical appliances, Japan's comparative advantage is slightly greater than the United States'. For general industrial machinery and professional, scientific, and control instruments, Japan had a weaker comparative advantage than the United States and the EC. For chemicals, wood products, clothing, beverages, and tobacco products, Japan has a decided comparative disadvantage while the United States and the EC have a strong comparative advantage in some of them. [19]

Table 2 shows strikingly lower import propensities for Japan than for the United States and the EC in virtually all product groups. This is true not only in cases where Japan has a strong comparative advantage but also in cases where similar comparative advantage would lead one to expect similar propensities. It is also true in the case of products for which Japan has a comparative disadvantage while the United States and/or the EC have a comparative advantage while the United States and/or the EC have a comparative advantage. Since tariffs and quota restrictions are low in all of these countries for most affected product groups, this assymetry between comparative advantage and propensity to import in Japan suggests that its intangible barriers are in fact restrictive.

Table 2 also gives an estimate of the potential long-run increase in Japan's manufactured imports from a lowering of its intangible barriers for the products shown in the table to the level prevailing in the United States and the EC. Total manufactured imports could rise by 27 percent while total imports could rise by 7 percent. (This would raise Japan's total manufactured imports by about three-quarters of a percent of GNP.) Over half the increase should come in chemicals (including pharmaceuticals), computers, data processing equipment, and electrical machinery (including sophisticated telecommunications equipment). On the basis of current trading patterns, the United States' share of the overall gain should be at least half.

Table 2

Estimating the Long-Run Consequences of Eliminating Intangible Barriers to Japan's Imports

Products grouped according to Japan's comparative advantage relative to the United States and the European Community	Japan's imports in 1963 in millions of dollars	Japan	United States	European Community	Japan (estimated, intangible barriers lowered)*	Ratio of estimated actual imports for Japan	Japan's estimated imports in millions of dollars	In millions of dollars	Percent of total 1963 imports	Percent of 1983 imports of manufacturers
Much stronger	1,083						1,083	0		
Consumer electronics	464	0.038	0.352	0.284	0.038	1.00	464	0		
Motor vehicles	619	0.052	1.138	0.444	0.052	1.00	619	0		
Roughly similar or somewhat weaker	5,178						8,834	3,656	2.9	11.6
Office and data processing machinery	1,068	0.090	0.211	0.416	0.211	2.34	2,504	1,436	1.1	4.6
Electrical machinery (not elsewhere specified)	2,051	0.174	0.392	0.382	0.209 [a]	1.2 [a]	2,461	410	0.3	1.3
General industry machinery	1,004	0.085	0.150	0.231	0.150	1.76	1,771	767	0.6	2.4
Professional, scientific, and control instruments	1.055	0.089	0.063	0.177	0.177	1.99	2,098	1,043	0.8	3.3
Much weaker	9,096						13,965	4,869	3.9	15.4
Chemicals	7,008	0.593	0.341	0.660	0.858	1.45	10.140	3,142	2.5	9.9
Cork and wood products	172	0.015	0.045	0.083	0.045 [b]	3.00	516	344	0.3	1.1
Clothing	1,511	0.127	0.316	0.369	0.210 [b]	1.66 [b]	2.508	997	0.8	3.2
Tobacco Products	93	0.045 [c]	0.023 [c]	0.066 [c]	0.086	1.91	177	84	0.1	0.3
Beverages	312	0.026	0.089	0.028	0.052 [b]	2.00 [b]	624	312	0.2	1.0
Total of above	15,357						23,882	8,525	6.8	27.0

Memorandum:

Imports of Manufacturers [d]	31.532
Total Imports	125,017

Calculated percentages may not add to totals due to rounding.

* The basic assumption, that in the absence of barriers, countries with similar Comparative advantage have similar import propensities (defined as imports as a percent of GNP), is t aken to imply the following:

* Products for which Japan has a strong comparative advantage: no change in import propensities.
* Products for which Japan's comparative advantage or disadvantage is roughly similar to that of the United States or the EC: Japan's import propensity would rise to that of whichever has the more similar comparative advantage.
* Products for which Japan's comparative advantage is decidedly lower than that of the United States and the EC: Japan's propensity is raised to 1.3 times the higher of the United States EC propensities. This seems conservative in light of differences in ties for products where competitive advantages are similar.

Exceptions to this procedure are footnoted separately.

[a] In this heterogeneous product group (which includes consumer and sophisticated industrial equipment) the difference in income propensities to import is too large to be explained by Japan's slightly higher comparative advantage.. Japan's import propensity is therefore raised by 20 percent.

[b] Some of the discrepancy between Japan's propensity to import and the propensities of the United States and the EC are due to higher tariffs, in the case of wood products and alcoholic beverages, and to strict import restraints under the multi-fiber agreement for clothing. The increased in imports assumed to follow from elimination of intangible barriers only is therefore somewhat arbitrary, but smaller than the increased that could be expected if all trade barriers were eliminated.

[c] Tobacco and tobacco products. Trade in tobacco products not available separately.

[d] Standard International Trade Classifications 0.5, 0.6, 0.7, 0.8, 0.11, and 0.122. Processed foods omitted b because trade data unavailable.

The foregoing estimate is a maximum in the sense that it represents the rise in imports of specified products that could be expected if Japan's intangible barriers to those imports were reduced to the generally lower U.S. or EC levels. Since barrier reductions now in prospect are not complete, their import consequences are likely to be lower than these maximum estimates.

CONCLUSION

We have found that although Japan's tariffs and quantitative restrictions are lower than in other industrial countries, its intangible barriers have remained significant.   Such barriers — product standards, the distribution system, and government procurement — have included elements of discrimination against imports as well as systemic impediments to all newcomers, domestic and foreign. As a result of heavy pressure from its trading partners, Japan has already reduced measurably many discriminatory features of standards-setting and government procurement and is in the process of doing more. In two programs announced in 1983 and 1985, the Japanese government has undertaken to greatly reduce systemic barriers in standards by simplifying the standards themselves and the certification procedures required to meet them. Moreover, a natural evolution of the wholesale and retail distribution system — mainly a move toward larger, more enterprising, and independent retailers — is gradually reducing systemic barriers in that area.

Other things remaining the same, reduction of the intangible barriers to U.S. or EC levels for affected products would raise imports by 7 percent in the long run. However, barrier reductions on this scale do not seem likely.

These estimated long-term gains are not inconsequential. But they are too small to suggest that intangible barriers are the primary or even a major source of Japan's external trade surpluses — $56 billion total, and $42 billion of it with the United States in 1985. [20] Weak domestic demand growth and a high savings ratio, especially relative to the United States, and the stronger dollar appear to have been much more important forces behind Japan's rising trade surplus over the past several years. Nevertheless, the gradual restrictions of intangible barriers now in view should contribute modestly over time to reducing

Japan's external trade surpluses, both total and bilateral with the United States.

Notes

1   This is somewhat higher than differently derived estimates by W.F. Bergsten and William R. Cline in The United States-Japan Economic Problem, Institute for International Economics (October 1985).

2   Gary Saxenhouse, "Evolving Comparative Advantage and Japan's Imports of Manufactures," in K. Yamamura, ed., Policy and Trade Issues of the Japanese Economy (University of Washington Press, 1982). The averages included mine products.

3   Alan V. Deardorff and Robert M. Stern, "The Economic Effects of Complete Elimination of Post-Tokyo Round Tariffs", in W.R. Cline, ed., Trade Policy in the 1980s (Institute for International Economics, 1983).

     In those areas where industrial countries' tariffs are still protective (notably apparel and footwear, where imports from developing countries are considered a threat) Japan's tariffs are fully as high as those of all major industrial countries except the United States. But for those products where Japan has a clear competitive advantage, Japan's tariffs are significantly lower than in other industrial countries. This reduces its average tariff relative to the industrial countries.

4   Report of the Japan-United States Economic Relations Group (1981).

5   United States-Japan Trade Study Group, A Special Progress Report (April, 1980).

6   Operations of the Trade Agreements Program, 35th Report (1983) and United States International Trade Commission (June 1984).

7   In the foreseeable future, JT will not become privately owned, as the word "privatized" (used in the official description of the change) might suggest. The details of the privatization and market prospects for JT and foreign suppliers are discussed in "The Tobacco Monopoly Goes Private," Economic Eye, a Quarterly Digest of Views from Japan, Japan Institute for Social and Economic Affairs (June 1985).

8   This description of the evolution of the Japanese distribution system draws heavily on Edward J. Lincoln, "The Zebra Strips or a Tale of Distributus Japanicus and the Economists", in M. Harvey and R. Lusch, eds., Marketing Channels: Domestic and International Perspectives (University of Oklahoma Press, 1982). However, Lincoln focuses on the efficiency of the system.

9   "Home Electric Appliances: High Volume Retailers are Changing Distribution Patterns", Daiwa Bank Monthly Research Report (December 1985).

10 "Wholesalers Struggle to Ride Out Stormy Rationalization in Distribution", Mitsubishi Bank Review (May 1985).

11 A report by Japan's Council on Price Stabilization, summarized in Japan Economic Journal (November 23, 1985).

12 Italy, France and the United States were faulted for short bid deadlines, and Italy for publishing few tenders. The United States was criticized for

proliferation of "Buy American" requirements. United States International Trade Commission, op. cit., page 89.

13 The NTT Act of December 20, 1984 made NTT a private company as of April 1, 1985. However, the government still holds all of NTT's stock issued on that date. It will be sold to the public gradually, beginning in 1986, but foreigners will not be permitted to purchase it.

14 Operation of the Trade Agreements Program, US International Trade Commission, Publication 1725 (July 1985), pages 148-149.

15 Annual Report on National Trade Estimates, The US Trade Representative, Executive Office of the President (1985), page 119.

16 It might be argued that Japan's imports should not be expected to conform exactly to our basic assumption (i.e., that countries with similar comparative advantage in trade of a given product will have similar propensities to import that product) since Japan's higher propensity to raw materials might lead to lower propensities to import manufactures. However, these basic international differences in resource endowment are at least partially reflected in Japan's exceptionally high comparative disadvantages relative to other countries for raw materials, and its exceptionally high comparative advantages in some manufactured products.

17 This measure was developed by Bela Balassa in "Trade Liberalization and 'Revealed' Competitive Advantages," Manchester School of Economic and Social Studies (May 1965).

18 As a matter of convenience, OECD imports from all sources are taken as a proxy for world imports. The year 1983, the latest for which the desired data were available, has the advantage of being the year Japan seriously embarked on reducing its intangible barriers to trade. Processed foods, though affected by intangible barriers to imports, are omitted for lack of OECD trade data.

19 For wood products, clothing, and footwear, Japan, the United States, and the EC are all at a comparative disadvantage (Japan more than the others) — which may explain the universally high tariffs in those areas. Comparative advantage in these areas belongs to the developing countries.

20 Both balances are f.o.b. Japan.

5

Countertrade, Offsets, Barter, and Buybacks

Stephen S. Cohen with John Zysman

Barter, countertrade, buybacks, and offsets are not new. Indeed, money was invented, quite some time ago, to alleviate many of the more obvious inconveniences of those venerable forms of trade. For the longest time, they have been treated as marginal phenomena in a dominant and expanding system of monetized international trade. The enduring persistence of barter has always been acknowledged, but it was usually located in situations of greater interest to anthropologists than to economists. It was assumed to grow up quickly under conditions of disorder, but also presumed to disappear just as quickly once normalcy had been restored. Like so many other primitive and bureaucratic practices, barter was taken for granted as somehow incurably part and parcel of any deals with centrally planned economies. Like the suburban homeowners who get together and swap services to cut the taxman out of his take, international barter was seen as wrong and potentially upsetting to the system, but so marginal that it was no cause for concern as long as it was kept within bounds.

But barter and its more elaborate varieties (such as countertrade, buybacks, and offsets) have broken out of all imaginable bounds. Like some disease-causing microbe once thought safely eradicated by modern science, they have made a startling comeback in the past few years, and they now pose a challenge to the rules, procedures, and structures of international trade. Estimates of the extent of these practices vary widely. The U.S. Department of Commerce estimates that between 20% and 30% of world trade is now subject to some form of counterpurchase, buyback, or offset and that the proportion could reach 50% in fifteen years. [1] In surveys by the National Foreign Trade Council Foundation, the number of reported transactions involving some form of barter has been increasing at rates of 50%, 64%, and 117% respectively in each of the past three years. [2] *Business Week* and the General Electric Trading

Company each independently estimates the volume at 30% of world trade. [3] GATT, in a recent report, makes by far the lowest estimate: 8% of world trade. [4]   Since the volume of world trade is about $2 trillion, any point on this intolerably broad range of estimates nevertheless constitutes a staggering sum — especially for such an obscure and ill-regarded "marginal phenomenon."

When variance is in the hundreds of billions of dollars, we know two things. First, that something big is going on; and second, that we have no control over it. The imprecision of the data is significant for policy makers as well as for economic statisticians. It demonstrates the lack of a careful study of a substantial change in world trade patterns, and of even more fundamental changes in the economic roles of governments that lie behind it. Economic and business accounting conventions (such as balance of payments and corporate accounting) are largely blind to countertrade because they are designed for a cash-and-credit economy.   The complete inappropriateness of these basic economic information systems is likely, fairly soon, to be the cause of unwelcome economic, and ultimately political, drama.

HOW IT WORKS

Barter is a simple phenomenon. I will exchange a thousand barrels of crude oil for a given quantity of specific chemical solvents. *Countertrade* is rather the same, only the seller — let us say a German producer of electric turbines — is given a broader menu of products from which to choose those items he will take in exchange. For instance, the seller may be obliged to take payment of 50% or 100% or even 150% of the value of equipment sold to Indonesia in the form of any Indonesian product — except oil. *Buybacks* usually refer to the seller of a manufacturing plant taking a specified quantity of the future output of that plant as his payment. *Offsets* most often refer to a still broader category of non-cash payments.   In exchange for our purchasing $200 million of your telephone switching equipment, we ask you to locate production of a semiconductor plant in our country that will produce $100 million per year of memory devices, of which half will be exported. The techniques can be melded together: for example, in addition to the offset plant, you will also take as part of the payment package 40,000 barrels of vegetable oil, thirty tons of smoked ham, 50,000 wicker chairs, and perhaps some of our own countertrade obligations to dispose of Indonesian carburetors. [5]

Countertrade would not be a very substantial phenomenon if all international transactions were conducted company to company, without government playing a directive role. The swift acceleration of countertrade to its present importance and its continuing rapid growth are indicators — even a measure— of the extent to which the nation state now directs the terms of international sales and systematically sets policies and rules to influence the terms of supposedly private bargains. There simply would not be very much countertrade unless some nation state (the buyer) dictates that access to its market can be gained only by sellers willing to take payment in countertrade or to provide offsets.

Countertrade deals are elaborate, inventive, and extremely diverse. No two deals are identical. Each is created to circumvent an obstacle, or to slalom through a set of obstacles. The tighter the situation, the more original the deal. Poland, therefore, is doubly interesting. It is an Eastern bloc country that generally seeks countertrade to move its less easily marketable exports. It is also as strapped for hard currency as anyone in the world, with its export earnings for the near future, the far future, and also the hereafter mortgaged to Western bankers. Gabriel Wujek, of the Polish Embassy in Washington, recently described how countertrade provided a way for Poland to purchase industrial equipment from the West. An apple pulp factory in Poland needed equipment that could be provided by a number of Western firms. Due to the debt crisis, however, no U.S. banks were willing to supply the necessary financing. An Austrian bank came to the rescue. The bank guaranteed the promissory notes so the manufacturer (now an Austrian) could go ahead with the sale. The bank then made a deal with the Polish authorities to receive a substantial portion of the apple juice produced by the new plant. It took on the obligation of selling the apple juice in the West. Everyone gained. The Austrians got business they wouldn't normally have gotten. The manufacturer was able to charge a far higher price than a normal market transaction would permit. The bank got fees that were a large multiple of those generated by just opening letters of credit. The Poles got their apple processors. Everyone gained except the holders of the Polish debt (who thought export earnings would go towards servicing the debt), the American manufacturer that lost the sale because its bank was not organized to accept payment in apple juice, and the Polish apple producers (or perhaps taxpayers) who overpaid for the machinery. [6]

In partial payment for aircraft equipment it sold to Rumania, McDonnell Douglas found itself with, among other countertraded items, a rather stupendous supply of canned ham "which the firm's staff is expected to munch its way through at the company's canteen for years to come." [7]   The Algerian wine that Caterpillar Tractor took on in countertrade, and found itself unable to sell, "was served in the company's cafeterias for many years." [8]

NATO countries — as well as third world countries — invariably demand offsets (production of the same or a different product located in their country) as a counterpart to arms purchases. Almost one half of U.S. aerospace exports now involve countertrade in some form or another. [9]   According to William Evonsky, Manager of Countertrade, Offset and Barter for the General Electric Trading Company, the average countertrade obligation during the 1960s was about 35% of the value of the expected sale. During the 1970s, that figure increased to almost 60%. At present, the average countertrade or offset requirement exceeds 80% of the value of the expected sale, and sometimes the commitment exceeds 100%. [10]   As a result of a number of recent large export sales — in particular, aircraft engine sales to Sweden and Spain — GE's countertrade commitments now exceed $2.2 billion. [11]   Countertrade is not even confined to goods. Services are beginning to enter the game. Deerfield Communications (USA) took payment from Jamaica in the form of data-processing services. [12]

The instances of countertrade abound. *Indonesia* recently legislated countertrade obligations of a very strict sort onto any major purchase, and the take-back goods cannot be oil or any other product that would "displace Indonesian cash sales." [13] *Mexico* is making major steps in a similar direction. [14] *Israel* has just changed the name of its countertrade authority. The Central Authority for Reciprocal Purchases, now known as the Board of Industrial Cooperation Agreements, requires foreign suppliers to the Israeli public sector to buy Israeli products worth 25% of the value of the contracts they receive (and the buy-back must be in industrial, not agricultural goods). *Austria* (as a buyer) has worked out offset purchase agreements with a host of Western companies. "The engagement of the foreign suppliers to buy in Austria is strictly voluntary because of the Austrian dedication to free market and free trade." But McDonnell Douglas has been taking offset production in partial payment for an airplane sale, and a similar system has been worked out with Airbus for the purchase of aircraft later in the 1980s. The Austrians have also worked out similar arrangements with automakers — including arrangements for Japanese cars where offset purchases result in percentage reductions of import duties. [15] The list of countertrades can be very long; the arrangements, very intricate.

CHANGES IN THE STRUCTURE OF THE INTERNATIONAL ECONOMY

The growth of countertrade is not merely a new wrinkle in traditional economic transactions prompted by superficial—and transient—events. Behind it lie fundamental changes in the structures of the international economy. The most important change is the rise of developmental states—most prominently Japan and the Asian NICs—as primary actors on the international scene and the imitation of their methods in sector after sector by more traditional, "regulatory" governments.

By "developmental state" (a term first and best used by Professor Chalmers Johnson in his excellent study, *MITI and the Japanese Miracle*), we mean countries where the central and ordering principle of government is the direct promotion of national economic growth and power. Japan invented and perfected the modern form; other countries have been quick to copy — or to adapt aspects of the system to their own circumstances. Governments as diverse as Brazil, France, and Korea have acted to create advantage and alter, in enduring ways, the international competitive position of their national firms and economies. These efforts by governments to shape outcomes make the distinctive capacities of governments and their willingness to support their national firms an element in the market competition among those firms. As a result, international trade has become less and less the private actions of private companies operating by market rules and constraints and more and more the instrument of national development policy. Where not too long ago international competition pitted the strengths and capacities of companies against one another, the competitive equation now includes the capacities of governments to shape market outcomes — and crucially, their ability and willingness to use those powers. Across a growing range of nations — but nowhere as well, as successfully, and at such a colossal scale as Japan — governments control (or significantly channel) the strategic allocation of capital to industries and try, to the best of their abilities, to control what enters and leaves the country. These efforts by governments to shape outcomes in international markets challenge the very premises of the open trade system.

There is no need for another sketch of how the Japanese system works. Let us simply point to one objective result of that system's operations: Japanese trade data — not the amounts of surpluses with different nations, but the peculiar pattern of Japanese trade and its relation to the growth of mercantilism in the international system.

After World War II, when the open international trade system was designed, the real problem was not trade in tractors to the tropics in exchange for coffee beans or exotic minerals. It was that the major trading nations of North America and Western Europe all made the same sorts of products — manufactured goods — and all expected to continue making them. The only way open trade could conceivably work at a large scale — without some parties being devastated, without it shifting from a system of mutual gains to one of winners and losers — was through the exchange of goods within the same broad sectors. That is precisely what happened. That is what is still happening, at least in most sectors across the Atlantic and within Western Europe. It is what was supposed to happen in a world where market forces are given free play and production costs and technologies converge. It has not been a very smooth process; adjustments — such as temporary protection and devaluations — have been necessary throughout. But the body of evidence is strong and supportive. Theory predicted it; experience has confirmed it. [16]

France is a major exporter of aircraft and autos. Yet France imports about four automobiles for every six she exports; she imports about 3.6 dollars of steel for every $5 she exports, and $2.7 of aircraft for every $3.5 exported.

Germany's trade pattern is similar. Germany also imports in the same sectors in which it exports. For every eight autos exported, about three are imported. For every $4 of steel exported, about $3 are imported. Even in chemicals, for every $3.5 exported, over $2 are imported.

But Japan is different. Its trade presents a completely different picture — one that strikes at the basic underpinnings of the trade system.

Unlike all the other advanced industrial countries, Japan does not import substantial amounts in those sectors in which it is a substantial exporter. Most dramatically, it imports less than one auto for every hundred it exports (compared to France's 4 for 6). It imports almost no consumer electronics products; it imports no commercial vehicles, practically no finished steel, practically no domestic appliances. The list is very long. [17]

Whatever the reasons behind it — deliberate government policy, cultural practices, whatever — the existence of such a trade pattern by itself, and from the second largest national economy in the international system, strikes at the very foundations of the GATT system.

First, such a pattern of trade creates winners and losers. The policies and practices that create such a trade pattern convert a system of mutually beneficial exchange through increasingly efficient sub-specialization into a predatory conflict. The existence of the pattern is evidence of the transformation. In the new system, whole sectors and regions can suddenly be devastated — and with them, long chains of industries, both upstream and downstream, that depend on those sectors. These are not marginal adjustments. And after the first round of consumer gains, they are not mutually beneficial. Such a trade pattern calls into question the entire basis for open international trade. It strips away the rationale behind most of our policies and the relevance of the economic theories that justify and generate those policies.

Second, where such patterns exist, open trade does not. They demonstrate that in fact markets do *not* determine the flows of commodities or discipline firms in an automatic, or self-regulating, system. Companies compete in the new international economy, but many of them are no longer creators of disinterested market forces; they are the agents of government policies for national economic development.

Reinforcing this principal cause (that trade and investment is more and more an instrument of active national economic development policy and less and less the affair of private buyers and sellers) is a confluence of additional sources that swell the stream of countertrade.

Arms Trade — The first, and most important, is the rapid growth of international trade in big-ticket, sophisticated armaments. International arms sales are estimated at some twenty-five billion dollars, with the United States way out in front, selling some forty percent, followed by the Soviet Union solidly in second place at about thirty percent, and France holding onto third place, while the UK, Germany, and Italy eagerly seek to increase their sales, and Japan waits in the wings. [18] For some of the newer arms-merchant nations, such as Brazil and Israel (exports, respectively an official 2.5 billion and a good deal more unofficially), the armaments industry is a major focus of governmental development and trade policies. [19]

In many ways, the arms trade is the model for the new mercantilism. The market is characterized by discrete, giant contracts, rather than by marginal adjustment of commodity flows. A large initial sale — say, for a fighter aircraft — locks in a large stream of follow-up sales for such items as spare parts, up-grade kits, support equipment, and training and maintenance services. Armaments is the sector where it is the most difficult to distinguish between economics and politics, between the state and the private sector. Governments are the clients — they buy the arms. But they are also the key economic players on the seller's side. [20]

The arms sector is probably the largest generator of countertrade and offset deals, with about one-half of U.S. aerospace exports subject to some kind of countertrade or offset and quite likely an even higher ratio for the other arms exporters. Not only developing countries, but such developed and market-oriented nations as Canada, Belgium, and Holland routinely demand — and get — major compensating offsets before they make an armaments purchase. Indeed, it is the growth of offsets in the arms trade that is prompting the first serious American inquiry into the extent and consequences of countertrade. The U.S. Congress is beginning to hold hearings on countertrade in the armaments sector. [21]

Surplus Capacity —The need to manage surplus capacity is a second major reinforcing factor in the growth of countertrade. When productive capacity exceeds demand at price levels that permit sustained production and employment, companies scramble to sell their goods in imaginative ways. Sometimes they resort to "dumping." When overcapacity is felt in a range of industries important to the economics and politics of nations — such as steel, autos, textiles, dairy, aircraft, and oil — governments act to assist sales and sustain employment. They also act, quite as frequently, on the other side of the transaction to demand some non-market benefits, such as offsets or technology transfers, in exchange for access to their markets when their nationals become important buyers in overcapacity situations. Countertrade arrangements are a favorite device for such overcapacity situations, in part because of the extreme difficulty of putting a simple market price on a complex countertrade transaction.

Dumping — pure and simple in substance, but opaque and elaborate in form — is, of course, a major motive for the surge in barter and countertrade. Gary Banks, who is writing the briefing book that will serve for initial discussions by GATT members in their efforts to begin to formulate a countertrade policy, is quite clear on the subject:

> The main attraction for countertrade for dumping or price-cutting purposes...is its reduced transparency. In trade with non-market economies...it is already difficult enough to determine from price information whether dumping has taken place, particularly for manufactured goods. [But,] this need not mean that some additional opaqueness would be unwelcome. [22]

When the objective is to unload (discretely) primary commodities that have been stockpiled, then countertrade can serve as a technique to dump or to cut prices. The marketing of surplus commodities appears to be the most dominant objective.

> The problem is that when markets soften, many commodity producers are barred from slashing prices to market-clearing levels by international commodity agreements as well as by fears of anti-dumping measures. [23]

Barter can provide a means by which individual countries may dispose of their export surpluses without having to stipulate the price. Eroding real prices, in the face of international commodity agreements such as OPEC, generate an increase in barter. Thus one can speculate about the motives behind the sudden proclivity for oil-barter deals in Nigeria, Iran, Libya, and Indonesia — the four OPEC members worst affected by the recent oil glut. And the recent gigantic barter deal between Saudi Arabia and Boeing raises similar concerns. [24] Saudi Arabia paid for the Boeings in oil — not cash. We know the spot price of a barrel of oil and the quantity of oil Boeing received. The question is the price of a Boeing 747, and that of course can vary considerably depending upon the terms of sale and the way the aircraft is rigged-out. In the end, it becomes difficult to determine the price of either the aircraft or the oil, and that may be the reason for both parties deciding on barter. (The bauxite for powdered milk deal between the U.S. and

Jamaica in 1983 also excited some controversy in this respect.) The strongest evidence of an intent to dump or to get around price agreements can often be found in the agreements governing such transactions, which frequently contain a clause forbidding re-sale of the bartered products on third markets!

Increase in Funds — Barter was also encouraged by a sharp increase in funds for countries pursuing ambitious and state-centered development strategies in the mid-seventies. For some countries, mostly OPEC nations, the funds came from trade; for others, such as Brazil and Mexico — and also Eastern Europe — they came from borrowings. Their suddenly expanded role in international trade translated as an expansion of the role of state-controlled trading. Trade transactions were increasingly used as extensions of government development policies. Thus, buy-back agreements increasingly became the price for sales of the production plants that embodied national development and import-substitution strategies.

Economics is not physics. In economics, an opposite cause can very well produce (or reinforce) the same effect. The sudden and vast increase in "free funds" in the 1970s (mostly loans or oil revenues to countries with ambitious, government-oriented trade and development strategies) increased the volume of state trading, barter, buy-backs, and countertrade. Ten years later, the even more sudden drying up of those funds had the same result. The weakening oil market has been an important accelerator of countertrade, but more important is the Latin American debt crisis. As hard currency has all but vanished from the major trading nations of Latin America, and uncommitted Free Money dried up in the OPEC nations, governments have turned to countertrade — and the state controls of trade they developed in the earlier cycle — to control the volume and kind of imports. Companies — both importers and their foreign suppliers — have become rather ingenious in living with and sometimes circumventing those controls through extremely elaborate countertrade deals. Indonesia has been a pioneer in erecting rigorous countertade obligations for large sales into Indonesia. Countertrade requirements are 100% of the purchase and must not be taken in goods that Indonesia would normally export without the countertrade deal. Mexico is now trying to copy the Indonesian model and is instituting countertrade requirements at a substantial rate. Malaysia, finding that Indonesian countertrade promotions come at its expense, is now instituting a similar countertrade policy for defensive reasons. [25]

Expanding trade with East Bloc countries was an important stimulus for the growth of barter in the 1970s. The volume of Western exports into Eastern Europe increased from $6 billion in 1970 to $26 billion in 1980. [26] This spectacular spurt in trade was fueled by loans from Western banks, and much of it took forms other than simple market transactions, with offsets, buybacks, and countertade deals figuring prominently. A most recent, but quite typical, arrangement has been the Volkswagen deal to construct an automobile engine plant in East Germany and take engines produced in that plant as payment. The institutional capacity developed by German companies, banks, and specialized trading companies (such as Metallgesellschaft) in their trading with Eastern Europe has served as a base for the further development of countertrade with such nations as Indonesia and Brazil. But the continued expansion of countertrade in the 1980s cannot be explained as a peculiarity of growing East-West trade because, beginning in 1980, the volume of trade with Eastern Europe began to fall — from 26 billion in 1980 to 18 billion in 1982 [27] — as net lending by Western banks to Eastern Europe dried up.

THE SCOPE OF THE PHENOMENON

The Short-Term View — The view of barter as exceptional — as well as exceptionable — remains dominant. Barter is still seen as overwhelmingly related to short-term expedients and as fundamentally bounded by time and scope, even though those boundaries are so terribly relaxed at the moment. It is a way to circumvent temporary difficulties caused by currency crises or by excess capacity that generates disguised, though tolerated, dumping in third markets. And, of course, it is accepted as an enduring practice in the special and circumscribed domains of trade with the East Bloc and trade in armaments.

Barter is an expedient, a means to survive bad times. But once the tactic becomes part of competition, even the strongest competitor will, sooner or later, be obliged to follow suit. In this view, which fits nicely into conventional modes of economic analysis and leads to conventional policy formulation, barter is part of an overcapacity problem. The sources of its sudden expansion are on the producers' side, as will be the causes of its contraction: the extent of the practice should diminish once excess capacity is written down, and the world economy picks up, and special problems, such as the hard currency problems in Latin America, are settled. Normal trading practices — so much swifter, cheaper, and more flexible — will then return to their rightful position of dominance. And so will normal, traditional market shares and trading patterns. Except that some producers will find their traditional markets flooded with years of accumulated countertrade obligations, and once the flood works down, re-entry will be extremely costly and, perhaps, impossible.

This conventional view of barter often carries the additional hypothesis that some producers, especially in less-developed economies, may lack marketing skills and resources. Consequently, they may be willing to let prices shift against them in order to transfer that selling task to their trading partners. Through countertrade, they are paying for marketing in a disguised way. This, essentially, is an adaptation of a classical argument. It finds that there exist substantial imperfections in the market for international sales expertise facilities. The condition should also self-correct in a reasonably short time, as international trading companies grow to fill the need. And indeed, they are. Such powerful international trading companies as Metallgesellschaft and Mitsubishi are expanding their countertrade operations rapidly; and new players, American industrial firms (such as GE and GM) and American banks (such as Bank of America), are opening countertrade divisions. [28] The new countertrade specialist firms in effect remonetize barter. That is, the producer company saddled with extraneous commodities as part of a transaction can, for a fee (often considerable), transfer the responsibility for sale of those goods to a specialized trading company. Since no sensible trading company wants to get stuck with unsaleable commodities (such as the pink telephone dials GTE found itself holding in exchange for a sale of telephone equipment to Poland [29]), the countertrade specialists are increasingly consulted before the deal is concluded. The producer can then calculate the deal in more traditional financial terms. An international barter mart (and there is occasional talk of one opening in Amsterdam) — to function as a clearinghouse for multilateral swaps of palm oil, peanuts, pliers, and pants — would be a major step towards formalizing the restoration of the market.

The Long-Term View — An alternative explanation of the growth and function of barter is more interesting and more threatening to the international trade system as currently constituted because it suggests that barter will be more permanent.   In this view, international transactions are not necessarily about exchanging one product for another, as in classical trade theory's example of Portuguese wine exchanged for English wool. Ricardo assumes transactions are between private actors. If transactions are not about exchanging wine-for-wool, what are they about? When governments are involved, trade may be about the use of political power to alter a nation's economic structure, that is, the profile of what it produces. Governments intervene in the wine for wool trade, not just to get the wool cheaper, but to control access to its national market for wool products for the deliberate purpose of gearing up domestic companies to produce wool and sweaters too. Trade is then about strategic efforts to change a nation's economic situation, to re-position its industry in the international division of labor, wealth, and power. It becomes not a short-term, self-regulating game of optimal use of the world's resources for maximizing consumer welfare, but a long-term, strategic game about the Wealth of Nations.   The Brazilian petrochemicals story and the competition between Airbus and Boeing illustrate this view particularly well. [30] Japanese semiconductors and computers, a few years back, were a parallel illustration; so were French process engineering, Saudi petrochemicals, Korean steel, Brazilian automobiles, and Japanese aerospace. Once again, the list is very long.

THE POLICY IMPLICATIONS

The policy implications are two-fold. The first is that barrier tactics may affect the competitiveness of American companies. The second is that a mini-version of the third-world debt crisis may be preparing itself, as unknown but substantial quantities of countertrade obligations pile up on the books of major industrial companies.

(1) Feeling both that countertrade is basically wrong and should not be encouraged, but that American industry is at a decided disadvantage in countertrade against such institutionally organized and experienced players as the French and the Japanese, the U.S. is moving in several different directions at once. In the government, different departments

take different — and contradictory — positions. "Treasury says it is 'flatly opposed' to it, Commerce helps companies do it, the Department of Labor objects to it, and the Ex-Im Bank has no policy for dealing with it." [31]   In Congress, legislation has been introduced both to curtail countertrade and to encourage the countertrading of U.S. surplus commodities (mostly agricultural) for foreign strategic minerals. [32]

The response of American business is also mixed. Some companies, most prominently IBM, simply stay away from any form of barter — or claim they do. Most others, feeling threatened by substantial losses of markets unless they accept barter deals, are reluctantly engaging in such transactions. Still others are greeting it as an opportunity. Such manufacturing giants as GE are actively involved in barter deals all over the world and are using their experience to set themselves up in a new line of business as trade and barter specialists. The Export Trading Company Act of 1982 is proving to be an important instrument for creating American countertrade specialists. Enacted to encourage exports — especially by small and middle-size U.S. companies who lack international trade experience — it has led to the rapid creation of American export trading companies, including bank trading companies, to compete with such established giants as C. Itoh and Mitsubishi. Within the past two years or so, such major American firms as Sears, First Chicago, and Bank of America, have established (or, like GE, substantially beefed up) export trading companies. And though the Sears venture has folded, new ones continue to be created. Many of them are actively pursuing countertrade deals. The Bank of America Trading Company, for example, estimates that a full third of its business will come from countertrade. [33]

(2) The scale of countertrade obligations (that is, the quantity of goods that U.S. companies are obliged to purchase from foreign producers and dispose of) is an unknown. Last year, the Treasury department circulated a voluntary survey among major defense contractors. Some twenty-six companies responded, but there is no way to know which big ones did not. The sum of such obligations they held exceeded $10 billion. [34] Completely informal and unofficial inquiries indicate that some major U.S. companies are each sitting on substantially more than a billion dollars of such obligations.

It is quite possible that firms (such as GE or United Technologies or McDonnell Douglas in the U.S., or Aerospatiale in France, or C. Itoh or

Sumitomo in Japan, or whoever) have collectively (but unknowingly) agreed to move exports out of particular countries far in excess of what those countries have ever — or will ever — export. This could mean that on the books of those companies sit dubious assets of colossal proportions: millions of dollars of non-oil Indonesian products; or Portuguese non-vegetable oil, non-cork, and never-before-exported products, carried at values far in excess of that which could conceivably be realized.

The absence of any central data file on countertrade obligations — organized by country (whose exports various companies worldwide are obligated to move) and by product — could help precipitate a minor international crisis in a fairly short time. It is uncomfortably reminiscent of the lack of any central intelligence on Latin American debt a few years back.

A simple measure that could be taken by the international community before it is too late would be to open a central countertrade information clearing house so that companies, banks, and countries could know if they are about to contract to export Portuguese shirts or Indonesian wicker or Malaysian sneakers at twenty times the quantity the Portuguese, Malaysians, or Indonesians have ever exported. It would also make interesting reading for the traditional suppliers of those countertraded commodities.

THE IMPLICATIONS FOR OPEN TRADE

The GATT system was constructed around a set of definable premises. First, trade arrangements that are built on multilateral negotiations among all nations are preferable to bilateral or other partial arrangements. Second, trade will be conducted by private actors in markets in which prices are set by a free interplay of supply and demand. Third, free trade will generate the expansion of all economies, if only each will bear the strains of internal expansion and adjustment. Fourth, government intervention is seen as a distortion to international price signals.

When considering trade among advanced countries, the premises of the GATT system ignore or deny the potential influence on trade of development strategies working through domestic structures. Thus, they only awkwardly fit many of the new realities of international trade. The assumption — half fact and half fiction — that governments are negotiating about the rules of trade and leaving the market to settle the outcomes is increasingly less tenable. Governments are increasingly negotiating directly about trade outcomes. Equally important, the state-centered development strategies are entangled with the changes in patterns of world economic power and trade. They have served both as an instrument of policy and as a device to mobilize political support for those policies. Moreover, the rules of the domestic economy and the appropriate use of national government power in the world economy have themselves become the subject of negotiation.

Even a few years ago, it seemed that the exceptions to reasonably free trade could be contained and the goals preserved by some system of "organized muddling through." It was believed that the reduction of non-tariff barriers could be negotiated in the same fashion that had so successfully removed more direct limitations on trade during the previous generation. But bargaining over external barriers and negotiating over the arrangements of the domestic political economy in fact involve very different things.

Several developments set the informal agenda of preoccupations. The Americans discovered that the American economy (as well as the other national economies) was "interdependent," that is, sensitive and even vulnerable to developments abroad. Two emblems of the new era focused attention on powerful new forms of private actions in international trade and obscured the enduring ability of governments to shape economic outcomes: the dramatic ability of the multinational corporation (MNC) to formulate international strategies and to operate across national boundaries; and the rapid expansion of the Eurocurrency market to produce an international private financial system of similar size to the one inside the United States, but outside the control of any government authority.

Compared to these new and powerful forces, government interventions were treated as relatively negligible, rather rearguard exceptions to a transforming liberal order.

Though attention and concern were focused on the MNCs and the Eurodollar market, their preeminence was not the inevitable market outcome of improved communications and transport technology. Critically, the bargains that host countries struck with the American MNCs depended, in the end, on the administrative resources and will of the government and economic structure of the country. The Japanese first showed that a government could act as doorman to the national economy, breaking up the package of management, finance, technology, and control represented by the MNC and forcing the pieces to be recombined under national authority. Other countries quickly learned those lessons. Government and politics had mattered all along; their influence had simply been obscured.

CONCLUSION

We are left with the question we began with. Do the instrumentalities of mercantilist strategies and practices require specific policy responses at the international level, perhaps even re-design of the international trade system? Let us consider our categories in turn. Most of the tactics of developmental strategies which involve domestic subsidy and closed or semi-permeable markets fall under the purview of GATT, although GATT has been notably unable to contend with the kind of non-tariff barriers nations have created, Japan being the most important case. In part, it is their use in combination and their frequent revision and redeployment that is difficult to address. Most important is the reality that the tactics, once implemented, created enduring advantages and permanently altered the structure of markets. Once a *fait accompli* is achieved, there is no trade remedy. Equally, the remedies under formal procedures are slow and tortuous, leaving governments tempted to implement unilateral solutions restricting their own markets or providing comparable assistances to their producers. In separate studies, the BRIE has examined these strategies in the Japanese case and has developed a theoretical model to account for both the sectoral and aggregate patterns of trade. Surplus capacity is a traditional concern, and explicit techniques have emerged to manage, albeit with difficulty and conflict, such problems. As we have seen, state trading bred such techniques as barter and countertrade. They spill their problems over into other realms.

The real question is whether these exceptions have become the rule. Have we in fact established a mercantilist suborder within a liberal system and justified it in the language of liberal trade? If we add together the trade dramatically affected by development strategies, managed in bilateral and unilateral arrangements, conducted between governments or in the form of barter, we might conclude we have. Recognizing it is difficult because doing so could legitimate a strategy of closure.

Perhaps it is simply the other way around. Perhaps managing trade relations more explicitly than in the past has allowed new players to enter the system in big ways, has allowed trade to continue to expand (even with wild fluctuations of unmanaged currencies), and has allowed dramatic changes in market advantage. Perhaps in a world without managed currencies, expanding trade means managed trade.

Notes

1   Cited in *Business Marketing* (January 1984); *Forbes*, March 12, 1984, p. 41.
2   *Forbes*, op. cit, p. 42.
3   *Business Week*, July 19, 1982; GE Trade in *Countertrade*, March 19, 1984.
4   See Gary Banks, in *World Economy, A Quarterly Journal on International Economic Affairs* (June 1983). Mr Banks is preparing the GATT briefing book on countertrade policy. See also, *International Management*, (August 1984), p. 25.
5   Leo G. B. Welt, Trade Without Money: Barter and Countertrade (New York, NY: 1984) provides careful and elaborate definitions and examples of each kind of barter and countertrade. Gary Banks, op. cit., provides brief, but clear definitions.
6   *Countertrade,* Vol. II, No. 15.
7   McDonnell-Douglas in *Finance and Development,* published by IMF, January 1984.
8   Caterpillar in David Yoffie, "Profiting from Countertrade," *Harvard Business Review* (May/June 1984), p. 8.
9   *Forbes,* March 12, 1984, p. 42.
10 Speech to World Trade Institute Conference on Countertrade, in *Countertrade,* Vol. II, No. 12.
11 Ibid.
12 Ibid., Vol. II, No. 5.
13 See Cathleen Maynard, *Indonesia's Countertrade Experience,* American-Indonesian Chamber of Commerce, November 1983; see also, *Countertrade,* January 9, 1984.
14 *Countertrade,* November 21, 1983.
15 Speech by Gerhardt Vogt, Director, Centrobank, Vienna, in *Countertrade,* January 9, 1984.
16 For a discussion of the theoretical background see Borrus, Tyson, and Zysman, "Creating Advantage," Export-Import Bank, 1984.
17 Data from Professor Bruce Scott, *American Competitiveness: Problems, Causes, and Implications,* paper presented at Harvard Business School, 75th Anniversary Colloquium, 1984. (In print, Harvard University Press.)

18   Market shares from Andrew J. Pierre, *The Global Politics of Arms Sales*, Princeton, 1982, p. 81.

19   *Wall Street Journal*, January 4, 1985.

20   John Zysman and Stephen S. Cohen, "Double or Nothing," *Foreign Affairs* (Summer 1983).

21   See hearings on Countertrade and Offset Arrangements, House Banking Committee, Sub-Committee on Economic Stabilization, May 1984; and hearings before House Armed Services Subcommittee on Seapower...for HR 3544.

22   See Banks, op. cit.

23   Ibid.

24   See *Financial Times*, October 25, 1984.

25   See *Countertrade*, November 21, 1983, on Mexico; May 16, 1983, and October 24, 1983, on Indonesia; September 12, 1983, on Malaysia.

26   United States Central Intelligence Agency, *Handbook of Economic Statistics*, September 1983, table 69.

27   Ibid.

28   See *Business Marketing*, January 1984.

29   Ibid.

30   See Zysman and Cohen, op. cit., for Brazilian petroleum discussion.

31   *Business Marketing*, op. cit.

32   See speech by Ed Barber, Trade Finance Foreign Affairs Officer at the Treasury to Institute of International Trade and Development, October 1983; see HR 3544 and S 1683, "The Barter Promotion Act."

33   See *Countertrade*, February 20, 1984.

34   Ibid., August

II

STRATEGIC TRADE POLICY, COMPETITIVENESS & DEINDUSTRIALIZATION

In the last decade a new issue in the debate over trade policy has emerged in the United States. Many economists, business people and politicians have begun to talk about the decline of U.S. "competitiveness", particularly with respect to Japan, and about the "deindustrialization" of the American economy. They point out that, one by one, many U.S. industries have lost market share to the Japanese: first the automobile and steel industries, then the TV and consumer electronics industries, then the semiconductor industry. Recently, the Japanese have also challenged the Americans for dominance in the banking and financial service industries while another Asian competitor, South Korea, entered the steel, auto, and consumer electronics industries.

Many observers argue that Japan's trade and industrial policy bears little resemblance to the free trade policies endorsed by Adam Smith, David Ricardo and most economists today. Motivated by the Japanese example, some economists in the U.S. seriously criticize the basic tenets of a free trade policy and question whether the U.S. should continue to follow such a policy.

The first reading supports the position that a free trade policy may not be the best answer-- that some sort of industrial policy may be needed. Bruce Scott, a Harvard Business School professor, argues that the traditional notion of comparative advantage presented by Ricardo is a static one and is not applicable to a world of rapidly changing technology. In his view a country can create a comparative advantage by choosing to invest in the sectors of the economy which are subject to the most rapid technological progress. Scott contends that Japan has succeeded in world trade through a specific set of industrial and trade policies which: (a) systematically targeted certain key industries where Japan could become a leader in technology; (b) subsidized and supported those industries; (c) excluded foreign competition from domestic markets.

In the second article, Krugman examines the contributions of the "new international economics." He points out that the traditional theories of trade as expressed by Ricardo and by the Heckscher-Ohlin-Samuelson model cannot adequately explain the pattern of trade by industrialized countries. Instead, it appears that trade among developed countries can be better explained by models of imperfect competition. Interestingly, the policy implications of these new models of international trade may be quite different from the traditional theory of trade. Krugman shows that in the context of the new international economics, certain types of strategic trade policies, such as Europe's subsidy of Airbus may indeed be advantageous (for Europe). However, he cautions that the new models of trade yield no clear policy prescriptions: one can demonstrate that strategic trade policies either help or hurt a country depending upon what assumptions are made. In the end, Krugman contends that the main argument for a free trade regime may rest on the politics of protectionism. Although one country may be able to profitably pursue a strategic trade policy, if all countries follow this policy, all will ultimately be worse off.

In the final article, by Hatsopolous, Krugman and Summers, "U.S. competitiveness: beyond the trade deficit," the authors conclude that the main problem facing the U.S. in terms of its international competitiveness has been lagging productivity which stems from a low savings rate. They propose that the U.S. needs to raise its savings rate if it is to maintain a position of leadership in the world economy.

6

Creating Comparative Advantage

Bruce Scott

Comparative advantage, free trade, and competition among firms are central features of theory behind the trading system built since World War II. It is a system in which all countries gain if each specializes in its areas of comparative advantage and exchanges products with other countries in the free market system. "A much larger (world) market permits increased specialization, increased productivity, and higher incomes. Free trade among the fifty states allows productivity not possible in a single state, for example, and all states should gain in terms of a higher standard of living and improved welfare. In this system, firms should discover what can be produced best in a given locale, and governments should prohibit all forms of protection.

The theory of comparative advantage was first articulated by David Ricardo in 1817. He argued that England and Portugal would each gain by trading even if Portugal produced both wine and cloth more cheaply than England. If the British had less of a cost disadvantage in cloth, they should specialize in exporting cloth and import wine. The Portuguese should do the reverse. Both countries would be better off through specialization and trade in an open market than with a strategy of protection.

The theory was originally worked out for two commodities, wine and cloth, and a single measure of value — hours of labor. The basic idea is still one of the central pillars of Western economic theory. As stated in a current best-selling economics text, the theory is deceptively simple: ". . . countries export commodities whose production requires relatively intensive use of productive resources found locally in relative abundance." [1]

The theory is based on a number of important assumptions, including full employment, balanced current accounts, the existence of productive factors that are "homogeneous and mobile between sectors" and which can thus "costlessly be reallocated from one sector to another," [2] and the comparability of knowledge and technology from one country to another. There are obvious problems with each of these assumptions: for example, the possibility of high and continuing levels of unemployment; frictional unemployment and/or retraining costs as labor shifts from one skill area or level to another; social costs as plants and sometimes whole communities are shut down while plants or even whole communities are built elsewhere; institutional factors that permit current accounts to remain substantially out of balance for extended periods of time; and different and unequal levels of knowledge and technology, some of which is proprietary to particular firms. Each of these abstractions from reality limits its applicability in some measure and thus calls for care in its use. However, there seem to be two additional abstractions that are not so much inevitable simplifications as distortions, which in the present international context cause the theory to obscure rather than illuminate some of the most important dynamics of international competition. [3]

As presently used in Western economics, the theory of comparative advantage assumes that 'the laws of increasing costs' prevails [4] and that productive resources are "found locally" rather than created. If resources are "found" and costs rise once they are fully utilized, then production levels are determined by natural endowments and they will tend to be self-limiting. Agricultural land is a good example: even a rich Portuguese vineyard will only yield so much wine. Increasing investments of fertilizer and labor have diminishing returns at some point. Much the same reasoning has been applied to industry, as there will inevitably be diminishing returns and rising costs in the production of cloth as well.

The assumption is critical. Diminishing returns and rising costs mean that there are few if any natural monopolies other than pubic utilities, and that competition among numerous producers is the natural state of affairs. Any advantage a country has is both "natural" and "self-limiting." Given these assumptions, specialization and trade will yield higher incomes than the attempt to be self-sufficient, and it will be mutually beneficial given any reasonable distribution of the gains.

The resulting perspective is a positive-sum game based on an essentially static trade theory. Advantages rest largely on endowments that must be "found" rather than created, and one assumes rising costs as one exploits those resources more intensively. The fact that critical resources can be imported or created is overlooked, as is the possibility of continually declining costs (except temporarily in the case of an infant industry). The fact that a firm might continually cut prices to expand volume and in so doing drive all others out of the market is an example of monopolistic and antisocial behavior unjustified by economic reality. The fact that a nation might pursue a similar approach through an export promotion policy is likewise unjustified.

A DYNAMIC THEORY OF COMPARATIVE ADVANTAGE

One of the key innovations of the new East Asian competitors is a revised theory of comparative advantage, a theory focused on opportunity as well as resources, and one that shows how a country can mobilize whatever limited resources it has to seize opportunities. Instead of focusing on static factor endowments and rising (short-run) costs, it focuses on factor mobility and the possibility of declining long-run costs based on the learning curve as well as economics of scale. It is a theory that focuses on the opportunities for change through time — a dynamic theory of comparative advantage which supplements the traditional, static Western one. [5]

With the advantage of hindsight, it is obvious that the short-term and long-term growth and productivity prospects for cloth and wine were quite different in the original Ricardian example. For Portugal, the short-term advantage come from specialization in wine; the long-term advantage comes from making a success in cloth, the "high-tech," high-growth," rapidly changing industry of the period. If the Portuguese follow the Western theory of comparative advantage, they are sacrificing long-term growth for short-term gains and implicitly accepting a lower standard of living than the British. Concluding otherwise implies that for some reason the Portuguese are "unable" to compete in textiles, a proposition much like the once-popular notion that the Egyptians could not operate the Suez Canal. While there is still merit in the static theory, its implications for an economic strategy are likely to lead to second-rate performance at best.

In addition to recognizing the contrast between long-run and short-run gains, the dynamic theory recognizes that the benefits of the static system are not necessarily symmetrical. For example, those countries with a favored position in a high-growth, high value-added industry have an advantage over others. Those with advantages in low-growth industries or those with a low rate of technological change have "advantages" that are second rate in comparison. To stick with these natural advantages is to accept a lower rate of growth and technological development simply because it is a "natural state of affairs," for which, unfortunately, there is "no remedy."

A world of static comparative advantage and free trade favors the rich and the strong — those with natural resources and high levels of productivity in major growth industries. They can undersell newcomers in less-fortunate or less-developed countries and maintain their favored position. The issue is not so much "exploitation" of the weak as a "natural state of affairs" governed by an efficient, impersonal marketplace. And it should not be surprising that the leading advocates of free trade have been those who were the strong at the time, first the United Kingdom, then the United States, and then Germany. Free trade, like free competition, has political as well as economic content: taken literally it is a system that enhances the power of the powerful and makes it all the more difficult for the poor to catch up.

Assuming a connection between theory and national strategies, it should not be surprising that the foremost challenge to the world of static comparative advantage and free trade has come from those nations that were unwilling to accept the second-class citizenship implied by their lower standard of living. The driving motive is political more than economic: "The need for economic growth in a developing country has few if any economic springs. It arises form a desire to assume full human status by taking part in an industrial civilization, participation in which *alone* enables a nation or an individual to compel others to treat it as an equal." [6]

In a world of technological change, differential rates of growth in volume and productivity across industries, and declining costs — especially in the high technology, rapid-growth industries of the era — the rational choice for Portugal, as for other less-developed countries, is to select growth industries and to use the powers of government to supplement those of the market in marshalling the resources necessary for entry and successful participation. Portugal needs to think in terms of acquiring or creating strength in promising sectors rather than simply accepting its existing mix of resources and attempting to exploit that "endowment" as efficiently as possible. *In short, the Portuguese should specialize in textiles, not wine, regardless of whether their costs are lower or higher than those prevailing in Britain at the time.*

Portugal should in some measure choose the industries in which it wishes to participate and adapt its policies and institutions as required to participate successfully. While it cannot be best at everything, it has considerable leeway in choosing the industries in which it wishes to participate and in creating the conditions necessary for successful participation. In other words, it has a considerable measure of freedom to create the comparative advantages it wishes, provided it has the will and ingenuity to create or borrow the necessary mix of policies and institutions to achieve the cost and quality positions required for success.

Miyohei Shinohara, former head of the economics section of the Japanese Economic Planning Agency and longtime member of the Industrial Structure Council, explains the need for a new view of cooperative advantage as follows:

> In modern economics it has been considered that in an economy of abundant labor and scarce capital, the development of labor-intensive production methods would naturally bring about a rational allocation of resources.
>
> On the other hand, in an economy with abundant capital and a shortage of labor, it has been taken for granted that capital-intensive industries would grow by becoming export industries. It has also been assumed that any measure taken contrary to this theorem would be going against economic principles, thus distorting resource allocation.
>
> If this reasoning is correct, the industrial policies adopted by MITI in the mid-1950s were wrong. Ironically, however, Japan's industrial policies achieved unprecedented success by going against modern economic theory.
>
> The problem of classical thinking undeniably lies in the fact that it is essentially "static" and does not take into account the possibility of a dynamic change in the comparative advantage or disadvantage of industries over a coming 10- or 20-year period. to take the place of such a traditional theory, a new policy concept needs to be developed to deal with the possibility of intertemporal dynamic development. [7]

The Japanese appear to have been the first to recognize that advantages could be created through the mobilization of technology, capital, and skilled labor, not just to nurture a few infant industries to supply the domestic market, but as a way of nurturing the whole industrial sector toward areas of growth and opportunity in the world market. Furthermore, government could create policies and institutions that accelerated the attack of new sectors on the one hand and the abandonment of declining or threatened sectors on the other. [8] In so doing, the Japanese discovered or created a strategy of dynamic comparative advantage at the national level which in many ways parallels the strategy of a diversified firm as it shifts resources from less promising to more promising areas.

Once this visible hand or strategy was discovered, the label "Japan, Inc." followed. This term, typically rejected in the U.S. academic community as unduly simplistic, was found useful by business executives familiar with the lack of tidiness of decision-making processes in large firms. As a consequence, when American academics and business executives meet to discuss how the Japanese economy works and to assess its impact on the U.S. economy, they often talk past one another. Business people sense the Japanese are doing something different but lack a theory to explain it. Much of the academic community clings to a static theory that obscures what the Japanese are doing, which leads inevitably to the conclusion that it involves nothing new or different. Even though the Japanese have explicitly indicated that rejecting Western theory was an essential ingredient in their growth strategy, some of our leading experts refused to listen.

> Those who attribute Japan's economic success principally to MITI's industrial policy seem to be suggesting that without MITI the huge 30 to 35 percent of GNP that the Japanese invested in the past several decades would have gone mainly into such industries as textiles, shoes, plastic souvenirs and fisheries. This is sheer nonsense. Given the quality of Japanese business executives, those massive investment funds probably would have wound up roughly where they actually did. And to the extent that there would have been differences, there is no reason to believe that MITI's influence, on balance, improved the choices in any major way .[9]

There have also been misunderstandings between some U.S. officials and their Japanese counterparts, with the former alleging that Japanese industrial policy was more significant than the latter were willing to acknowledge. This problem was analyzed by Yoshizo Ikeda, senior adviser to the board of Mitsui & Co., as follows:

> In my view, the real problem is a perception gap. Americans focus on the fact that the Japanese government is more successful than the U.S. government in promoting industry, while Japanese officials emphasize the fact that they have less power over the economy than they did several years ago. In order to close this perception gap, both sides must communicate more closely. The United States certainly needs to improve its understanding of Japanese policies. But Japan also has a responsibility to explain its policies candidly and credibly. In my

judgment, its failure to do so has contributed considerably to the friction over this issue.

My central theme . . . is that Japanese government industrial policies, although less powerful than in the past, continue to play an influential role in Japan's economic development. But this influence does not derive from dictatorial controls or unfair practices that violate international trade rules. Rather, it is based on effective policy implementation and a variety of cultural traits that enable the government and the private sector to cooperate effectively for the common good of the nation. [10]

In 1972, the Organization for Economic Cooperation and Development (OECD) published one of the early, formal explanations of the basic concepts underlying Japanese industrial policy based on a speech by the then MITI vice minister, as follows:

Should Japan have entrusted its future, according to the theory of comparative advantage, to these industries characterized by intensive use of labor? That would perhaps be a rational choice for a country with a small population of 5 or 10 million. But Japan has a large population. If the Japanese economy had adopted the simple doctrine of free trade and had chosen to specialize in this kind of industry, it would almost permanently have been unable to break away from the Asian pattern of stagnation and poverty, and would have remained the weakest link in the free world, thereby becoming a problem area in the Far East.

The Ministry of International Trade and Industry decided to establish in Japan industries which required intensive employment of capital and technology, industries that in consideration of comparative cost of production should be the most inappropriate for Japan, industries such as steel, oil refining, petrochemicals, automobiles, aircraft, industrial machinery of all sorts, and later electronics, including electronic computers. From a short-run, static viewpoint, encouragement of such industries would seem to conflict with economic rationalism. But, from a long-range point of view, these are precisely the industries where income elasticity of demand is high, technological progress is rapid, and labor productivity rises fast. It was clear that without these industries it would be difficult to employ a population of 100 million and raise their standard of living to that of Europe and America with light industries alone; whether right or wrong, Japan had to have these heavy and chemical industries. [11]

The Japanese, placed in a position similar to that of Portugal in Ricardo's famous example, rejected the notion of specializing in "wine" and chose "cloth" instead. Less than a generation later they had become the world's low-cost producer of many of the items in which they had started with a high-cost position (e.g., steel, ships, automobiles, and consumer electronics).

The criterion used by the Japanese in selecting which industries to emphasize or target is often loosely described as higher value added. This is true in a rough sense; after the fact, however, their criteria appear to have been more subtle, less mechanical, and above all appear to have required sophisticated judgments about the future. Shinohara explains:

> The two basic criteria to which the industrial structure policies adopted by MITI conformed . . . were an "income elasticity criterion" and a comparative "technical progress criterion. . . ."
> The "comparative technical progress criterion" pays more attention to the possibility of placing a particular industry in a more advantageous position in the future through a comparatively greater degree of technical progress, even if the cost of the products is relatively high at this stage.   This term could be called the "dynamized comparative cost doctrine." [12]

The argument is not the same as pursuing higher value added per employee or higher technology sectors, as can be seen in the current U.S. context. U.S. industries ranked by level of R&D spending as a share of sales for the year 1979, with value added per employee for different industry groups stated in relation to the U.S. industrial average for the year expressed as 100. Value added correlates to some degree to level of technology, but the correlation is obviously weak. The correlation to the level of investment per employee is, however, much stronger. Literal pursuit of higher value added per employee in the U.S. context would put chemicals and oil refining above all other sectors, without adequate regard either for growth, technical prospects, or profitability. That these sectors could be high value added per employee and low profit at the same time should be noted. Literal pursuit of higher value added per employee would lead to gross misallocation of capital resources and to impoverishing the nation rather than improving its economic performance.

A STRATEGY TO CREATE ADVANTAGES — THE JAPANESE MODEL

The emergence of industries characterized by rapid growth, technical change, and declining costs opens the possibility of an industrial strategy for a nation as well as for a firm. A *firm* can accelerate its run down the experience curve through increasing its market share and hence its volume relative to competitors. Aggressive if not predatory pricing becomes a way to trade lower short-run earnings for a stronger, presumably more profitable long-run position. A firm can also accelerate its run down the curve by acquisition of the latest technology, either through internal R&D or through licensing from a competitor. A *nation* can build upon these ideas by protecting the home market during the initial period of relatively high costs, by helping provide low-cost, long-term finance to promote capital investment, and by a variety of measures to maintain or promote the mobility of resources — both capital and labor. In extreme situations in which the political motivation to catch up allows government not only a visible hand but a heavy one, government can push firms toward accepting the latest technologies by setting minimum sizes on new plants, thus requiring them to be brought rapidly to world scale. Excess capacity can be avoided by requiring firms to take turns building new plants, with the requirement that they supply competitors until they have had opportunity to build their own new facilities. A "very visible hand" has been described in the Japanese context as follows:

> The process is quite straightforward. Japan imports a technology . . . .from the West. It then protects the industry in question from foreign competition to whatever extent and by whatever means may be required while it gains scale, experience, cost parity, and momentum in Japan itself — the world's second largest and fastest growing market, exporting aggressively, further enhancing its cost position. Gradually it converts a part of its cost advantage into improved product quality. At some point the Japanese competitor is able to offer a better product, profitably, and at a lower price. . . . [13]

Givens describes the Japanese practices as "a sophisticated strategy of selective protectionism." The sophistication is in protecting "a narrow moving band" that gradually moves up the technology scale. Successive industries are targeted and protected for a time. Once a superior position is achieved the protection is dropped. [14]

Selective protection is vital but only a part of the strategy. Without more detail, we cannot decide if the Japanese strategy is essentially an unfair trade practice or a more competitive, better strategy. The distinction is important. To see the Japanese strategy essentially as an unfair trade practice, for example, leads to demands that they change. To see the Japanese as having a holistic strategy of creating advantages rather than accepting the status quo is to recognize that their approach may be more competitive than ours. It also implies that they have little reason to change and are increasingly likely to resent demands that they do so. For the moment it begs the question of whether such a strategy would still be "better" if many, much less all, countries attempted to follow it.

Americans tend to be forced to one of two positions as they observe these developments in Japan. Economists steeped in a static theory that has no place for a strategy of creating comparative advantage claim that the Japanese are misunderstood, that there never was such a strategy, but even if there had been it is a thing of the past. Business executives, who have a continuing awareness of the differences of doing business in competition with the Japanese, are inclined to dwell on those aspects of the Japanese strategy that are the most aggressive and not infrequently constitute unfair trade practices. American academics, for example, explain the demise of the U.S. television industry in terms of superior Japanese technology, typically treating the dumping and other unfair competition claims of U.S. manufacturers as"legal harassment." They may even omit the fact that the importers were assessed $75 million in fines for dumping and criminal fraud. Industry executives, for their part, were slow to match an awareness of unfair trading practices with comparable recognition either of superior Japanese manufacturing practices or the strategy that was reshaping the structure of Japanese industry.

Targeting, or exerting a concentrated effort to catch up in a particular industry, is of course not a new idea. On the contrary, it has long been known as the infant industry argument. What is new, however, is applying the argument to build export-oriented industries rather than focusing on import substitution; to include a very broad range of industries instead of just a few; to achieve domestic rather than foreign control; and to systematically upgrade the portfolio of industries over time. The infant industry paradigm has traditionally been seen as a defensive response permitting a country to catch up in a sensitive area. As used by the Japanese it has become the paradigm for a broad-scale industrial offensive.

> In general, the nurturing of infant industries is limited to a certain period of time and to a certain number of industries. In Japan, however, these measures were across-the-board and applied to almost all industries. This Japanese-type of infant industry may not be admissible from the generally accepted premises of international economics, for one of its fundamental concepts is the international division of labor through free trade. Because of the vastly extended promotion of infant industries and across-the-board encouragement of exports, MITI's approach ran counter to the basic principles of modern international economics. [15]

The goal was to "strengthen the international competitiveness" of essentially all of the industries under MITI's jurisdiction by a set of incentives, through a consultative process in which MITI played a very influential but far from dictatorial role. In addition to the targeted incentives, the exchange rate was kept undervalued until 1971 and then allowed to rise only when there was no alternative. Probably of equal importance, but much less understood outside Japan, the results of its successful export promotion strategy were not allowed to accumulate as rising foreign exchange reserves. Instead, the Japanese began deliberately to accelerate their growth rate, starting in 1957, under the slogan "A hundred billion yen tax cut is a hundred billion yen of aid."

Some American observers discount the Japanese claims of a program to build export competitiveness to the point of using familiar national income data to prove that it never happened. Thus, Japanese exports do not rise appreciably as a share of GNP, and they remain a smaller share than for a number of other (typically much smaller) countries. This argument misses the point. By deliberately accelerating domestic growth, the domestic market grew at about the same rate as exports, but at a rate twice that of Japan's leading competitors. Another argument, that Japan was not mercantilist because it did not accumulate foreign exchange reserves, also misses the point. Domestic growth was allowed to run as fast as it could, subject to a balance of payments constraint, until the early 1970's. Then, as domestic growth slowed, Japan began to accumulate the now familiar surpluses.

If one accepts that industries can be targeted and nurtured from infancy for the world market, that it can be done on a very broad scale, and that it need not result in balance of payments surplus if domestic growth is accelerated to generate offsetting imports, then one has the broad outlines of a supply-side strategy for rapid economic growth. Macroeconomic policy must help assure the savings necessary to finance the high levels of investment required to sustain it and accelerate growth to keep the external accounts in balance. And, as the economy approaches or reaches full employment, it is increasingly urgent to recognize that further progress comes from shifting resources from low-growth, low value-added sectors to higher-performance sectors. Mobility of resources is an essential ingredient of continued progress. Further, the capacity to mobilize and concentrate resources on key sectors permits the possibility of decisive breakthroughs, for a country as for a company or a military commander.

How aggressively a country wishes to use such ideas seems to depend on political priorities. How successfully it can implement them depends on translating them into a consistent, coherent strategy.

Notes

1 Richard Caves and Ronald W. Jones, *World Trade and Payments* (Toronto: Little, Brown & Co., 1981).
2 Caves and Jones, *World Trade*, 115.
3 For other discussions of the inadequacy of the theory of comparative advantage in depicting aggregate trade flows of manufactured goods, see John Zysman and Laura Tyson, *American Industry in International Competition* (Ithaca, N. Y. : Cornell University Press, 1983); Paul Krugman, "New Theories of Trade Among Industrial Countries," *American Economic Review,* Papers and Proceeding, May 1983.
4 Caves and Jones, *World Trade*, 116.
5 Earlier discussion on dynamic comparative advantages may be found in (1) Bruce R. Scott, "Can Industry Survive the Welfare State?" *Harvard Business Review* (September-October 1982): (2) John Zysman and Stephen S. Cohen. The *Mercantilist Challenge to the Liberal International Trade Order*, a study prepared for the use of the Joint Economic Committee, U.S. Senate, 97th Cong., December 1982: and (3) Robert Reich, "Beyond Free Trade," *Foreign Affairs* (Sprint 1983).
6 Ernest Gellner, "Scale and Nation," *Philosophy of the Social Sciences 3* (1973): 15-16, as quoted in Chalmers Johnson, *MITI and the Japanese Miracle* (Stanford, Calif.: Stanford University Press, 1982), 16.
7 Shinohara, *Industrial Growth*, 24.
8 Zysman and Cohen, *The Mercantilist Challenge*, 10.
9 Charles L. Schultze, "Industrial Policy: A Dissent," *Brookings Review* (Fall 1983).

10   Yoshizo Ikeda, "Japanese Industrial Policies," address given at John F. Kennedy School of Government, Harvard University, 11 October 1983. See also Shinohara, *Industrial Growth,* chapters 2 and 3.
11   OECD, *The Industrial Policy of Japan,* Paris, 1972, 15.
12   Shinohara, *Industrial Growth,* 24-25.
13   William L. Givens, "The U.S. Can No Longer Afford Free Trade," *Business Week,* 22 November 1982, 15.
14   Givens, "U.S. Can No Longer Afford Free Trade"; and Shinohara, 48-49.
15   Shinohara, *Industrial Growth,* 49.

7

Is Free Trade Passé?

Paul R. Krugman

If there were an Economist's Creed, it would surely contain the affirmations "I understand the Principle of Comparative Advantage" and "I advocate Free Trade." For one hundred seventy years, the appreciation that international trade benefits a country whether it is "fair" or not has been one of the touchstones of professionalism in economics. Comparative advantage is not just an idea both simple and profound; it is an idea that conflicts directly with both stubborn popular prejudices and powerful interests. This combination makes the defense of free trade as close to a sacred tenet as any idea in economics.

Yet the case for free trade is currently more in doubt than at any time since the 1817 publication of Ricardo's *Principles of Political Economy*. This is not because of the political pressures for protection, which have triumphed in the past without shaking the intellectual foundations of comparative advantage theory. Rather, it is because of the changes that have recently taken place in the theory of international trade itself. While new developments in international trade theory may not yet be familiar to the profession at large, they have been substantial and radical. In the last ten years the traditional constant returns, perfect competitive models of international trade have been supplemented and to some extent supplemented by a new breed of models that emphasizes increasing returns and imperfect competition. These new models call into doubt the extent to which actual trade can be explained by comparative advantage; they also open the possibility that government intervention in trade via import restrictions, export subsidies, and so on may under some circumstances be in the national interest after all.

To preview this paper's conclusion: free trade is not passé, but it is an idea that has irretrievably lost its innocence. Its status has shifted from optimum to reasonable rule of thumb. There is still a case for free trade as a good policy, and as a useful target in the practical world of politics, but it can never again be asserted as the policy that economic theory tells us is always right.

RETHINKING INTERNATIONAL TRADE THEORY

From the early nineteenth century until the late 1970s, international trade theory was dominated almost entirely by the concept of comparative advantage, which we can define loosely as the view that countries trade to take advantage of their differences. In formal models, economies were assumed to be characterized by constant returns to scale and perfect competition. Given these assumptions, trade can arise only to the extent that countries differ in tastes, technology, or factor endowments. The traditional Ricardian model emphasizes technological differences as the cause of trade; the Heckscher-Ohlin-Samuelson model emphasizes differences in factor endowments. Additional models can be generated by varying assumptions about the number of goods and factors, by placing restrictions on the technology, and so on. These alternative models have different implications in important respects; for example, income distribution effects are absent in the Ricardian model, extremely strong in the Heckscher-Ohlin-Samuelson model. Nonetheless, the underlying commonality among conventional trade models is such that until a few years ago international trade theory was one of the most unified fields in economics.

Thoughtful international economists have long known that comparative advantage need not be the whole story, that increasing returns can be an independent cause of international specialization and trade. [1] Ohlin himself repeatedly emphasized this point. Furthermore, at least since the late 1950s empirical workers and informal observers have been dissatisfied with formal trade theory, so that there has been a sort of "counter-culture" in international trade research, a set of informal arguments stressing sources of trade other than those represented in the formal models. Authors such as Steffan Burenstam-Linder (1961) and Raymond Vernon (1966) emphasized endogenous technological change, while many authors have discussed the possible role of economics of scale as a cause of trade separate from comparative advantage. A few papers attempted formal models of trade under increasing returns. However, all such efforts were plagued by the problem of modeling market structure. Except under the implausible hypothesis that economies of scale are completely external to firms, increasing returns must lead to imperfect competition. Yet until the late 1970s, there was no generally accepted way to model imperfect competition in general equilibrium. Since mainstream trade theory derived its power and unity from being stated in formal general equilibrium terms, alternative views were relegated to the footnotes. As recently as 1980, many textbooks — and even survey articles on the theory of international trade — failed even to mention the possibility that trade might arise of reasons other than exogenous differences in tastes, technology, and factor endowments.

During the 1970s researchers in industrial organization began to develop models of imperfect competition that, while admittedly lacking generality, were easy to use and apply. In particular, Chamberlinian large-group competition was given a grounding in utility maximization and placed in a general equilibrium framework by such authors as A. Michael Spence (1976) and Avinash Dixit and Joseph Stiglitz (1977). It quickly became clear to trade theorists that these new models supplied the necessary framework for formal modeling of the role of increasing returns as a cause of international trade. Simultaneously and independently, Victor Norman (1980), Kelvin Lancaster (1980), and this author (1979) published papers in which economies of scale led to arbitrary specialization by nations on products within monopolistically competitive industries. These models immediately established the idea that countries specialize and trade, not only because of underlying differences, but also because increasing returns are an independent force leading to geographical concentration of production of each good. Indeed, at a logical level, increasing returns are as fundamental a cause of international trade as comparative advantage. [2]

The role of increasing returns in trade was not, as already noted, a new idea, although the new models gave it more clarity and precision than in the past. The main new insight from these models was that to, the extent that trade driven by economies of scale is important in the world economy, imperfect competition is important as well. International trade theory thus becomes inextricably intertwined with industrial organization. In retrospect this conclusion is obvious. After all, most trade is in the products of industries that economists classify without hesitation as oligopolies when viewing them in their domestic aspect. For international economics, however, this was a radical reorientation.

Although the new models of trade challenged the traditional view that all trade represents exploitation of comparative advantage, the new trade theory did not at first challenge the proposition that trade is of mutual benefit to the trading nations.   Indeed, if anything, the introduction of increasing returns and imperfect competition into trade theory strengthens the case that there are gains from trade. In addition to benefitting from complementary differences in resources and technology, trading countries can specialize in the production of different goods, achieving increased scale of production while maintaining or increasing the diversity of goods available. Admittedly, a second-best world of imperfect competition offers no guarantee that potential benefits from trade will necessarily be realized. In most formal models, however, it turns out that the presence of increasing returns increases rather than reduces the gains from international trade. Furthermore, by creating larger, more competitive markets, trade may reduce the distortions that would have been associated with imperfect competition in a closed economy. Thus the initial implication of new trade theory seemed, if anything, to reinforce the traditional view that trade is a good thing, and thus to strengthen the case for free trade.

However, showing that free trade is better than no trade is not the same thing as showing that free trade is better than sophisticated government intervention. The view that free trade is the best of all possible policies is part of the general case for laissez-faire in a market economy, and rests on the proposition that markets are efficient. If increasing returns and imperfect competition are necessary parts of the explanation of international trade, however, we are living in a second-best world where government intervention can in principle improve on market outcomes. Thus as soon as the respectability of non-cooperative-advantage models in international trade was established, international trade theorists began to ask whether the new view of the *causes* of trade implied new views about appropriate trade *policy*. Does acknowledging economies of scale and imperfect competition create new arguments against free trade?

NEW ARGUMENTS AGAINST FREE TRADE

The new view of international trade holds that trade is to an important degree driven by economies of scale rather than comparative advantage, and that international markets are typically imperfectly competitive. This new view has suggested two arguments against free trade, one of which is a wholly new idea, the other of which is an old idea given new force. The new idea is the *strategic trade policy* argument, which holds that government policy can tilt the terms of oligopolistic competition to shift excess returns from foreign to domestic firms. The old idea is that government policy should favor industries that yield *externalities*, especially generation of knowledge that firms cannot fully appropriate.

STRATEGIC TRADE POLICY

The strategic trade policy argument begins with the observation that in a world of increasing returns and imperfect competition, lucky firms in some industries may be able to earn returns higher than the opportunity costs of the resources they employ. For example, suppose that economies of scale are sufficiently large in some industry that there is only room for one profitable entrant in the world market as a whole; that is, if two firms were to enter they would both incur losses. Then whichever firm manages to establish itself in the industry will earn super-normal returns that will not be competed away.

⁕ A country can raise its national income at other countries' expense if it can somehow ensure that the lucky firm that gets to earn excess returns is domestic rather than foreign. In two influential papers, James Brander and Barbara Spencer (1983, 1985) showed that government policies such as export subsidies and import restrictions can, under the right circumstances, deter foreign firms from competing for lucrative markets. Government policy here serves much the same role that "strategic" moves such as investment in excess capacity or research and development (R & D) serve in many models of oligopolistic competition — hence the term "strategic trade policy."

The original Brander-Spencer analysis and the literature that followed it uses the machinery of duopoly analysis: firms choose levels of R & D and/or output conditional on other firms' choices, and an equilibrium occurs where the reaction functions of firms intersect. The essence of the strategic trade policy concept, however, is so simple that it can be conveyed with a numerical example. Indeed, focusing on such an example may convey the essentials more clearly than a more formal treatment.

Suppose, then, that two countries are capable of producing a good. For concreteness, let the good be a 150-seat passenger aircraft, and call the "countries" America and Europe. Also, let there be one firm in each country that could produce the good: Boeing and Airbus, respectively.

To focus attention on the competition for excess returns, assume that neither America nor Europe has any domestic demand for the good, so that the good is intended solely for export; this allows us to identify produce surplus with the national interest. Also, assume that each firm faces only a binary choice, to produce or not to produce. Finally, assume that the market is profitable for either firm if it enters alone, unprofitable for both if both enter.

Given these assumptions, the game between Boeing and Airbus may be represented by a matrix like that shown in Table 1. Boeing's choices to produce (P) or not to produce (N) are represented by upper case letters, Airbus's corresponding choices by lower case letters. In each cell of the matrix, the lower left number represents Boeing's profit (over and above the normal return on capital), the upper right number represents Airbus's profit.

As the game is set up here, it does not have a unique outcome. To give it one, let us assume that Boeing has some kind of head start that allows it to commit itself to produce before Airbus's decision. Then in the absence of government intervention, the outcome will be Pn, in the upper right cell: Boeing will earn large profits, while deterring entry by Airbus.

Clearly Europe's government would like to change this outcome. The strategic trade policy point is that it can change the outcome if it is able to commit itself to subsidize Airbus, at a point before Boeing is committed to produce. Suppose that Europe's government can commit itself in advance to pay a subsidy of 10 to Airbus if it produces the plane, regardless of what Boeing does. Then the payoff matrix is shifted to that represented by Table 2. The result is to reverse the game's outcome. Boeing now knows that even if it commits itself to produce, Airbus will still produce as well, and it will make losses. Thus Boeing will be induced not to produce, and the outcome will be Np instead of Pn. The surprising result will be that a subsidy of only 10 raises Airbus's profits from 1 to 110! Of this, 100 represents a transfer of excess returns from America to Europe, a gain in Europe's national income at America's expense.

Table 1
Hypothetical payoff matrix

		Airbus P	Airbus n
Boeing	**P**	-5 / -5 (100)	0
	N	100 / 0	0

Table 2
Hypothetical payoff matrix after European subsidy

		Airbus P	Airbus n
Boeing	**P**	5 / -5 (100)	0
	N	110 / 0	0

The strategic trade policy argument thus shows that at least under some circumstances a government, by supporting its firms in international competition, can raise national welfare at another country's expense. The example just presented showed this goal being achieved via a subsidy, but other policies might also serve this purpose. In particular, when there is a significant domestic market for a good, protection of this market raises the profits of the domestic firm and lowers the profits of the foreign firm in the case where both enter; like and export subsidy, this can deter foreign entry and allow the domestic firm to capture the excess returns. As businessmen have always said, and as economists have usually denied, a protected domestic market can — under some circumstances! — promote rather than discourage exports, and possibly raise national income.

The strategic trade policy argument is immensely attractive to non-economist, since it seems to say that views always condemned by international trade theorists as fallacious make sense after all. In defense of free trade, a number of analysts have quickly acted to point out the weakness of strategic trade as a basis for actual intervention. Before considering these arguments, however, I turn to the other justification for government intervention in trade suggested by the new theory.

EXTERNAL ECONOMIES

There is nothing new about the idea that it may be desirable to deviate from free trade to encourage activities that yield positive external economies. The proposition that protection can be beneficial when an industry generates external economies is part of the conventional theory of trade policy. [3] However, the rethinking of international trade theory has given at least the appearance of greater concreteness to the theoretical case for government intervention to promote external benefits.

It is possible to imagine bees-and-flowers examples in which externalities arise from some physical spillover between firms, but empirically the most plausible source of positive externalities is the inability of innovative firms to appropriate fully the knowledge they create. The presence of problems of appropriability is unmistakable in industries experiencing rapid technological progress, where firms routinely take each others' products apart to see how they work and how they were made. In traditional international trade models with their reliance on perfect competition, however, externalities resulting from incomplete appropriability could not be explicitly recognized, [4] because the knowledge investment by firms that is the source of the spillover could not be fitted in. Investment in knowledge inevitably has a fixed-cost aspect; once a firm has improved its product or technique, the unit cost of that improvement falls as more is produced. The result of these dynamic economies of scale must be a breakdown of perfect competition.

As a result, perfectly competitive models could not explicitly recognize the most plausible reason for the existence of external economies. This did not prevent trade theorist from analyzing the trade policy implications of externalities, and in fact this is a well-understood topic. Since investment in knowledge was not explicitly in their models, however, external economies seemed abstract, without an obvious real-world counterpart. In traditional trade models, one industry seems as likely as another to generate important external economies — so that the theory seems remote from operational usefulness.

Once increasing returns and imperfect competition are seen as the norm, this problem of abstractness is reduced. The dynamic scale economies associated with investment in knowledge are just another reason for the imperfection of competition that has already been accepted as the norm. External economies can now be identified with incomplete appropriability of the results of R & D, which immediately suggest that they are most likely to be found in industries where R & D is an especially large part of firms' costs. So by making tractable the modeling of a specific mechanism generating externalities, the new trade theory also seems to offer guidance on where these externalities are likely to be important.

The emphasis on external economies suggested by new trade theory is similar to the strategic trade policy argument in offering a reason for government targeting of particular sectors. However, the external economies argument differs in one important respect: Policies to promote sectors yielding external economies need not affect other countries adversely. Whether the effect of one country's targeting of high-externality sectors on other countries is positive or negative depends on whether the scope of the externalities is national or international. There is a conflict of interest if knowledge spills over within a country but not between countries. Suppose that the research of each computer firm generates knowledge that benefits other computer firms. This is only a case of sponsoring production of computers in the United States as opposed to Japan if U.S. firms cannot benefit from Japanese research. [5] In many cases it seems unlikely that spillovers respect national boundaries; a firm can "reverse engineer" a product made abroad as well as one make at home. The best candidates for nationally limited externalities are where knowledge spreads largely by personal contact and word of mouth. This is a much more restricted set of activities than R & D in general, although it is presumably the force behind such spectacular agglomerations of high-technology industry as Silicon Valley and Route 128.

Despite the restriction that only externalities at the national level make industrial policy a source of international conflict of interest, it is clear that the changes in trade theory have strengthened the view that nations are competing over who gets to realize these externalities. This reinforces the new strategic trade policy argument in offering a more respectable rationale for deviating from free trade than has been available until now.

CRITIQUE OF THE NEW INTERVENTIONISM

The positive economics of the new trade theory, with its conclusion that much trade reflects increasing returns and that many international markets are imperfectly competitive, has met with remarkably quick acceptance in the profession. The normative conclusion that this justifies a greater degree of government intervention in trade, however, has met with sharp criticism and opposition — not least from some of the creators of the new theory themselves. The critique of the new interventionism partly reflects judgments about the politics of trade policy, to which we turn below. There are also, however, three economic criticisms. First, critics suggest that it is impossible to formulate useful interventionist policies given the empirical difficulties involved in modeling imperfect markets. Second, they argue that any gains from intervention will be dissipated by entry of rent-seeking firms. Third, it is argued that general equilibrium considerations radically increase the empirical difficulty of formulating interventionist trade policies and make it even more unlikely that these policies will do more good than harm.

EMPIRICAL DIFFICULTIES

The previous numerical example assumed that the European government knew the payoff matrix and knew how Boeing would respond to its policy. In reality, of course, even the best informed of governments will not know this much. Uncertainty is a feature of all economic policy, of course, but it is even greater when the key issue is how a policy will affect oligopolistic competition. The simple fact is that economists do not have reliable models of how oligopolists behave. Yet the effects of trade policy in imperfectly competitive industries can depend crucially on whether firms behave cooperatively or non-cooperatively, or whether they compete by setting prices or outputs. [6] Furthermore, in many oligopolistic industries firms play a multistage game whose rules and objectives are complex and obscure even to the players themselves.

The externality argument for intervention runs up against the empirical problem of measuring external economies. By their nature, spillovers of knowledge are elusive and difficult to calculate; because they represent non-market linkages between firms they do not leave a "paper trail" by which their spread can be traced. A combination of careful case study work and econometrics on the history of an industry may be able to identify significant external economies, but what we need for trade policy is an estimate of the future rather than the past. Will a dollar of R & D in the semiconductor industry convey ten cents worth of external benefits, or ten dollars? Nobody really knows. [7]

By itself, the argument that making policy based on the new trade theory is an uncertain enterprise would only dictate caution and hard study, not inaction. When it is linked with the political economy concerns described below, however, it raises the question of whether the political risks associated with action outweigh any likely gain.

ENTRY

Suppose that a government is somehow able to overcome the empirical difficulties in formulating an interventionist trade policy. It may still not be able to raise national income if the benefits of its intervention are dissipated by entry of additional firms.

Consider first the case of a strategic trade policy aimed at securing excess returns. Our example was one in which there was room for only one profitable firm. Suppose, however, that the market can actually support four or five firms, a sufficient number so that the integer constraint does not matter too much and free entry will virtually eliminate monopoly profits. In this case, as Ignatius Horstmann and James Markusen (1986) have emphasized, a subsidy, even if it succeeds in deterring foreign competition, will be passed on to foreign consumers rather than securing excess returns for domestic producers. Or as Avinash Dixit has put it, when there is a possibility of new entry we need to ask, "Where's the rent?"

A similar issue arises with policies aimed at promoting external economies. Suppose that external economies are associated with the manufacture of semiconductor chips, seemingly justifying a subsidy to chips production. If additional resources of labor and capital are supplied elastically to the industry, the external benefits of larger production will not be confined to the promoting country. Instead, they will be passed on to consumers around the world in the form of cheaper chips. The *national* advantage can come only to the extent that some factors are supplied inelastically to the industry — Santa Clara valley real estate? — or external benefits conveyed by the semiconductor industry to other industries. The point is that entry of new factors and new firms further reduces, though it does not eliminate, the extent to which competition for external economies represents a valid source of international conflict.

GENERAL EQUILIBRIUM

Even in a world characterized by increasing returns and imperfect competition, budget constraints still hold. A country cannot protect everything and subsidize everything. Thus interventionist policies to promote particular sectors, whether for strategic or externality reasons, must draw resources away from other sectors. This substantially raises the knowledge that a government must have to formulate interventions that do more harm than good.

Consider first the case of strategic trade policy. When a particular sector receives a subsidy, this gives firms in that sector a strategic advantage against foreign competitors. However, the resulting expansion of that sector will bid up the price of domestic resources to other sectors, putting home firms in these other sectors at a strategic disadvantage. Excess returns gained in the favored sector will thus be offset to at least some extent by returns lost elsewhere. If the government supports the wrong sector, the gain there will conceal a loss on overall national income.

The implication of this general equilibrium point is that to pursue a strategic trade policy successfully, a government must not only understand the effects of its policy on the targeted industry, which is difficult enough, but must also understand all the industries in the economy well enough that it can judge that an advantage gained here is worth advantage lost elsewhere. Therefore, the information burden is increased even further.

A similar point applies to externalities. Promoting one sector believed to yield valuable spillovers means drawing resources out of other sectors. Suppose that glamorous high-technology sectors yield less external benefit than the government thinks, and boring sectors more. Then a policy aimed at encouraging external economies may actually prove counterproductive. Again, the government needs to understand not only the targeted sector but the rest of the economy to know if a policy is justified.

The general equilibrium point should perhaps not be emphasized to much. Sectors of the economy differ radically and visibly in both the extent to which they are imperfectly competitive and in the resources they devote to the generation of knowledge. There may not be a one-to-one correspondence between small numbers of competitors and excess returns, or between high R & D expenditure and technological spillovers, but there is surely a correlation. Governments may not know for sure where intervention is justified, but they are not completely without information. However, the general equilibrium critique reinforces the caution suggested by the other critiques.

To say that it is difficult to formulate the correct interventionist policy is not a defense of free trade, however. Thus the economic critique of the new interventionism is only part of the post-new-trade-theory case for free trade. the other indispensable part rests on considerations of political economy.

THE POLITICAL CASE FOR FREE TRADE

Like most microeconomic interventions, the interventionist policies suggested by new trade theory would affect the distribution of income as well as its level. The well-justified concern of economists is that when policies affect income distribution, the politics of policy formation come to be dominated by distribution rather than efficiency. In the case of trade interventions, this concern is at two levels. First, to the extent that the policies work, they will have a beggar-thy-neighbor component that can lead to retaliation and mutually harmful trade war. Second, at the domestic level an effort to pursue efficiency through intervention could be captured by special interests and turned into an inefficient redistributionist program.

RETALIATION AND TRADE WAR

Strategic trade policy aimed at securing excess returns for domestic firms and support for industries that are believed to yield national benefits are both beggar-thy-neighbor policies that raise income at the expense of other countries. A country that attempts to use such policies will probably provoke retaliation. In many (though not all) cases, a trade war between two interventionist governments will leave both countries worse off than if a hands-off approach were adopted by both. For example, consider the case of the European telecommunications equipment industry. This industry is a likely candidate for targeting on both oligopoly and external economy grounds. It is also a sector where nationalistic procurement by government-owned firms allows countries to pursue protectionist policies without violating agreements on international trade. The result of such protectionist policies, however, is by most accounts harmful to all concerned. Each country tries to be largely self-sufficient in equipment, and no country is able to realize the scale economies that would come from supplying the European market as a whole. Arguably, the structure of the game between countries in telecommunications equipment, and probably in other sectors as well, is that of a prisoners' dilemma where each country is better off intervening than being the only country not to intervene, but everyone would be better off if nobody intervened.

The way to avoid the trap of such a prisoners' dilemma is to establish rules of the game for policy that keep mutually harmful actions to a minimum. If such rules are to work, however, they must be simple enough to be clearly defined. Free trade is such a simple rule; it is easy enough to determine whether a country imposes tariffs or import quotas. New trade theory suggests that this is unlikely to be the best of all conceivable rules. It is very difficult to come up with any simple set of rules of the game that would be better, however. If the gains from sophisticated interventionism are small, which is the import of the economic critique of the last section, then there is a reasonable case for continuing to use free trade as a focal point for international agreement to prevent trade war.

DOMESTIC POLITICS

Governments do not necessarily act in the national interest, especially when making detailed microeconomic interventions. Instead, they are influenced by interest group pressures. The kinds of interventions that new trade theory suggests can raise national income will typically raise the welfare of small, fortunate groups by large amounts, while imposing costs on larger, more diffuse groups. The result, as with any microeconomic policy, can easily be that excessive or misguided intervention takes place because the beneficiaries have more knowledge and influence than the losers. Nobody who has followed U.S. trade policy in sugar or lumber can be very sanguine about the ability of the government to be objective in applying a policy based on the Brander-Spencer model.

How do we resolve the problem of interest group influence on decision-making in the real world? As in the case of the problem of international conflict, one answer is to establish rules of the game that are not too inefficient and are simple enough to be enforceable. To ask the Commerce Department to ignore special-interest politics while formulating detailed policy for many industries is not realistic; to establish a blanket policy of free trade, with exceptions granted only under extreme pressure, may not be the optimal policy according to the theory but may be the best policy that the country is likely to get.

THE STATUS OF FREE TRADE

The economic cautions about the difficulty of formulating useful interventions and the political concerns that interventionism may go astray combine into a new case for free trade. This is not the old argument that free trade is optimal because markets are efficient. Instead, it is a sadder but wiser argument for free trade as a rule of thumb in a world whose politics are as imperfect as its markets.

The economic cautions are crucial to this argument. If the potential gains from interventionist trade policies were large, it would be hard to argue against making some effort to realize these gains. The thrust of the critique offered above, however, is that the gains from interventions are limited by uncertainty about appropriate policies, by entry that dissipates the gains, and by the general equilibrium effects that insure that promoting one sector diverts resources from others. The combination of these factors limits the potential benefits of sophisticated interventionism.

Once the expected gains from intervention have been whittled down sufficiently, political economy can be invoked as a reason to forgo intervention altogether. Free trade can serve as a focal point on which countries can agree to avoid trade wars. It can also serve as a simple principle with which to resist pressures of special-interest politics. To abandon the free trade principle in pursuit of the gains from sophisticated intervention could therefore open the door to adverse political consequences that would outweigh the potential gains.

It is possible, then, both to believe that comparative advantage is an incomplete model of trade and to believe that free trade is nevertheless the right policy. In fact, this is the position taken by most of the new trade theorists themselves. So free trade is not passé — but it is not what it once was.

Notes

1   There have been many surveys of the new developments in international trade theory. For a synthetic presentation of much of the positive side of this work, see Elhanan Helpman and Paul Krugman (1985); for an informal presentation of arguments for and against new forms of trade intervention, see the volume edited by Paul Krugman (1986); for a survey that also covers related topics in the border area between trade and industrial organization, see Paul Krugman (forthcoming).

2   One need not, of course, abandon comparative advantage entirely. From early in he development of new trade theory most models have represented trade as arising from both increasing returns and some form of comparative advantage, such as differences in factor endowments. This behavior of such models depends on the underlying parameters. For example, if scale economies are large and countries are similar in their factor endowments, the model will behave very differently from when scale economies are weak and countries differ greatly; in the latter case traditional trade theory yields the right predictions, in the former it does not.

3   See, for example, W. M. Corden (1974). As the conventional literature points out, however, protection is only s second-best policy; direct correction of the domestic market failure is preferable.

4   The one exception is the case of *zero* appropriability. In this case technobiological progress will occur only through learning-by-doing,

because there will be no incentive for firms to invest deliberately in knowledge creation; since the fixed costs associated with knowledge investment are absent, perfect competition may be preserved.

5   Even if externalities are national in scope, one might argue that no conflict need be involved; simply let each country provide the optimal subsidy. There are three answers to this. First, in practice countries often pursue industrial policy objectives with second-best trade policy tools. It is interesting to ask why they do this, but as long as they do the attempt to promote sectors is an attempt to promote them at other countries' expense. Second, much of the practical argument over industrial policy in the US concerns the urgency of domestic sectors, then the costs of not subsidizing become larger. Finally, if economies of scale (internal or external) are large enough, conflict of interests becomes unavoidable. Suppose there is room for only one Silicon Valley in the world, yet the agglomeration will yield valuable external economies to the country that gets it. Then the conflict cannot be avoided except through side payments.

6   In a widely cited paper, Jonathan Eaton and Gene Grossman (1986) showed that in a duopoly model where the optimal strategic policy was an export subsidy with quantity competition, it was an export *tax* with price competition.

7   Of course, one response is to try to find out. The central direction of current research in the new trade analysis is the effort to produce quantitative models of competition in imperfectly competitive industry. These efforts are currently primitive, and even the authors are skeptical about the robustness of the results (forthcoming), Richard Baldwin and Paul Krugman (forthcoming), Anthony Venables and M. Alasdair Smith (1986), Dani Rodrik (1987), and Richard Harris and David Cox (1984).

8

U. S. Competitiveness: Beyond the Trade Deficit

George N. Hatsopoulos, Paul R. Krugman,
Lawrence H. Summers

Large trade deficits and the corresponding increase in U.S. international indebtedness have raised concerns about the long-run competitiveness of the United States. But being competitive requires more than balance in our foreign trade; it requires an improving standard of living. The long-term U.S. competitive problem is largely caused by low saving rates, high costs of capital, and the resulting inadequate level of both visible and invisible investment. As long as the U.S. national saving rate remains far below that of all our major competitor nations, there is little chance for restoring America's international economic position.

The extraordinary rise in the U.S. trade deficit from 1981 to 1987 and the corresponding rapid shift of the United States from the world's largest creditor to its largest debtor have focused national attention on the problem of U.S. competitiveness. Although public alarm over the trade deficit has served the useful function of bringing the problem into focus, it has also distorted the debate: the U.S. trade deficit is only a symptom of America's lagging competitiveness. The trade deficit represents, in essence, a U.S. economy that has been living beyond its means; bringing our spending into line with our income will be difficult, but the really serious problem is how slowly our income has been growing.

Does it matter if the United States is competitive? Unless the United States is able to turn its performance around, the future looks bleak. At best, the United States will experience a period of declining growth in living standards as the trade deficit is brought down, followed by a long period of slowly rising living standards associated with a steady relative decline of the United States in the world, comparable to that of Britain in the 20th century. At worst, the mismatch between our aspirations and our achievement could bring financial crisis on the Latin American model.

Warnings about U.S. competitiveness are now being widely sounded. We argue that these warnings do not put the emphasis where it belongs. Much of the explanation of the long-term U.S. competitive problem rests with low saving, a high cost of capital, and the resulting inadequate level of investment in both visible and intangible capital. As long as the U.S. national saving rate remains far below that of all our major competitor nations, there is little chance for restoring America's international economic position.

In this article, we examine the long-term problem of U.S. competitiveness. What it is, why it has emerged, and what we can do about it. First, we characterize the U.S. competitiveness problem and present evidence on its extent. Second, we analyze the roots of the problem. Third, we turn briefly to the relatively short-run issues of the U.S. trade deficit and the problems that the United States is likely to encounter in bringing it down. Finally, we offer some prescriptions for dealing with the U.S. competitive problem.

WHAT DO WE MEAN BY COMPETITIVENESS?

There is a strong temptation to identify the issue of competitiveness with the single measure of the trade balance. However, while trade balances sometimes indicate competitive strength, they do not always do so. For example, from 1980 through 1986 Bolivia consistently ran a trade surplus. Exports exceeded imports by more than 60% in most years, and the trade surplus as a percentage of gross national product was usually larger than that of Japan. Yet nobody would consider this a demonstration of Bolivia's competitive strength — from 1980 to 1986 the per capita output of the already desperately poor Bolivian economy fell by 26%. What was happening, of course, was that Bolivia was forced to run large trade surpluses in order to service the large debts it had incurred in earlier years. Meanwhile, the real productive capacity of the economy was declining, in part because of the burden posed by the need to run large short-run trade surpluses. (This experience, although extreme, is not without relevance to the prospect that the United States now faces.)

The proper test of competitiveness, then, is not simply the ability of a country to balance its trade, but its ability to do so while achieving an acceptable rate of improvement in its standard of living. Neither rising living standards nor balanced trade are themselves enough to make a country competitive, since rising living standards can be achieved through growing trade deficits (as in the United States since 1981), whereas trade can be balanced through a steady decline in a country's relative standard of living (as in Britain since World War II and, perhaps, the United States in the 1990s). What is an acceptable rate of improvement in living standards? An advanced country like the United States, which possesses many natural advantages, should be able to maintain a living standard at least as high as that of other advanced countries; thus, we would not view the United States as competitive unless it is able in the long run to maintain a rate of growth in living standards that keeps pace with that of the rest of the industrial world.

THE U.S. STANDARD OF LIVING

The United States retains the highest standard of living of major nations. However, our success in raising that standard of living for the past 15 years has been disappointing in comparison with our own past achievements, the experience of other countries, and our own potential.

Figure 1 shows median family income [1] along with the real earnings of the median full-time adult male worker in the United States in constant dollars since 1960. Like any simple measures, these are imperfect guides to how well we are doing; nonetheless, the picture is a striking one. Real family income peaked in 1973, and has failed to resume sustained growth despite the economic recovery since 1982. It is no exaggeration to speak of the United States in the past 15 years as passing through a "quiet depression" in which the income of families has stagnated or declined, forming a sharp contrast with the rapid growth in income that characterized the postwar years up to the early 1970s. Movements in median family income are affected by demographic changes — the trends towards more single parent families tend to reduce it, increased female labor force participation tends to increase it. However, the alternative measure provided by the incomes of full-time adult male workers has also stopped growing in recent years, confirming the fact of stagnation.

The stagnation of U.S. income need not, of course, represent a competitive problem. One could imagine a world in which shortages of raw materials or a slowing of technological progress led to stagnation of income everywhere. However, comparison with other countries makes it hard to blame the problem on such external factors: The stagnation in U.S. income has been accompanied by a steady erosion of the U.S. lead in income compared with other nations, as real income continues to rise elsewhere.

Figure 1.

Median adult male worker income and median family income [2]

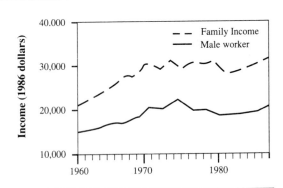

PRODUCTIVITY IS THE FUNDAMENTAL PROBLEM

The main source of the stagnation of real income in the United States has been inadequate growth in production. U.S. overall economic growth has been slower since 1973 than it was in the 1950s and 1960s: 2.2% annually from 1973 to 1985, compared with a 3.8% annual rate of growth from 1960 to 1973. Equally important, this growth has been achieved primarily through increases in employment rather than increases in productivity. With the growth in the labor force, due to the maturing of the baby boom generation and the movement of women into the labor force, the United States has been able to expand its work force rapidly (and it is an important achievement that these jobs have been made available), but the output of each worker has grown hardly at all. Output per worker rose at an annual rate of 1.9% per year during the period 1960 to 1973; it rose at an annual rate of only 0.3% per year from 1973 to 1985.

Over the long term, productivity growth is always the main determinant of trends in living standards. Figure 2 shows rates of growth of productivity and rates of growth in real consumption per capita for the period 1960 to 1985 for the major industrial countries. Clearly the results lie very close to a 45-degree line — that is, the rate of growth of consumption is nearly equal to that of productivity.

The extent to which U.S. productivity growth, broadly defined, has lagged behind that of other advanced countries may be most sharply seen by focusing on one fact: the wages that U.S. firms have been able to pay their workers have steadily lagged behind those that their foreign competitors can pay. U.S. workers have been able to compete in international markets only by steadily cutting their wages. Because labor income is most of national income, lagging wages are central to the relative decline in the U.S. position.

Figure 2

Consumption per capita as a function of output per worker (average annual percentage growth rates, 1962-1985) [3]

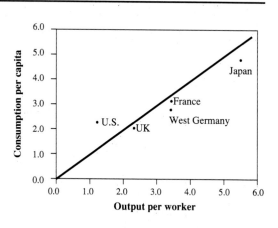

Let us briefly focus our attention on the manufacturing sector for which international comparisons are most easily made. Figure 3 shows how U.S. wages in manufacturing have fallen compared with those in Japan (converted into dollars at the going foreign exchange rate) since 1970. In 1970 our wages were 4.5 times those of Japan; through a combination of lower wage growth and repeated devaluations of the dollar the ratio had fallen to 1.1 in October 1987. (This comparison reflects an exchange rate of 140 yen per dollar; when the yen rises above 120, Japanese wages will overtake those in the United States.)

If the United States had maintained its one-time advantage over Japan in productivity, technology, and product quality, the fall in U.S. relative wages would have given U.S. manufacturers a huge advantage over their Japanese rivals. Obviously, this did not happen. Instead, the U.S. relative wage decline was matched by a decline in the ability of U.S. firms to compete in world markets, leaving the United States with a far bigger trade deficit in 1987 than in 1970. To put it another way, the decline in U.S. relative wages was necessary to compensate for a loss of other U.S. advantages.

Figure 3

Wages in manufacturing: United States wages as a percentage of Japanese wages. [4]

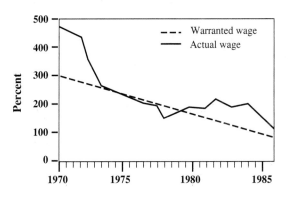

Table 1 shows rates of growth of wages, expressed in U.S. dollars, and productivity in manufacturing for major industrial countries. We note that U.S. wages rose 7.1% more slowly than Japanese wages from 1970 to 1986, yet the United States moved into a deep trade deficit and Japan into a huge surplus during this period. The clear implication is that the U.S. relative wages needed to fall at least this rapidly in order to allow U.S. producers to sell their goods on world markets. The dotted line in Fig. 3 shows the "warranted" wage suggested by this observation: it shows a trend line that declines 7% a year (and that is assumed to reach 100, that is, equality of wage rates, in 1986). In periods when the U.S. relative wage has been close to this trend line, as during most of the 1970s, the United States has also been able to export roughly as much as it imports; in the 1980s, as the actual wage diverged from the warranted level, the U.S. moved into massive deficit. With the falling dollar, the U.S. relative wage has declined sharply, and over time we should begin to see the trade deficit shrink. Yet the long-run problem of competitiveness is not measured by the trade deficit but by the need for an ever-declining relative wage, and this shows no signs of reversing.

Table 1

Productivity and Wage Growth in Manufacturing 1970 to 1986 [4]

Measure	Average annual growth rates %				
	U.S.	U.K.	France	Germany	Japan
Productivity growth	2.9	3.4	4.2	3.8	6.0
Difference from U.S.		0.5	1.3	0.9	3.1
Wage growth in dollars	7.2	10.5	11.3	11.2	14.3
Difference from U.S.		3.3	4.1	4.0	7.1

The necessity for lower wage growth in the United States compared with other advanced countries is a result of lagging U.S. productivity in the broadest sense — that is, both a lower rate of growth in physical output per worker and a declining advantage in technology and quality.

Official measures of productivity, which are difficult to adjust fully for changes in quality and technology, do not fully show the extent of U.S. relative decline. As Table 1 shows, the decline in U.S. relative wages has been more rapid than the relative decline in measured productivity. For example, Japanese manufacturing productivity has grown 3.1 percentage points faster than that in the United States since 1970. If that were the whole story, the United States could have held its own as long as its wages grew only 3.1% more slowly than Japan's. Yet in fact U.S. wages grew 7.1 percentages points more slowly than the Japanese, even though the United States was moving into a massive deficit in manufacturing trade and Japan into a massive surplus. The clear implication is that the United States needed to cut its wages by an additional 4 to 5 percentage points per year over and above the decline necessitated by slower measured productivity growth.

This is not surprising. Measured productivity growth rates do not fully take account of the decline in U.S. technological advantage. At the end of the 1960s, the United States had an overwhelming advantage over other countries in both innovation and the ability to convert ideas into useful products. As a result, in any given year the United States had a virtual monopoly in many products that had just recently been developed and that other countries could not yet make. The United States could afford to pay wages that made it uncompetitive in many goods because it could export goods that nobody else could supply. Over time this advantage has steadily eroded, as other countries — Europe as well as Japan — have challenged U.S. technological leadership. Today the product cycle is as likely to begin with Japan's introduction of a new product, emulated only later by U.S. firms, as the other way around. Since the United States no longer has a monopoly of the new, it needs labor cheap enough to let it compete on the old.

Another factor that is probably inadequately accounted for by conventional productivity measures is the perception of quality. Although no simple way exists of measuring this, it is clear that many purchasers of manufactured goods, both consumers and businesses, are willing to pay a premium for Japanese or European goods, where once they would have preferred those made in the United States.

Clearly both technology and quality are closely related to productivity. In fact, ideally both would be included in a definition of productivity. The key point is that the combination of a measured productivity lag, an eroding technological edge, and a perceived decline in relative quality have all contributed to the fact that the United States finds itself with a growing trade deficit unless it steadily reduces its relative wage rate at a very rapid rate. Indeed, the available evidence suggests that in order to remain competitive, wages in the United States will have to decline by a factor of about one-half relative to Japan each decade if current productivity trends continue.

WHY IS U.S. PRODUCTIVITY GROWTH SO SLOW?

Capital formation and economic growth. Although many explanations have been offered for lagging U.S. productivity and trade performance, one key factor stands out on even the most preliminary examination of the data. This is the relation between productivity growth and capital formation.

"Capital" is a broad concept. Fixed capital — plant and equipment — is only part of the total capital employed in business. Businesses must undertake a variety of activities that cut into current cash flow if they are to improve their situation in the future. Some of these activities, such as buying plant and equipment, are acknowledged by accounting practice as investments and, therefore, do not reduce reported profits. Other equally important activities, however, are not counted in this way. These activities create a stock of "invisible" capital that is potentially as important as the physical stock, yet they are expensed rather than capitalized.

Figure 4

Productivity as a function of the capital-labor ratio in manufacturing (average annual percentage growth rates, 1970-1985) [3, 4]

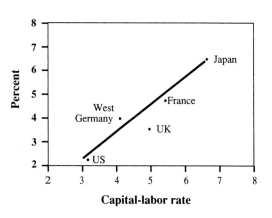

The most obvious kind of invisible investment is research and development expenditure. We estimate that in 1985 U.S. manufacturers spent over 75% as much in nondefense R&D as they did in fixed assets. In addition, there are more subtle kinds of invisible investment. For example, if a firm accepts low earnings temporarily in order to move down a learning curve on a new product or establish itself in a new market, its accounts will show the value of its earnings is low during the initial period. Fundamentally, there is no difference between investing by buying a new piece of equipment and investing by accepting initial losses to break into a market. Statistics on investment, however, count only the first but ignore the second.

A proper definition of capital should include, in addition to plant and equipment, investments in such activities as knowledge acquired through R&D, skills acquired through the willingness of firms to take losses while learning through experience, the creation of marketing and distribution networks, and so on. In what follows, we focus on what is most easily measured, realizing that this is a proxy of a much broader range of assets.

Figure 4 compares the rates of growth between 1970 and 1985 of manufacturing productivity with the rates of increase in the quantity of physical capital per worker for five major industrial countries. The relation is strikingly close and also is essentially proportional, as indicated by the closeness of the scatter of points to a 45-degree line. The United States is, of course, the low performer in both productivity growth and capital accumulation.

It might be objected that the causality could be running the other way — that countries with high rates of productivity growth for other reasons are able to raise their capital-labor ratios over time. To check on this point, we plot in Fig. 5 productivity growth as a function of the rate of national savings as a fraction of income, which should not be strongly affected by the rate of economic growth [5] . (Savings rates are, as we explain below, one of the main determinants of the rate of capital accumulation in the long run.) The relation remains very strong, suggesting that the causation does indeed run from capital to growth, not the other way around.

The strength of the relation between capital and growth is so great that it actually poses a problem for economic theory. Traditionally, economists have approached the role to capital in contributing to economic growth using the technique of growth accounting developed by Solow [6]. Solow's approach involves estimating capital's contribution to economic growth by evaluating the share of capital income in total income. Essentially, his calculation involved asserting that a 1% increase in both the amount of labor and the amount of capital employed in production would raise output by 1%. Because capital's share in total income was about one-quarter, Solow's methods led him to conclude that the elasticity of output with respect to the capital stock was about one-quarter. That is Solow's conclusion; that of an extensive subsequent literature [7] was that a 1% increase in the capital labor ratio would raise output by much less than 1%.

Figure 5

Manufacturing productivity growth as a function of net national saving (average annual percent, 1962-1985) [3,4]

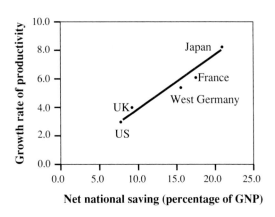

If valid, this conclusion conflicts with the apparent strength of the relation between capital and growth as indicated in Fig. 4 and 5. For example, a Solow-type calculation implies that much of the difference in productivity growth rates between the United States and Japan cannot be attributed to differences in capital accumulation. As we have seen the capital-labor ratio in Japan has increased at about 6.4% per year during the period 1970 to 1985, compared with 3.3% per year in the United States during the same period. This allows us to attribute to Japan's higher rate of capital investment only about 0.8 percentage points per year of the 3.2 percentage points per year difference in Japanese and U.S. growth rates.

The strong relation, however, between capital formation and growth is a clear fact of the data, and not an artifact of the countries we have selected. Romer [8] finds a strong statistical relation between investment rates and growth rates using a sample of 115 countries.

There are substantial theoretical and empirical reasons for thinking that conventional growth accounting calculations understate the role of capital formation in accounting for productivity growth.

First, capital investment embodies technical change. Countries where the rate of investment is high are likely also to have more modern capital stocks. A good example is provided by the Japanese and U.S. steel industries. During the past 20 years Japanese steel producers have been investing heavily in the basic oxygen and continuous casting processes whereas their U.S. counterparts, constrained by limited capital resources, invested in repairing their outdated equipment. Since many innovations are embodied in capital goods, innovation is more likely to occur in industries and nations where the rate of investment is high. Schmookler [9] found clear evidence that rates of patenting in different industries were closely tied to rates of investment.

Second, the traditional approach to estimating the contribution of capital to economic growth presumes that the total social return to capital is equal to its private return as reflected in the rate of profit. Increased production and installation of capital goods may generate learning-by-doing effects of the type stressed by Arrow [10], as costs of production fall with production experience. In this case, the social return to investment will exceed its private return. Alternatively, if labor is able to extract more than its marginal product, the social return to investment will be underestimated by the rate of profit.

In any case, investment in fixed capital is only part of the story, since capital, as we have already emphasized, contains a large invisible component as well as the visible stock of buildings and machines. The key point is that both visible and invisible investment are strongly influenced by a common factor — the cost of capital to firms.

Fixed capital formation and the cost of capital. The higher rate of the Japanese capital-labor ratio is, of course, the result of higher capital spending per employee. Figure 6 shows the gross fixed investment per employee in U.S. and Japanese manufacturing. On average, Japan has been investing 50% more per employee than the United States. Recently the disparity has increased to 100%.

The ratio of capital to labor that minimizes overall production costs for a firm depends on the relative costs of capital and labor. It follows that a major determinant of the rate at which capital is invested per employee is the cost of capital divided by the cost of labor. As mentioned previously, the cost of labor in Japan has been lower than in the United States and is presently about the same. Why then do the Japanese spend more on capital than we do? A good part of the answer is that their cost of capital is much lower than ours.

Figure 6

Gross fixed investment per worker in manufacturing [3]. Japanese data have been converted to U.S. dollars at the 1980 exchange rate of 220 yen per dollar.

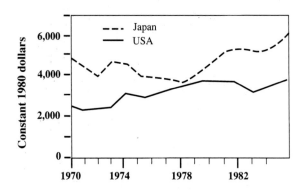

Several investigators [11] have studied the cost of capital in the United States and Japan. This is not a simple task because firms raise money both from borrowing and from equity (that is, retained earnings and new stock issues). This means that the cost of capital cannot simply be measured by the interest rate, the cost of borrowing. Normally, the cost of equity is much higher than the cost of debt, principally because interest payments are tax deductible to corporations whereas returns to equity holders are not. Moreover, investors generally demand higher returns on equity investments because they are more risky. On the other hand, corporations cannot rely solely on debt to finance investment because this would concentrate too much risk on their existing stockholders. Thus, two countries may have roughly equal real interest rates — as is currently the case for Japan and the United States — yet have very different costs of capital [12].

Despite the conceptual difficulties, reasonable estimates of the overall cost of capital can be made. Figure 7 shows the results obtained by Hatsopoulos and Brooks [13]. It can be seen from this figure that Japanese manufacturers have generally enjoyed a cost of fixed capital before depreciation about one-third that of their American counterparts.

If one takes into account depreciation costs, which are common to both, U.S. costs are on average 50 to 75% higher than Japanese costs. Accordingly, capital spending in the United States and Japan appears roughly consistent with the cost of capital in the two countries.

Invisible capital formation and the cost of capital. It is fairly obvious that the extent of a firm's investment in physical assets will depend on its cost of capital. What is less widely appreciated is that investment in invisible assets — or even more generally, the planning horizon adopted by firms — also depends on the cost of capital.

Figure 7

Real cost of fixed assets in the United States and Japan (excluding depreciation) [13]

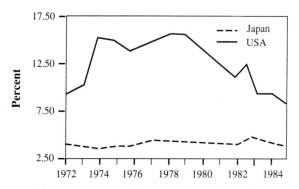

Perhaps the most common indictment of American management holds that it is myopic. Critics charge that this myopia not only leads managers to forego profitable long-term investments in R&D, but also that it influences their behavior in other ways. For example, it is argued that U.S. firms are more reluctant than their foreign competitors to reduce prices and accept losses in order to penetrate markets and that U.S. firms forego investing in their work forces to the same extent as foreign competitors. Business myopia is blamed on a variety of factors ranging from the management techniques taught in business schools, to contemporary accounting rules, to the tyranny of a stock market driven by short-term traders.

We think that the critics are correct in emphasizing the difference in the planning horizons of U.S. and Japanese firms but suspect that they have misdiagnosed the problem. Suppose that managers systematically erred on the side of myopia. Then one would expect that there would have been strong incentives for those with longer horizons to displace myopic managers through hostile takeovers. In fact, hostile takeovers have been common in recent years. But almost invariably raiders have cited excessive investment as the reason for the takeover. Acquires have been able to substantially increase corporate market values by scaling back investment and concentrating on increasing current profitability.

If anything, this suggests that U.S. managers are judged by the market to be operating with too long a horizon. The real question is, why does the market penalize U.S. managers for taking the long view? The answer is the high cost of funds.

Figure 8

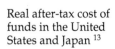

Real after-tax cost of funds in the United States and Japan [13]

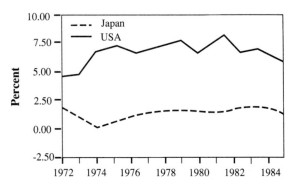

The point is that the cost of funds plays a crucial role in determining how much a firm values future as opposed to current earnings. It determines how much patience on the part of a firm is actually rational. A decision that lowers earnings by $1 now while raising them by $2 ten years from now is a profitable decision if the firm's cost of funds is 5%, but it will lower the firm's value if the cost of funds is 10%. It follows that both visible and invisible investments will rationally be lower in a firm facing a high cost of funds than in one facing a low cost.

Estimates of the real cost of funds in the United States and Japan are shown in Fig. 8. (These numbers differ slightly from those in Fig. 7

because of the differing tax treatment of visible and invisible investment.) In 1985 the figure indicates that American firms had a real cost of funds of 6%; Japanese firms had a real cost of funds of only 1.5%. This means that a U.S. firm should be willing to undertake a project that lowers earnings by a dollar today and raises them by 1.2 constant dollars at some future date, only if the payoff comes in less than 3 years in the future. By contrast, a Japanese firm should be willing to sacrifice a dollar now for 1.2 dollars 12 years in the future. Thus, a U.S. firm would be irresponsible not to adopt a much shorter time horizon than its Japanese counterpart.

It is well known that Japanese manufacturers of automobiles and consumer electronics spent vast sums on distribution, service, and product promotion in order to penetrate the U.S. market. For example, in 1965 when Honda Motors, then a $400-million company, decided to develop automobiles for the U.S. market, its return on assets fell sharply — from a 9% average before that time to only a 3% average for the ensuing 15 years. By the mid-1980s, the investment had begun to pay off: Honda became a $20-billion company with an average return on assets of 8.5%. Clearly, there was a very long-term process of invisible investment taking place which is also very difficult to measure. The point, however, is straightforward: not only would a U.S. firm not have been willing to do what Honda did, but, more importantly, it should not have been willing to do so. Given the much higher U.S. cost of capital, an investment with such a long delayed payoff would not have been in the stockholders' interests.

If differences in the cost of capital persist for extended periods, their effects will run deeper than rational calculation. The type of people who rise to the top in a corporation and the culture of the firm evolve in response to what works best in its prevailing environment. Place a firm in an environment where the cost of capital is very low, and it will do best when it takes a long view, largely disregarding current profitability. In time, this long view becomes part of the company's way of doing business. Place a firm in an environment where the cost of capital is high, and the firm's interests will be best served by a short-term focus, and this too becomes part of the company's culture. These differences in approach may eventually come to seem cultural, and they will indeed be slow to change even if the cost of capital is altered. Nonetheless, the behavior of firms is ultimately conditioned by the cost of capital they face.

The short-term focus of American managers, then, is a rational response to their market situation. If anything, the evidence from takeovers and market valuations suggest that American managers take a longer view than is in the best interests of their stockholders. The appropriate strategy for lengthening business planning horizons and encouraging long-term investments is not to criticize corporate cultures but to change the market incentives that shape them.

We do not mean to deny that there are many ways in which U.S. industry could and should be improved that are independent of the cost of capital. However, it is important to emphasize the role of the macroeconomic environment, of which the cost of capital is a key feature, in our competitive performance. When analysts study competition in individual industries, as is the case in most studies of competitiveness, they naturally tend to focus on industry-specific sources of success or failure. Thus, it is important to stress that the unsatisfactory performance of U.S. industry across the board must have broader causes — and that a high cost of capital is a key problem that all U.S. industry faces.

There is a further reason for focusing on the cost of capital in addressing U.S. productivity problems. Many other possible sources of productivity difficulties are much less amenable to public policy. Insofar as the productivity problem is a consequence of the depletion of good ideas, as suggested by Nordhaus [14], or the changing attitudes of workers, or the behavior of managers, there is relatively little that public policy can do to address it. On the other hand, public policy can do a great deal to lower the cost of capital.

Why does the United States invest so little? The high cost of capital in the United States is the most important proximate cause of low investment rates, which, in turn, are the major explanation of lagging U.S. competitiveness. The cost of capital, however, is not a price that is arbitrarily short by fiat. Like other prices, it reflects supply and demand. Specifically, the high cost of capital to the U.S. manufacturing sector reflects the limited availability of funds, to that sector. Our manufacturing sector finds access to capital limited both by an extremely low overall national savings rates and because the United States puts a large fraction of its savings into nonbusiness uses such as residential housing. Of course, the cost of capital is affected by tax, monetary, and fiscal policies. These policies influence the cost of capital by altering the supply and allocations of savings.

Figure 9

Net national investment as a function of net national saving (average annual percentage of gross domestic product, 1962-1985)[3]

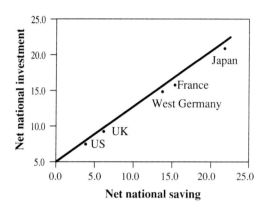

In the long run the ability of a country to invest is constrained by its willingness to save. International capital flows have not historically been large enough to allow major countries to finance more than a small fraction of their investment through foreign borrowing; the close relation between national savings rates and investment rates is shown in Fig. 9. In this respect, U.S. experience since 1982 represents an aberration. For several years the United States has had extremely low and declining national savings, but has been able to avoid the full consequences of this savings decline because massive inflows of foreign capital have financed most of our investment (Table 2).

For some time now, the U.S. national saving rate has been the lowest among the advanced industrial countries and has fallen recently to its lowest nondepression level in history. It is true that measured national savings fail to account for the invisible investments, which are just as important as visible ones. We offer the conjecture, however, that both the gap between the United States and other industrial countries and the decline in national saving in the 1980s would be even larger if we could measure invisible investments as well as tangible ones.

Table 2

Net National Saving and Net National Investment in the Unites States and Japan

as percentages of gross national product [3,4]. Japanese data are adjusted for accounting differences between OECD and the U.S. Department of Commerce.

	Japan			United States		
	National saving	National investment	Foreign investment	National saving	National investment	Foreign investment
1966-1970	16.0	16.4	0.4	7.6	7.2	0.4
1971-1975	15.7	14.7	1.0	7.3	6.8	0.5
1976-1980	11.6	11.3	0.3	6.7	6.7	0.0
1981-1985	10.6	9.1	1.5	3.2	4.5	-1.3

National saving may be divided into two components, that of the federal government and that of the rest of the economy. Both have been inadequate and declined in recent years (Table 3). There is no mystery regarding the decline in federal saving or more accurately, the increase in federal dissaving. It is a consequence of the imbalance between spending and taxation ever since the massive 1981 tax cut. Declining private saving is more mysterious. Summers and Carroll [15] reviewed a number of possible factors that may explain the low level of private saving and concluded that it is probably a consequence of a number of institutional factors in this country, including the easy availability of consumer credit, increasingly generous Social Security and pension benefits, and the spread of life and disability insurance. These explanations suggest that without major changes in public policy, it is unlikely that private saving will rebound strong in coming years, let alone reach levels needed to make our industry competitive.

It is tempting to ascribe the low U.S. national saving rate entirely to cultural factors: a get-rich-quick society, the yuppie mentality, the frontier ethic. However, as in the case of understanding the sources of differences in productivity growth, it makes sense to focus on what can be measured — and changed — before blaming the whole problem on culture. What is clear is that the U.S. fiscal policies, the ways in which the government finances its expenditures, redistributes income among segments of the population, give strong disincentives to save and, conversely, strong incentives to consume now rather than later.

Table 3

United States Net National Saving Rates for Selected Years
as a percentage of gross national products [16]

Year	National saving	Federal governments	Rest of economy
1969-1970	7.6	-0.6	8.2
1971-1975	7.3	-1.8	9.1
1976-1980	6.7	-1.9	8.6
1981-1985	3.2	-4.2	7.5
1986	1.8	-4.8	6.6
1987	1.9	-3.4	5.3

It is useful to bear in mind that Japan's extraordinarily high savings rate has not been a permanent feature of the culture. Before World War II Japanese savings rates were not out of line with those of the United States; it is only in the postwar period that the countries have followed divergent course [17]. Thus, it makes sense to focus on the ways in which U.S. institutions and government policy encourage current consumption at the expense of saving.

There are three major ways in which the U.S. government in effect subsidizes current consumption and taxes saving. These are: the recently rampant budget deficit, the effect of which is to subsidize the present at the expense of the future; the Social Security system, which subsidizes the consumption of present generations at the expense of future ones; and the income tax, both corporate and private, which biases consumption toward the present.

The budget deficit. The recent emergence of huger peacetime budget deficits is a new phenomenon, but it should be viewed in context as the latest in a series of government actions that have the effect of subsidizing current consumption at the expense of the future.

In 1986, dissaving by the federal government absorbed 90% of the private saving generated by households and corporations (although this effect was slightly mitigated by a surplus on the part of state and local governments). Although the measured federal deficit fell by almost one-third between 1986 and 1987, this decline was largely a reflection of transitory factors relating to the Tax Reform Act and the sale of federal assets. As a consequence, official projections call for federal deficits approaching $200 billion in coming years if substantial policy changes are not enacted. There is every reason to expect that even these projections are too optimistic. Historical experience suggests that budget forecasts tend to under-predict actual deficits, and the current projections assume that the U.S. economy will for the first time in its history enjoy ten consecutive years of economic growth between 1982 and 1992.

Ever since the 1981 tax cut, the government has let taxes fall short of its spending without any credible promise that spending will fall in the future. This makes it inevitable that taxes will have to be raised, both to close the current gap and to service the national debt that has arisen. Since the part of government spending not covered by current tax revenues still represents resources diverted form other uses, the deficit does not make the private sector any richer. The deficit subsidizes the consumption of those now working at the expense of future generations. The benefits of taxes lower than spending accrue now and are spent on consumption. The costs of higher taxes later on when the debt must be serviced will be paid in part by future generations who cannot begin saving now. So, the result is a subsidy to current consumption that is paid by the future.

Social Security. The Social Security system is in outward form like a national pension fund. However, unlike private sector pension plans, Social Security has traditionally been unfunded — that is, it has not accumulated a base of assets out of which to meet its obligations. Instead, it relies on the current contributions of those now working to pay for the receipts of those who are retired.

This is not a small issue. If in the past, Social Security liabilities had been fully funded, as with private pension funds, Social Security would have accumulated a $5.5-trillion surplus by now compared with a total fixed capital stock in U.S. industry at $3.7 trillion [18].

The present Social Security law, enacted in 1983, calls for the accumulation of substantial surplus in coming years so that large tax increases will not be necessary when the baby boom generation retires early in the next century. If these surpluses are accumulated and are not offset by deficits in the remainder of the federal budget, they will make a substantial contribution to increasing national saving.

The income tax. The impact of the income tax may be seen by comparing the rate of return that the economy earns on investment in the manufacturing sector with the return that an individual investing in that sector is likely to receive net of taxes. Suppose, not too unreasonably, that the rate of return in manufacturing is 10% in real terms — that is, that a dollar of output devoted to investment in plant and equipment will raise the output of a firm next year by 10%. Translated into compound interest, this means that a dollar's worth of consumption foregone today can be traded for two dollar's worth 7 years from now. If individuals were able to receive the rate of return that the U.S. economy as a whole gets form deferring consumption, many would voluntarily consume considerable less and save considerable more.

However, individuals do not get the 10% rate of return, because taxes drive a wedge between the economy's return and what individuals receive. First, the firm must pay taxes on profits. Although inflation has been greatly reduced, taxable corporate profits are still exaggerated by valuing investments at historical cost. At 4% inflation, a 10% real rate of return may appear form the point of view of the Internal Revenue Service as a 14% nominal rate, on which taxes of 34% — about 4.75 percentage points — will be levied. This leaves the firm with nominal after-tax profits of 9.25%, which it can pass on to its stock holders. The latter, in turn, must pay taxes — say about 30% or 2.75 percentage points. What is left, then, is a nominal return of 6.5%, or a real rate of return of only 2.5% — only a quarter of what their saving is worth to the economy.

To put it another way, from the point of view of the economy , deferring a dollar's worth of consumption allows it to substitute two dollar's worth after only 7 years. From the point of view of individuals, however, they can only trade a dollar today for two dollars 30 years from now. This massive distortion of incentives surely plays an important role in explaining the remarkably low U.S. savings rate.

In addition to reducing savings, the income tax encourages diversion of an excessive fraction of these savings into residential housing. The key pint here is that the services provided by an owner-occupied house — although they represent a return on an investment, in the same way as interest on a bond — are not counted as income and therefore not taxed.

We should finally note that during the high inflation years of the late 1970s these incentives were even worse than they are now. for an extended period the real after-tax rates of return facing U.S. households were substantially negative: a dollar spent now purchased more than that dollar saved for the future (unless that dollar was used to buy a house). Consumption behavior, like the behavior of firms, gradually adapts to its environment. The low savings that now appear to be a part of U.S. culture may well be the delayed response to the extreme disincentives to saving created in the 1970s.

The disincentives to saving provided by the U.S. tax system are not inevitable. They are not the unavoidable price of the welfare state or our defense burden. Better alternatives exist that would raise the same revenue. for example, a tax on consumption rather than income would avoid the bias toward consuming now rather than later that is so strong in our current system [19]. Despite major political action on taxes in the 1980s, we have not make progress toward a system that would provide more incentives to save. The 1980s have been marked by major changes in U.S. tax policy: first the major tax cuts of 1981, then the tax reform of 1986. One mighty have expected that these changes would have helped correct the problems we have pointed to earlier. They have not. Although a detailed discussion of the implications of recent tax changes is beyond the scope of this article, a careful analysis shows that the overall "wedge" — the difference between the return on investment form the point of view of society and from the point of view of an individual deciding whether to consume or save — has if anything gotten wider since 1980 [20]. Meanwhile, the massive federal deficit and the decline in private savings have cut sharply into the overall savings pool.

How much sacrifice is needed? Fifteen years ago, the United States had an advantage in technology, resources, and the size of its internal market that allowed it to be the richest and most productive nation in the world, despite having what was even then an annually low rate of national savings. This is no longer possible. With rough technological parity between the United States and other advanced nations, we cannot expect to compete with other countries unless we save and invest as much as they do.

The magnitude of the change this will require should be apparent from the preceding discussion. The United States is currently saving only 2% of its national income. Thus, even to return to a historically normal saving rate of 5 to 6 % will require more than a doubling of our current savings rate. Yet this is not nearly enough to make the United Stated competitive. We must expect that we will need to save as much as other advance countries. Even if we do not try to match Japan, with its extraordinary saving rate, the average saving rate of advanced countries other than the United States is 11%. There is no reason to believe that the United States can remain a first-rate economy unless it comes close to matching the average saving rate of our competitors.

To achieve such a high savings rate (even though this is a perfectly normal rate elsewhere in the world) will, as our discussion has suggested, require major adjustment. We will need, first of all, to eliminate our federal budget deficit — something that is still not being discussed realistically in the political arena. We will also need to make major reforms of long-standing institutions, notably our tax system. All this will be extremely difficult.

What will make it even more difficult is the fact that in the last few years, instead of moving in the direction of increasing savings, the United States has moved in the opposite direction It treated itself to an unearned consumption boom largely financed by foreign borrowing.

From 1979 to 1986 U.S. net national product per worker, in constant dollars, rose only 2.2%, with slow productivity growth and declining income form our diminishing net investments overseas. In other words, the consumption the United States could afford increased at a snail's pace. Yet, actual U.S. consumption per worker rose 8.8%. People were in fact living substantially better in 1986 than in 1979.

This rise in consumption was possible for two reasons. The main one was the growth of the trade deficit, which allowed the United States to spend more than it earned. A significant extra reason was that U.S. net investment failed to keep pace with the economy's growth: net private investment per worker was actually 16% lower in 1986 than it was in 1979. Both reasons for rising consumption, of course, share a common aspect: they are ways in which current consumption was increased at the expense the future.

The extent to which consumption growth has outstripped production growth during the past 7 years means that now the reverse must happen. A minimum estimate of the belt-tightening ahead is the difference between consumption and production growth since 1979, that is, more than 6%. Even the savings rates of the late 1970s, however, were much lower than those of other industrial countries and, in our view, clearly inadequate to restore U.S. long-term competitiveness. so the trimming down of consumption relative to production that the United States must now undertake could be large, quite easily as large as 10%.

GETTING FROM HERE TO THERE: THE TRADE DEFICIT

So far we have left aside the whole question of the U.S. trade deficit. Important as it is, we think that it is a mistake to use the trade deficit as a measure of the U.S. competitive problem. It is a symptom of the problem, but a symptom that has only appeared recently and that will inevitably prove temporary. By contrast, the underlying competitive problem has been growing steadily for a long time and will still be with use when the trade deficit is gone.

The trade deficit is commonly viewed in isolation, as a special problem in an otherwise prosperous economy in which employment and real consumption per worker have been rising. At first glance it might seem that everything has been fine except for the trade deficit. In fact, this picture is backward. Everything has seemed fine because of the trade deficit, which has masked the underlying disappointing performance of the United States as a producing nation.

To understand this, we need to realize that on the whole running a trade deficit is a pleasant experience for a nation, until the bills come due. There are many useful angles form which to view the U.S. trade deficit, but the most fundamental is that it represents the excess of what the United States spends over what it earns. As long as a country can run up its trade deficit, it can raise its consumption without either raising its output or cutting its investment. It simply imports the resources needed to satisfy the increased consumption. And this is exactly what we have done since 1979.

In an important sense, the, the U.S. trade deficit represents a sort of luck. We have experienced a decline in saving that should have severely squeezed our already inadequate investment. But we were able temporarily to avoid the consequences because we were able to attract a large inflow of foreign capital. This was in a sense a lucky accident — but it may not turn out to have been so lucky in the end. By cushioning the United States from the consequences of its savings collapse, the willingness of foreigners to finance our trade deficit has created a false sense that the situation is acceptable. The capital inflow cannot continue indefinitely and is already starting to dry up. When it does, the United States will find that in order to maintain even a barely adequate level of investment, let alone raise investment to levels comparable to that of other advanced countries, it will have to hold its rate of consumption growth well below its rate of growth in production.

The recognition of the need for a sharp slowdown in the growth of U.S. consumption has not yet been fully appreciated even by informed opinion. There is still a widespread belief that somehow an appropriate policy mix, especially with cooperation form foreign governments, can allow the United States to balance its trade without making any sacrifices. It is important to understand that this comfortable view is wrong. Concessions from foreign governments can somewhat reduce the size of the required U.S. adjustment, but the bulk of the belt-tightening is inevitable whatever the rest of the world does.

The essential point is that the United States must produce more exports, must do with few imports, and therefore produce more substitutes for imports, and must produce more capital goods. All three actions require commitment of resources of capital, labor, and raw materials. Since we do not have large unemployed resources, resources have to be diverted from producing goods for domestic consumers. Regardless of what the rest of the world does, we must slow the growth of our consumption.

CONCLUSIONS

The United States still has great advantages that should ensure it as high a living standard as any other country — considerable natural resources, political stability, a unified internal market, and a highly flexible and innovative society. For 15 years, however, U.S. productivity and living standards have stagnated, due largely to a chronic unwillingness to make sufficient provision for the future. The consequences of that stagnation were masked in the 1980s by a consumption boom fueled by budget deficits and massive borrowing from abroad. But the twin deficits will be resolved one way or another in the next few years, and as they decline our standard of living will once again be constrained by our productivity.

The questions that will determine America's economic future are these: will we face reality and make the adjustment necessary to provide for rapid growth into the 21st century? Or will we instead continue to consume as much as possible for as long as possible without regard to the future?

It is politically attractive to deny that the dilemma exists. Concern over low productivity growth in the late 1970s led, not to a realistic response, but to economic policies based on wishful thinking. These policies boosted consumption without boosting production and have left the economy in worse shape than it was before. The current political debate is hardly encouraging — few candidates have the courage to speak plainly about the difficulties we face, and the voters have not encouraged those that do.

Nonetheless, we believe that ultimately America will face the challenge and regain the economic leadership of which it is still capable. It is encouraging to remember the experience of the energy crisis. In 1974 when that crisis first hit, many commentators believed that the national propensity to consume energy was immutable. In the face of a real crisis, however, the country responded: from 1973 to 1987 the Uniteed States proved able to increase gross national product by 38% in real terms with no increase in energy consumption at all. Not immediately, but eventually, the political system proved willing to do what was necessary by allowing energy prices to rise and by providing incentives to conserve. And there was a change in the national energy "ethic" — toward insulated homes, smaller cars, and more efficient factors — a change stimulated by public rhetoric and promoted by public policy.

The U.S. competitive problem, like its energy problem, must be resolved at many levels. In this article we have emphasized the need for a sharp rise in U.S. savings, which is the *sine qua non* of any effort to maintain U.S. relative standing in the world economy. Of course this increase is not a panacea; increased savings must be used well, which means that they should be accompanied by changes in tax policy, regulation, government research, and monetary policy that ensure an effective application of increased investable resources. The important point is to realize that any other policies cannot work unless the United States also restrains its consumption growth.

Although this will be difficult, the task is not impossible. We have already pointed out that Japan did not always have an extraordinarily high savings rate. The high savings rate emerged only in the recovery after World War II when the imperative of economic growth was clear to the Japanese government and to the Japanese public. The United States remains a fortunate nation, which will not need such an extraordinarily turn around; we should be able to meet our more modest challenge. If the rate of growth of U.S. consumption could be kept even 1% below the rate of growth of U.S. output from now until the year 2000 — and the reduced consumption to be replaced by increased exports and investment — the U.S. would be strongly placed to regain the position of international economic leadership that its natural advantages should entitle it to. The energy crisis was in the end met with political realism and courage, but only after the failure of old policies was dramatized by shortages and gas lines. The challenge for policy toward U.S. savings, the key to competitiveness, is to act without the help of a similarly dramatic crisis.

Notes

1   The U.S. Congressional Budget Office (CBO) has released a report in which the official measures of family income is adjusted to account for changes in family size and contain technical problems with the Consumer Price Index ['Trends in Family Income: 1970-1986" (Congressional Budget Office, Washington, DC, February 1988)]. The adjusted family-income series shows more improvement during the 1970s and 1980s than the official series. However, the CBO series does not adjust for the increased number of workers per family and therefore fails to account for the increased work effort required to sustain improvements in family income.

2   U.S. Department of Commerce, Bureau of the Census, as reported in *The Economic Report of the President* (Government Printing Office, Washington, DC, February), table B-30, p.282

3   Data from selected publication of the Organization for Economic Cooperation and Development (OECD), Paris, France (1987): National

Accounts of OECD Countries, vol. 1; National Accounts of OECD Countries, vol. 2; Flows and Stocks of Fixed Capital; Labour Force Statistics.

4   "Output per Hour, Hourly Compensation, and Unit Labor Costs in Manufacturing, Twelve Countries, 1950-1986" (U.S. Department of Labor, Bureau of Labor Statistics, Office of Productivity and Technology, Washington, DC, December 1987).

5   In Fig. 5, national saving rates are compared with manufacturing-sector productivity. The relation between national saving rates and economy-wide productivity is similar to that shown in Fig. 5.

6   R.M. Solow, Rev. Econ. Stat. 39, 312 (1957).

7   For a state-of-the-art use of growth accounting to analyze U.S. performance, see D. Jorgenson, f. Gollop, and B. Graument [Productivity and U.s. Economic Growth (Harvard Univ. Press, Cambridge, MA, 1987)].

8   P.M. Romer, Macroecon. Annu. 2, 163 (1987).

9   J. Schmookler, Invention and Economic Growth (Harvard Univ. Press, Cambridge, MA, 1966).

10 K.J. Arrow, Rev. Econ. Stud. 29, 155 (1962).

11 G. N. Hatsopoulos and S. H. Brooks, in Technology and Economic Policy, R. Landau and D. Jorgenson, Eds. (Ballinger, Cambridge, MA, 1986), pp. 221-280; G. N. Hatsopoulos, "High Cost of Capital: Handicap of American Industry," Thermo Electron Corporation, Waltham, MA, 26 April 1983; C. Y. Baldwin, in Competition in Global Industries, M. E. Porter, Ed. (Harvard Business School Press, Boston, 1986), pp. 185-223; B. D. Bernheim and J.B. Shoven,k "Taxation and the cost of capital: An international comparison," paper presented at the American Council for Capital Formation Conference on "Consumption Tax: A Better Alternative?" Washington, DC, 3 September 1986; A. Ando and A. J. Auerback. "The cost of capital in the United States and Japan: A comparison," paper presented at the Joint NBER — Ministry of Finance Conference on U.S. and Japanese Economics, Tokyo, Japan, 16 and 17 October 1986. For additional references to studies on the cost of capital, see Hatsopoulos and Brooks [10]

12 It is often argued that the opening of capital markets in Japan will tend to equalize costs of capital. This is not true. The cost of capital in Japan is lower than in the United States (despite similar real interest rates) because of two things: the tax system and the financial structure of Japanese industry. Equity investors in Japan are taxed much less than those in the Unities States because in Japan capital gains on equities are tax-free and dividends are partially deductible at the corporate level. Equalization of after-tax returns to investors will still produce very different costs of equity to the firm. Moreover, in Japan national risk sharing, through the interlocking ownership of industry and banks, allows for much higher debt-to-equity rations without an increase in the risk premium on equities. Since debt is much cheaper than equity, a higher debt-to-equity ratio will lower the cost of capital in Japan.

13 G. N. Hatsopoulos and S. H. Brooks "The cost of capital in the United States and Japan," paper presented at the International Conference on the cost of Capital, Kennedy School of Government, Harvard University, Cambridge, MA, 19 to 21 November 1987.

14 W.D. Nordhaus, Europe. Econ. Rev. 18, 131 (1982).

15 L. H. Summers and C. Carroll, in Brookings papers on Economic Activity (Brookings Institution, Washington, DC, 1987), vol. 2, p. 607. Crucial policy steps contained in the Tax Reduction Act of 1986 working to increase the

cost of capital for business include the repeal of the investment tax credit in 1986, the deceleration of depreciation allowances, and the elimination of capital gains preferences. These steps primarily apply to new investment. On the other hand, the effective tax rate reductions primarily apply to old capital.

16   U.S. Department of Commerce, Bureau of Economic Analysis, National Income and Product Accounts, 1988.

17   For the period from 1920 to 1939, the average net national saving in Japan was 5.2% of the gross national product, see K. Sato, in *The Political Economy of Japan: The Domestic Transformation*, K. Yamamura and Y. Yasuba, Eds. (Stanford Univ. Press, Stanford, CA, 1987), vol. 1, p. 137.

18   Office of the Secretary, Department of Treasury, as footnote to "Statement of liabilities and other financial commitments of the U.S. government as of September 30, 1987," *Treas. Bull.* (Winter issue, March 1988).

19   See D. Bradford, "The choice between income and consumption taxes," New *Directions in Federal Tax Policy for the 1980s* (Tax Notes, Tax Analysts, Arlington, VA, 1984), p. 224.

20   L.H. Summers *Harv. Bus. Rev.* 65, 53 (1987).

III

TRADE POLICIES AND DEVELOPING COUNTRIES

Although over 70% of the world's population lives in developing countries, most of the discussion of international trade policies centers on the developed, industrialized countries. Most economists would agree that the circumstances facing developing countries are quite different from those faced by developed countries. This section examines specifically the types of problems and potential strategies that developing countries face.

The first selection, "Trade conflicts in the 80's" examines some of the central problems facing developing countries. Many developing countries rely on primary product exports for much of their foreign exchange; since the demand for most primary commodities is inelastic, the prices of these commodities is notoriously unstable. To make matters worse, the terms of trade for most countries exporting primary products has worsened over the last decade. Another problem that the article points out is that developing countries face many trade barriers for their exports to developed countries.

The second article, "Import substitution versus export promotion" examines two of the major trade policies that developing countries have followed. Under an import substitution policy, a country attempts to create its own indigenous industries to produce goods which were formally imported. In contrast, under export promotion, a country specializes in producing goods for export. As Kruger points out, export promotion policies have been much more successful than import substitution policies. One of the key reasons for this is that import substitution policies have often merely protected inefficient local industries or have provided trade barriers for multinational corporations to produce in the developing country's domestic market without exporting.

9

Trade Conflicts of the 1980s

Robert H. Girling

Thus far, the 1980s, with its good news/bad news punchline about world trade, seems like an exercise in black comedy. First, the good news. During the 1970s, according to the IMF, the international economy was a hotbed of activity: world exports soared from $283 billion in 1970 to $1,845 billion in 1980. The world economy seemed ever more productive and integrated. East-West trade was stimulated by the opening of China, the initiation of massive joint ventures such as the trans-Siberia pipeline, and a boom in grain sales. In just three years, 1977-79, U.S. exports of agricultural products to the Soviet Union doubled to more than $2 billion. Meanwhile, the Western European economies, which stood at the center of East-West commerce, enjoyed a booming trade with Soviet bloc countries. In 1980 alone, West German trade with the U.S.SR grew by over 20 percent (Bressard 1982).

The bad news was implied by events in the Third World. Although trade was also booming there, was it a sign of life or of impending instability? The answer is not immediately clear. On the one hand, Third World manufacturing exports grew and much of that trade was South-South, suggesting that regional integration of markets was occurring and that whole groups of Third World economies were reaching the takeoff point in self-sustained development. On the other hand, most third World nations were running massive and chronic trade deficits, and foreign MNCs were actually spearheading and dominating the growth sectors of various national economies.

So, which way was up? The growth of manufacturing exports and South-South trade seemed to indicate that the Third World's desires for increased industrialization, a reduction in dependence upon primary commodity exports, and increased regional interdependence were being realized. Between 1970 and 1980 Third World exports of manufactured goods grew from $24 billion to $60 billion in constant prices (UNCTAD 1981). Meanwhile, intraregional and interregional South-South trade rose from $3 billion to $30 billion (Bressard 1982, p. 99). However, the growing trade deficits and the dominance of MNCs implied that growing Third World trade was not resolving structural contradictions and generating self-sustaining growth. Much of the growth in Third World trade seemed precariously nonindigenous, the result of MNCs shifting their foreign investment focus from production of commodities to production of manufactures. A prime example was the global shift in electronics production from the United States and Western Europe to the Far East — Taiwan, Singapore, and Hong Kong.

The internationalization of capital is not new; it dates to the nineteenth century. Since the early 1960s, however, a new feature has appeared — what one writer has called the "globally integrated manufacturing system" (Moxon 1974). Offshore production, in which plants are established in many countries by U.S. corporations for export back to the United States, is now very common. This process has raised a host of issues that bear on trade relations, the rise of protectionism, and the performance of the international economy (see NACLA 1976). "Up," then, seems to point north, to the advanced industrial economies.

In many respects this new dance step — two steps forward, one step back — symbolizes contradictions in the world economy:

a.   The fragile basis of the international trade that sustained postwar growth is becoming evident. The resurrection of the Japanese and Western European economies brings those countries increasingly into conflict with the United States. Emerging trade and investment wars will set the tone for the 1980s.

b.   The political role of trade has been heightened by confrontations provoked by the U.S. government in 1982 over West-East technology transfers.

c.   Third World economic insecurities stemming from deteriorating trade balances are heightening political insecurities and may push the underdeveloped nations into greater economic cooperation.

THIRD WORLD-FIRST WORLD TRADE CONFLICTS

In times of economic boom and rapid growth, expanding trade benefits the rich and the poor. In times of economic weakness and decline, the bottom drops out of trade, and conflicts arise as countries seek to shore up domestic industries and employment. Both positive and negative effects are magnified in the Third World. Since the Third World economies are hinged to the advanced capitalist world. According to World Bank estimates, the growth elasticity of trade is about 1.5. That means that a 3 percent growth rate of GDP in the industrialized capitalist countries generates a 4.5 percent growth rate in the Third World. As the rate falls off by 2 percentage points in the advanced capitalist countries, it falls more steeply — by 3 percentage points in the Third World (UNCTAD 1981).

The worldwide recession/depression of the early 1980s has increased tensions between the First and Third Worlds on economic policy. Three issues stand out as areas of particular conflict: commodity prices and the deteriorating terms of trade between the advanced capitalist countries and the Third World; hidden trade barriers that discriminate against Third World exports; and export enclaves that result in unequal exchange, a process by which the Third World's earnings from trade are limited to producers connected with the enclave. Each of these issues is complex and needs closer examination.

COMMODITY PRICE STABILIZATION

The economies of most Third World nations are heavily dependent upon export income. Commodity sales account for the bulk of that revenue, but the price structure for staples such as coffee and tin is volatile. Unstable export earnings for a few key products can reverse the gears of the entire economy. when export income falls, purchases in other sectors decline, resulting in sharp reductions in investment, employment, and government revenue. It is particularly difficult to plan investments because fluctuations in revenues frequently produce discontinuities in long-term, capital-improvement project and development programs. That uncertainty results in higher-risk premiums on borrowed funds and higher costs of fixed capital formation.

Although this snowball theory is logically coherent, it is not universally accepted. One neoclassical critique (MacBean 1966) attempts to demonstrate that wide swings in profit and loss margins are only marginally attributable to price fluctuation, and that the impact on other economic sectors has not been as damaging as had been supposed. A later study by Knudsen and Parnes (1975) corroborated these results on methodological and statistical grounds. Meanwhile, a further study by

Gkzakos (1973) tested the effects of export price instability by using cross-national data to measure the rate of growth of export income and then of the growth of real per capita income. The study concluded that export instability clearly inhibits economic development.

Despite the continuing theoretical controversy and the evidence, M.J. Lord of the IDB concluded that "On the basis of the evidence. . . it appears that export instability has been a justifiable preoccupation for several Latin American countries" (Lord 1980, p. 223). He found that the economies of countries dependent upon exports of sugar, copper, and beef were especially vulnerable, then went on to conclude that "Important potential gains may consequently be derived by a number of countries in Latin America from international agreements because of the disruptive effects that could otherwise hinder their economic development progress. . . . There is little doubt that export instability can produce serious disruptions in the growth of an economy"(Lord 1980, p. 235).

What kinds of commodity price stabilization agreements have been proposed, and why are they important? Most proposals concentrate on a few key commodities (the UNCTAD proposals deal with ten "core commodities": sugar, cocoa, sisal, copper, cotton, coffee, rubber, tea, tin, and jute). These measures have the dual objectives of maintaining price fluctuations within a band of plus or minus 15 percent of the average price for the past five years, while limiting the deterioration in the comparative values of primary commodities and industrial goods. Some proposals reach further, to propose measures to raise commodity prices over time.

To accomplish these objectives, price stabilization proposals focus on one or more of the following six steps. First, buffer stocks of various commodities would be set aside. Second, a "common fund" for financing international commodity stockpiling would be set up (UNCTAD 1976). Third, wider access to compensatory financing has to be provided to Third World countries experiencing balance-of-payments deficits from export shortfalls. Fourth, trade barriers in the AICs that restrict imports of primary products and processed commodities from the Third World need to be lowered. Fifth, Third World countries need to diversify their activities into the processing, distribution, and marketing of commodities, where the lion's share of profits is made. Finally, additional research and development that will improve the marketing and competitiveness of primary commodities vis-à-vis substitutes (for instance, cotton vs. synthetics) must be subsidized (Behrman 1979).

In order to understand why commodity price stabilization is important, one has only to chart the recent history of price movements. According to UNCTAD:

> Commodity prices (excluding petroleum) in real terms declined steadily throughout the period 1950-1972. After a short recovery in 1973-1974, they fluctuated sharply during the remainder of the 1970s, drifting generally downwards towards a level even below the nadir of the early 1970s. By the end of 1980, commodity prices in real terms had reached the lowest level for the past 30 years. (1981, p. 66)

The commodity trade of the Third World is acutely sensitive to world economic conditions. Sniffles can rapidly become pneumonia. Instability, measured by the deviation from trend purchasing power, during the 1970s was from two to four times greater than in the 1960s. Moreover, the shortfalls in earnings grew systematically from 2.5 percent in 1970-71 to 14 percent in 1974-75 and 18 percent in 1979-80. The increased earnings during 1972-73 and 1976-78 did not offset the bad years. Meanwhile, neither import prices nor volumes declined sufficiently to compensate for unstable export receipts. Therefore, the drop in export earnings in poor years was due to deteriorating terms of trade as well as to poor export volumes.

An example of the extreme volatility of prices appears in Figure 1. For example, the price of sugar rose from 8.1 cents per pound in 1970 to 65.4 cents in 1974, only to fall to 17.2 cents in 1978. At the moment of writing (June 1984) sugar stands at a fraction over 6 cents per pound.

Such extreme fluctuations make meaningful planning of output or marketing hazardous not only for policy makers in the developing countries, but also for the farms and enterprises that produce and market the commodities, and for eventual processors and refiners. For example, in August 1982 Exxon canceled a $1 billion project in Chile after a nose dive in copper prices, and many workers were laid off. The Dominican Republic saw substantial profits from its sugar exports in 1980 evaporate into a disastrous $200 million loss in 1982. Swings of this magnitude place extreme strain on governments, reducing public revenues while increasing the need for public services. If the swings are too violent, governments — like strings — can break.

Figure 1   *Commodity Price Instability, 1973-82*

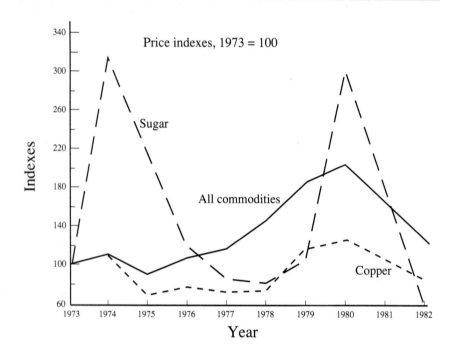

Price indexes, 1973 = 100

The side effects extend beyond national boundaries. Price fluctuations of imported raw materials generate inflationary pressures in consuming nations, as was seen throughout the 1970s. Import prices that rise even temporarily to extreme levels cause ripples throughout domestic economies (Cline 1979). There also tends to be a ratchet effect; higher retail prices for manufactured goods rarely fall back to their previous levels. In this way the extreme movements in commodity prices exert a magnified effect upon the international price level and further reduce the Third World's terms of trade.

Several factors contribute to the wild swings in commodity prices of Third World primary exporters:

1. Crops such as cotton and coffee are vulnerable to changing weather, which can sharply reduce harvest, thereby driving prices up. (For example, the Brazilian crop failure in 1974-75 pushed coffee up by

over 200 percent.) On the other hand, unexpectedly "perfect" weather can lead to record yields and falling prices.

2. The demand schedules for primary products are relatively inelastic. Small variations in supply can lead to large swings in prices and earnings.

3. A few MNCs often control the marketing of raw materials. For example, through collusion and use of their market power, the major oil companies (known as "The Seven Sisters") were able to maintain low crude oil prices until 1973. Then they joined forces with OPEC and switched tactics, boosting oil prices to their present level (Schneider 1975).

4. Econometric studies covering the 1950s and 1960s indicate that variations in production and the commodity concentration of producing countries, rather than price swings, are the dominant causes of income fluctuations in the Third World (MacBean 1966). However, the problem with these analyses is that production varies with prices: producers reduce output when prices are low. The time lag involved in matching supply with demand so as to increase profits can be considerable, however. If reserves of commodities are inadequate, producers can go bankrupt. This of course is the logic behind U.S. and EEC farm price supports, which make agriculture in the United States and Europe profitable.

5. Access to markets in advanced countries is often restricted. For example, a series of quotas and tariffs provides U.S. sugar growers with preferential treatment in the United States and Europe. Ironically the Third World is prevented from competing in its area of greatest comparative advantage, thereby substantially reducing incomes and employment, while meager sums of foreign aid and loans are given to fund development.

Earnings from commodity exports represent 55 percent of the Third World's nonpetroleum exports. The massive swings in earnings have contributed to recurrent balance-of-trade deficits and rising indebtedness. Estimates by Jere Behrman for the Overseas Development Council project that price stabilization could increase the annual incomes of producer countries from $500 million to $5.1 billion, depending upon the number of commodities involved. Estimated savings for industrial countries — even after subtracting the costs of operating the stabilization schemes — would net $4.6 billion annually due to the macroeconomic benefits from lower inflation (Cline 1979).

An accurate appraisal of costs and benefits depends on understanding how a buffer stock scheme — the central measure for commodity price stabilization — would operate. The classic case among primary commodities involved the combination of a relatively inelastic supply schedule and an inelastic demand schedule. In any given year the world supply of sugar will vary with the acreage planted, prevailing weather conditions, and yield per acre. Meanwhile, the demand for sugar remains relatively unresponsive to price changes; traditionally, consumers have not substantially reduced or increased their consumption of sugar, even when prices skyrocketed or fell precipitously. (With some variation this basic situation prevails for all of UNCTAD's ten core commodities.) Appendix A provides a more detailed analysis of what happens in this kind of supply-and-demand relationship, and the impact a buffer stock arrangement would have.

Between 1963 and 1972 developing countries would have realized potential gains of $5.4 billion if a buffer scheme including eight commodities ($24 billion for 13 commodities) had been in operation (Behrman 1979, p. 96). Consumers would have received indirect savings from reduced inflationary pressures. Subtracting the costs of operating the buffer stocks from the net gains in revenue (but not the benefits derived from reduced inflation) would have produced gross revenues of $2.2 billion for eight commodities and $28.8 billion for 13 commodities (Behrman 1979, p. 97). An initial fund of between $6 and $10 billion to purchase and store commodities would have been required to finance such a scheme (UNCTAD 1976; Behrman 1979). (Behrman maintains that the consumers and producers of copper and tin would be net losers under a commodity price stabilization scheme and would bear a substantial part of overall costs in maintaining such a system.) While there would have been winners and losers during any period, the winners and losers would change from one period to another. However, the main advantage is that the collective world welfare could be enhanced by such a scheme.

Commodity price stabilization promises much larger incomes for producer nations, but those benefits may be the tip of the iceberg. Oligopolistic industries dominated by MNC's often utilized fluctuating commodity prices as "cost justifications" for their own price increases.

"Cost savings" when commodity prices fall are seldom fully passed on to the consumer. For example, retail sugar prices in the United States soared in 1975 when bad weather damaged the crop in several cane-growing countries. The price of refined sugar has subsequently remained well above trend even though record crops have been produced. Distributors simply chose to widen their profit margins. Behrman suggests that reduced inflation in the U.S. economy alone might save $15 billion in a decade. There would be similar but smaller benefits to European and Third World economies.

The net gains from reduced inflation far outweigh the operating costs of a price stabilization system. A World Bank team has concluded that systemic benefits will extend to all commodity crops — that is, total gains from stabilization are positive and gainers can compensate losers, leaving everyone better off (Brook et al. 1978). Its empirical analysis found that Third World countries would earn greater export revenues for cocoa, coffee, wool, and jute, and the price stabilization of wheat would lower import expenditures. The data for sugar and cotton are statistically inconclusive but indicate higher profits.

To conclude, the stabilization of commodity prices can greatly reduce the volatility of investment income, unemployment, and government revenues in the Third World. The most thorough current assessment suggests that the Third World would earn $5.4 billion over a decade if eight key commodities were controlled. In addition, producer governments and businesses could improve their planning for investment and qualify for lower-risk premiums on loans. Such "secondary" savings will probably exceed, and will certainly magnify, the effective use of larger commodity profits. Meanwhile, there seem to be rather limited prospects for increasing the future trend of export prices via commodity price stabilization (any such consequence would be anathema to the advanced capitalist world). Paradoxically, the advanced countries may gain most from commodity price stabilization through reduced worldwide inflationary pressures. Such systemic savings would benefit everyone: the Third World, the ACCs, even the socialist world.

HIDDEN BARRIERS TO TRADE

In October 1982 the French government decreed that all imported video-tape recorders (mainly Japanese) must clear customs at Poitiers, a small city in the interior of France, rather than Le Havre, the main port of Paris. the delay in entry and processing of the machines will raise their costs (Lohr 1982). When U.S. baseball bats arrive in Japan, each must be unwrapped, inspected, and rewrapped. Indian exports of shirts and blouses to the United States are restricted by quota, and an internal consumption tax is levied by the EEC on coffee imported from the Philippines (Anjaria et al. 1982). These are examples of hidden, nontariff barriers that restrict international trade flows.

Non tariff barriers are multiform. They range from import licensing requirements that may be applied in a discriminatory fashion, to import quotas for sugar, to a variety of surveillance practices, quarantines, and arbitrary requirements and standards, to outright prohibitions against the exports of a particular nation — for instance, Cuban exports to the U.S. market. The U.S. government has initiated antidumping investigations, and will impose counterselling duties if it finds that foreign steel producers are being subsidized by their governments to undercut U.S. producers in the U.S. market. Other governments require that certain kinds of imports, such as TVs or autos, must contain a minimum number of domestically produced components. In general, any practice that restrains exports from one country to another or impedes the entry of one class of products constitutes a nontariff trade barrier.

The first group singles out methods of government participation in trade that either restrict imports from or subsidize exports to Third World countries. They may take the form of grants, tax credits, "buy-national" purchasing, or state trading. A second group involves customs and administrative entry procedures — such as the levy of antidumping duties, arbitrary methods of customs clearance, and requirements for certificates of origin — that discriminate against foreign products.

A third group applies nonmarket quality or "safety" standards as a "cover" for inhibiting imports. For example, arbitrary testing of a product may increase the wholesale cost and thereby make it less competitive with domestically produced goods. A fourth group concerns specific limitations on trade, which include numerical quotas for imports from a particular country or for a certain product, "voluntary" export restraints, and licensing requirements. It also includes minimum pricing devices, such as the now defunct American Selling Price (ASP), which levied a duty not on the invoiced cost but on the comparable American manufacturer's list price. The final category, charges on imports, covers a variety of items from prior deposits to cover the costs of customs services, to discriminatory taxes on specific products or the application of special duties — for example, the special tax on imported liquors.

Additionally, the GATT listing conspicuously omits restrictive business practices. These methods allow large firms to squeeze small firms out of a market. The practices may be overt, such as lobbying for export restrictions for specified domestic markets, or covert, such as selling below cost in a market to drive a competitor out of business (see United Nations 1969, 1978).

Recently the UNCTAD secretariat has begun to monitor the use of non tariff barriers by the major trading nations. The data show that the barriers are concentrated against agricultural exports, predominantly through the use of variable levies. Other measures include discretionary licensing, global quotas, tariff quotas, and voluntary export restraints. The percentage of imports restricted by nontariff barriers for highly protected sectors — plant products, foods and beverages, leather products, and footwear — ranges from less than 5 percent to over 90 percent.

TRADE DEVELOPMENT AND THE INTERNATIONALIZATION OF CAPITAL

Intel Corporation is located in the heart of California's "Silicon Valley," the rapidly developing center of the U.S. electronics industry. More than 3,000 Intel workers produce a variety of components for use in computers, calculators and other devices that require memory systems. When Intel's engineers develop a design for a new electronic circuit or process, technicians in the Santa Clara Valley, California plant, will build, test and redesign the product. When the new item is ready for production, however, it is air freighted to Intel's plant in Penang, Malaysia. There, Intel's Malaysian workers, almost all young women, assemble the components, tediously hand soldering the fiber-thin wire leads. Once assembled, the components are flown back to California for final testing and/or integration into a larger end product. And, finally, they're off to market, either in the United States, Europe, or back across the Pacific to Japan (NACLA 1976).

Third World export platforms have become increasingly common. Large corporations searching for cheap labor and resources have increasingly moved their production facilities to Asia, Latin America, the Caribbean, and Africa. This is part of a process termed "the internationalization of capital." Although it dates back to the late nineteenth century, when British banks commonly purchased shares in foreign companies, the 1960s began a new phase. MNCs chiefly based in the United States began to establish overseas subsidiaries for assembly and export. In 1961 the first Mexican facility to assemble electronic components was started. In 1964 General Instruments set up the first U.S. electronics factory in Taiwan, in 1968 National Semiconductor moved into Singapore, and Intersil opened a semiconductor operation in India in 1974 (NACLA 1976, p. 13).

Several factors contributed to this expansion. Beginning in 1963, section 807 was added to the U.S. Tariff Schedule. This provision reduced duties on any product whose parts originate in the United States and are sent abroad for assembly. Duty is paid only on the value added abroad. Section 806.30, which applies the same provision to any metal product, has been in effect since 1930. Articles that are imported into the United States under this section include semiconductors, aircraft parts, iron and steel products, and electronic components. Items covered by section 807 include apparel, electronic parts, sewing machines, and office machines. By 1975 over 70 percent of all U.S. electronics imports entered under sections 806.30 and 807 (NACLA 1976).

The new internationalization of capital also has been stimulated by the export processing zones (EPZs) that have sprung up in many Third World countries. EPZs are usually set up along international borders or around ports, and include tax and foreign ownership exemptions that make them attractive to investment by foreign corporations.

Although the boom that occurred throughout the 1960s and 1970s from EPZ-related activities was designed to spur domestic economies, actual development was more limited. When corporations produced their goods in several countries or vertically integrated their production on a world scale — for example, producing semiconductor crystals in the United States, assembling them in Barbados, and marketing them in Europe — it reflected a growing international division of labor. In effect, technology remained concentrated in the developed countries while the Third World provided cheap labor for the less-skilled assembly-related tasks.

While production by these subsidiaries for export nominally enhances the host countries' trade balances, the transactions are largely fictitious, in the sense that they represent internal transferring within the MNC. Thus, a section 807 textile plant in downtown Kingston, Jamaica, imports ready-cut cloth to be sewn into training brassieres for export to the United States. The only local content is the labor of the 60 women who in 1982 were paid a subsistence wage of $30 a week. The textiles are supplied ready-cut by J.C. Penney, the U.S. distribution chain, for reexport to J.C. Penney. Consequently, there is little likelihood that the Kingston assembly operation will diversify or spark related growth in the Jamaican economy. This is development inside hermetically sealed test tubes.

Such operations, however, do raise important issues. If the export processing factory was not located in Jamaica, wouldn't local workers have fewer jobs, and wouldn't the Jamaican economy earn less foreign exchange? The answers to these questions are not obvious. First, we must recall that plants locate in a Third World count v to take advantage of lower wage scales. Wage rates typically start very low; if labor costs pass a threshold of relative advantage, a firm will move to another location. Jamaican workers may be learning job skills and making money today, but tomorrow their jobs may be exported. One electronics executive explained that once wages reach "about 60¢ per hour [in electronics] it is uneconomical to use offshore facilities because of other costs involved. Offshore facilities have only a three-to-five-year useful labor advantage" (NACLA 1976, p. 16).

Even where employment is transient, it has been argued that MNC subsidiaries broaden and diversify a country's labor pool by employing large numbers of women workers. On the one hand, this is positive because it often brings women into jobs from which they may have been excluded, and provides them with income and on-the-job training. On the other hand, the motives for such "equal-employment" policies are not always egalitarian. In Singapore plans to hire 75,000 female factory workers were developed in order to avoid local minimum wage laws, which did not apply to women.

Finally, multinational subsidiaries are vulnerable to a variety of trade-related pressures, both internal and external. The activity of the EPZ may be curtailed via a "voluntary" export restraint or the imposition of some other form of non tariff barrier. Or a domestic credit squeeze may restrict needed imports for processing and lead to layoffs and reduced exports. This occurred in Mexico's border EPZ industries in late 1982.

The two main export industries — electronics and textiles — experienced high instability during the 1970s. Between 1969 and 1971 a recession caused a 15 percent drop in sales. The textile industry responded by laying off 400,000 workers around the world. In Mexico's border EPZ, where garment production is common, 37 factories closed while 53 new ones opened. There is little job security, and the industry makes a limited contribution to regional development. A 1979 study of Mexico's border EPZ concluded: "The Border Industrialization Program (BIP) has neither solved the employment problem nor made any contribution to integrated development in the region. The BIP is a stop-gap measure of a government confronted with crisis-level unemployment, yet unable and unwilling to undertake the necessary structural changes" (Baird and McCaughan 1979, p. 139).

Similarly, a World Bank study of Colombian textile exports tracked the roller-coaster ups and downs of that industry. Clothing exports rose from less than $1 million before 1970 to over $50 million in 1974. Then they plummeted to $30 million in 1975 and have remained at about that level. Fluctuating prices and exchange rates, and the lack of internal economic transportation crippled the industry before it could take off (Morawetz 1980).

More recently, evidence has been accumulating that even the foreign-exchange earnings from the EPZs appear to be evanescent. A study of economic development in the Far East found that exporting sectors had to borrow increasingly to meet their import requirements — especially agricultural imports — because production for export interfered with domestic production. As countries such as Brazil, Mexico, and South Korea have belatedly discovered, export-led growth requires extensive imports of components, raw materials and state subsidies. Agricultural labor is drawn off the land to work in higher-paid industrial sectors — far more workers than the limited number of new jobs — raising the cost of food production and often increasing reliance on imported foodstuffs. When world markets are favorable, these added costs are easily managed, but when export markets grow slowly or even decline, the country has to borrow increasingly to pay for industrial and agricultural imports (Frank 1982).

APPENDIX A

COSTS AND BENEFITS OF COMMODITY PRICE
    STABILIZATION

In Figure 2, P and Q represent the trend sugar prices and quantity, respectively, which are determined by the normal supply schedule S. If, however, there is a bad sugar crop, supply is reduced to S^* and the price rises to P_2. If there is a particularly good crop due to extraordinarily good weather or the planting and harvesting of more acreage following a period of prevailing high prices, then supply increases to S^{**} and the price falls to $P_1 Q_1$ What is significant is that relatively small fluctuations in supply produce pronounced swings in price.

A buffer stock facility would help stabilize prices by stockpiling surplus production in good years to sell during a bad year when supplies are scarce. Consumers would benefit by paying P_0 instead of the higher price P_2 in low-output years, while producers would gain by receiving P_0, instead of the lower price P_1, in high-production years. Behrman's (1979) analysis demonstrates that under most conditions the sum of benefits is positive, although in some cases (depending upon the slopes of the demand and supply curves) only producers benefit.

In surplus years, when production exceeds the trend, consumers pay A+B+C, while the benefit to producers from selling their production, Q, at a higher price is A+B+C+D. The buffer stock scheme must bear the cost C+D+E. The excess of costs over benefits in a good, high-output year (excluding storage costs) is C+E.

When a poor crop yields shortfall, the supply curve shifts to S^*, stocks accumulated during the high-output year are sold at price P_0, preventing the price from rising to P_2. Consumers save the amount F+G, while producers lose F in excess profits. The buffer stock scheme earns B+H, and the net benefit to all parties is B+G+H.

Figure 2   *Commodity Price Stabilization*

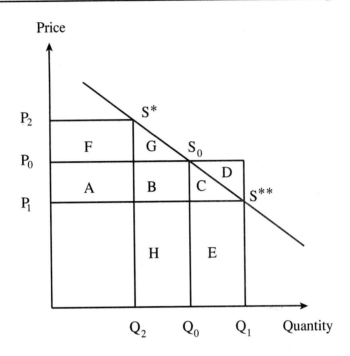

Summing up, over a period of years in which surpluses and shortfalls are equally likely, the net profit for producers is A+B+C+D-F — that is, incomes will rise. Consumers will realize a net loss of F+G-A-B-C through higher prices. For all parties the net result is positive: B+G+H-C-E. In reality, the actual configuration of net beneficiaries will vary with the exact slope of supply and demand schedules. It is possible that with altered assumptions, consumers might end up ahead.

Operations of a buffer stock incurs overhead costs. In order to maintain prices within a narrow range, commodities will have to be stockpiled for various periods of time and buffer stock managers will need sufficient financial as well as commodity resources. The overall cost of buffer stock operation is composed of four elements: the present discounted storage costs; present discounted value of the losses on sales of commodity holdings: stock deterioration costs; and transaction costs.

10

Import Substitution versus Export Promotion

Anne O. Krueger

In the 1950s and 1960s, there was considerable debate among academics and policy makers on the relative advantages of inward-oriented (or import substitution) policies and outward-oriented (or export promotion) policies, and on the effects of such policies on economic growth in developing countries. Essentially the argument for protection and inward orientation of the economy rested on the presence of imperfections in the market mechanism that made it difficult for developing economies to compete and to develop. Proponents of outward-oriented policies pointed to the costs associated with protectionist policies. Meanwhile, a number of developing countries proceeded either to abandon or substantially reduce their trade barriers and other controls on economic activity. The result was a spectacular growth of their economies, leading to the conclusion that outward-oriented policies had a dynamic effect on the domestic economy and helped accelerate growth rates. See Table 1.

Three main points have emerged from the experience of the countries that opted for export-led growth. First, their remarkable rates of growth were associated with the rapid growth of exports; second, for all countries where it was possible to contrast performance before and after the policy changes, the growth rate clearly jumped sharply after adoption of the export-oriented strategies; and third, the sustained high growth indicated that outward-oriented policies created dynamic effects in the economies and did not merely produce static gains from improved allocation of resources.

This article examines the links between export orientation and general economic performance by contrasting inward- and outward-oriented strategies and attempts to explain the reasons for differences in performance of economies that adopted each strategy.

DEFINING EXPORT-LED GROWTH

The terms "export-led growth," outward-oriented," "export promotion," and "export substitution" are all used to define policies of countries that have been successful in developing their export markets. While different countries have had different policies, their common features are that there is at least as much incentive to earn as to save foreign exchange and that incentives to export are fairly uniform and not discriminatory across commodity groups.

Table 1

Experiences of the Successful Exporters

Country/Territory	Period	Annual rate of growth of:		Exports	Investment
		Real GDP	Dollar value of exports		
		(In percent)		(As percentage of GDP) [1]	
Brazil	1960-67	4.1	3.7	7	14
	1968-73	11.5	16.5	8	23
Hong Kong	1963-78	8.2	9.2	99	28
Korea	1953-60	5.2	5.7	3	11
	1960-78	9.6	28.4	29	35
Singapore	1965-78	8.6	8.7	187	39
Taiwan Province of China	1960-76	8.7	20.9	47	28

Sources: United Nations, *Yearbook of National Accounts Statistics* 1966, 1975, and 1979; and World Bank, *World Development Report* 1978 (for Taiwan Province of China) and 1981.
[1] In the last year of the period indicated.

An export-oriented set of policies could be no more than the absence of policies that discriminate in favor of sales in the domestic market. The criterion for optimal allocation of resources is that the marginal rate of transformation of domestic production should equal the international marginal rate of transformation, in the absence of monopoly power in trade. One must bear in mind that developing countries, with their relatively smaller economies, are unlikely to have monopoly power to import manufacturing goods, which are most often the subject of protection. (The marginal rate of transformation is defined as the amount of one commodity that must be forgone in order to free resources to produce a specified amount of another commodity. One good (A) can be "transformed" into another (B), if production of the first is reduced and resources transferred to the production of the second good. The marginal rate of transformation shows how much extra output of B could be obtained by reducing the output of A by one unit.)

In principle, a government could protect some industries in the domestic market while providing sizable export subsidies to other industries. In practice, however, the scope for such two-way protection is limited, for a number of reasons: (1) protective devices for export subsidies are meaningful only if they discriminate against some other activities; (2) protection of a large number of activities is generally inconsistent with encouraging exports, because exporters of manufactured goods require relatively easy access to international markets for their inputs of raw materials and intermediate and capital goods; and (3) protection at the levels deemed necessary to induce import substitution usually requires a great degree of control (to prevent smuggling, false invoicing, etc.) to ensure that the domestic market is profitable enough, and to prevent export of the protected goods.

Thus most analysts would agree that an export-oriented strategy is one in which there is no bias of incentives toward production of import substitutes. Whatever incentives exist must favor production for export as much as, if not more than, production for the domestic market. Such a strategy generally entails less of a departure from free trade and equalized incentives than does an inward-oriented strategy.

A glance at some countries and territories that have been successful as exporters (at certain periods or consistently) indicates the range of policies followed. Singapore appears to have followed interventionist policies while Hong Kong was genuinely *laissez-faire*, with Brazil, Korea, and Taiwan Province of China lying somewhere in between. Interventions generally were in the form of incentives rather than imposition of direct controls. Most successful exporters also provided incentives across the board instead of differentiating by commodity groups.

SALIENT CHARACTERISTICS

The characteristics of import-substitution and export-oriented regimes vary widely according to local conditions, especially those prevailing in factor markets. Nonetheless, there are some fairly uniform features, and for present purposes a few stylized facts can be presented to highlight the differences between import substitution and export-oriented regimes.

Import-substitution regimes generally have strict and time-consuming licensing procedures for imports of manufactured producer goods; *export-oriented* regimes permit ready access to imports of intermediate and capital goods, at least to exporters.

Import-substitution regimes are characterized, *inter alia,* by overvalued exchange rates (fostering excess demand for foreign exchange, which is held in check by the licensing process). Since domestic producers of import substitutes would receive a substantially lower price for their products in the world market than they do behind the wall of protection under the import-substitution regime, it rarely pays them to expand production beyond the demand of the domestic market; *export-oriented* regimes have fairly realistic exchange rates and provide at least as much, if not more, incentive to sell abroad as to sell domestically.

Generally, virtual prohibition of imports is needed to sustain *import substitution;* either imports are prohibited, or a wide range of tariffs is imposed on different products at a level high enough to make their import uneconomic. Under *export promotion* most incentives apply uniformly to all exporters and are based on either the value or value added of export sales.

Import-substitution regimes are characterized by quantitative restrictions or prohibitive tariffs for many commodities; *export-oriented* policies normally avoid quantitative restrictions and use (generally low) tariffs with relatively simple procedures to permit exporters access to the international market at international prices for their inputs.

The chief rationale for import substitution in many developing countries is to stimulate industrial growth. The rate of industrial growth normally exceeds that of the rest of the economy under both import-substitution and export-oriented strategies. However, the industrial growth rate appears to be higher and output of primary commodities seems to grow more rapidly under export promotion than under import substitution.

Import substitution, which is rationalized in many countries as a means of reducing dependence on the international economy, actually seems to increase it as import-substitution activities are import- intensive and require both intermediate and capital goods from abroad to sustain production and growth.   Thus, the economy becomes vulnerable to declines in availability of foreign exchange.   By contrast, export promotion seems to reduce dependence, in the sense that foreign exchange earnings grow rapidly, markets become increasingly diverse and the economy increasingly flexible.

It is relatively easy to launch an import-substitution policy; initially simple and administratively straight forward regulations offering protection and prohibiting competitive imports provide adequate incentives for the first few new investments. As investments multiply it becomes increasingly difficult and costly to monitor and sustain this strategy. On the other hand, starting an export-oriented growth strategy is difficult and requires a combination of policies and determination on the part of the government that is politically difficult to achieve. However, once started, an export-oriented growth strategy is more likely to be self-sustaining and to gather momentum.   The increasing supply of foreign exchange permits additional liberalization of the import regime. This strengthens the bias of the regime toward exports.

WHAT AFFECTS PERFORMANCE?

Three sets of factors account for the difference in performance of economies under inward- and outward-oriented regimes. Their relative and absolute resistance probably varies considerably between countries, depending on local circumstances (such as size and resource endowment), and political and cultural differences that affect both the behavior of politicians and bureaucrats and the relations between the government and business.

The three sets are: (1) technological factors; (2) economic factors; and (3) politico-economic considerations. Technological factors cover the nature of production functions including the extent of indivisibilities and economies of scale, and the capital intensity of import-competing domestic production. Economic factors refer to such phenomena as peoples' responses to incentives and direct controls, the impact of industry structure on behavior, and the flexibility of the economy. Politico-economic considerations relate to the factors that influence decision makers in making or altering economic policies.

TECHNOLOGICAL FACTORS

Size of markets. The small size of domestic markets in developing countries constrains their economic growth under import-substitution policies. Even some of the populous developing countries have markets, however measured, that are relatively small in contrast with the developed countries. Bangladesh, for example, has a nonagricultural income approximately 3 percent that of Sweden and less than 2 percent that of Canada, neither of which is regarded as an economy large enough to forgo the benefits of specialization and international trade. Despite a large population, the Indian market is estimated to be less than one quarter that of Germany's, based on the value of industrial output.

Import substitution policies inherently tend to encourage expansion of any industry only up to the size of the domestic market (which itself may be smaller when commodities are high priced), and the expansion of an activity beyond the amount sold in the domestic market is seldom profitable under import substitution. In an outward-oriented economy, efficient activities can expand well beyond that point.

Indivisibilities and economies of scale. For processes and activities that are highly divisible and have constant returns to scale, the size of the production unit does not matter. There are other processes, however, where one or more indivisibilities are important, or where there are sizable economies of scale. Capital equipment (e.g., heavy presses) requires a substantial volume of production if it is to be fully utilized. Likewise, many processes or industries (e.g., fertilizers and tires) demand a minimum size for a plant to be efficient. Other processes do not allow production to be divided into numerous steps that can easily be changed. I n most metal casting, pressing, and shaping activities, for example, the die or mold has to be changed whenever a new shape or form is to be produced. No intermediate alteration is possible. The longer the length of the production run for a given metal product, the smaller the fixed costs relative to variable costs.

Import substitution policies, because they generally restrict local industries to reliance upon sales in the domestic market, lead to short production runs and high average variable costs. An export-oriented strategy, however, permits a developing country, regardless of the size of its domestic market, to establish plants of economically efficient size and to maintain long production runs. Thus, the limitations of a small size of domestic market can be largely overcome, at least for traded goods, in an export-oriented economy. Under such a regime, producers in a small developing country can obtain specialized products, which are not produced domestically, at internationally competitive prices. By contrast, under import-substitution regimes, either there are substantial delays in obtaining items not domestically produced because of import licensing procedures and restrictions, or producers must obtain them from high-cost (possibly monopolistic) domestic sources.

Factor intensities. Developing countries are usually relatively well endowed with unskilled labor. The rate of human and physical capital formation (broadly defined) is the constraint upon expansion of the industrial sector in these countries. When the proportions of the human and physical factors employed differ significantly among industrial sectors, export promotion permits a more rapid growth of value added and employment of unskilled labor in industry for the same rate of human and physical capital formation. Under these conditions, the larger size of the international market encourages expansion of exporting industries that use relatively unskilled labor. Import substitution, however, limits the expansion of these industries to the rate of growth of domestic demand once production has expanded sufficiently to replace imports; thereafter growth of output is tied to increases in real income and demand (unless costs and prices are falling).

Infant industry. The infant industry argument has long been used to justify protection. Given the experience of the export-oriented developing countries, there are important grounds for believing that, if there are infant industries, once developed, they can — and indeed should--- be expanded well beyond the size of the domestic market. Restriction of their output levels to the quantities demanded in the domestic market would necessarily reduce the dynamic gains from the development of the industry to far smaller magnitudes that would be possible if the industry could be induced to export. Viewed in this light, there is nothing in the infant industry argument that indicates that import substitution, or more generally protection, is preferable to an unbiased or export-oriented trade-and-growth strategy.

Interdependence and quality.   Efficient production of most manufactured goods entails the use of a wide variety of inputs. As mentioned earlier, countries adopting inward-oriented trade strategies have generally (because of foreign exchange shortage and in order to enforce a degree of protection) required producers to obtain their intermediate inputs from protected domestic producers, if possible. When such protected producers have not maintained satisfactory standards of quality control, because of lack of competition, use of their products has raised costs and lowered the quality of output in other firms.

The demands for intermediate inputs are generally fairly specialized. This, in turn, has implied that there were few domestic producers of any particular item. Consequently, production stoppages (or even inadequate quality of inputs) in one sector of the economy very quickly affect other firms and industries. These phenomena, in turn, raise costs for users of the intermediate goods.

Under a liberal trade regime, exporters have access to international markets for their intermediate inputs. Their freedom of choice permits them to tap the cheapest and most reliable source, thus reducing their own production costs. That this may be important is suggested by the fact that in Korea, even with its relatively labor-intensive consumer goods exports in the 1960s, approximately 50 percent of the value of exports represented imports of intermediate goods and raw materials.

ECONOMIC BEHAVIOR

The relatively small size of most domestic markets implies that, when industries are encouraged by protection, there will be either few firms producing a given product or the firms will be very small. Any policy encouraging competition by increasing the number of firms in a given line of activity will result in the reduced size of each firm and hence the loss of economies of scale. Moreover, many import-restricting mechanisms indeed preclude the entry of new firms and reduce the possibility of competition regardless of the number in the industry. To cite but one example, a frequently encountered licensing mechanism allocates intermediate goods and raw material imports to firms in proportion to their share of industrial capacity or output. To the extent that outputs and inputs are in more or less fixed proportions to each other and resale of inputs is either costly or prohibited, these mechanisms tend to render market shares fairly rigid, thus inducing a lack of competition among firms. That, together with the small size of market and the limitation of expansion of individual industries to the rate of growth of the domestic market, generally implies that growth rates of most firms and industries will be fairly uniform. Hence, changes in shares would come about more slowly than they would in a more competitive environment. The absence of competition itself probably cuts down the extent to which individual entrepreneurs concern themselves with engineering and economic efficiency.

When industrial growth is based upon the competitive international market, firms can be of optimal economic size without regard to the size of price and demand characteristics of the domestic market. Low-cost firms in individual industries can expand at their desired rate, unconstrained by availability of raw material or the price elasticity of domestic demand for the product. This leads to greater reduction of costs and expansion of output than that observed under protection. Moreover, industries with comparative advantage can increase their shares of industrial output at a more rapid rate when they can profitably export than when their growth is restricted to their shares of the less dynamic domestic market.

Thus, to the extent that competitive markets induce lower-cost activities in individual firms, there is a presumption that an export-oriented trade strategy will induce greater economic and engineering efficiency. For any given distribution of costs within an industry, the possibility of exporting permits more rapidly changing market shares. Finally, changing individual industries' shares of industrial output can further accelerate the average rate of increase of factor productivity and of the industrial sector.

POLICY FORMULATION

Government policy instruments that seek to regulate and control through negative means (e.g., import restrictions) are less likely to achieve the intended results than those that create incentives for particular types of economic activities. Nonetheless, there seems to be a widely present temptation for politicians to regulate economic activity rather than to create incentives.

There are obvious limits to the extent to which quantitative controls can be imposed in an export-oriented regime. Since exporters must have ready access to the international market for their inputs, provision of that access substantially reduces the scope for quantitative restrictions upon any category of imports. If quantitative restrictions are highly restrictive, the reward for evading them will be substantial. Their enforcement is possible only with fairly detailed scrutiny of all incoming goods. That scrutiny, in turn, is inconsistent with the ready access required for exporters. Thus, the fact that some imports are intermediate goods used by exporters imposes a limit on the level of protection accorded to any productive activity through quantitative import restrictions. (Of course, imports of luxury consumer goods do not fall in this category.)

Export-oriented policies by their nature reward those who export and do not discriminate against exportables. Since rewards are based upon performance, which in turn is highly correlated with the social profitability of the activity, there is a greater inherent tendency toward less variability in incentives under export promotion than under import substitution.

The feedback to policy makers on the negative effects of policies is much stronger under an export-oriented policy stance than it is under import substitution. For example, an overvalued exchange rate is much more clearly reflected in lagging exports under an outward-oriented policy than would be evident through rising premiums for import licenses under import substitution. It is quite possible that constraints upon the nature of policies that can be followed, and the quicker feedback to policy makers on the effects of their policies, are at least as important in explaining the success of outward-oriented regimes as are the economic and technological factors considered above. However, quantifying their role would provide a significant research challenge.

One other potentially important, but probably unmeasurable, aspect of feedback should be noted: under import substitution and direct controls over imports, firms have built-in incentives to misrepresent their activities in ways that will induce the receipt of more import licenses and other permissions and privileges. Government officials naturally suspect information presented to them, and thus require verification or check producers' claims before acting on their applications. Under an export- oriented regime with a fairly realistic exchange rate, the incentive to misrepresent performance is far smaller, as is the scope for doing so: surrender of foreign exchange proceeds is sufficient proof of exports.

OVERVIEW

The growth rate of the outward-oriented countries certainly suggests that something more than the direct impact of exports was at work in accounting for the superior growth performance of these countries. When one examines critically some of the bases upon which that superior performance may have rested, most of the factors earlier thought to have justified protectionist regimes in fact become arguments for intervention supporting exports instead of production for a protected domestic market.

Whether that "something more" is because export-oriented regimes are *de facto* closer to the optimal allocation of resources under free trade or whether their superior performance is the result of their ability to capture the dynamic gains associated with an export-oriented strategy is still an open question. What seems certain is that the existence of dynamic factors in no way creates a presumption that growth induced via protection of the domestic market will be in any way superior to growth under neutral or outward-oriented trade strategies.

Insofar as the superior results achieved under export orientation have been the result of the behavioral differences rather than the technological factors discussed earlier, the fact of openness itself, rather than of export growth, is a critical ingredient for rapid increases in output and productivity. This consideration is significant in evaluating the prospects for future growth of developing countries in the context of a potentially slower expansion of world trade: if it is openness itself that conveys benefits due to competition and the nature of policy instruments employed, the gains from export orientation will be almost as great (provided the world economy remains open) with slower growth of world trade as with more rapid growth.

IV

ECONOMIC INTEGRATION AMONG DEVELOPED COUNTRIES

Economic integration among industrialized countries is again a topic of debate; the central focus of the debate is on Europe in 1992. What will be the effects of 1992 on the U.S. and Japan? Will Europe really unite in 1992? Will Europe have a common currency?

The first article is from a survey by the British magazine, *The Economist*. The article points out many of the potential pitfalls in trying to unify Europe in 1992. A truly unified Europe would require that the individual countries which comprise it will have to give up some of their sovereignty. Border restrictions must be relaxed; products must be standardized to prevent hidden barriers (see the article "Japan's intangible barriers to trade in manufactures" in a previous section) ranging from such things as pollution control devices for automobiles to electric sockets for household appliances; government subsidies must be eliminated and the value added tax must be uniformly applied across Europe. A true monetary union of Europe would require an even greater loss of sovereign power as countries must give up control over monetary policy and to some extent fiscal policy in order to achieve a common currency. According to this article, all of these changes will be much more difficult than many realize and many of the necessary changes will not occur until well after 1992. The article strongly supports unification, however, and argues in particular that the elimination of red tape alone will save Europe billions of dollars.

11

Europe's Internal Market (Survey of Europe in 1992)

The Economist

AFTER THE FIREWORKS

There is a spring in the step of European civil servants that they have not known since the late 1960's. In February the heads of the European Community's governments managed to sweep an interminable wrangle about money to one side. The cost of Europe's farms; the spending power of the European Commission; the amount that should be spent on the infrastructure of the EEC's poorer regions; the depressing subject of Britain's contribution to the EEC budget — all were shelved for a while. Eurocrats could at last turn undistracted to the EEC's great project of the moment, a campaign to turn its 12 countries into one barrier-free market by the end of 1992.

It has taken more than two years, since the commission lit the fuse of this project, for "1992" to burst upon the world. The French, West German and British governments have mounted campaigns to raise their countrymen's eyes to it. Conference organizers are doing a brisk trade explaining it. Squads of Japanese corporate planners fly to Europe to assess it. Non-EEC European countries like Sweden, Switzerland and Austria worry about its portent for them. America eyes it warily for any unfriendly protectionist message. "1992" is the European phenomenon of the spring of 1988, and this summer will probably be remembered as the high-point of unquestioning hope for it.

What is it, and what difference will it make? Project 1992 is a clever campaign to bounce the EEC's 12 nations towards what the six original members agreed they wanted in their Treaty of Rome 30 years ago: a common market in which goods, people, services and capital could move without obstacle. Part of the power of 1992 is that it is so hard to reduce to essentials. At its simplest it is presented as "Europe without frontiers"; but to this graspable notion have been added extra after extra, all consistent with the aim of a single market but not necessarily vital to it: patent law, broadcasting standards, labelling rules, corporate structure, vocational training for young people, the pedigree of bovine animals, and so on and so on.

There is power in the diversity of this firework display. It means that there is something in 1992 for everyone. Now that most branches of European business are aware of it, 1992 has become a state of mind, a set of expectations that has political force, an obsession that amounts almost to a new reality. This survey cannot tell every reader how the big influences in his/her walk of life are responding to this display and what new business facts they are thereby creating. That would require a reference work. Instead it will burrow down to the core of the project that has caused all this excitement and guess what underlying changes will have been wrought by the middle of the next decade, when the fireworks are over.

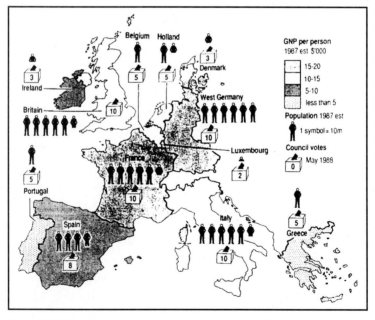

Source: OECD; EEC

As billed, 1992 will not be achieved this century. Equally, it is already clear that the successful parts of this project will do more for the coming together of the countries of Europe than any European initiative since the Treaty of Rome. The first reason for this success is that the designers of 1992 learnt from the mistakes of the past.

HISTORY LESSONS

Robert Schuman, a French founder of the EEC, said in 1950 that "Europe will not be made all at once or according to a single general plan. It will be built through concrete achievements, which first create a de facto solidarity." Another founder, Jean Monnet, held that progress towards united Europe would be made only where clear goals and timetables were laid down. Both bits of advice were honored in the Treaty of Rome of 1957 which set a pragmatic first task and a timetable — the removal of tariffs and quotas between European countries within 12 years.

Subsequent, failed attempts to move the EEC forward showed what avenues to avoid. The Fouchet plan of 1961 envisaged a joint European foreign policy; both it and Fouchet Mark II died because they were too direct in their attempts to compromise the sovereignty of members. The Werner plan in 1970 for Economic and Monetary Union (EMU) by 1980 had a deadline going for it; but it, too, went straight for the jugular of national independence, and had the bad luck to do this on the eve of the everyman-for-himself era of floating exchange rates and oil crisis. EMU became the butt of hollow laughter in the late 1970's; though it found some vindication later in the founding of the European Monetary System (EMS) in 1979. A programme for "European Union", presented by the Belgian prime minister, Leo Tindemans, was another ambitious Eurovision that member governments asked for and then ignored — though it too smouldered on to reappear later in the tale of 1992.

Before Mr. Jacques Delors, a former French finance minister, became president of the European Commission at the beginning of 1985, he toured the member states and tried on them four ideas to push Europe forward: closer collaboration on defence, development of the Community's system of government, another move on the monetary front, or a renewed campaign for a proper European market.

The last of these was the one that appealed to members the most, for various reasons:

- Mrs. Margaret Thatcher's government, long the black sheep of the EEC for its general stand-offishness and its maddeningly justified complaints about the European budget, wanted some pragmatic, non-airy-fairy European goal that it could advocate.

- France had lost any remaining illusions about go-it-alone economic management with a brief and painful adventure in socialist reflation in 1981-82. It was ready for less dirigisme, and more competition and interdependence.
- West Germany had a freshly installed liberal-conservative government making new, if rather empty, promises of liberal economic management.
- High unemployment right across Western Europe created a hunger for some new initiative that might cure it. The Reagan administration (before its own economic come-uppance) suggested freer markets as an antidote to "Eurosclerosis."
- European industrialists, notably Mr. Wisse Dekker of Philips and Mr. Jacques Solvay of Solvay, were campaigning energetically for an end to the EEC's economic divisions. They saw it as part of the answer to the challenge presented by Japan and the Asian dragons.

At Mr. Delors' bidding, Lord Cockfield, a doughty British conservative ex-businessman and tax-supremo, who had arrived in Brussels with no great fanfare as commissioner for the Internal Market, took to the task of preparing a white paper with almost alarming gusto. His tactics would have delighted Monnet and Schuman. He rapidly cobbled together a list of 300 measures that were needed for a wholly unified European market. He laid out the hectic timetable that would have to be followed to get those directives (European laws) adopted by the end of the next commission's reign, December 1992. The cleverness of the approach lay in the absence of priorities — which always favor one member-state's interests over another's — and in the strict focus on practical ends such as "no security checks at frontiers", rather than on political consequences, in other words, "this means a common immigration policy."

The magic of those 300 directives was potent — 20 or more have since been quietly dropped or replaced, but the mystique of Leonidas's round number remains. After years of piecemeal fiddling, European governments were suddenly presented with the full measure of what they said they wanted. The challenge of so much lawmaking bounced those governments into passing the Single European Act, the second reason why 1992 must already be deemed a success.

ODD PARENTS, ODD NAME

The Single European Act started life as an attempt by an avid European, Altiero Spinelli, to re-ignite Tindemans's ideal of European Union by increasing the powers of the EEC institutions, and of the European Parliament in particular. As such, it probably would have died the normal death at the hands of those governments, notably Britain's, which instinctively mistrust any shift in the balance of power towards the EEC's institutions.

The pragmatic lure of the great market won the sceptics round. The act was greatly watered down before being adopted by the governments at the end of 1985; nevertheless it moved the scope and power of the Treaty of Rome forward on several fronts and, vital for 1992, ordained that most of its 300 directives would be adopted by "qualified majority voting" between ministers, rather than by unanimity.

The act was an early, irreversible triumph for the 1992 project. It took referendums in two countries — Ireland and Denmark — before it was ratified, but its precarious passage showed clearly how a practical goal could ginger EEC countries into concessions of sovereignty that would have got nowhere if presented only as woolly ideals.

The act also embodied reason number three why 1992 has already delivered something: mutual recognition, two dry words whose importance is worth a great number of frontier posts. Until the end of the 1970's the route to a common market was thought to lie through "harmonization". Frontiers would wither as the pasta, taxes, company laws, and anti-terrorist policies on either side of them were forced by the Eurocracy to conform to Euro-norms that would make the Community a seamless continuum. It was a hopeless prospect wherever countries were asked to take unanimous decisions over national quirks that were dear to them.

But in 1978 along came a West German company called Rewe Zentral AG, an unsung European hero, whose contribution to the great market should be toasted regularly in kir. This firm wanted to import Crème de Cassis, a liqueur otherwise known as Cassis de Dijon, into West Germany. It found it could not, because the elixir did not contain enough alcohol to be deemed a liqueur by West German standards. Rewe started legal proceedings which led to the European Court of Justice in Luxembourg, a body that will loom larger and larger as the 1992 story unfolds. The court looked at West Germany's claim that its liqueur norms did not discriminate between West Germans and foreigners, and ruled that it would not wash. West Germany had no right to block the import of a drink that was on sale in France, unless it could show that it was blocked for reasons of health, fiscal supervision, fair trading or consumer protection. West Germany could not.

1 ecu =	1987 average	mid-June 1988
$	1.15	1.21
£	0.71	0.66
BFr	43.0	43.4
DKr	7.88	7.90
DM	2.07	2.08
Esc	162	171
FFr	6.93	7.01
Guilders	2.33	2.33
lire	1495	1544
Ptas	142	137
IR£	0.78	0.78

On this unlikely base was built a whole new technique for demolishing the EEC's unseen barrier — not those at frontiers but the barriers within. The technique is enshrined in the Single European Act — "the Council may decide that provisions in force in a member-state must be recognized as being equivalent to those applied by another." A new approach to industrial standards has evolved from Cassis de Dijon. Banks in one EEC country will be able to establish themselves in all. Insurance can be sold across frontiers. All benefited from this case.

More generally, the Cassis ruling means that 1992 offers the prospect of competitive lawmaking in European countries. Europe's companies and people will, in principle, be allowed to vote with their feet, or their wallets, for the member-state that offers them laws with the right blend of freedom and responsibility. Might freedom without responsibility be the unwanted victor? The scope for argument is obvious and already bedevils the attempt to apply mutual recognition

Who trades where
EEC trade, 1987

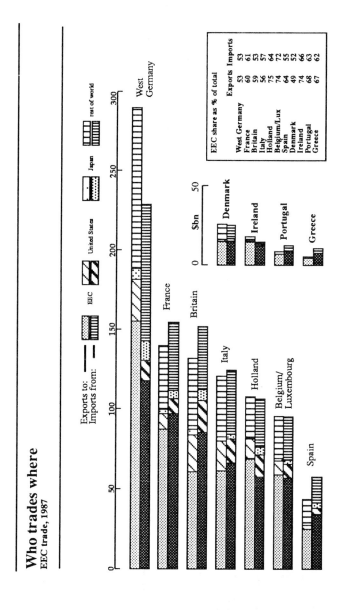

Exports to: ▬
Imports from: ▬

EEC | United States | Japan | rest of world

EEC share as % of total		
	Exports	**Imports**
West Germany	53	53
France	60	61
Britain	59	53
Italy	56	57
Holland	75	64
Belgium/Lux	74	72
Spain	64	55
Denmark	49	52
Ireland	74	66
Portugal	68	63
Greece	67	62

West Germany

France

Britain

Italy

Holland

Belgium/Luxembourg

Spain

Denmark

Ireland

Portugal

Greece

$bn

0   50

0   50   100   150   200   250   300

Source: OECD

more widely. But, equally, an analysis of America's internal market, later in this survey, shows that "competitive rulemaking" has not led to anarchy there.

However far this Cassis approach is ultimately taken, 1992 has here achieved a lurch towards a Europe that is alien to French or West German eyes. The extreme reluctance of Mr. Helmut Kohl's government to deregulate the West German economy shows how attached that society is to norms and standards painstakingly connected, and how unwilling it is to see them undermined by those of less fastidious nations. What would the Meistersingers say to an Italian tenor who breezed into Nuremberg claiming mutual recognition for his Venetian singing diploma unless he could be shown to be a health risk?

For France, with its long-established tradition of unchallenged dirigisme from the center, the prospect of competition in rules seems insidious in a different way. A senior French diplomat, Mr. Henri Froment-Meurice, has written one of an impressive series of studies of 1992 commissioned by the French government. In it he says that one of the dangers of the 1992 approach is that the EEC could be governed by a government of judges inadequately balanced by institutions of political power. Compare that with the evident relish with which Sir David Hannay, the British ambassador to the Community in Brussels, notes that case law is now shaping the EEC just as the evolution of common law shaped Great Britain.

In truth, this 1992 project is an adventure in deregulation: that is why Britain likes the sound of it. That, curiously, is why the French and the West Germans go along with it. Deregulation is the economic treatment of the decade — a fashionable medicine which European countries know they should swallow like good patients, even if they dislike its taste.

A practical-sounding goal; a much-trumpeted deadline; a new, deregulatory basis for drafting Community laws; a new majority-voting system to push those laws through; all playing upon a wide-spread susceptibility: these are what have given 1992 a trampoline start in bouncing the European Community towards greater unity. The technique has put off the moment when the members see the consequences of the project for their sovereignty and for the national system, phobias, principle and habits that they hold dearest. But it cannot remove those hard choices forever. The second half of the 1992 project, which starts at the end of this year, will be the half in which sovereignty fights back. Its earliest resistance is already showing in the symbolically important matter of frontier controls.

BORDER WARS

The European Commission has put about the idea of "Europe without frontiers" as the shorthand for what it is trying to achieve by the end of 1992. This has always been both a gamble and something of a fast one. Britain and Denmark still feel that the Treaty of Rome, and the Single Act's modifications of it, are for an economic community (the initials EEC used throughout this survey reflect that British viewpoint) and not the free movement of people tout court. Nevertheless, the commission is adamant that frontiers are the most potent symbol of the EEC's divisions. It insists that if frontier-posts remain for any reason at all, they will be used, willy-nilly, as a convenient place to carry out less justifiable checks.

As for the gamble, a brief review of what is needed before the EEC can become a zone without passport controls gives an idea of the odds against them: a harmonized law of gun control; police collaboration and mutual trust in guarding Europe's external frontiers against drugs and terrorists collaborations, trust and consistent laws for immigration, visas, and rights of asylum for people from outside the EEC. Small wonder that the 1992 progress report issued by the European Commission in March said bluntly that there had been no progress in such matters.

The complications are legion. West Germany has extremely strict gun controls: France has an American-like right to bear arms. Denmark insists upon maintaining a passport-free arrangement with the Nordic countries, so someone flying into London from Copenhagen could be a Dane, or a Swede, or a blonde alien let into Sweden from elsewhere. Britain, with its sea frontiers, finds it convenient to check its people only at frontier ports; it eschews identity cards. France, with unpoliceable land frontiers, cares less about border posts and monitors its people from within. Entirely different patterns of government snoopiness have developed around such facts of geography. They will not be discarded this century.

The outlook is not uniformly bleak. By the end of next year all new passports issued in Europe will be slim Euro-passports bearing the name of country beneath that of the Community. Britain's, Holland's and West Germany's will be "machine readable" for rapid computer scrutiny, but the commission is keeping up a campaign to trim formalities for the bearers of such passes so that, wherever possible, they need do little more than wave them.

There is, moreover, the prospect of a "two-speed Europe" emerging in the matter of passport controls. In 1984 Chancellor Kohl of West Germany and President Mitterrand of France surprised their own officials by vowing to remove their mutual border controls completely. The Benelux countries, which already run a passport union, joined the other two in the Schengen agreement of 1985. Italy now wants to join as well, suggesting that the original EEC six may move ahead of the rest in letting people cross land frontiers unchecked.

Given the variety of types of port, of border and of combinations of contiguous countries that exist in the EEC, the commission should welcome such à la carte removal of immigration controls, and alter its sales-pitch for 1992 accordingly. In contrast to the trade-deadening insulation provided by customs posts, the economic benefits of a passport-free Elysium do not seem worth the trouble.

RENDER UNTO COCKFIELD

Customs posts are above all a matter of tax. There is no issue like taxation to show how the good intentions behind the 1992 project are running into the sands of sovereignty. If readers have to engage mental four-wheel-drive to plough through what follows it is because this survey will suggest, in the end, that tax is crucial to the expectations for 1992 that governments have raised among their electorates.

The contents of the battered box held up each budget day by the British chancellor of the exchequer have not yet been greatly compromised by Britain's membership of the EEC. Broadly, in choosing whether to tax people's income or what they do with it, and in deciding where for the good of society to make life cheaper or more expensive, European governments have remained their own masters.

A custom-free internal market will put an end to that. Customs controls protect one European country's indirect taxes (taxes, that is, on things not people) from relative tax bargains available in others. And they allow governments to make sure that they collect the VAT that is due to them. The prospect of 1992-as-billed is not merely of shoppers with large station-wagons taking day trips to Luxembourg to buy lightly taxed whisky and luxuries. It is of businesses buying components and capital equipment across borders and sending lorries to collect them, and of a booming trade in mail-order tax avoidance. If there is to be a Europe without customs halls, Europe's governments will have to accept heavy diversions of revenue and local business nonsenses — unless they move their rates of indirect tax close enough for such tax dodging to become uninteresting. The experience of the United States shows that contiguous states can maintain differences in sales tax of up to about five percentage points without the tax leakage becoming unbearable. Europe will, one way or another, have to achieve such an American order of tax-sameness if it is to get rid of its tax-frontiers.

Of all the problems of creating an open market, the tax issue was the one on which the white paper lavished the most attention. In fact, the commission's approach here departed from the general 1992 tactic of getting members committed to a simple-sounding goal, chivvying them towards it, and letting them cope with the consequences later. Rather than opt for a fiscal version of mutual recognition — you charge your tax; I'll charge my tax; and we'll see how we manage — the commission went straight for preemptive harmonization. Why?

The commission feared that far from allowing market forces to determine what tax-differences could be sustained, as the British government proposed (from beyond a stretch of sea that would do its old duty in keeping continental forces at bay), high-taxing countries with land frontiers like Denmark, Ireland or even France would not lift their barriers to let those forces do their bit.

Europeans already have an allowance of 350 ecus-worth (roughly $400) of goods that they can take across intra-EEC frontiers without tax paperwork and payments. This amount alone has prompted Ireland and Denmark illegally to restrict their allowances to "genuine" travellers: that is, those staying outside their country for some arbitrary length of time, or those lugging suitcases but not washing-machines. The amount of tax lost was already more than these two governments were willing to shrug off. What chance of them keeping their booms open in a free-for-all?

Table 1

VAT Rates in the EEC, %

	Reduced Rate	Standard Rate	High Rate
Belgium	1 and 6	19	25 and 33
Britain	0	15	None
Denmark	None	22	None
France	2.1 to 7	18.6	33.33
Greece	6	18	36
Holland	6	20	None
Ireland	2.4 and 10	25	None
Italy	2 and 9	18	38
Luxembourg	3 and 6	12	None
Portugal	8	16	30
Spain	6	12	33
West Germany	7	14	None
Commission proposal	4 to 9	14 to 20	None

So Lord Cockfield proposed a practical form of harmonization. He started with the American example of the spread of tax rates that seemed sustainable. Then he tried to fit such spreads as best he could around the scatter-shot pattern of European tax rates. This was a challenge, as the table shows. The standard rates of VAT range from 22% in Denmark down to 12% in Spain and Luxembourg. The Italians charge a hefty 38% on consumer gadgetry: Holland and Britain do not have a luxury rate at all. Britain does not charge any tax on a range of things including books, food and children's clothes. The commission's answer was to propose two VAT brackets — a normal rate of tax stretching between 14% and 20% and a reduced rate of 4-9% that would apply to a list of basic goods and services. Countries would choose their rates within those brackets.

Alas, the commission had to propose more than just new VAT bands. The quest for a frontier-free VAT system involves changes in the way that VAT on traded goods is levied. Although VAT is a value added tax, levied stage by stage as a product evolves, governments persist in viewing it as a sales tax. They expect to receive all the VAT on a product, even if some of its value has been added in another country: that is, they want their rate of VAT on the final sale price. Until now, such payment has been arranged by exporting countries demanding no VAT on export sales and refunding to the exporter all the VAT it has paid on the ingredients of the exports. An importing country, in contrast, levies VAT at the border on the import price and then tops this up with more VAT when the imported good is finally sold to the consumer. So border posts are vital both for tax-levying by the importing country, and for tax-policing by the exporting country, which uses the border papers to make sure that the zero-rated, exported product really did leave the country.

To get round this border-dependence, the commission proposes scrapping the zero-rating of exports. The exporting country will collect tax on the value-added up to the point of export. The importing country will apply its tax to the value added thereafter. To get all the VAT levied on traded goods into the hands of the country of final sale, the commission has thought up a clever clearing system. Countries will tot up all the VAT they have refunded to companies that have bought imports — money they want back from exporters' exchequers, and all the tax they have collected on their own export sales — which they owe to other countries. They will lodge/demand the balance at a central clearing-house. Honesty will be at a premium.

UNPLEASANT DUTIES

Whisky, cigarettes, motor fuel and other things liable to excise duties present similar problems of rates and collection, but the issue of rates is even more intractable. The differences across the EEC are large and are compounded by VAT, and most of these goods are easily transportable across frontiers. A liter of pure alcohol in Britain, for example, would carry 24.83 ecus in tax, in France 11.49 ecus, and in Dionysian Greece just 0.48 ecus. The commission felt bound to come up with a list of fixed compromises that would markedly alter the price of a tipple in some countries.

In the three years since the white paper appeared, these proposals have got nowhere. The finance ministries have had two committees study them. Both have nodded gravely at the grave problems involved; neither has been able to propose a better way of doing away with tax controls at frontiers. So the ministers have set up yet another committee.

Governments have varied reasons for finding the commission's proposals impossible. The British government regards them as bureaucratic meddling. It insists that high rates of duty on drink and tobacco be maintained for health reasons. It cannot entertain the idea of VAT on food because it promised never to impose it during the campaign for last year's general election. It wants to be left to see what rate-differences it can get away with, given its particular geographic position. Unfortunately, one country's experiment will be another's problem: Britain's Mothercare, for example, would be wonderfully set up to wage mail-order war on the continent's purveyors of children's clothing if the British zero VAT on children's clothes remained. France would then have to decide whether and how to block the advantage.

France's general attitude is shaped by such prospects. It fears that the commission's proposed tax bands are too wide and that France could not coexist openly with West Germany because both France's VAT rates and its public spending are higher. It is staring at a single-market-imposed reshaping of its fiscal policy; and it knows it. The Danes face the prospect of losing 6% of GDP's worth of tax: neighboring Germany's standard VAT rate is eight percentage points lower than theirs. The clearing-house plan is generally pooh-poohed as being unworkable.

All in all, the way things are going at the moment, it is most improbable that 1992 will bring even the prospect of frontiers without tax checks. The British are already toying with a scheme to delay their removal, suggesting that another increase in the quantity of duty-free goods will somehow produce the market-driven convergence it is so keen on. (This is pure self-delusion: it is a sad fact that, however automatic the pressures, it is governments in the end that have to take the nasty political decisions.) The French, too, are talking about larger duty-free allowances and more policing of VAT away from frontiers. They are already adept at stopping the unwary smuggler in his car some way from the French border. Exit the spirit of 1992, pursued by a frontier-post-on-wheels.

AND THE WORLD BEYOND

One more knotty problem before leaving the matter of frontiers: in a customs-free Europe the only trade policy that a member-state can have towards the outside world is a Community one. Such a prospect does not square with Article 115 of the Treaty of Rome, which authorizes the commission to allow member states to take their own protective measures to shield themselves from "economic difficulties." The white paper tiptoes round the problem of Article 115. Logically it should be got rid of; but its future has barely been discussed between member-governments.

Article 115 underpins a number of practical blockages that are inconsistent with project 1992.

- Some European countries, the most blatant being France and Italy, limit the number of Japanese cars imported each year by "Voluntary Restraint Agreements." They buttress these with the fact that there is no uniform "type approval" for cars in the EEC, so they can use technical quibbles to block any flow of Japanese cars via other EEC countries.

- The quantity of textile products that come to Europe under the Multi-Fibre Arrangement is divided up country by country. Frontier controls make sure that the quotas of jeans and T-shirts do not leak from one member to another.

- Britain has a number of special trading arrangements with ex-colonies. It sensibly enjoys New Zealand's cheap lamb. Frontier controls on the continent make sure that this pleasure does not spread there. On the other hand, Britain chooses to import expensive bananas from Caribbean ex-dependencies and to hold down the inflow from cheaper rivals. Frontier controls make sure that banana-running into Britain via, say, West Germany does not undermine this act of self-denial.

Commission officials admit that foreign trade is an unopened book, but assert (to *The Economist* at least) that they want the great market's trade policy towards the outside world to be a liberal one. Recent anti-dumping actions and crack-downs on Japanese "screwdriver plants" make one wonder. The French point of view is wonderfully laid out in the paper by Mr. Froment-Meurice. He considers the commission's approach to be "far too legal." He wants the commission to identify sensitive trade sectors, negotiate bilateral deals on them with countries outside the Community, and only when these are in place open up the internal market for the products involved. Here is another 1992 argument waiting to happen.

Pile together the problems of immigration control and those of tax, stir in external-trade policy, season with others not touched upon here — plant and animal-health checks, and the strange price-shifts for farm goods that must take place as they cross intra-European frontiers — and the conclusion is bleak. The European governments that are getting people excited about the prospect of a frontier-free Europe have not remotely summoned the political will to deliver what it involves.

Does this really matter? The durability of frontiers will be a blow to the 1992 campaign. If it had one identifiable target to match the disappearance of tariffs in the 1960's, the removal of the border posts was meant to be it. [It has been suggested] that the absence of internal borders is a crucial psychological feature of America's surprisingly imperfect home market. A survey by the commission found that European business men, too, place frontier delays, and the administrative and tax paperwork that takes place at frontiers, high on their list of difficulties in trading across Europe. If that is what businessmen perceive, that is what shapes their enthusiasms.

EXECUTIVE MISCELLANY

These selected bones are the only parts of the grand 1992 vision that this survey will pick out. What do they add up to for industrialists who are in the grip of the fashionable awareness that "Europe is open for business," and that they ought to do something about it fast?

First, there is no "Big Bang" in prospect for 1992 — no red-letter day towards the end of that year on which some new system of trading will swing into action. There might, perhaps, have been a ceremonial burning of border posts. But, adding up all the concessions needed for such a party, one is forced to conclude that it will not happen. Borders will continue to reinforce Europe's natural divergences: different languages, different mass media, different tastes, different habits. Europe will remain a Europe of national markets that become steadily more accessible.

Second, there will not be a European equivalent to America's dollar by 1992, though the pressure for one will build up faster than most people imagine. So selling or subcontracting in the European market will still be bedevilled by transaction costs and by exchange-rate uncertainty that cannot be avoided (for it is as painful to lose a windfall profit you might have made as to suffer a windfall loss you did not cover against). The Bureau Européen des Unions de Consommateurs found recently that moving 100 ecus across an EEC frontier cost an average of 9% and took an average of five days. Price lists in foreign currencies; exchange losses that are hard to calculate; lingering customs formalities — these will suffice to stop the arbitrage-on-whim that would otherwise bring different national markets for the same products together.

Third, there will, for most managers, be no post-1992 set of Euro-rules equivalent to the national ones they are used to. In principle, mutual recognition of regulations will have opened up markets; in practice, it will be up to businessmen to discover what they can get away with. It is going to take more European case law to discover what Dutch banks can do in Wiesbaden, whether tiles built to a British interpretation of a European standard can get building insurance in France, or whether Tiefbau of West Germany really has a chance of getting a public-works contract in Huddersfield.

So where is the good news? First, the cost of transport across Europe will come down. A newly introduced "Single Administrative Document" for taking goods across frontiers is a big step in the right direction; and if there is any area in which governments will be under pressure to honor the expectations they have generated for 1992, it is in trimming commercial frontier delays to an absolute minimum. Meanwhile a deregulated road-haulage business will lower its prices, and the airline industry will be under sustained pressure to cut its overpricing, too.

Frustrations will switch to transport infrastructure. Shortage of airspace, runways and motorway lanes will become the limiting factor. There will be argument over the impact of cheaper transport on the environment. (Austria, a non-member of the EEC which provides one of the main truck-routes to Italy, will figure prominently here.) Rail transport will undergo a renaissance. The construction industry will profit.

Moral for businessmen: There will be mounting competitive pressure to concentrate production in fewer plants, made flexible enough, through automation, to serve Europe's variable tastes. Unilever, for example, will make all its dishwasher powders for Europe at one plant in Lyons and all its "toilet-soap" at one plant in Port Sunlight. The distribution of consumer products will, however, remain mainly in national hands.

Second, there will be less protectionism-through-standards than there was in the past, and much less of the nonsense of working up competing national standards for new technologies before trying to reconcile them into European ones. No breakthroughs will happen here: the example of the new machinery directive shows what a slog lies ahead. But the 1992 spirit has altered the psychology with which governments and national champions are approaching this matter.

Moral for businessmen: As in finance, they need to be closely aware of and involved in the development of the industrial norms that will shape their products in the European market. In the shadow of IBM, for instance, Bull of France, ICL of Britain, Nixdorf and Siemens of West Germany, Olivetti of Italy, and Philips of Holland have all been pushing constructively for a common standard that will allow competing computers to interconnect freely. This is a campaign in a war that stretches well beyond Europe; but it helps with project 1992.

Third, there will be slow but steady progress towards greater openness in government procurement; partly because the rules will be policed more effectively, partly because the right of jinxed bidders to appeal to national courts will concentrate the minds of buyers in the public sector, and partly because of a more cost-conscious approach to public spending throughout Europe. Progress on industrial standards will help here, too: public procurers often use national standards to specify what they want. As for the customers of the traditional state enterprises — telecommunications, airlines and so forth — they will tend to shop around increasingly anyway, particularly if privatized. Even the conservative Bundespost of West Germany recently placed an order for "data-over-voice" equipment with Racal of Britain.

Moral for businessmen: Any company that relies on (non-defense) public procurement in one country for more than 25% of its sales ought to look for the custom of other governments, or spread its sales away from government.

Fourth (some businessmen will see this as bad news), the reduction of frictions and restraints in the European markets will make competition from non-European companies stiffer. Although the

Community's external-trade policy, post-1992, has not yet been worked out, and despite recent campaigns against dumping and "screwdriver plants," the effect of a more open European market will be to align European trade policy with that of its more liberal members. Non-tariff-barriers like voluntary restraint agreements will be tougher to organize.

Curiously, even though 1992 should make life easier for non-European multinationals, it may sap their relative advantage. They have, till now, been able to exploit big-company efficiencies against fragmented competition in a fragmented Europe: that position of relative superiority will be undermined.

Moral for businessmen: Even big, pan-European multinational companies should re-examine their structures in Europe with project 1992 in mind. IBM, for example, organizes its manufacture by continent, but its sales by country. It thinks this structure should suffice, post-1992. Will it? Perhaps customers will buy where margins and VAT rates are lowest and then freight their computers in. They might, in these software-dominated times, prefer to deal with a Europe-wide IBM specialist for their industry rather than a less-specialized salesman in their own country.

RIDING THE WAVE

None of this is in itself the stuff of panic. Project 1992 presents businessmen with a gradually expanding opportunity in a European market that has long been there; and a gradual threat to any "nice little earners" at home that have not already been spotted. Viewed in isolation, project 1992 should not force companies to do something fast, at the expense of something sensible.

Unhappily, this gentle prospect has been overlaid with a takeover wave that upsets calm reflection. Shearson Lehman Hutton, says that the number of its assignments to "find something to buy" for European companies is running at three times what it was a year ago. Project 1992 provided a pretext for Mr. Carlo De Benedetti's takeover forays into France and Belgium. It also created a political climate that has made possible deals that would have been blocked by governments five years ago. In the mid-1970's, for instance, GKN of Britain tried to strengthen its position in the European motor-components field by bidding for Sachs of West Germany. The deal was stopped by the West

German Cartel Office on narrow, technical grounds. The spirit of 1992 would almost certainly have tipped the scale the other way today, just as it did recently when the French finance ministry tried unsuccessfully to block the purchase by the Financial Times of a French business newspaper, Les Echos.

So, given a sudden imperative to make more of the European market, what should a medium-sized European company do? One specific answer comes from two little-known companies, one Dutch the other French, that have just joined forces to exploit the European market for pet food.

B.V. Safari is a Dutch private company making dried foods for livestock and pets. Continentale de Conserves is a French private company that makes upmarket tinned foods and tinned pet foods. Both companies are the same size, with annual sales of something over FFr300m ($50m).

Their 1992 plan has a nice symmetry to it:
- Each will take a stake of about one-third in the other
- Each will have the exclusive right to market its own products, and the products of the other, in its own country.
- They will jointly own a marketing subsidiary which will sell the products of both firms across the rest of the European Community.
- They will jointly run and finance a research and development unit.

The virtues of the plan? There is a good fit between the products of the two companies, within a clearly identified business. Each partner will go on playing to its existing strengths in the country that it understands, but with a wider range of things to sell. The effort, emotion and cost of a takeover are avoided. Relatively little day-to-day collaboration is required. On the other hand, the cross-shareholdings make sure that both companies gain from the success of the whole adventure.

Europe must be full of companies that have a fine market or brand position at home and that want to "Europeanize" themselves rapidly without losing their independence. For them, a "twinning" formula of this sort would seem to have much going for it.

12

At Stake in the U.S.-Canada Free Trade Agreement: Modest Gains or a Significant Setback

Jane Sneddon Little

On January second 1988 President Reagan and Prime Minister Mulroney signed the U.S.-Canada Free Trade Agreement, which eliminates all tariffs and removes or moderates a host of other barriers to the free flow of goods, services and investment between the two countries. The agreement, which requires implementing legislation from both Congress and Parliament, [1] would create the world's largest free trade area over a 10-year period. Because the text breaks new ground in dealing with trade in services and foreign investment flows, it would also serve as a model in multilateral trade negotiations, in particular, the current Uruguay Round of the General Agreement on Tariffs and Trade (GATT).

This article provides a synthesis of current economic thought on the potential opportunities and costs associated with this agreement. Because trade barriers between the two countries are on average already relatively low and the two economies are already closely linked, the article concludes that the agreement would involve minimal risks and modest gains for both countries. Modest though these gains may be, failure to ratify the agreement would represent a significant loss because a return to the current status quo cannot be taken for granted. Moreover, failure of these two very similar countries to proceed with a comparatively simple step would cast doubt on their commitment to further multilateral trade liberalization and would undermine their credibility in the GATT forum.

The first part of this article describes the developments and motives that led Canada and the United States to free trade negotiations, while section two summarizes the resulting agreement. The article then discusses two different sources of gains from free trade and provides a synthesis to studies that have sought to measure the impact of a U.S.-Canada free trade agreement. Section four explores possible adjustment costs and addresses some specific U.S. and Canadian concerns regarding the agreement. The conclusion suggests some possible consequences of failure to proceed.

NEW IMPETUS FOR AN OLD IDEA

The idea of a U.S.-Canada free trade area is hardly new. Indeed, in 1854 the United States and the British North American colonies actually concluded a treaty providing for free trade in natural products, free navigation of the St. Lawrence and the Great Lakes and reciprocal fishing rights in the Atlantic. The agreement lasted 12 years — until the United States abrogated it, because Britain was supporting the Confederacy during the Civil War. From time to time thereafter the issue has re-emerged, negotiations have ensued and the effort has been abandoned — generally because many Canadians have feared that free trade would limit Canada's freedom of action in social and political as well as economic spheres. As a result, it was argued, Canada's national identity would be diminished. [2]

Nevertheless, by the 1980s the dangers inherent in the current situation and the opportunities expected from a free trade agreement had become sufficiently compelling that Prime Minister Mulroney proposed another try and President Reagan accepted the invitation. In the first place, despite Canada's efforts to promote closer ties with the United Kingdom (primarily in the 1950s under Prime Minister Diefenbaker) and Europe (primarily in the 1970s under Prime Minister Trudeau), the Canadian economy has actually grown increasingly dependent on the United States. In the 1960s, Canada exported less than a fifth of its national output and less than 60 percent of its exports went to the United States. By 1986, in contrast, exports accounted for a quarter of its GNP and the United States for over 75 percent of those exports. [3] In certain commodities the dependence is even greater than the totals indicate, as is suggested by Table 1, which shows the share of Canadian exports sold to the United States by industry.

The United Kingdom's accession to the European Economic Community (EEC) in 1973 undoubtedly proved a turning point. At that time Canada lost the privileged access to the British market accorded Commonwealth members and became a disadvantaged outsider beyond

Table 1

Canadian Exports, 1986
Percent of Value

	Industry Share of Exports	U.S. Share of Exports
Total Merchandise Exports	100.0	76.6
Food	9.0	39.0
Energy Materials	9.2	83.7
Crude Petroleum	3.1	99.4
Natural Gas	2.1	100.0
Coal	1.4	.8
Petroleum and Coal Products	1.7	94.9
Electricity	.9	100.0
Other Natural Resource Materials	31.8	67.7
Lumber and Sawmill Products	5.2	78.3
Pulp and Paper	9.4	67.7
Metals and Minerals	12.8	64.2
Iron and Steel and Alloys	2.0	88.4
Precious Metals and Alloys	2.5	95.2
Aluminum and Alloys	1.9	77.3
Chemicals and Fertilizers	4.6	66.4
Motor Vehicles and Parts	28.3	98.0
Vehicles	19.2	98.8
Parts	9.1	96.3
Other Manufactured Goods	17.0	73.5
Aircraft and Parts	1.9	76.0
Other Transportation Equipment	1.2	78.9
Agricultural Machinery	.4	81.7
Communications and Electric Equipment	3.3	73.2
Industrial Machinery	2.8	63.7
Other Equipment and Tools	2.3	84.5
Other Consumer Goods	1.8	80.7
Other Industrial Goods	3.3	66.0
Special Transactions	.3	82.3

Source: *Bank of Canada Review*, October 1987, Tables J4 and J10

the EEC's common tariff. This change underscored Canada's vulnerable position as one of the few industrialized countries without unimpeded and secure access to a market of one hundred million or more customers. The United States and Japan both have large domestic markets, and the Europeans trade tariff-free within the EEC common market and European Free Trade Area (EFTA). To make matters worse, from the Canadian perspective, access to the United States market has become progressively less assured.

As successive rounds of GATT negotiations have reduced average tariff levels, many governments have felt their producers to be increasingly vulnerable to "unfair" foreign trade practices such as dumping and subsidizing exports; thus, they have tended to broaden and toughen their trade remedy laws. In the United States these laws require the President to impose countervailing duties to offset a subsidy or dumping action if the Commerce Department finds that unfair practices have occurred and if the U.S. International Trade Commission finds that they are causing or threatening to cause "material" damage to a U.S. industry. Over time the U.S. government has defined the terms "subsidy" and "dumping" more and more broadly. For instance, in the case of subsidies, which have been a particular bone of contention between Canada and the United States, this country originally confined its attention to measures specifically designed to promote exports. In 1973, however, a Canadian regional development grant to a Michelin tire plant was deemed a subsidy requiring countervailing action. More recently, Canadian methods of assessing stumpage fees for the lumber industry, which were found not to involve a subsidy in 1983, were declared countervailable in 1986.

Canadians have complained that the administration of these trade "remedy" laws — with unilateral changes in ground rules and lengthy and expensive hearings — amounts to harassment and "contingent protection." [4] Because Canadian producers are so heavily dependent on the U.S. market, these contingencies can have particularly devastating consequences for them. Indeed, Canadians suggest that the mere threat of such actions deters investment in Canada and, in particular, in plants of optimum size.

Without secure access to the U.S. market, Canadian producers say they are discouraged from building plants large enough to take full advantage of economies of scale and specialization. Instead, protected by Canada's relatively high tariffs and thwarted by actual and contingent

---

Table 2

Average Shipments per Establishment, 1982
Millions of U.S. Dollars

	United States	Canada
All Manufacturing	5.6	4.2
Food and Kindred Products	12.7	6.1
Tobacco Manufactures	98.5	50.4
Textile Mill Products	7.2	3.6
Apparel and Other Textile Products	2.2	1.5
Lumber and Wood Products	1.3	1.7
Furniture and Fixtures	2.4	.8
Paper and Allied Products	12.5	15.5
Printing and Publishing	1.6	1.2
Chemicals and Allied Products	14.3	9.3
Rubber and Miscellaneous Plastics Products	4.1	3.5
Leather and Leather Products	3.6	2.1
Primary Metal Products	14.8	22.5
Fabricated Metal Products	3.4	1.9
Machinery, except Electrical	3.6	3.7
Electric and Electronic Equipment	9.0	6.3
Transportation Equipment	21.3	15.2

Source: U.S. Bureau of the Census, 1982 Census of Manufactures and Statistics Canada, *Canada Yearbook, 1985.*

---

trade barriers in the United States, Canadian manufacturers focus on the domestic market and supply the whole range of products within each industry. As a result, in many industries Canada has a plethora of small plants producing too many products in short, fragmented production runs. Table 2 provides data on average shipments per establishment to illustrate the difference in average plant size in Canada and the United States. The connection between high tariffs, short production runs and relative inefficiency was made almost 30 years ago in the Bladen Report,[5] which, in turn, led to the Auto Pact of 1965.[6] More recent work by Baldwin and Gorecki (1983) has drawn the same correlations. Because of all these concerns about the disadvantages of Canada's small domestic market, its increasing dependence on the U.S. economy and growing protectionist activity in this country, obtaining secure access to the large U.S. market has been a primary Canadian goal in the free trade negotiations.

Why did the United States agree to the Canadian invitation to negotiate? Although U.S. trade is much less focused on Canada than is Canadian trade on the United States, Canada is nevertheless this country's primary trading partner. Canada buys 21 percent of U.S. exports, almost twice as much as Japan, our second best customer. Naturally then, many U.S. producers encouraged the Administration to negotiate the removal of Canada's tariffs, which, as Table 3 shows, are on average higher than those levied by the United States. Moreover, although even Canada's post-Tokyo Round duties may seem low, these rates are averages of tariffs on many commodities weighted by the value of trade in those goods. Thus, they actually understate the tariffs' deterrent effect: unusually high or prohibitive rates get little or no weight. And high tariffs do abound. A glance at the 600-page Canadian tariff schedule reveals numerous tariffs in the 9 to 10 percent range. Many are higher. Tariffs on textiles, clothing and footwear generally run from 20 to 25 percent , while those on rubber gloves, coffee makers, telephone sets and brooms — just to pick some random items — are, respectively, 25.0, 14.3, 17.5 and 17.5 percent. Then too, while the Canadian market is only one-tenth the size of the U.S. domestic market, gaining unrestricted access to it could represent a considerable boon to firms in mature or niche industries as well as to those located near the border.

Another equally important goal for U.S. negotiators was proving that further progress in trade liberalization is possible. In particular, they hoped to develop agreements on some difficult new issues, such as trade in services, foreign investment and intellectual property rights, to use as models in the ongoing GATT discussions in Uruguay. Previous multilateral negotiations have already reduced tariffs considerably; thus, with the easiest tasks accomplished, momentum has slowed to the discouraging pace permitted by the minimum consensus. Indeed, in the

Table 3

Average Post-Tokyo Round Tariffs, [a] United States and Canada

	U.S. Tariffs on Imports from		Tariffs on Imports from	
	Canada	Other	U.S.	Other
Agriculture	1.6	1.8	2.2	1.8
Food	3.8	4.8	5.4	6.1
Textiles	7.2	9.1	16.9	16.4
Clothing	18.4	21.4	23.7	22.1
Leather Products	2.5	3.8	4.0	8.7
Footwear	9.0	8.9	21.5	21.9
Wood Products	.2	3.8	2.5	4.9
Furniture and Fixtures	4.6	2.9	14.3	14.1
Paper Products	0	1.3	6.6	5.5
Printing and Publishing	.3	.7	1.1	1.0
Chemicals	.6	3.5	7.9	7.0
Petroleum Products	0	.1	.4	.1
Rubber Products	3.2	2.0	7.3	6.0
Non-Metal Mineral Products	.3	7.2	4.4	8.5
Glass Products	5.7	5.8	6.9	7.9
Iron and Steel	2.7	3.9	5.1	5.5
Non-Ferris Metals	.5	.8	3.3	2.7
Metal Products	4.0	4.4	8.6	8.9
Non Electric Machinery	2.2	3.2	4.6	4.8
Electric Machinery	4.5	4.1	7.5	7.1
Transportation Equipment	0	2.5	0	2.5
Miscellaneous Manufacturers	.9	2.0	5.0	5.3
Average	.7	4.3	3.8	7.4

[a] Weighted by bilateral trade.
  Source: Brown, Drusilla K. and Robert M. Stern. 1987. "A Modeling Perspective." In *Perspectives on a U.S.-Canadian Free Trade Agreement*, Robert M. Stern, Philip H. Trezise and John Whalley, ed..s Washington, D.C.: The Brookings Institution. Reprinted by permission of the publisher.

face of the oil shocks, severe recessions, LDC debt crises and major exchange rate movements of the late 1970s and early 1980s, "managed" trade (in the form of orderly marketing arrangements and voluntary export restraint programs) and less transparent forms of protection (elements of industrial and foreign investment policies) have become increasingly widespread. While some observers have argued that a bilateral approach to these issues may undermine multilateral efforts and most-favored-nation principles,[7] long the keystones of U.S. trade policy, U.S. trade negotiators undoubtedly hope that a U.S.-Canadian agreement will spur movement on several fronts. In the past, the formation of the European Economic Community and the European Free Trade Area appear to have encouraged progress in the Dillon and Kennedy Rounds of the GATT, because non-Europeans were eager to negotiate multilateral arrangements to reduce the disadvantages of exclusion from the free trade areas. Currently, moreover, a Japanese government task force is studying the possibility of creating a free trade zone encompassing Japan, Australia, Canada, the United States and possibly some other Pacific countries. As long as such (prospective) trading blocs remain open to additional members, such developments could lead to progressively freer trade.

THE AGREEMENT IN BRIEF

According to U.S. Trade Representative Clayton Yeutter, the U.S.-Canada Free Trade Agreement is the most ambitious bilateral economic accord the United States has ever made.[8] It is more comprehensive than many observers had anticipated and will clearly set a new standard for free trade arrangements, in part because it takes steps concerning services which other groups are only beginning to consider.

TARIFFS AND OTHER BARRIERS

The Agreement will eliminate all tariffs on bilateral merchandise trade by January 1, 1998. Some tariffs will be removed immediately, others in equal instalments over five years, and a final group over 10 years. The Agreement also eliminates virtually all import and export restrictions such as quotas, embargos and minimum price requirements.[9] In addition, it removes or reduces many less visible barriers, such as those related to government standards and government procurement practices. In the case of government procurement, the Agreement extends the GATT Government Procurement Code downwards (from $171,000) to cover procurements over $25,000 and in such cases prohibits discrimination between U.S. and Canadian suppliers.

RULES OF ORIGIN AND DUTY DRAWBACKS

Because manufacturers use imported parts and materials, rules of origin must determine when a good qualifies for favored treatment under a bilateral trade agreement. (With multilateral free trade the issue does not arise.) The U.S.-Canada accord states that in order to qualify as North American, goods incorporating imports generally must have sufficient value added within the United States or Canada to permit them to be exported under a tariff classification different from the one under which the imported inputs first entered. In some cases, a specified share (generally 50 percent) of the manufacturing cost must also have been added in North America. Duty drawbacks (returns of duties paid on imported materials when the goods incorporating them are re-exported and customs users fees will end for bilateral trade on January 1, 1994.[10]

SECTORAL ISSUES

Overall, a great deal of negotiating time was devoted to sectors where sensitive issues have arisen or special arrangements have grown up over the years. These sectors include agriculture, automotive products, cultural products, energy, and wine and spirits.

Agriculture. The accord's provision eliminating all tariffs within 10 years applies to the agricultural sector. The Agreement also makes a few other liberalizing changes. However, because agricultural support programs have become a complex global problem, the negotiators concluded that more substantial progress would have to wait for the multilateral meeting in Uruguay. The two countries agreed that they would work together there to eliminate all subsidies that distort agricultural trade.

Automotive Trade. Because of the provisions of the 1965 Auto Pact, 95 percent of U.S.-Canadian auto trade is already duty-free. Not coincidentally, auto products, which accounted for less than 1 percent of bilateral trade in the early 1960s, now make up one-third of the total. Nevertheless, problems have been festering in this area for some time, particularly because the Canadians have been encouraging Asian auto makers to invest in Canada by offering duty remissions based on exports to any country, including the United States. In other words, Korean and other foreign investors are earning remissions of duties on imported parts by exporting, duty-free because of the Auto Pact, to this country. The Agreement eliminated most of these frictions. Duty remissions earned through exports to the United States will end as soon as the Agreement comes into force. Other duty remission schemes linked to export or production requirements (except for those which apply to Auto Pact manufacturers) will be phased out. The new rule of origin for duty-free treatment of automotive products will require North American content equal to 50 percent of *direct* manufacturing costs. This new rule is stricter than the Auto Pact requirement, which counted some indirect costs as North American content.

Culture.   Protecting Canada's cultural identity was a nonnegotiable issue; thus, production and sale of books, magazines, newspapers, films, video and audio recordings and broadcasting are exempt from the Agreement, except for the elimination of tariffs. Accordingly, many Canadian regulations that hinder trade in this sector remain in effect. For example, Canadian postal rates are lower for Canadian than for foreign magazines. Canada, has, however, agreed to provide copyright law protection for the retransmission of copyrighted programs and will remove the "print in Canada" requirement for tax-deductible advertising.

Energy. The Agreement prohibits restrictions on the export and import of crude oil, petroleum products, natural gas, electricity, coal and uranium with limited exceptions, as permitted by the GATT, for shortages, conservation and national security. In the event of shortages, the reduced supplies must be allocated proportionately according to historical use in *both* countries. Over the long run, increasing the accessibility and reliability of relatively low-cost imported power could be one of the accord's most important benefits for energy-short regions like New England where a lack of adequate power could become a constraint on growth (Henderson, Kopcke, Houlihan, and Inman 1988).

Wine and Spirits. In Canada the retail sale of alcoholic beverages is conducted almost exclusively by provincial marketing boards which discriminate against wines and spirits from other provinces as well as from the United States. The accord will eliminate some of these barriers for wines and spirits, but Canadian regulations on the sale and distribution of beer remain unchanged.

INVESTMENT

The Free Trade Agreement states that investments from partner countries will receive national, that is, nondiscriminatory, treatment during and after entry. While the United States has never subjected foreign investment to mandatory official review or made performance requirements, such as domestic content provisions, a condition of their acceptance, the Canadian government has frequently used these policy tools to try to tilt the benefits of investment toward Canada. Because such measures distort capital and trade flows, however, the accord limits screening to direct acquisitions of Canadian assets of more than C$150 million (with adjustments for inflation) and prohibits the future use of most performance requirements.

FINANCIAL SERVICES

The Agreement on Financial Services is this country's first bilateral agreement covering the entire financial sector. It ends essentially all of the discriminatory practices, such as restrictions on market share, asset growth and capital expansion, currently faced by U.S. financial institutions operating in Canada. Canadian financial service firms will continue to enjoy national treatment in the United States.

OTHER SERVICES

The U.S.-Canada accord is the first international agreement addressing trade and investment in the service industries. It extends the principle of national treatment to most commercial services and provides that future regulations affecting this sector must be nondiscriminatory. Transportation, basic telecommunications (like telephone service) and health, education and social services are not covered. Because U.S. and

Canadian professionals and other service personnel sometimes have difficulty entering the other country to work or to service previous exports, the two governments have agreed to change immigration regulations to ease business travel.

DISPUTE SETTLEMENT

A Canada-U.S. Trade Commission will supervise implementation of the agreement and defuse problems of interpretation and application as they arise. Unresolved disputes will be referred to a panel of experts, and those regarding safeguard or escape clause actions (measures providing temporary relief for industries where imports are a "substantial cause of serious injury or the threat thereof") [11] will be subject to binding arbitration. In other cases either party may retaliate. Special provisions apply to disputes concerning financial services, which will be handled by the finance ministers, as well as to those concerning countervailing duties and dumping.

The free trade agreement provides that each country will continue to enforce its own countervailing duty and anti-dumping laws. If requested, however, a special binational panel will review the final administrative decision — applying the *domestic* laws of the importing country. Its decision will be final. The two countries have five to seven years to work out a better regime governing subsidies and dumping. If they do not succeed, either may terminate the accord.

Altogether, these dispute settlement provisions give Canada more secure access to the U.S. market, they limit the potential damage from safeguard actions and probably stabilize the definitions of "subsidy" and "dumping." Clearly, however, access is not totally assured.

One popular way of assessing the merits of a trade agreement consists of comparing the concessions made by the negotiation parties. By this standard, the United States achieved most of its aims for the Free Trade Agreement, while Canada — the country taking the initiative and the country historically most interested in bilateral free trade — did not get complete satisfaction on its primary goal, securing access to the U.S. market. Nevertheless, stacks of concessions give little indication of the size of the gains to be reaped over the long run or the division of those gains between countries. Presumably, after all, Canadian negotiators agreed to many U.S. requests because they believed the benefits to free trade would more than balance any concessions they may have made. The next section will discuss these gains: how they may arise and to whom they may go.

THE POTENTIAL GAINS

Studies assessing the economic impact of the U.S.-Canada Free Trade Agreement come to diverse conclusions.[12] While some report that bilateral free trade would lead to large increases in Canadian real income, others anticipate small losses. For the United States, the results range from small gains to small losses. The conclusions of specific industry studies are equally contradictory. The explanation for these disagreements lies in the different approaches and assumptions made in these studies. Economic analysis has identified two major sources of gains from free trade — allocative efficiencies stemming from comparative advantage and production efficiencies stemming from economies of scale. Consequently, studies can be categorized according to which source they emphasize: in other words, whether or not they allow for economies of scale. This section describes these two basic approaches and summarizes their general conclusions about the size and division of gains from a bilateral free trade agreement. Possible dislocations caused by trade liberalization are discussed in the following section.

GAINS FROM COMPARATIVE ADVANTAGE

The first, more traditional approach depicts a world in which markets are competitive and economies of scale do not exist. In these studies gains from international trade stem from comparative advantage. Because of differences in climate, endowments of raw materials, technological prowess, and so forth, production costs vary from country to country. Countries gain by exporting the goods that they can produce relatively cheaply to pay for low-cost imports from countries that have a comparative advantage in those other products. By so doing, countries indirectly trade the factors that each has in relative abundance.

For example, in the simplest case, when Canada removes existing trade barriers, Canadian prices for imports and for import-competing goods fall. Accordingly, Canadian producers are worse off, as is the Canadian government, which no longer collects tariff revenues. Canadian consumers, however, can purchase more goods at lower prices. If nothing else changes, the consumers' gains in real income generally exceed the losses suffered by the producers and the government by a small amount. Of course, under a bilateral free trade agreement, the United States also removes its trade barriers, and Canadian producers gain from exporting more to this country. Developments in the United States mirror those in Canada. Removing U.S. trade barriers leads to net gains — reaped by U.S. consumers — while removing Canadian barriers leads to gains in real income for U.S. producers penetrating the Canadian market. Accordingly, both countries gain because both sets of producers increase production of the goods in which they have a comparative advantage and consumers enjoy lower-cost goods.

The analysis becomes more complicated if removing trade barriers changes demand enough to alter world prices. In some circumstances these price effects can offset the gains from comparative advantage just described. These price effects can occur if the trading partners differ in size or if their products are not considered perfect substitutes. Accordingly, even within the group of studies that ignores economies of scale, conclusions differ as to whether the United States or Canada benefits from free trade. The results depend on whether Canada is treated as a small country and whether U.S. and Canadian products are perfect substitutes.

When Canada is treated as a small country unable to influence world prices, it tends to benefit from free trade. Under this small country assumption, when Canada removes its own tariffs, the resulting increase in Canadian demand is too small to change U.S. export prices; thus, Canadian consumers gain, as described above. However, under bilateral free trade, when the United States removes tariffs on Canadian imports but leaves them in place for goods from other countries, Canadian producers can export to the United States at unchanged U.S. prices — the world price plus the tariff which other countries still face. Canadian producers, thus, gain an amount equal to the tariff revenue the U.S. government previously collected on Canadian exports plus any third-country exports that duty-free Canadian goods now replace. The resulting increase in Canadian output is — by assumption — too small to cause a decrease in world prices. In this small country case, therefore, the gains from bilateral free trade accrue to Canada. One study which attributes Canada's gain from bilateral free trade primarily to its small size is that by Hamilton and Whalley (1985). In their study, when tariffs are eliminated, the United States suffers a small loss in real income (largely because duty-free imports from Canada replace more efficiently produced third-country output), while Canada achieves a small gain.

If, by contrast, Canadian and U.S. goods are not perfect substitutes, then changes in demand do affect prices, and U.S. and Canadian terms of trade are likely to change with the formation of a free trade area.[13] Models making this assumption tend to emphasize that Canadian tariffs are on average higher than those in the United States. As a result these studies are likely to conclude that Canada loses from a bilateral free trade arrangement.

In this case, when Canada removes its tariffs, Canadian consumers buy fewer goods from Canadian producers, as before. Because Canadian goods are assumed to be different from other countries' products (beer and magazines come to mind) the decline in demand reduces the world price of Canadian output. But, when U.S. tariffs disappear, U.S. consumers buy more Canadian goods, thereby raising Canadian prices. Where the price of Canadian goods settles depends on whether the fall in Canadian demand for Canadian goods is greater than the increase in U.S. demand for Canadian goods. The outcome largely reflects relative tariff levels (as well as the degree of substitutability between U.S. and Canadian goods).

Because Canada's tariffs are on average higher than U.S. tariffs, their removal may cause a relative decline in the demand for Canadian products as compared with the demand for U.S. goods. Accordingly, the price of Canadian goods will fall relative to the price of U.S. goods, and Canada's terms of trade will worsen. Because Canada will have to export more to earn a given level of imports, the result is a loss of real income for Canada — a loss that may offset any efficiency gains based on comparative advantage. Indeed, Brown and Stern (1987) conclude that Canada would experience a small welfare loss (less than 1 percent of its GNP) while the United States would enjoy an even smaller welfare gain (in terms of GNP) from bilateral free trade.

Although these two groups of studies based on competitive markets and constant returns to scale differ on the division of gains flowing from a bilateral free trade agreement, they agree that the gains (or losses) would be quite small — almost certainly less than 1 percent of GNP. In this respect, they are consistent with empirical studies of other geographical areas which assume constant returns and find — almost universally — that the welfare cost of protection is less than 1 percent of GNP (Wonnacott 1987). (This finding also reflects the fact that tariffs are already fairly low.)

GAINS FROM ECONOMIES OF SCALE

In the alternative approach to measuring the benefits of a free trade arrangement, economies of scale play a crucial role. Studies using this approach conclude that large welfare gains are possible. Economies of scale stem in part from the existence of overhead and fixed costs. In the presence of such fixed costs, it becomes advantageous to increase production in order to spread these expenses over greater output. Specialization and long production runs also contribute to reducing average costs. Economies of scale and specialization thus provide a powerful incentive to trade. However, when firms expand, markets may become concentrated. This link between economies of scale and increased market power makes the benefits of increased trade less certain.

On their, own, economies of scale provide important gains from trade beyond those resulting from comparative advantage. When domestic markets are too small to support efficient producers, as is the case even in some markets in the United States (jumbo jets, for instance), then countries can reap large gains from international trade. With economies of scale, trade always offers the *opportunity* for a simultaneous increase in the diversity of products available and in the scale at which each product is produced. If firms respond to this opportunity, countries will enjoy benefits from trade above those accruing from comparative advantage. With imperfect competition, however, there is no guarantee that firms will actually take advantage of these possibilities. Nevertheless, according to innovative theoretical work by Helpman and Krugman (1985), while gains from trade cannot be proved, under many circumstances trade can be presumed to be beneficial in the presence of economies of scale.

The scale economies approach to trade differs from the comparative advantage approach in another important respect. The comparative advantage analysis suggests that the owners of productive factors that are relatively scarce in each country are likely to lose from trade, because imports will increase the supply of those factors and reduce their price. By contrast, the scale economies approach suggests that if unexploited economies of scale are large enough and if the countries are similar enough so that the changes in relative factor returns are not too big, then everyone could gain from trade. Like a technological improvement, trade based on economies of scale would enhance the productivity of all factors. In important examples of trade liberalization, like the formation of the EEC and EFTA, little resource reallocation between industries appears to have occurred; instead, firms rationalized and specialized and increased their intra-firm and intra-industry transactions.[14] As a result, trade seems to have permitted increased productivity of existing resources which left everyone better off.

Accordingly, models that incorporate economies of scale tend to suggest much larger welfare gains from a move to free trade than do those based on constant returns. While gains in constant returns studies reflect shifts that affect a fraction of exports and imports, opportunities to exploit economies of scale affect the whole tradeable goods sector — not just goods actually entering into trade (Petri 1987). For example, one study which focuses on economies of scale (and which undoubtedly influenced the course of the trade negotiations) is that by Harris and Cox (1985). Based on tariff rates and other data from the mid-seventies, it concludes that *multi*lateral free trade would improve Canada's welfare by 8 to 9 percent of gross national expenditure. Using the authors' most conservative estimates regarding possible economies of scale, pricing mechanisms and the sensitivity of imports and exports to price changes reduces the estimated gains by about half. Since the post-Tokyo tariffs are lower than they were in the mid-seventies,[15] current Canadian gains from a *bi*lateral free trade agreement might be assumed to be in the vicinity of 2 to 3 percent of Canadian GNP, according to an increasing returns approach.[16] The relatively modest gain remains large compared to those estimated by constant returns analysis and certainly would not be negligible in an era of slow economic growth.[17]

Cox and Harris did not estimate the gains for the United States, but given that the U.S. market is 10 times the size of the Canadian market, unexploited economies of scale are presumably less plentiful in this country. As Helpman and Krugman point out, however, it may not matter very much which country's industries expand to take advantage of economies of scale.[18] If total production of decreasing-cost goods expands because of a free trade agreement, whether the expansion occurs in Canada or the United States, the importing county will still benefit by being able to buy lower-cost goods.

Altogether then, the potential for efficiency gains — even the presumption of gains — exists. Nevertheless, the link between economies of scale and concentrated markets does pose the risk that firms will not take advantage of this potential. Indeed, in a study of the impact of the Canada-U.S. Auto Pact of 1965, which created a duty-free market for the major U.S. producers, Fuss and Waverman (1986) conclude that the Pact did not induce much improvement in Canadian production efficiency compared to that in the United States. Although Canadian automobile production and U.S.-Canadian trade in automotive products both expanded rapidly, their study finds that the Pact led to a mere 3 percentage point improvement in the Canadian plants' relative efficiency. The authors suggest that the expected productivity gains did not materialize because the Pact did not increase competition in the U.S.-Canadian auto industry in any way. Surely, however, the example of the auto industry is an extreme case. In no other industry do the same four firms account for over 90 percent of industry shipments in both countries. If trade liberalization contributed to even minor gains in efficiency in this extreme case, competitive pressures in less concentrated industries might well lead to more substantial improvements in productivity.[19]

So far this section has concentrated on the gains from bilateral free trade. However, bilateral, as opposed to multilateral, free trade also entails some costs. Welfare losses will occur to the extent that duty-free partner exports replace lower-cost, third, country exports still encumbered by trade barriers. Because Canada and the United States are already each other's best customers and because their average post-Tokyo Round tariffs are quite low, the scope and cost to trade diversion resulting from the Free Trade Agreement is likely to be limited. Moreover, most U.S.-Canadian bilateral exports compete with products from other OECD countries, many of which belong to regional trade groups like the EEC and EFTA which already discriminate against the United States and Canada. One obvious remedy for these distortions is for all countries to reduce trade barriers further on a multilateral basis: if a free trade accord contributes to progress in that direction, so much the better. Indeed, creating that kind of pressure was one of this country's major motivations for negotiating the Free Trade Agreement. Nevertheless, the accord could cause some problems for developing-country manufacturers, especially those producing textiles, clothing, steel, and (replacement) auto parts. It is to be hoped that U.S. and Canadian policy-makers will be sensitive to these potential hardships, particularly, say, when the orderly marketing arrangements governing some of these products come up for renegotiation.

The studies and estimates discussed in this section have focused on the effects of removing tariffs and, in a few cases, some highly visible nontariff barriers to trade. None of these studies has quantified (How could they?) the impact of reducing less visible barriers — regulations, standards, government procurement policies, and so forth [20] — or of the steps taken to encourage a free flow of services and investment. None has measured the gains from the increased efficiency of business travel permitted by the agreement, for instance. And no one who has ever looked at either country's tariff code — each 600 pages of excruciating detail — could imagine that administering and complying with those systems is anything but terribly cumbersome. Yet no study has incorporated the benefits of reducing these administrative costs. Most importantly, finally, no study has included the impact of decreased uncertainty on investment or examined the dynamic gains which should flow from increased investment and income — wherever they occur. These considerations reinforce the presumption for gains from freer trade.[21]

ADJUSTMENT PAINS?

If gains from a free trade agreement largely depend on whether or not firms actually take advantage of possible economies of scale and specialization, it is no wonder that some producers and workers on both sides of the border are wary. After all, rationalization could imply the death of a number of firms. And it is probably not much comfort to people concerned that their own plant may close to know that consumers theoretically should be better off because the scale of production has increased — somewhere else. This section will explore major U.S. and Canadian concerns about possible adjustment problems and other difficulties resulting from the Free Trade Agreement. U.S. concerns tend to deal with industry specifics. Canadian concerns are more fundamental.

CANADIAN CONCERNS

Canadians particularly fear that U.S. firms may rationalize by closing their Canadian affiliates and serving the Canadian market from the United States. Since some of these affiliates are in fact tariff-jumping operations these fears are not entirely unfounded. Indeed, some U.S. manufacturers have quietly indicated that the new trade agreement would cause them to reassess the need for their Canadian subsidiaries.

Canadian concerns are obviously aggravated by the role U.S. firms play in the Canadian economy. For example, of the firms listed in the Summer 1987 issue of *The Financial Post 500* (akin to the *Fortune 500*), almost one-fourth are U.S. affiliates. Moreover, as Table 4 shows, U.S. affiliates account for well over one-half of Canadian shipments in several manufacturing industries. While most major Canadian firms also have affiliates in the United States, they do not have anywhere near the same weight in the U.S. economy. Indeed, even taking affiliated shipments and U.S. imports from Canada, together, the output of Canadian firms amounts to no more than 10 percent of U.S. shipments in any major industry, as Table 5 indicates. Industries where Canadian firms (some owned by U.S. investors, of course) play the largest role are primary metals, paper and chemicals (because Canadian investors own Du Pont).

However, while some firms may indeed close with the creation of a free trade area, Canadians' worst fears — of a substantial migration of industry from Canada to the United States — cannot possibly be realized. The same mechanism that ensures that countries can afford to trade on the basis of their comparative advantage also ensures that a country's locational advantages must remain attractive over the long run. This mechanism is the exchange rate. If a country's goods are all too expensive, the exchange rate will fall until foreigners will buy the goods in which it has a comparative advantage. Similarly, should capital flow from Canada to the United States, the Canadian dollar will decline until investing in Canadian factors of production becomes irresistible.

Table 4

Sales of Canadian Affiliates of U.S. Firms as a Share of Canadian Shipments, 1985
Percent

Manufacturing	42.5
Food	21.2
Chemicals	85.6
Primary Metals	8.3
Fabricated Metals	27.3
Machinery, except Electrical	109.5 [a]
Electric and Electronic Equipment	50.9
Textiles and Apparel	9.3
Lumber and Furniture	12.2
Paper and Allied Products	28.0
Printing and Publishing	9.3
Transportation Equipment	106.0 [a]

[a] Clearly, sales of Canadian affiliates of U.S. firms cannot in fact amount to more than 100 percent of Canadian shipments, and the data series used here are not entirely consistent. The figures for shipments of Canadian manufacturers are estimates based on a monthly survey of a sample of manufacturing establishments, benchmarked to the annual census of manufactures. The timing of currency conversion provides another possible source of discrepancy.

Source: U.S. Bureau of Economic Analysis, *U.S. Direct Investment Abroad: Preliminary 1985 Estimates, and Statistics Canada, Canadian Statistical Review.*

At present, without a free trade agreement, trade barriers, real and contingent, favor locating new investment in the United States. In the face of the current uncertainties, an investor seeking to serve the North American market from a single plant would surely locate in the United States. Should contingent protection befall, he still has access to the larger part of the market. Indeed, in part for.this very reason, Canadian investors have increased the pace of their investments in the United States to the point that from 1981 to 1986 direct investment capital flows from Canada to the United States exceeded flows from the

United States to Canada in most years. Creating a unified North American market would, by contrast, remove these uncertainties and

---

Table 5

Sales of U.S. Affiliates of Canadian Firms and Imports from Canada as a Share of U.S. Shipments, 1985
Percent

	Sales of U.S. Affiliates of Canadian Firms as Share of U.S. Shipments	Imports from Canada as a Share of U.S. Shipments
Manufacturing	1.8	2.4
Food	.8	.5
Chemicals	d	1.0
Primary Metals	3.5	4.6
Fabricated Metals	.8	1.0
Machinery, except Electrical	.9	1.5
Electric and Electronic Equipment	d	1.1
Textiles and Apparel	.7	.6
Lumber and Furniture	.3	5.3
Paper and Allied Products	1.2	6.2
Printing and Publishing	3.0	.3
Transportation Equipment	.1	7.9

---

d = data withheld to avoid disclosing individual firm data.
Sources: U.S. Bureau of Economic Analysis, *Foreign Direct Investment in the United States: Operations of U.S. Affiliates of Foreign Companies, Preliminary 1985 Estimates*; U.S. Bureau of the Census, *1985 Annual Survey of Manufactures: Statistics for Industry Groups and Industries*, M85 (AS)-1; and U.S. Bureau of the Census, *U.S. Imports for Consumption and General Imports*, IA275 and IM175, January-December 1985

---

permit investment to occur in both countries on the basis of real locational advantages. Canada has abundant natural resources, secure power supplies, and a well-educated labor force. At current exchange rates, Canadian wage rates are also lower than those in the United States for many industries.

Table 6

Canadian and U.S. Affiliates:
Exports as a Share of Total Sales, 1985
Percent

	Exports to U.S. by Canadian Affiliates of U.S. Firms	All Exports by U.S. Affiliates of Canadian Firms
All Industries	22.5	5.4
Petroleum	16.7	.3
Manufacturing	33.3	8.0
Food	3.7	1.6
Chemicals	9.4	d
Metals	16.9	4.6
Primary	29.6	4.9
Fabricated	12.2	3.7
Machinery, except Electric	17.7	15.1
Electric and Electronic Equipment	15.2	d
Transportation	56.1	3.8
Other Manufacturing	25.2	d
Textiles and Apparel	12.6	2.0
Lumber and Furniture	34.0	14.5
Paper and Allied Products	42.6	d
Printing and Publishing	d	1.2

Memo: Other Foreign Affiliates of U.S. Firms: Exports to the U.s. as a Percentage of Total Sales, 1985

	EC	Japan	Latin America	Other Asia
All Industries	2.6	7.8	8.4	17.0
Manufacturing	3.0	13.6	12.2	33.3

d = data withheld to avoid disclosing individual firm data.
Sources: U.S. Bureau of Economic Analysis, *U.S. Direct Investment Abroad: Operations f U.S. Companies and Their Foreign Affiliates, Preliminary 1985 Estimates,* Tables 7 and 19; and *Foreign Direct Investment in the United States: Operations of U.S. Affiliates of Foreign Companies, Preliminary 1985 Estimates,* Tables E-5 and G-6.

Moreover, in the event of free trade, firms currently operating in Canada would not rush to close these operations — for a variety of practical reasons.   For instance, multinational corporations are increasingly finding it advantageous to be able to produce, market and service their products in local markets. In some cases, for instance, they must be able to provide quick response to customer needs, especially in this era of just-in-time inventories. Moreover, while the Agreement prohibits discrimination in federal government procurement, buy-local policies persist at the state-provincial level. In addition, multinational operations help diversify against various risks, from labor unrest to exchange rate fluctuations, Indeed, U.S. multinationals are maintaining their affiliate operations in Europe despite rising production costs associated with the declining dollar for just these many reasons.

More importantly, while the Free Trade Agreement will assuredly cause companies to reassess their plants' futures, many operations will be able to specialize in product lines compatible with Canada's long-run comparative advantage.[22] In fact, considerable rationalization has already occurred within U.S. firms operating in Canada. As Table 6 indicates, exports to the United States currently account for a significant share of the total sales of their Canadian affiliates. Indeed, the ratio of exports to sales is higher for Canadian manufacturing affiliates than for any other group except those in the Asian countries other than Japan. These figures suggest that Canadian affiliates are not just serving the protected Canadian market but that output at various U.S. and Canadian production sites is already somewhat specialized. The high ratios for the transportation and paper industries-[23] suggest that the rationalization process will proceed even further in other sectors once free trade occurs. By contrast, the figures for the U.S. affiliates of Canadian firms indicate that their output is less integrated with parent production and that these affiliates' primary purpose is serving the U.S. market.

Altogether then, if and when bilateral trade barriers disappear, we should not expect to see a big decline in the number of plants in operation. Rather we should anticipate increased specialization and the continued growth of intra-firm and intra-industry trade, just as occurred in Europe after the formation of the EEC. The adjustment costs associated with such developments should not be large.

U.S. CONCERNS

As congressional hearings get under way, U.S. industry and labor are beginning to focus on the Free Trade Agreement and to voice some concerns of their own. Generally, these comments reflect the specific problems of particular industries, those which are frustrated by continued Canadian protection and those which fear increased competition. Among those criticizing Canadian trade restrictions are members of the film, plywood and textile industries and of the United Auto Workers. U.S. film makers, for instance, are distressed that the distribution of U.S. films in Canada remains restricted because domestic politics exempted the Canadian cultural sector (like the U.S. maritime industry) from the Agreement. Similarly, U.S. plywood makers point to Canadian construction standards which disqualify most U.S. plywood for use in housing financed by the Canada Housing and Mortgage Corporation.[24] The textile industry has also been aroused by a Canadian Finance Department proposal to rebate customs duties on imported fabric made into clothing in Canada. These rebates would offset the advantages the U.S. textile industry had hoped to gain from the Agreement and appear to contravene its standstill provision on actions not in keeping with its spirit.

As for the UAW, its members see the Agreement as an unacceptable substitute for a complete renegotiation of the Auto Pact. They dislike the Pact because it includes Canadian content requirements for Auto Pact members and because it permits duty-free imports of parts from third countries (Asia, for instance) by Canadian auto assemblers. Neither provision benefits U.S. labor. Nevertheless, the automotive portions of the the accord clearly address many U.S.-Canadian frictions in this area and probably represent, as part of a broader agreement, the best deal the United States could make at this time. The realistic alternative to the Free Trade Agreement is the current unsatisfactory situation.

U.S. sectors resisting increased Canadian competition include energy, nonferrous metals and agriculture. Some U.S. coal producers, worried that imports of Canadian power will replace coal, argue that Canadian generating companies take advantage of government subsidies and less stringent environmental standards. Accordingly, a West Virginia Congressman has introduced a bill that would prohibit imports of electricity from Canadian generators and transformers determined by the U.S. Environmental Protection Agency not to meet U.S. environmental standards. U.S. wheat growers also complain about remaining Canadian transportation subsidies.[25] In addition, they are concerned that the Agreement removes the U.S. tariff on Canadian wheat but permits the Canadian Licensing Board to restrict Canadian imports of U.S. wheat until price and income supports provided by the two countries are equalized. A recent U.S. Department of Agriculture estimate indicates that Canadian subsidies amount to 10 to 24 percent of Canadian farmers' gross receipts from wheat sales while the equivalent U.S. figure is 25 to 49 percent.[26]

Obviously, many U.S. concerns stem from Canada's widespread use of subsidies. Because the U.S. government provides relatively few subsides,[27] while many other countries use them extensively to promote a variety of policy goals, the subsidy issue has become one of the most intractable in all recent trade talks.

From an economist's viewpoint, consistent subsidies do not necessarily hurt the importing country. *Their* treasuries subsidize *our* consumers (as well as their producers), and our consumers' gains are likely to exceed our producers' losses. Nevertheless, because a subsidy provided to some narrowly defined group can reduce costs artificially and distort trade flows, the GATT outlaws the use of most subsidies to promote exports. It does not, however, prohibit subsidies to encourage domestic policy goals such as regional development. On the whole, this distinction is economically sound (as well as politically practical in a world of sovereign nations) because in a period of flexible exchange rates, the advantages inherent in a widely available subsidy will be offset by an appreciation of the subsidizing country's currency. While U.S. trade remedy laws no longer permit a focus on export subsidies alone, the U.S. Department of Commerce does apply a general availability standard in determining whether a foreign practice involves a subsidy. Nevertheless, whether under GATT or U.S. standards, the terms "export subsidy" and "generally available" are both subject to conflicting interpretations.

In its broadest terms the Free Trade Agreement tries to stabilize the current level of the dispute over subsidies while the United States and Canada seek to resolve this complicated issue. The Agreement provides that over the next five to seven years Canada and the United States will work to develop new rules on subsidy practices, rules that will obviate the use of trade remedy laws. They will try to define what is and is not acceptable and explore the use of domestic commercial law to curb abuses. In the meantime, the accord creates the dispute settlement machinery described above and limits the extent to which changes in existing antidumping and countervailing duty laws can apply to the other partner. Since the Agreement does not provide an immediate resolution of this issue, Canadian subsidies will continue to plague U.S. producers and U.S. contingent protection will continue to harass Canadian producers. While the accord's provisions in this area may seem inadequate to some, they represent the limit of U.S.-Canadian agreement at this time. Again, the realistic alternative to the Free Trade Agreement is a negative spiral of friction and retaliation.

Moreover, we might want to remember how well the United States common market functions without countervailing duties in the face of myriad state and local incentive programs. And it does so without any help from fluctuating state exchange rates. Of course, firms have been free to move around within the United States to take advantage of these incentives. Now that the Agreement provides equal treatment to U.S. firms investing in Canada, however, U.S. firms will be able to benefit from Canadian subsidy programs as well.

As it stands, the Free Trade Agreement is far from perfect. It is natural, thus, that dissatisfied U.S. sectors should seek to press their points now, while the enabling legislation is being drafted; however, the Agreement smooths many sources of U.S.-Canadian friction and provides many opportunities. If the Agreement is implemented, the remaining problems will clearly be anomalies screaming for action. If the Agreement fails, all recent problems — resolved and unresolved — return to the table. Those too difficult to accommodate within the current accord are unlikely to get more favorable treatment or higher priority in the more hostile atmosphere likely to prevail.

IF THE EFFORT FAILS

At this point it is not at all clear that the Free Trade Agreement will be implemented. On the whole, interest in the Agreement has been much keener in Canada than in the United States. While the topic occasionally gets treated on the front page of the business section in this country, it has been headline news in Canada for months, and emotions are strong on both sides of the issue. The differences in depth of concern are not surprising,   After all, while the overall risks appear minimal and the probable gains modest, both are likely to be proportionately greater for the Canadians. Although the current Parliament appears certain to enact the implementing legislation, Prime Minister Mulroney must call a general election by September 1989. The Free Trade Agreement will clearly be a major issue, because the leaders of both opposition parties have denounced it. Indeed, John Turner, leader of the Liberal Party, has said that he would abrogate the Agreement if the Liberals form the next government.

Table 7

Share of U.S. Imports that are Duty-Free, by Area, and Average Duty Applied for Area Imports, 1986
Percent

	Share of U.S. Imports that are Duty-Free	Average Duty Applied to Imports from that Area
Average	33.0	5.4
Developed Countries	32.2	4.4
Developing Countries	35.5	7.2
Canada	71.3	3.4
Central American Common Market	84.0	15.7
Latin American Free Trade Area	35.6	4.5
Mexico	28.2	4.9
Brazil	47.8	10.8
European Economic Community	22.8	4.9
United Kingdom	36.7	4.1
West Germany	10.5	4.0
Japan	6.8	4.2
Asia, n.e.c.	32.4	10.2
Australia and Oceania	46.6	3.4

Source: U.S. Bureau of the Census, *Highlights of U.S. Export and Import Trade* (FT990), December 1986.

Should the Agreement collapse, a great deal will be lost — more, perhaps, than the modest gains discussed above. If the effort fails at this point, conditions may not return to the status quo. In a possibly strained, resentful atmosphere, the cycle of trade frictions, contingent protection and retaliation which led up to the free trade negotiations could well begin again with new vigor. The resulting uncertainties would be greater than before.

Even worse, failure to proceed would represent a real setback to multilateral trade liberalization and to U.S. and Canadian credibility in the GATT negotiations. These two very similar countries already have the world's largest trading relationship, and most major U.S. and Canadian companies already operate on both sides of the border. Many U.S. affiliates in Canada already appear to serve the North American, not just the Canadian, market. In other words, some specialization has already occurred. And, as Table 7 shows, U.S. tariffs are lower for and apply to a smaller fraction of imports from Canada than for any other major trading partner, while average Canadian tariffs are also lower for imports from the United States than from other industrial countries. Surely these are the conditions that minimize the risks and adjustment costs involved in a move to free trade. If these two countries cannot take this relatively simple, sensible step — phased in over 10 years, moreover — who can? And if the United States and Canada prove unwilling to risk freer trade with each other, their commitment to further, more difficult multilateral trade liberalization must not appear very strong. In other words, even if the gains associated with U.S.-Canada free trade are expected to be modest, not proceeding with the Agreement would mean a significant loss.

Notes

1   In the United States Congress must approve the Agreement and pass enabling legislation. (In Canada the Cabinet can approve the Agreement but Parliament must provide the implementing laws.) Because the agreement was negotiated under "fast-track" authority granted by the U.S. Trade Act of 1984, the enabling legislation will not be open to amendment on the House or Senate floor. Congressional committees will have 45 to 75 legislative days to review the text and the enabling legislation once it is officially submitted to them.

Thereafter the House and Senate have 15 legislative days to vote the entire package up or down by a simple majority. A letter from congressional leaders to the Administration commits Congress to voting on the Free Trade Agreement before the end of this legislative session and, if possible, before the August recess. If approved, the agreement will come into force on January 1, 1989.

2   Such fears appear largely unfounded, however, judging by the experience of the European Community where progress toward economic and, a fortiori, political union has proved considerably more elusive than many supporters would wish. For more information on the history of U.S.-Canada free trade, see Wonnacott (1987a)

3   The United States also supplies almost 70 percent of Canada's imports. See the box for basic facts on U.S.-Canadian trade and investment.

4   A phrase used by Canadian trade representative Rodney Grey (Grey 1983, pp. 243-57). For more information on Canadian subsidies and U.S. countervailing duty laws, see Wonnacott (1987a), pp. 71-108.

5   Royal Commission on the Automobile Industry 1962.

6   The Auto Pact established bilateral free trade in vehicles and original equipment parts as part of a plan to encourage U.S. auto manufacturers to increase the size and efficiency of their Canadian affiliates. This Canadian goal was reinforced by Canadian content requirements for cars sold in Canada. From the U.S. viewpoint, the scheme was a means of ending a nasty confrontation over Canadian export subsidies directed against the United States. See Wonnacott (1987b) for further discussion of the Auto Pact.

7   The U.S.-Canada Free Trade Agreement appears to meet GATT obligations. Although the GATT is based on most-favored nation principles of nondiscrimination, Article XXIV permits the creation of free trade arrangements that meet three conditions. The agreements must eliminate tariffs and other restrictions on "substantially" all trade between the parties; the remaining barriers to nonmember trade must be no more restrictive than they were previously; and the agreement must be implemented within a "reasonable" length of time. Thirty-four regional agreements are currently in force.

8   Yeutter 1987. For more detailed summaries of the Agreement text, see "U.S.-Canada Free Trade Agreement: Summary of Major Provisions," from the Office of Public Affairs, Office of the U.S. Trade Representative, Washington, D.C. and The Canada-US. Free Trade Agreement Synopsis, from the International Trade Communications Group, The Department of External Affairs, Ottawa.

9   Exceptions include restrictions on log exports from the United States and Canada and the U.S. Jones Act provisions restricting coastal shipping to U.S.-built ships.

10   The Agreement establishes quotas for the duty-free treatment of apparel made of imported fabric. If Canadian exports exceed the duty-free quota, Canadian manufacturers may apply for a drawback of the duty paid on the imported fabric used in the exports. While this scheme is nowhere near as onerous for U.S. producers as the duty drawbacks Canada has offered foreign auto producers to encourage them to invest in Canada, U.S. textile manufacturers are not keen on this provision.

11   If Free Trade Agreement duty reductions cause serious injury to an industry, the pre-Agreement tariff may be restored once for a period of three years.

The accord also sets limits on the application of escape clause actions to the partner country when imports from several countries are causing injury.

12   Good surveys of these studies are provided by Brown and Stern (1987), by Hill and Whalley (1985) in Appendix B, and by Wonnacott (1987a), pp. 21-56.

13   An example is the model developed by Brown and Stern (1987) and discussed in their chapter in Stern, Trezise and Whalley.

14   Helpman and Krugman 1985, p. 3 and p. 190.

15   Harris and Cox also used tariff rates weighted by mutilateral trade, which tend to be higher than U.S. and Canadian tariff rates weighted by bilateral trade. See Brown and Stern (1987), pp. 165-67.

16   This estimate is similar to Petri's "back of the envelope" estimate.

17   In addition to the effect on real income, much concern has also focused on the impact of a free trade agreement on employment. The Cox-Harris model indicates that Canadian real wages and labor productivity would rise just under 30 percent from their level in 1976 while employment in the sectors on which their study concentrated (textiles, steel, agricultural equipment, urban transportation equipment and chemicals) would rise 5 percent (Cox and Harris 1986). A very recent Canadian study reports that Canada would gain 76,000 to 251,000 jobs (as compared to the employment level in the absence of the Free Trade Agreement) by 1998. The larger number reflects assumed productivity improvements in 20 manufacturing industries. These figures represent less than 2 percent of Canadian employment. (See Magun, Rao and Lodh 1988. See also Frank 1988 which finds an employment gain of 150,000 by 1997.)

18   Helpman and Krugman (1985), p. 189 and p. 265.

19   Another study by Daly and Rao (1986) also expresses doubt that unexploited economies of scale will permit Canada to enjoy large gains from bilateral free trade. This skepticism reflects their finding that as Canadian manufacturing output expanded between 1958 and 1979, the economies of scale actually experienced were small at best. While the ex post economies of scale measured by this study may not provide much information about potential economies of scale, the authors are surely correct to stress that a major benefit of the free trade agreement will be its stimulus to competition.

20   One exception is the Magun, Rao and Lodh study (1988), which calculates the tariff equivalent of a good many U.S.-Canadian non tariff barriers but concludes that the Agreement's provisions concerning these restrictions will have little impact because numerous non tariff barriers in agriculture and the food and beverage industry will be largely unaffected. While the Office of the U.S. Trade Representative values U.S. and Canadian government procurement business opened by the agreement at $3 billion and $500 million respectively, Magun, Rao and Lodh find the government procurement provisions will also have a limited impact on net trade, output and employment. The Frank study also addresses procurement and attributes a small part of the Canadian gains from the Free Trade Agreement to additional sales to the U.S. government.

21   Philip H. Trezise (1988) describes the modeling efforts discussed above as "indicative" and "not wholly relevant" and mentions many of the important considerations which have not or cannot be incorporated in this approach.

22   Of course, conditions such as age of individual plants will play a role in the outcome. In the steel industry, for instance, the older facilities tend to be in the United States, while in paper the opposite is true. In the auto industry

the situation is mixed. See Crandall (1987), and Royal Commission on the Economic Union and Development Prospects for Canada (1985), p. 343.

23 In 1986 more than three-quarters of U.S. paper imports entered duty free. The average tariff on the dutiable portion was less than 3 percent.

24 An attachment to the accord provides that Canada will review these standards by March 15, 1988. If they are not broadened, the U.S. tariff on plywood will remain in force.

25 On shipments through Thunder Bay, Ontario. The Agreement eliminates those on shipments through the western ports.

26 "Farm Belt Grows Uneasy Over Canada-U.S. Free Trade," Journal of Commerce, January 19, 1988.

27 Except on agricultural products. Moreover, foreigners argue that this country's huge defense expenditures often subsidize industrial R&D. In addition, state and local governments offer a vast array of incentive programs.

V

THE MULTINATIONAL CORPORATION AND WORLD TRADE

Most standard models of international trade have little to say about multinational corporations even though these companies are responsible for a great deal of international trade and often transfer technology and capital (and sometimes even labor) from one country to another. In this section we examine multinational corporations.

In the first article, "Multinational are mushrooming," Raymond Vernon, one of the leading experts on multinational corporations, examines the importance of multinationals in world trade. In the second article, King examines one particular aspect of multinational corporations, their role in the development of the third world. The article presents two different schools of thought on multinational corporations. The first school of thought contends that multinationals foster the growth and development in the third world by transfering valuable capital and technology. The second school of thought, often referred to as the dependency school, contends that multinationals do not foster economic development, but rather help to create and maintain a system by which the developed countries are able to exploit the cheap labor and cheap raw materials available in the third world.

13

Multinationals are Mushrooming

Raymond Vernon

Since the end of World War II, most of the world's largest manufacturing firms have been transformed from national firms into multinational enterprises. By building up a network of subsidiaries and affiliates outside the home country in which the parent company is located, these multinational enterprises have greatly enlarged the scope of their production and marketing operations, covering much larger areas of the globe than in the prewar period.

The development has been worldwide, affecting large enterprises headquartered in all countries, from Holland to Hong Kong. But the development has been especially evident with respect to enterprises in which U.S. policy-makers are obliged to take a special interest, namely, those headquartered in the United States, such as General Motors and IBM, and those headquartered in foreign countries with subsidiaries operating in the United States, such as Toyota, Philips Electric, and ICI.

The growth and spread of multinational enterprises has contributed heavily to opening up the borders of the U.S. economy, enlarging and strengthening its direct links with the economies of other countries. Some crude indications of the importance of those new links to the U.S. economy are provided by the data in Table 1 Because the direct investments of U.S. firms abroad are of an earlier vintage on the whole than the investments of foreign-based firms in the United States, the book figures in the table are not altogether comparable, tending to understate the relative size of U.S. holdings abroad. Nevertheless, the figures in Table 1 firmly establish two points: that the foreign links achieved through direct investments in the United States are growing rapidly, and that in absolute terms they have already achieved very considerable proportions.

In terms of the manufacturing jobs they provide, multinational enterprises have become a major factor. In 1977, U.S.-based manufacturing firms employed 3.9 million persons outside the United States. And in 1980, the U.S. manufacturing subsidiaries of foreign-based firms employed about 1.1 million persons. For purposes of comparison, the total U.S. work force engaged in manufacturing in these years was in the neighborhood of 20 million.

Table 1

U.S.-based Firms' Direct Investment in Foreign Countries and Foreign-based Firms' Direct Investment in the United States

(based on year-end book values in billions of U.S. dollars)

U.S.-based firms in foreign countries	1950	1960	1970	1980	1984
Manufacturing	$ 3.8	$ 11.0	$ 31.0	$ 89.0	$ 93.0
Petroleum	3.4	10.8	19.8	47.0	63.3
Other	4.6	10.0	24.7	77.5	77.0
Total	11.8	31.9	75.5	213.5	233.4
Foreign-based firms in the U.S.					
Manufacturing	n.a.	2.6	6.1	24.1	50.7
Petroleum	n.a.	1.2	3.0	12.3	25.0
Other	n.a.	3.1	4.2	29.1	83.9
Total	n.a.	6.1	13.3	65.5	159.6

Sources: Various issues of Survey of Current Business.
Note: n.a.— not available.

In addition to the role that multinational enterprises have come to exercise as a source of employment in manufacturing, their role in the U.S. balance of payments also has acquired significant dimensions. In 1984, for instance, the income that U.S.-based parents received from their foreign establishments came to $66 billion, representing 18 percent of all U.S. exports of goods and services. The payments made to foreign firms in connection with their direct investments in the United States in 1984 were much lower, amounting in 1984 to less than $11 billion, but that figure can be expected to climb rapidly in the years to come.

The international trade generated directly by these multinational enterprises also was impressively large. The aggregate merchandise exports and imports of these enterprises have not been fully reported in recent years, but in 1965 U.S.-based multinational enterprises accounted for 66 percent of all U.S. merchandise exports, and by 1977 the figure had climbed to 70 percent.

This growth in the inward and outward flows of foreign direct investment has profoundly affected the outlook of U.S.-based enterprises, turning them from firms focusing on the U.S. market to enterprises that make production and marketing decisions in a context of global competitors and global markets. Once again, various statistics reflect this shift in focus. By 1980, for instance, Ford, IBM, and ITT reported that over 50 percent of their sales arose in foreign markets. For U.S.-based corporations as a group, the analogous figure in 1977 was 32 percent, and for the manufacturing firms in the group, 29 percent.

To be sure, not all U.S.-based firms have been expanding their multinational networks in the past decade. In a few industries, in fact, the predominant tendency has been withdrawal and retrenchment. In copper and petroleum, for instance, and in branches of the chemical industry, some observers have speculated that the multinational trend might be coming to an end. History tells us, however, that the decline of multinational firms in some industries is no indication of an overall decline in multinational networks as a whole.

Since the time when such networks first developed about a century ago, some firms that had developed a multinational structure have been obliged to give up that structure in reaction to certain other changes in their industry. In a cycle that is sometimes referred to as "the obsolescing bargain," enterprises are often compelled to shrink back when they no longer possess special competitive advantages — advantages that are usually embodied in a special capability to mobilize capital, to provide difficult managerial or technological skills, or to provide access to hard-to-enter foreign markets. In earlier eras, multinational enterprises have lost their own advantages in tropical agriculture, in various types of mining, in the electricity-generating industry, and in traction companies. More recently, multinational enterprises in some other industries, including oil, appear to have lost these special advantages and have been obliged as a result to cut back the scope of their foreign operations. But by and large, the underlying trend to multinationalization has been sustained.

Table 2

Transfers of Innovations by 57 U.S.-based Multinational Enterprises to their Foreign Manufacturing Subsidiaries: Classified by Period of U.S. Introduction

Percentage transferred abroad by number of years after U.S. introduction

Period of U.S. introduction of innovations	Number of innovations	Same year or 1 year after	2 or 3 years after	10 or 4 or 5 years after	6 to 9 years after	more years after	Total
1945	34	8.8	14.7	2.9	11.1	43.3	82.8
1946 - 1950	79	11.4	15.2	10.1	14.1	39.3	90.1
1951 - 1955	57	7.0	5.3	15.8	25.4	32.5	86.0
1956 - 1960	75	16.0	21.3	16.0	20.0	18.7	92.0
1961 - 1965	63	26.9	17.6	14.3	7.9	8.1	74.7
1966 - 1970	64	28.2	17.2	12.5	6.2	n.a.	64.1
1971 - 1975	34	38.2	26.2	n.a.	n.a.	n.a.	64.4
Total	406	18.7	16.3	11.6	14.3	20.2	81.1

Source: Raymond Vernon and W. H. Davidson, "Foreign Production of Technology-Intensive Products by U.S.-Based Multinational Enterprises, Report to the National Science Foundation, no. PB 80 148638, January 1979, Table 11. *Note*:: n.a.— not applicable.

Indications of the strength of the underlying trend are ubiquitous. One telling sign is reflected in the data in Table 2. The figures reflect the profound consequences of a fundamental learning process that U.S.-based firms experienced in the years from 1945 to 1975. In the earlier years, U.S. firms were in no great rush to set up facilities abroad to produce the innovations that were coming out of their laboratories and being introduced in U.S. markets. By the end of three decades, however, the lag between their first U.S. production ad their first overseas production had shortened considerably. What is more, the degree of such shortening was a faithful function of the firm's prior experience in the particular country and with the particular product.

More recently, indications of the persistent vitality of the multinational enterprise have been seen in the rapid expansion of foreign-based enterprises in the U.S. market (already mirrored in Table 1), a result of increased direct investment mainly on the part of European-based and Japanese-based enterprises. At the same time, increasing numbers of smaller firms have taken to forming multinational networks. In the United States, for instance, by 1977 the number of manufacturing firms with less than $25 million in assets that had acquired one or more foreign subsidiaries reached 622, and preliminary results from a 1982 survey indicated that the figure would be substantially higher for that date.

PATTERNS OF OPERATION

Until quite recently, economists in the United States felt no great need to puzzle out the economic implications of the growth of multinational enterprises, leaving that line of inquiry largely to their colleagues in the developing countries, in Canada, and in Europe. It was obvious that multinational enterprises tended to internalize various international flows of goods, services, and money, so that the flows took the form of transfers between related units in a single multinational network. But it was widely assumed that the internal decisions of the multinational enterprise would create international flows of goods, services, and money that roughly approximated those reached by unrelated firms operating at arm's length. Today, however, few economists who have studied the multinational-enterprise phenomenon would cling to that assumption. Although serious efforts to articulate those differences in conventional economic terms and to measure the differences econometrically are still fairly rare, some strong hints of the nature of those effects already exist.

The decisions of multinational enterprises in expanding, contracting, or shifting their productive facilities around the globe are likely to produce patterns that are significantly different from those that would develop from the decisions of independent national producers.

The likely sources of those differences are numerous, but a few are worth mentioning.

One factor is simply the cost to the firm of acquiring knowledge about alternative locations in foreign countries, as well as the credibility attached to that knowledge after it is acquired. As was pointed out earlier, the prior experience of an enterprise with producing in a given foreign country measurably hastens the decision to set up more production facilities in that country. The information that planners at the headquarters of multinational enterprises receive from their subsidiaries in the field is likely to be less costly and to appear more credible than information gathered from external sources. Enterprises that are in a position to receive credible information swiftly and at low cost, one can assume, are likely to react more swiftly and more sensitively than others.

Another reason for anticipating that multinational enterprises will produce a distinctive locational pattern stems from their ability to play off competing national jurisdictions against one another, especially when they are locating plants whose purpose is to produce for export. In such situations, in addition to looking for an environment with a favorable cost structure, enterprises often look for the most attractive package of subsidies and tax exemptions being offered by competing governments. The implications of that practice should not, of course, be exaggerated. Factors other than these government blandishments have a considerable influence on the locational decisions of firms. For instance, multinational enterprises cannot place their exporting plants in locations that might bar them from their intended market. Despite the caveats, however, the subsidies that governments offer cannot fail to affect the locational decisions of the multinational enterprises.

Perhaps the most effective device by which governments have influenced the investments of multinational enterprises in their productive facilities, however, is through the so-called performance requirement. Most governments in developing countries and some in industrialized economies make a practice of imposing specific performance requirements on the subsidiaries of multinational enterprises, such as the requirement to export more and import less; subsidiaries that fail to measure up to such requirements are usually threatened by the possibility of being barred from selling those products in the national market.

Performance requirements, it is apparent, represent a relatively new and virulent form of beggar-thy-neighbor tactics among competing governments. A typical response by a multinational to Mexico's demands, for instance, would be quietly to reduce the production of subsidiaries in, say, Brazil or the United States, in order to expand production in Mexico. When more than one government is making demands of this sort on a multinational enterprise, the enterprise is forced to mediate between the demands of different governments by inconspicuously redistributing production among its various affiliates. All told, then, the multinational enterprise introduces a relatively new force in the distribution of international trade and investment, a force that operates on patterns that may be quite different from those contemplated in the traditional view of international trade and investment conducted at arms length between independent parties.

LINES OF POLICY

The mushrooming of multinational enterprises has been affecting various areas of U.S. policy with increasing frequency. In some cases, the growth of such enterprises has exacerbated some long-standing issues, such as the protection of the foreign assets of U.S. citizens, the U.S. taxation of foreign income, and the U.S. prosecution of antitrust suits. In other instances, the growth of multinational enterprises has figured in some quite novel situations, such as the use of such enterprises to promote human rights, the avoidance of injury in the international sale of harmful products or technologies, and the avoidance of threats to the safety of bank deposits in the United States. Many of these issues are of sufficient importance in U.S. international economic relations to merit a few words of elaboration.

THE ANTITRUST ISSUE

One familiar set of problems that promises to grow in intensity over the years stems out of the antitrust policies of the United States. By law, the Federal Trade Commission and the Department of Justice are responsible for worrying whether proposed mergers, consolidations, and joint ventures among competing U.S. firms are likely to impair competitive conditions in U.S. markets. In making such judgments in individual cases, these institutions are guided by various rules of thumb that are incorporated in precedent and in law. Those guides have been fashioned on the assumption that whenever the sales of a given product become more heavily concentrated in the hands of a few sellers in the United States, the increase in concentration my constitute a threat to competition in the U.S. market.

The measures used to determine if competition is being threatened, however, are anachronistic in light of the rapid growth of multinational enterprises. However relevant they may have been some decades ago, they have been rapidly losing their meaning under modern conditions of competition. In a world increasingly populated by multinational enterprises, measures that rest on the degree of concentration of sales in the U.S. market become unreliable. Multinational enterprises, relying upon their existing outposts in the principal markets of the world, are in a better position to recognize new market opportunities in foreign countries than national firms would be. Their ability to compete in those markets is measured not by their past sales in such markets, but by their capacity to respond to the opportunity created by abnormal profit margins. Measures of concentration, therefore, can be acutely misleading; where high concentration exists in an industry, it need not mean that the existing sellers can act with impunity. And, in fact, multinational enterprises that have dominated U.S. markets in given product lines are often acutely aware of their vulnerability.

The challenge of antitrust doctrine is to find some operational standards that reflect this changed state of international competition. Obviously, actual imports and the threat of imports have to be taken into account in such revised standards. But beyond that, the extent to which competitors may set up new subsidiaries in U.S. markets also ought to be reflected in any ideal measure.

Another problem for antitrust doctrine that arises out the growth of multinational enterprises is one of longer standing — but one that is gradually growing in intensity. This is the problem of jurisdictional clash, especially between nations with incompatible approaches to the subject of restrictive business practice, or incompatible interests in the maintenance of some specific restrictive practice.

The efforts of U.S. prosecutors to command data from alleged foreign "co-conspirators" and even from innocent foreigners not partaking in the alleged violations, as well as the efforts of U.S. courts to shape remedies that would apply to foreign enterprises engaged in such violations, have produced bitter reactions in foreign countries, notably the United Kingdom, France, Canada, and the Netherlands. Some governments, indeed, have enacted laws prohibiting their residents from responding to the requests of U.S. agencies for data in antitrust cases. The problem is particularly difficult for the United States because of the separation of powers between the U.S. courts and the U.S. executive; while some judges have been sensitive to the problems of jurisdictional conflict, others have felt free to make demands on foreigners without regard to the political consequences of such demands.

In years past, the U.S. government has made sporadic efforts to develop some modus vivendi for dealing with these jurisdictional conflicts. A provision for consultation on restrictive business practices has been worked into a number of bilateral treaties with other industrialized countries. The United Nations Conference on Trade and Development has developed some nonbinding principles that might guide governments in the handling of international restrictive business practices. But these have been cosmetic gestures rather than serious efforts to reconcile conflict.

The possibility that some resolution could be achieved in the years ahead is enhanced by a number of developments. First, measures taken by the European Economic Community in this field, such as the prosecution of IBM on antitrust grounds, have occasionally appeared objectionable in jurisdictional terms to the United States. Second, Europe-based and Japan-based multinational enterprises have greatly expanded direct investments in the United States. Developments such as these suggest the likelihood that in future the U.S. economy will find itself on the receiving end of measures taken by other governments that seem inconsistent with U.S. concepts or interests in the field of restrictive business practices.

In the absence of some resolution of conflicts such as these, one can easily foresee two possible consequences: The United States and other countries will clash over these issues with increasing frequency; or countries will draw back from enforcing their national antitrust statutes whenever foreign interests are involved, simply because they are unwilling to take on the burden of the international political consequences. Some evidence exists for the prevalence of both tendencies. Needless to say, either outcome will be costly to U.S. interests.

Accordingly, the time may be ripe for resuming U.S. support for an effective international modus vivendi in this area. The tendency of the United States to limit its support to hortatory statements of large principles may no longer be sufficient. Instead, changing circumstances call for an explicit set of guidelines for the resolution of conflict, plus some means for finding facts and reconciling conflicts in undecided cases.

PRESSURES FOR POLITICAL ENDS

The U.S. government has repeatedly used the foreign networks of its multinational enterprises to apply economic pressure on other countries for political ends, with results that have sometimes been politically disastrous. As a rule, the American strategic objective has been to hold down the war-making capabilities of the communist countries, including not only the U.S.S.R and Eastern Europe, but also Cuba, Angola, and Nicaragua. At other times, however, the U.S. government has had other aims in applying economic sanctions, including efforts to enforce its concept of human rights, as witnessed by the Southern Rhodesian and South African cases.

These uses of the multinational enterprise tread on extraordinarily delicate ground, but the delicacy of using multinational enterprises for political ends has not registered very strongly in the United States as long as foreign direct investment has not played an important role in the U.S. economy. Countries adversely affected by such U.S. policies might occasionally express their discontent over our measures, but, as long as the United States was not the aggrieved party, their complaints carried little weight in the U.S. process.

Today, however, foreign direct investment in the United States is approaching $200 billion. Other countries, therefore, are increasingly in a position to play a similar political game. Domestic reactions to the efforts of Arab countries to boycott Israel hint at the political storm that could be provoked as other nations attempt to exploit the participation of their multinational networks in the U.S. economy. From the U.S. viewpoint, the Arabs' goals were much harder to defend than are the goals that the United States seeks to achieve in South Africa, but in the absence of any international standards regarding the use of multinational enterprises for such restrictive actions, the intrusive character of such measures is bound to evoke bitter political reaction.

The larger issue in which these cases are embedded is the extent to which governments should use subsidiaries of multinational enterprises for political ends. The problem is usually thought of as one in which the country of the parent firm seeks to influence the country in which the subsidiary is located. But the possibilities of political pressure actually can run as well in the opposite direction. Governments in which important subsidiaries of multinational enterprises are located can attempt to hold the subsidiaries hostage in order to squeeze changes in policy out of the governments of their parents; oil-exporting countries in the Middle East toyed with such a strategy repeatedly during the decade of the 1970's, hoping to alter the direction of U.S. policy toward Israel.

Problems such as these are often indistinguishable from two related issues. To what extent should foreign subsidiaries of multinational enterprises be entitled to engage in the normal political activities of the countries in which they are located? And to what extent should they be entitled to call upon the governments of the parents for diplomatic support? These questions have been a source of many bitter disputes in international relations, disputes that have produced little more than unilateral declarations by the various parties.

Although disputes of this kind are less frequent today than they were five or ten years ago, the lull is almost certainly transitory, the result of governments' being prepared for the moment to overlook such problems in order to acquire new sources of foreign capital. In the longer run, these controversies are bound to grow in number and intensity. Because many governments are identified with long-held positions in such disputes, reaching agreement on principles will not be easy. Yet in the absence of agreement, the issue will constitute another significant source of strain in international relations.

PRESSURE FOR ECONOMIC ENDS

Multinational networks offer a tempting target for governments to pursue not only political objectives but economic ones as well. Perhaps the most obvious maneuver of that sort is the so-called performance requirement mentioned earlier, a requirement that usually takes the form of directing the subsidiaries of multinational enterprises to export more and import less, on pain of losing access to the domestic market of the country in which they are situated.

Once again, however, it is well to emphasize that the problem of performance requirements does not always run from subsidiary to parent. When parents limit a foreign subsidiary's sales to specific markets, such as the national market of the country in which the subsidiary is located, in effect they are imposing a performance requirement on the subsidiary, obliging it to surrender export business to other affiliates. When that allocation is influenced by the home government of the parents, as has been the case in a few well-publicized instances, the parallel with the performance requirements of host countries is even more marked.

These practices are well known to the policymakers of the United States and other countries, a growing form of beggar-thy-neighbor tactics on which no vigorous international assault has yet been made. In importance, the problem takes its place alongside other, more visible, barriers to trade. Perhaps, in the end, it can be dealt with most efficiently as a trade barrier. Meanwhile, however, it is important that the problem should be recognized as one peculiarly associated with the growth and spread of multinational enterprises, hence one likely to grow in importance as such multinational enterprises grow.

THE TAX ISSUE

The various affiliates that make up any multinational network commonly draw on a joint pool of resources including management, technology, and capital and commonly pursue a strategy that is related to that of other affiliates in the same network. IBM's centralized research, for instance, affects the products of all its manufacturing subsidiaries, and IBM's sales force in any country relies on the general reputation and explicit technical support of the entire global network. Accordingly, the profit that each affiliate reports in any national taxing jurisdiction in which it operates has to be arbitrarily determined to some extent. To be sure, every taxing jurisdiction has its regulations and guidelines to assist the enterprise in determining that profit. But as a rule, there is still plenty of room for the allocation of central-office overheads, the fixing of prices for the sale of technology and intermediate products among the affiliates, and other decisions determined according to the accountant's craft.

Recognizing some of the arbitrary elements that are involved in the division of taxable income among affiliates in the same multinational network, governments in most industrialized countries have entered into bilateral tax agreements with other industrialized countries, aimed at ensuring some degree of consistency in what each jurisdiction defines as taxable profits; the aim in such agreements is to spare the multinational enterprises the pain of double taxation, while ensuring that one or the other jurisdiction levies taxes on the income that has been generated.

For a time, these bilateral agreements seemed sufficient to deal with the problem, at least as it concerned relations between the advanced industrialized countries. Then some individual states in the United States, building on a practice that they had already applied when calculating the taxable income of U.S. firms, decided to calculate the taxable income of multinational enterprises falling in their jurisdiction as a percentage of the global income of these enterprises. States following that practice normally determine the appropriate percentage by calculating the proportions of global assets, sales, and employment of the enterprise that fall within the state and basing the allocation on those percentages.

From the viewpoint of any state, this is a perfectly plausible calculation, more transparent than a calculation based on the numerous arcane allocations that accountants are obliged to make in pursuing the fiction that the activities of the enterprise in the state constitute a distinctive business unit with a distinctive profit. From the viewpoint of the multinational enterprise, however, the method suffers from two drawbacks: it prevents them from allocating their costs, as they would otherwise be inclined to do, in order to avoid having too much of the global profit appear in high-tax jurisdictions; and it exposes them to the possibility that each taxing jurisdiction will elect the method it thinks will generate the highest taxable profit in its jurisdiction, thus exposing the enterprise to the risks of double taxation.

The protests of a number of countries against having the various states in the Unites States elect the global allocation approach may succeed in pushing U.S. policymakers toward banning such state practices, forcing a reversion to the accountant's use of arcane and arbitrary allocations of income and expense among the states. A more defensible approach would be explicitly to acknowledge the fact that, for many enterprises, it makes no sense to think of a profit arising within a single state, or even a single nation. In such cases, the objective should be to secure the widest possible adoption of the global allocation approach at all levels, national and subnational. Otherwise, the determination of profit in any jurisdiction is almost certain to remain opaque, being determined largely by the arbitrary allocations of the taxpayers' accountants. This is an issue that promises to increase in intensity as multinational enterprises based in many different countries expand their networks over the globe.

UNFINISHED BUSINESS

The subjects explored above should be thought of as no more than illustrations — illustrations of the consequences of jurisdictional conflict arising out of the growth of multinational enterprises. In fact, numerous other illustrations could have been used: problems arising from the transmission of dangerous industrial technologies or products, such as those involved in the Bhopal affair; problems involving the protection of bank depositors; problems involving the disclosure of corporate affairs for the protection of investors; and so on.

The list of such issues is daunting, given their number and variety. The temptation is to sweep them all together in a single package, to label the package "multinational enterprise" or "transnational corporation," and to hope that some single international institution will be able to deal with them all. Any such expectation, however, would be illusory. Within any country, each of these diverse problems characteristically evokes its own unique set of responses. Some are handled at local levels of government; some at national levels. some are dealt with by rule of law, some by administration, some by contract, and some by benign neglect. Similar choices will have to be made at the international level. And if these international efforts are to be more than gestures of exhortation, the institutional arrangements for implementing those efforts will probably prove as varied as those efforts will probably prove as varied as those devised within national jurisdictions.

14

The Multinational Corporation: Pro and Con

Philip King

The role of Multinational Corporations in the development of the Third World has been widely debated for years. Depending upon one's perspective, Multinational Corporations are seen either as the engine of development, or the agents of imperialism. This paper will examine two perspectives on the role of MNCs in Third World development: Dependency Theory, and what has been variously termed as the neoconventional perspective or the "sovereignty at bay" perspective. After a brief explanation of each of these points of view, the paper examines two case studies involving investment by Multinational Corporations in the Third World. The first case study concerns bauxite mining in Jamaica, the second case study examines petroleum exploration and development in Indonesia.

DEPENDENCY THEORY AND THE MULTINATIONAL CORPORATION

While there are probably as many theories of dependency as there are authors, all of these theories share certain common themes. The general view is that Capitalism is a zero sum game in which the northern, Developed Countries, gain at the expense of the Third World. Thus dependency theorists share with Marxists a belief that Capitalism is fundamentally flawed and that "free" markets are not really free, but rather serve as a mechanism of exploitation.

Central to many versions of Dependency Theory is the concept of the center and the periphery. The center represents groups, institutions or social structures which may in some sense be referred to as "developed." Wealth and power are concentrated in the center and it is the center which benefits from trade with the periphery. As opposed to the center, the periphery represents those areas that do not benefit from trade. The periphery is exploited by the center for its raw materials and its cheap labor. High value-added processes are located in the center and thus the periphery receives an unfairly low compensation for its own inputs.

According to Dependency Theory, the relationship between the center and the periphery is an ongoing, dynamic process in which the center systematically keeps the periphery underdeveloped. Capitalism does not foster development in the periphery but instead leads to what Andre Gunder Frank refers to as the "development of under-development." This relationship is seen as an extension of former colonial ties, generally referred to as neo-colonialism.

The notions of center and periphery can refer to countries, groups, or social structures which benefit from Capitalism. Dependency theorists often refer to the Developed Countries such as the U.S., Japan or Western Europe as the center. Within the center countries one can also distinguish a center and a periphery. For example, within the United States a coal mining community in Appalachia would be considered on the periphery, whereas an investment banking firm on Wall Street would definitely be in the center. Similarly, a center exists within the Third World, although it is a much smaller center than that within a developed country.

The MNCs are the institutions which transfer the necessary technology and exploit the cheap labor and raw materials available in the periphery. They also forge the necessary bonds between the ruling elites in the center countries and the ruling elites within the periphery. Given the key role in the relationship between the center and the periphery that MNCs play, it is not surprising that much of the criticism levelled against the capitalist system by dependency theories has been levelled specifically against Multinational Corporations. The rest of this section will present specific critiques leveled by dependency theorists against Multinational Corporations.

The first major criticism of MNCs is that they enter a country with advanced capital-intensive technology and drive out local, more labor intensive technology. In the process, the MNCs wipe out the local entrepeneurial class and, since their technology requires little labor, they create large scale unemployment. In the textile industry, for example, MNCs have set up capital intensive production facilities which drive the local labor-intensive textile industry out of business. At the same time, the control of the production process shifts from local hands to a foreign company.

According to Dependency Theory, MNCs take the profits from their operations in the periphery and send them home. This repatriation of profits creates a drain on the Developing Country's economy and leads to a deterioration in the terms of trade. One aspect of this profit repatriation that critics of MNCs focus on, is transfer pricing. Often developing countries receive royalties from the MNCs which are based on a percentage of the profits that they receive. If the MNCs can under-report the profits that they make, they can pay less in royalties. Transfer pricing involves one division of a vertically integrated MNC selling some product to another division for an artificially low price. Since profits are equal to revenue minus costs, selling the product at an artificially low price implies that reported profits will be lower and thus the amount that the developing country receives in royalties will also be lower.

MNCs also play a key role in the process of political fragmentation which is central to Dependency Theory. MNCs coopt local elites who rely on them for taxes and incomes (and often kickbacks and other forms of corruption); MNCs may also coopt middle management and labor unions by paying them relatively high wages. Perhaps the most often cited case of MNC involvement in the local politics of a developing country is the case of ITT in Chile. Shortly after Salvador Allende, a left wing politician against foreign investment, was elected to power in Chile in 1974, ITT lobbied the American CIA to fund political groups opposed to Allende. The company also encouraged U.S. aid to the Chilean military (which was strongly opposed to Allende) and it systematically delayed shipments of spare parts to the Allende government in order to destabilize the regime.

Even where developing countries have nationalized the assets of the multinational companies (the formal ownership of the company now lies with the developing country itself), the actual control still rests with the company, according to Dependency Theory. The MNCs still control the technology and know-how, the international marketing networks, and usually the skilled personnel necessary to operate the company profitably. Thus, Dependency Theory argues, just as the formal political independence given to Third World Countries at the end of the colonial period did not change the fundamental economic relationship between the industrialized countries and the developing countries, nationalization of these firms also does not change their fundamental character.

Finally, critics of Multinational Corporations argue that MNCs encourage inappropriate patterns of consumption. In particular, they alter the consumption patterns of poor countries towards products which are perceived as more modern and more western, but which are not necessarily better. The case of Nestlés marketing of baby formula in the Third World is most often cited. The Nestlés corporation marketed infant formula as a modern, more nutritious formula for mothers in the Third World. Many have objected to Nestlés' approach since the general opinion among the medical community today is that the mother's natural supply of milk is more nutritious for a baby than any artificial formula. To compound the problem, many mothers often dilute the formula and use contaminated water, resulting in increased malnutrition and infant mortality.

ARGUMENTS IN FAVOR OF MULTINATIONAL CORPORATIONS

In contrast to the criticism of Multinational Corporations leveled by the dependency school, many other economists and scholars have argued that MNCs are the vehicle for the transfer of valuable capital, technology and other resources necessary for development. The paradigm here is of a world of interdependent nations all of which benefit from free trade. Thus, investment represents a positive sum gain in which all parties gain. The fact that many developing countries export raw materials or products based on cheap labor merely reflects their comparative advantage.

The chief difference between the dependency school and those who are in favor of MNC investment in the Third World is that the pro-MNC school sees MNCs as fostering growth and development. Proponents of MNCs tend to downplay the problems that the dependency school point to. For example, they contend that transfer pricing is not really a serious problem; instead they argue that MNCs provide valuable revenues that would not exist otherwise and thus improve the Developing Country's balance of payments. Proponents of MNCs also argue that MNCs do not replace indigenous production, but rather create industries which would not have existed before. They see the Nestlés case and case of ITT in Chile as anomolies which are not indicative of the general role of MNCs in the Third World.

Proponents of MNCs also point to South Korea, Taiwan and other East Asian countries as models of what type of development can take place with foreign investment. South Korea and Taiwan have achieved rapid development while maintaining a relatively equal distribution of income.

One of the best known proponents of the involvement of Multinational Corporations in the Third World is Theodore Moran. In his book, *Multinational Corporations and the Politics of Dependence: Copper in Chile*, Moran presents a theory of MNC-LDC negotiations and uses a case study of copper negotiations in Chile to support his theory. Moran points out that Chile, as well as a number of other developing countries gradually increased its share of the profits from mining.

Central to Moran's theory is the idea that developing countries gain skills in bargaining with the Multinationals and eventually even acquire some of the technical and managerial skills necessary to run the industry itself. He postulates that Chile's increasing share of profits over time stemmed from "moving up a learning curve of negotiating, operating and supervisory skills ... that lead from monitoring industry behavior to replicating complicated corporate functions" [Moran (1974, p. 154)]. The learning curve consists of three stages. First, the host country acquires the ability to monitor the industry in order to determine what share of profits it actually receives. The next two stages entail the gradual attainment of middle management "supervisory" skills by the host company and the "technical and operating skills" necessary to actually run the industry.

Moran also argues that the history of Chile's involvement with the copper corporations demonstrates that, in contradiction to the predictions of Dependency Theory, the interests of the political right (the "center") gradually evolved away from those of the Multinational Corporations and towards a more "nationalistic" stance. Consequently, over time a consensus developed to nationalize the corporations and increase taxes [Moran (1974, pp. 172-211)].

Moran presents solid and convincing evidence that Chile did indeed increase the share of profits it received from the MNCs and that it also gradually formed a class of mid-level managers and engineers who performed most of the tasks associated with the companies' day to day operations. He also points out that although Chile did indeed have an indigenous copper industry in the 19th century (before the involvement of foreign corporations) the best veins had been mined by the early twentieth century and Chile did not have the technological capacity to exploit the remaining copper ore, which was of a much lower quality. Thus, the indigenous copper mining industry in Chile was not replaced by the MNCs.

The next two sections of this paper present two different case studies involving investment by Multinational Corporations in the Third World. The first case study examines investment in bauxite extraction in Jamaica, the second case study examines the involvement of petroleum companies in Indonesia. Finally, we will examine each of the case studies in light of the contentions made by the depency school and by proponents of foreign investment by MNCs.

JAMAICA AND BAUXITE

With the expansion of the aluminum industry after World War II, three North American aluminum companies, Reynolds, Kaiser and Alcan, began exploration for new sources of bauxite. Because of its close proximity and its abundance of bauxite, these companies made substantial investments in Jamaica. In 1950, the Jamaican government signed the "Bauxite and aluminum industries encouragement law," a long-term agreement with Kaiser, Reynolds and Alcan, which provided that the companies would pay a royalty equal to 14¢ for every ton of bauxite exported and an income tax averaging about 24¢ per ton.[1] The combined tax was equal to about 3-4% of the value of bauxite exports.[2]

A British government commission report (the Hicks report), criticized the 1950 law, arguing that "it looks as if a better bargain could have been made by the Jamaican government." The Hick's report pointed out in particular that the Jamaican agreement provided more favorable terms to the aluminum companies than did contracts in other Carribean countries.

By 1957, the Jamaican government also became concerned that Jamaica might be earning too low a share of the bauxite revenues. The Jamaican government rescinded the terms of the old contract and increased the royalty from 14¢ to between 20¢ and 40¢ per ton of bauxite. [3] The income tax was also structured such that 50% of the tax varied directly with the value of aluminum ingot, instead of the price of bauxite [4]; the average income tax in the late 1950's was $1.54 per ton. Overall, the increase in taxes more than quadrupled the bauxite revenues that Jamaica received.[5]

Part of Jamaica's concern was that the aluminum companies were reporting too low a value for the bauxite produced in Jamaica in order to escape Jamaican taxes. (See the above discussion of transfer pricing.) The average income tax in the late 1950's was $1.54 per ton.

In 1962, Jamaica gained its independence from the British. A Parliamentary government was established modelled after the British government. At the time of independence, two political parties had already been established in Jamaica. The People's National Party (PNP) was formed in 1938 by Alexander Bustamante and Norman Manley, but by 1943 the two leaders split over ideology and Bustamante formed the opposition Jamaican Labor Party (JLP).[6]

For the first ten years after Jamaican independence, the JLP controlled the Jamaican Parliament. During this period, the Jamaican government did not increase the official bauxite tax rates; instead, the government stressed the expansion of Jamaica's refining of bauxite into alumina. Alcan, the only Canadian company, had already established two alumina refineries in Jamaica; however, the American companies were using refineries located in the U.S. During the late sixties, the Jamaican government was able to negotiate three new alumina refining plants built by the four U.S. companies operating in Jamaica at that time: Reynolds, Kaiser, Anaconda and Alcoa.[7]

When elections were held in 1972, Michael Manley and the Peoples National Party defeated the ruling Jamaican Labor Party. Soon after the election, Manley formed the National Bauxite Commission to study how Jamaica could best profit from the bauxite industry. The commission delivered six recommendations: (1) to repatriate the land owned by the bauxite companies, (2) to acquire 51% ownership in the bauxite companies, (3) to establish the Jamaican Bauxite Institute which would monitor prices and production levels of bauxite, (4) to form a cartel of bauxite producing countries, (5) to increase revenues by means of a tax which varies according to the price of aluminum ingot, (6) to develop an aluminum smelter in cooperation with Mexico and Venezuela. [8] In the next two years, Manley's government accomplished the first five of these goals.

In early 1973, Manley sent a mission to Australia to discuss forming a cartel of bauxite producing nations; Australia was receptive to the idea. In October of the same year, delegations from Jamaica, Yugoslavia, Guyana, Guinea, Surinam and Australia met in Yugoslavia to form the International Bauxite Association (IBA). The Dominican Republic, Haiti, Ghana and Indonesia also joined a year later. Together, these countries accounted for 85% of bauxite production outside of the Soviet block. [9]

In March 1974, Manley announced that a new levy was to be placed on all bauxite in Jamaica. The new levy would be set at 8% of the price of aluminum ingot derived from Jamaican bauxite. Previously, Jamaica received roughly 1.5% of the price of aluminum ingot for its bauxite production. Manley also announced that Jamaica would seek ownership of all bauxite mines in the country and a 51% share of the equity in the bauxite mining and refining operations. [10]

The aluminum companies objected to this announcement and refused to accept anything more than a small increase in the bauxite levy. They appealed to the World Bank's International Centre for the Settlement of Investment Disputes (ICSID), an international arbitration agency designed specifically to settle this type of dispute. However, shortly before the appeal Jamaica withdrew from ICSID's jurisdiction over its mineral disputes. Jamaica argued that any international arbitration represented an infringement on its sovereignty and it would thus refuse to honor any judgement. [11]

Ultimately, Jamaica did reach a compromise with the majority of the companies, a compromise which favored Manley's position. Instead of an 8% levy, the Jamaican government would impose a 7.5% levy, and to ensure that the companies did not reduce their production in response to the tax, each company was required to pay taxes on a minimum production quota. Jamaica also attained a stake in Alcoa's alumina refinery and a 51% equity share of Kaiser and Reynolds, both with the stipulation that the companies would retain managerial control for seven years. As part of the compromise, the companies were guaranteed access to Jamaica's bauxite for 40 years. Finally, the companies agreed to withdraw their appeal to ICSID. [12]

Most other members of the IBA also agreed to raise taxes, but no other country increased their taxes as much as Jamaica. Australia finally refused to go along with a substantially increased levy.

Although Manley's increase of Jamaica's bauxite levy lead to higher (short-run) revenues for Jamaica, these increases also discouraged the Multinational Corporations from investing in Jamaica. In the seventies Jamaica lost its position as the dominant producer of bauxite to Australia even though Jamaica had substantial unexploited deposits of bauxite. While Australia's bauxite output continued to increase, Jamaica's output stagnated. The aluminum companies were investing outside of Jamaica, particularly in three countries with lower taxes: Australia, Guinea and Brazil.[13]

Table 1

World Production of Bauxite
(millions of metric tons)[14]

Country	1971	1980
Jamaica	12.5	12.0
Australia	12.7	27.2
Brazil	0.6	4.2
Guinea	2.6	13.9

In 1980, Edward Seaga, the head of the Jamaican Labor Party called for new elections to remove Manley from office. When Manley refused, the JLP took to the streets in a wave of political violence forcing Manley to call for elections in the fall of 1980. [15] Just a few weeks before the American elections, Edward Seaga and the JLP won the Jamaican election receiving 59% of the votes and 51 out of 60 seats in Parliament.

Soon after Seaga was elected, the Reagan administration decided to set up Jamaica as a model of a free market government in the Caribbean. In March 1981, Reagan sent a committee of businessmen headed by David Rockefeller on a special mission to Jamaica to meet with Seaga to discuss new American business investment in Jamaica. The U.S. also increased foreign aid to Jamaica and encouraged multilateral agencies to do likewise.[16] To stimulate the Jamaican bauxite industry, Reagan agreed to buy Jamaican bauxite for part of a "Strategic Stockpile."

Despite these measures, Jamaica has attracted little foreign capital since 1980. [17] Although Jamaica lowered the bauxite levy to 6.5% in 1979 and 6% in 1984, the only major investment the bauxite industry received was $90 million for a giant conveyor belt.[18] During the same period, the aluminum companies spent many times this amount in Brazil, Australia and Guinea. [19] Last year Michael Manley was again elected as Prime minister of Jamaica; given Manley's election, it seems even less likely that the aluminum companies will invest in Jamaica.

INDONESIA AND PETROLEUM

Indonesia received its independence from the Dutch in the late 1940's. During its first ten years, the government consisted of a series of shifting parliamentary coalitions. In 1959, after several years of chaos, President Sukarno became "dictator for life" of Indonesia.[20]

The first few years of Sukarno's rule were relatively stable, but by 1964 Sukarno's regime was facing major political difficulties. Sukarno's policies and rhetoric were becoming more and more closely associated with the PKI, the Indonesian Communist Party. The United States expressed concerned about Sukarno's drift towards Peking and persistent rumors that the PKI would succeed Sukarno, whose health was failing. Indonesia's economy was also in trouble; inflation reached 600% in 1964 and Indonesia's foreign debt was rising rapidly. [21]

The PKI staged a coup in 1965, which the army, led by General Suharto, struck down. After the coup, the army, and in particular General Suharto, formed a joint cabinet with the now politically weak Sukarno. Gradually, the army assumed broader and broader powers and in 1968 Suharto received the full title of President. [22]

Suharto established a "new order" for Indonesia in which the army penetrated all realms of government as well as private enterprise. The army leaders declared that "the army does not have an exclusively military duty but is also concerned with all fields of social life." [23]

OIL

At the time of Indonesian independence, several foreign oil companies (mainly Stanvac, Caltex, and Royal Dutch Shell) operated under "let alone" agreements signed with the Dutch. These contracts came under attack from the Indonesian legislature and by 1954 a revised set of contracts yielding greater revenues to the Indonesian government were negotiated. Although the exact details of the agreement are not known, according to Alex Hunter:

> "it is generally presumed in petroleum circles that the net result ... for which the petroleum companies were liable amounted to something around a 50:50 division of net revenues (profits) between the companies and the Indonesian government. " [24]

No exploration or development of any oil fields took place during the fifties. According to the *Bulletin of Indonesian Economic Studies*, this was largely due to an overall retrenchment in the oil industry. [25]

Following a constitutional mandate that "natural riches be.... controlled by the state," in 1963, the Indonesian government nationalized all assets on Indonesian soil that were used to extract petroleum. The new "contracts of work" specified that the multinational oil companies would act as contractors for the State and that Indonesia would receive 60% of all profits from petroleum extraction. Formally, the new contracts gave managerial control to the Indonesian government, although it did not possess the technical or managerial skills to run the oil fields. The oil companies objected to the new arrangement and shortly after the contracts of work were established, one of the major oil producers in Indonesia, Shell Oil, left. [26]

Both the Indonesian government and the oil companies expressed dissatisfaction with the contracts of work; the Indonesians suspected that the oil companies were cheating them through transfer pricing and the oil companies wanted some guarantee of managerial control. To alleviate these difficulties, in 1966, Sutowo proposed a new set of contracts which entailed the following: (1) Indonesia would retain formal management control while leaving most working decisions to the oil companies themselves; (2) ownership of all project related equipment would be transfered to Permina as soon as the equipment entered Indonesia; (3) the oil companies would bear the risk of exploration and development, but could deduct expenses up to 40% of total oil production; (4) the parties would share oil production rather than revenues or profits. [27]

The new contracts, now referred to as production-sharing contracts, were designed to eliminate the above mentioned difficulties with the old contract-of-work agreements. First of all, although the production sharing contracts still gave Indonesia sovereignty over all capital invested in Indonesia, they also assured the multinational oil companies some degree of management control. Second, by placing a 40% ceiling on the total expenses that could be deducted and by requiring that Indonesia receive its share in petroleum, the contracts limited the companies' ability to engage in transfer pricing. The original production sharing contracts specified that 65% of the remaining production (after the 40% cost deduction) would go to Indonesia, and the remaining 35% would go to the oil company.[28]

Table 2

Indonesia's crude oil Production
(millions of barrels)[29]

1966	1967	1968	1969
170.7	186.2	219.9	270.9

A significant amount of new investment did occur after the creation of the production sharing agreements. However, the new investment did not come from the large oil companies but rather from Japanese firms and from small American "independent" firms. The Japanese were particularly interested in reducing their (89%) dependence on Middle Eastern oil and although the major oil companies disliked yielding ownership to Indonesia, the American independents were willing to accept this arrangement. Unlike previous exploration and development, much of the new activity took place offshore. [30]

According to *The Petroleum Press Service,* by the early seventies, the major companies were again looking at Indonesia for several reasons: (1) they viewed Suharto's regime as politically stable; (2) by the late sixties Indonesia's production contracts were more favorable to the oil companies than most contracts in the Middle East; (3) Indonesia's oil was low in sulfur, making it more desirable for environmental reasons; (4) it was by now becoming clear that Indonesia contained vast quantities of oil offshore. [31]

THE OIL TANKER CRISIS

In 1968, the Indonesian state-owned oil companies were all merged into one company, Pertamina, and Dr. Sutowo was appointed President-Director. For the next several years, Pertamina expanded rapidly: Pertamina purchased three refineries, its own telecommunications network, its own schools and hospital and even its own airline (P.T. Pelita). Sutowo also planned a fertilizer plant, a polypropylene plant and several modern service stations. As a result of its rapid expansion, Pertamina began to accrue huge debts and by 1971 the IMF restricted further borrowing by Pertamina as a condition for renewing credit to the Indonesian government. The IMF ruled that Pertamina could not take out any loans with maturities between 1 and 15 years.

Sutowo's solution to the problem was to take out 360 day loans. The commercial banks lending the money assumed that since Pertamina was a state-owned company, loans to Pertamina would fall under the category of country risk rather than company risk. [32]

Indonesia announced in October 1974 that Pertamina would not be able to pay $250 million in overdue income taxes because expenses on the Krakatau steel complex would be higher than expected.

To meet its budgetary crisis, the Indonesian government decided that it needed to increase its current revenues from the petroleum industry, even at the expense of reducing exploration activity. The old 65/35 (country/company) production split was altered to 85/15. For sufficiently high levels of production Indonesia's share rose to 90% and 95%. Pertamina also required the oil companies to sell part of the oil to Indonesia at below market rates thus raising the effective split to 89/11. Finally, the government tightened its 40% deduction for the companies' operating costs; where Pertamina had formerly granted the 40% deduction almost automatically, it would now try to reduce that figure to 35% where possible. [33]

The oil companies warned that these measures would reduce future investment considerably and soon after Indonesia announced its new increases, exploration and development fell. Several wells were capped and a number of drilling contractors gave their 30 day notices. The number of exploration wells drilled declined from nearly 200 in 1974 to less than 100 in 1976.[34]

In 1977, after the Pertamina crisis subsided, the government altered the contracts to encourage additional investment. Under the new agreement, the original, 65/35 (country/company) split would apply to the first $5 per barrel; the remaining receipts would be divided 85/15. Indonesia also liberalized depreciation allowances and added an "investment credit" of 20% to be added to the cost recovery component of certain high cost operations. Finally, the government guaranteed to purchase all "new" oil at the prevailing market price as opposed to the artificially low prices previously used. [35]

After the oil price hike in 1978-9, the oil companies increased their exploration and development in Indonesia. Exploration and development rose 19% between1979 and1980; expenditures exceeded $1 billion in 1980 and rose even further in 1981. According to *The Far Eastern Economic Review*, many of the revenues obtained from this oil boom were to be used to increase government subsidies before the upcoming elections. [36]

The government also launched an "Indonesianization" program designed to train Indonesians to take over jobs performed by foreigners. As of 1986, the Indonesianization program has not been very successful; the oil companies have been extremely reluctant to turn over multi-million dollar rigs to Indonesians. One difficulty is that the technical manuals needed to operate the rigs have not been translated into Indonesian. [37]

Exploration and development fell in the late 80's due to a glut in the oil market and lower oil prices. In 1985, the government also announced that foreign firms would be required to sell at least 20% of their equity to local firms by 1986. [38] It remains to be seen if, with low oil prices, this reform will actually be implemented.

CONCLUSION

Do the above case studies shed any light on the debate between the dependency school and proponents of Multinational Corporations? Yes, and no. First of all, only two case studies were examined and both of these cases involve resource extraction. Any conclusion drawn from these case studies is obviously rather tentative and may not apply at all to non-resource extracting industries. The two case studies above do not support either of the two views; they do however tend to confirm some of the propositions made by each side.

One of the major differences between the dependency school and the pro-MNC school is over whether MNCs actually provide revenues for the developing country and lead to an improvement in the balance of payments or whether, on net, MNCs actually drain the developing country and lead to a deterioration in trade. On this point the pro-MNC school seems to have the advantage, at least with respect to mineral and petroleum extraction. It is clear that in both Indonesia and Jamaica (as well as in Moran's case study of Chile) that the MNCs generated substantial revenues and that the share received by Jamaica and Indonesia increased over time. One can also cite many other instances of mining agreements in Third World countries which have lead to substantial and increasing profit shares for the host country. A steady increase in the developing countries' share of the profits is clearly in accordance with Moran's theory.

On the issue of transfer pricing, the pro-MNC school also seems to have an edge. It is clear that Jamaica and Indonesia learned fairly early to cope with the problem of transfer pricing. Both countries initially had contracts which specified that the country's share would come from the MNC's profits. Jamaica switched from this type of contract to a contract which linked its revenues to the final price of aluminum, a price which the MNCs could not manipulate. Similarly, Indonesia's switch to production sharing contracts placed a cap on the percentage of revenues that the oil companies could write off as costs and specified a minimum price for crude oil. These contracts guaranteed Indonesia a certain revenue for each barrel of crude oil produced.

Although it is clear that both countries received a great deal of revenue from resource extraction, it is much more difficult to assess the effect of this increased revenue on economic development in Jamaica and Indonesia. Despite a substantial increase in these revenues during the sixties and early seventies, Jamaica's economy stagnated; during the seventies, while bauxite revenues skyrocketed, Jamaica's economy actually deteriorated. One could argue that things would have been worse without the bauxite revenues, but Dependency Theory predicts that the deterioration in Jamaica's economy is precisely what one would expect from the involvement of Multinational Corporations in Jamaica's economy. In Indonesia some improvement in living standards has taken place over the last twenty years. It is also true, however, that much of the revenues from petroleum extraction have been wasted on corruption and have been used to support Suharto's military regime.

The development of managerial and technological capability that the pro-MNC school describes did not take place in Jamaica or Indonesia. This observation is in marked contrast to what Moran describes in Chile. In Jamaica and Indonesia, the learning that Moran describes seems to have stopped at an early stage. Both Jamaica and Indonesia quickly learned how to monitor their industries, what the tax rates in comparable developing countries were, and how to structure their taxes in order to avoid transfer pricing. Even though Indonesia later fully nationalized its petroleum industry and Jamaica partially nationalized its bauxite industry, neither country has acquired the technical or operating skills involved in these industries. Both countries rely upon the Multinational Corporations for both technical and managerial support. [39] In Indonesia, as we have seen, the corporations even use foreign workers to operate the drilling rigs despite attempts of the government at "Indonesianization." The Jamaicans have also failed to develop the technical and managerial skills to oversee the bauxite industry. Some observers doubt that Jamaica has even obtained the ability to monitor its bauxite industry completely:

> "Jamaica ... never had a laboratory to measure the quality of the bauxite exported, and simply accepted the figures of the companies concerned." [The Economist (2/10/79, p. 80)] .

In sum, although it appears that both countries attained some ability to monitor their industries quite early, neither country has attained the technical or supervisory skills that Moran describes in Chile. Despite this fact, both countries continued to increase their taxes substantially. Other countries, such as Zambia, Zaire and Papua, New Guinea have also continued to increase taxes even though they have failed to develop the managerial and technical skills that Moran describes.

It is also difficult to assess the effects that the bauxite and petroleum MNCs have had on Indonesian and Jamaican politics. The pro-MNC side would point to the degree of political stability that each side has achieved. Indonesia has had the same military regime for 25 years. While this regime has been favorably disposed toward foreign capital it also drove a hard bargain with the companies and, in the 70's, it was not reluctant to renege on contracts that it had signed with the oil companies. Jamaica has remained a democracy since receiving independence in 1962. Its two main political parties, the JLP and the PNP, have been in and out of office since then, each serving an 8 to 10 year term. Each party has maintained a relatively stable core of support over the years with the swing voters deciding the outcome of each election. The PNP has favored more radical measures toward MNCs; the JLP has been more accomodating. The official stances of each party toward foreign capital have not changed significantly over the last 30 years, nor has the relative percentage of the population who consider themselves loyal to each party.

Dependency theorists would point to the fact that Indonesia's military regime is very closely aligned with the U.S.; this, they argue, accounts for its favorable attitude toward foreign capital. According to this view the military, who run Indonesia's national oil company (Pertamina), receive most of the benefits from kickbacks and other forms of corruption and few of the revenues actually trickle down to the poor. Similarly, depency theorists would dispute the claim that Jamaica is politically stable. Unemployment and crime are high, particularly in the capital city of Kinston: political riots are commonplace. Indeed, the general opinion among bankers and corporate executives in the U.S. is that Jamaica is politically unstable.

In sum, while it is clear that resource extraction provided revenues to Jamaica and Indonesia, the effects of the investment on the actual economic development of Jamica and Indonesia remain unclear. It is difficult, particularly in the case of Jamaica, to see how significant these revenues have been as a source of development. It is also difficult, however, to argue that these investments have lead to the development of underdevelopment and the loss of autonomy that the dependency school describes. Indonesia has grown to some extent, and it is not clear that Jamaica's stagnation can be blamed on the bauxite industry which does not appear to have significantly affected Jamaica's political system.

Notes

1   Huggens (1965, p.106-7).
2   Lipton (1979, p.11).

3　The tax varied with production levels, decreasing with higher outputs.
4　Part of Jamaica's concern was that the aluminum companies were reporting too low a value for the bauxite produced in Jamaica in order to escape Jamaican taxes. (This method of escaping taxes is generally referred to as "transfer pricing.")
5　Lipton (1979, p. 8) and Huggens (1965, pp. 106-7).
6　Jamaica remains a democracy today and the PNP and the JLP are still the dominant political parties. The PNP is the more liberal of the two parties; throughout its history, the leadership of the PNP has espoused a socialist ideology. One of the PNP's chief concerns is the nationalization of all major Jamaican industries. The JLP, on the other hand, espouses a pro-market ideology. [Beckford(1980, pp. 62-63)]
7　The Financial Times (11/4/71), The Wall Street Journal (7/29/66) and (7/14/70).
8　Stephens (1983, p.385).
9　Pyndick (1977, p.344).
10　Lipton (1979, p.4).
11　The Wall Street Journal (6/18/74, p. 10).
12　The Wall Street Journal (10/26/78, p. 20), (11/21/74, p. 16), (2/3/77, p. 11), (4/1/77, p. 7), (6/19/75, p. 34), (5/17/74, p. 4).
13　See the Charles Rivers Study [Woods and Burrows (1980, pp. 90-4; 120-123)] andThe Economist (2/12/83, p. 12). Brazil was never a member of the IBA.
14　Data from Metal Statistics (1978, p. 21) and (1985, p. 19)..
15　The New York Times (2/12/85, p. 12).
16　The Economist (3/14/81, pp. 77-8).
17　Business Week (10/18/82 pp. 61-2).
18　The Financial Times (4/19/85, p. 34).
19　See the Charles Rivers Associates Study [Woods and Burrows (1980, p. 120-121)].
20　Pauker (1980, p. 127).
21　Pauker (1965, p. 88).
22　Pauker (1980).
23　Crouch (1976, p. 519).
24　Hunter (1965, p. 262).
25　The Bulletin of Indonesian Economic Studies (1967, p. 85).
26　Fabrikant (1975, p. 309).
27　Stoever (1981 p. 236).
28　The Petroleum Press Service (August, 1969, p. 291).
29　1966-68 data from The Bulletin of Indonesian Economic Studies (1970, p. 63),1969 data from The Petroleum Press service (April, 1971, p. 127).
30　The Bulletin of Indonesian Economic Studies (1967, p. 85).
31　The Petroleum Press Service (1968, p. 265).
32　Stoever (1981,p. 239).
33　The Far Eastern Economic Review (2/11/77., p. 95) andPetroleum News Southeast Asia (1975, p. 22).
34　The Far Eastern Economic Review (8/20/76,p. 35) and (8/20/76,p. 35).
35　The Oil and Gas Journal (4/25/77, p. 80).
36　The Far Eastern Economic Review (1/9/81. p. 58).
37　The Petroleum Press Service (June 1982, p. 42). According to one oil company spokesman, the companies did not "want to take a chance on damaging a well they've spent $2 million to drill and complete."
38　The Financial Times (7/10/85, p.4).

39   For example, see Girvan (1976), Stoever(1981) various issues of the The Economist and The Far Eastern Economic Review.

VI

OPEC

It is difficult to discuss any aspect of the international economy over the last fifteen years without some reference to OPEC. The two OPEC price hikes in the seventies had a dramatic effect on world trade and finance. In late 1985, however, the price of crude oil plummeted from just over 30 dollars a barrel into the teens. Since then, the price of crude oil has fluctuated between roughly 10 and 20 dollars a barrel. OPEC has periodically attempted to raise the price of crude oil, but as of 1989 all of these attempts have failed. The recent failures of OPEC have prompted many to ask whether the cartel has finally collapsed. In the following article, "Oil market instability and a new OPEC," the author argues that the factors which lead to OPEC's decline in the 80's- its loss of market share due to discoveries in Alaska, Mexico and the North Sea and the slow growth of demand for crude oil- will reverse again in the 90's. OPEC has control over much of the world's oil reserves; as other reserves become depleted and as the demand for petroleum increases further due to lower oil prices, OPEC will assume some of the power that it had in the 70's.

15

Oil Market Instability and a New OPEC

George C. Ceorgiou

World oil prices have moved in the 1980s as dramatically as they did in the 1970s. From a high of $35 per barrel in 1981, they fell as low as $10 per barrel in 1986. It was only after Saudi Arabia instituted a costly policy of disciplining OPEC (Organization of Petroleum exporting Countries) and non-OPEC producers by flooding the oil market that OPEC implemented a series of agreements to limit its production, which have pulled the price back up to $18 or $19 a barrel. These prices seem unlikely to hold, however — one more indication that the roller-coaster ride of the past decade and a half is by no means over.

Yet some observers appear to think that it is, pointing to the recent fall in oil prices as confirmation of OPEC's collapse and as a historic turning point. Even though some of this rejoicing has been cut short by the wrenching effects the price drop has had on U.S. oil producers, oil-producing Third World nations, and the international banking system, a certain amount of complacency remains. There is a fairly widespread belief that with the recent firming of oil prices, we now have the best of both worlds: prices are high enough to bring some relief to the depressed U.S. oil sector, but at the same time they are low compared to recent levels and therefore are conducive to world economic growth. OPEC is considered to have been badly weakened, unlikely to regain the power it had during the middle and late 1970s.

Such relative unconcern is shortsighted. The past 15 years should have made clear that the world oil market's problem is not high prices or low prices per se, but price instability, which underlies the boom-bust cycle not only in the world energy market but also, because of oil's centrality, in the world economy as a whole. Under the market's current organization, prices will inevitably rise again. To regard the current equilibrium as permanent is a dangerous mistake, since doing so discourages our taking the action necessary to secure our energy supply in the future.

The fall in oil prices has, for example, cut short the search for new energy sources, both fossil-based and renewable, and has drawn attention away from the costs that current oil price instability imposes on the economies of both producing and consuming nations. Moreover, while one new U. S. government study warns about the dangers of America's growing dependence on foreign oil imports, there are still many optimists in the West who are ignoring the possibility that a core group of OPEC members, a group that holds more than 50 percent of the world's proven oil reserves, may eventually be able to regain control over the world oil market and thereby develop into an even more dominant cartel than OPEC was in the 1970s.

This need not be the case. The present situation could be taken as an opportunity to reorganize the world energy market with an eye to forestalling an energy crisis in the 1990s. But if the current period is to be a respite during which we plan our energy future rather than a prelude to the next crisis, it will be necessary for the United States to put the energy question back onto the national political agenda and develop policies that promote producer-consumer cooperation, national and world energy planning, and increased investment in conservation and energy diversification. Such changes would bring benefits all around — steady income to the oil-producing nations, a steady supply of oil at stable prices to the oil-consuming nations, and some much-needed economic relief to the less developed countries. The stability that would be encouraged is crucial if the international economy is to avoid the kinds of shocks it has suffered in the 1970s and 1980s.

OPEC'S DEMISE?

For more that a decade, OPEC's future seemed assured. It had brought the price of oil from $3 to $35 per barrel, and a succession of experts was forecasting dwindling world energy reserves. Even during this period of success, however, economic forces of supply and demand were working toward OPEC's eventual decline: overall demand for oil continued to fall in response to the five-fold rise in oil prices, while world oil supplies continued to increase as both industrialized and Third World countries stepped up domestic production.

The decline in demand was spectacular — unlike anything seen since the oil industry's inception in the mid-nineteenth century. Before the 1973-74 price increase, world demand for oil had been growing rapidly; and it continued to rise, at a somewhat slower pace, between 1973 and 1979. Between 1979 and 1983, however, it fell from its 1979 peak of 65 million barrels per day by around 10 percent, and has since grown only slightly. [1] For OPEC, this fall-off was even more serious than these figures suggest; from a 1979 peak of 31 million barrels per day, world demand for OPEC oil has fallen almost 50 percent. [2]

Part of this drop may be attributed to the worldwide recession of 1981-83 during which the world economy languished, still suffering from the 1979-80 oil price shock. But another cause was the increase in conservation and energy efficiency that the oil-importing countries achieved in reaction to the oil price rises of the 1970s. In the Western industrialized countries, between 1973 and 1984, the ratio of energy consumed to gross national product fell by 19 percent. [3] The United States, being the most energy-intensive economy, was able to lower this ratio by 23 percent; Western Europe and Japan, starting with substantially more efficient economies, reduced their energy-to-GNP ratios by 16 percent and 29 percent respectively. [4] These figures suggest that what had been taken for granted as a strong complementary relationship between energy consumption and economic growth has been substantially weakened. Total consumption of energy, including oil, may well continue to rise in the future; but the rate of increase in consumption will certainly be lower.

In addition to increased efficiency of energy consumption, there has been an increased use of energy sources other than oil, which has further reduced world oil demand. Between 1973 and 1984, the use of coal, natural gas, nuclear power, and renewable energy sources increased greatly, while oil's share of world energy use fell from 41 percent to 35 percent. [5] Factors contributing to this trend include fears of a price rebound, higher consumer taxes on oil products, completion of conservation projects, and the desire of many developing countries to use indigenous gas and coal resources to earn foreign exchange and to encourage internal development.

Compounding the effects of decreased demand for OPEC oil was the increased worldwide oil supply. The oil price shocks of the 1970s spurred major investment and exploration that increased oil supplies in a number of areas. Since 1979, non-OPEC production has added more that 5 million barrels per day to world output. Mexican production has nearly doubled, adding 1.4 million barrels per day to the oil market; and production in the North Sea by Great Britain and Norway has risen from nearly nothing in 1973 to 3.3 million barrels per day in 1984. [6] These countries have captured an important share of the world market and are a major counterweight to OPEC dominance. In addition, five non-OPEC developing countries — Brazil, Egypt, India, Malaysia, and Oman — doubled their output between 1979 and 1985, bringing it to 3 million barrels per day. [7] Overall, oil output in the non-OPEC capitalist world increased from 16.8 million barrels per day in 1983 to 25.1 million barrels per day in 1985. [8]

One crucial factor behind the oil surplus of the 1980s has been performance of the world's two largest producers — the Soviet Union and the United States. The production of both countries was expected to decline in this decade, but just the opposite has occurred: between 1979 and 1984, the Soviet Union increased production by 0.5 million barrels per day, the United States by 0.3 million barrels per day. [9] Currently, the combined output of these two producers is about 3 million barrels per day more than oil analysts had predicted. [10]

Another major contributing factor to the world oil glut has been OPEC's inability to limit its production sufficiently to support a given price level. Between 1979 and 1982, demand for OPEC oil dropped by 40 percent; it has not yet risen. Nearly all OPEC members have had to bear some of the burden of limiting production. Although certain members have made larger cuts, with Saudi Arabia, Kuwait, and Libya reducing output by 65 percent, and 50 percent respectively, all members decreased production by at least 20 percent. Yet even with this drop in output, prices continued to fall. This put pressure on producers to make up for falling revenues by increasing their output. Eventually, in December 1985, Saudi Arabia announced that in light of other OPEC countries' repeated violations of their OPEC quotas, it would no longer play the role of swing producer and would instead attempt to increase its share of the world oil market by selling oil at whatever price the market would bear. As OPEC abandoned all production and pricing agreements, OPEC output rose by about 4 million barrels per day between August 1985 and July 1986 — a 25 percent increase. [11] Of course, this only added to the world oil glut, causing oil prices to fall below $10 a barrel, which in real terms is lower than the $3-per-barrel price that prevailed before the 1973 price shock.

UNDERLYING TRENDS IN THE WORLD OIL MARKET

The fall in oil prices and OPEC's various organizational problems are not the result simply of the interaction of supply and demand factors. Rather, OPEC's plight reflects underlying shifts that have taken place in the international oil regime.

The most important issue at stake has been responsibility for regulating the world oil market. When OPEC was formed in 1960, international oil companies dominated and regulated the world oil regime through long-term contracts with the oil-producing nations. At that time, OPEC lacked the strength to act as a truly effective cartel. Yet it did manage, during the 1960s, to force the major oil companies to accept tax system changes favorable to producers. And in 1968 it issued a declaration of goals, which included achieving control over its oil resources and nationalization of concessions.

No one outside OPEC paid much attention to this manifesto. But conditions were changing rapidly in such a way as to increase OPEC's power: in particular, excess productive capacity outside OPEC was virtually disappearing. By 1971, producers were able to apply enough pressure to obtain five-year price contracts with the oil companies that would favor OPEC — the Teheran and Tripoli Agreements. By 1973, they were in a position to dictate oil market conditions to the world. And by the middle of the decade, many OPEC countries had gained control of their oil resources by nationalizing them. This transfer of power from oil companies to OPEC — from consumers to producers — was a milestone in the history of oil.

Despite this transfer of power, OPEC still needed outside help to develop, produce, transport, and market its oil and to locate new reserves. Throughout the 1970s, OPEC countries relied on the major oil companies for assistance in most of these areas. In return, oil companies received preferential access to OPEC crude (and furthermore were able to maintain their profitability, as there was a lot of money to be made in trading oil). But in recent years, this arrangement has begun to break down: the oil companies' preferential access to OPEC crude has steadily diminished. In 1973, 93 percent of OPEC production was made available to the major oil companies under long-term supply contracts or on a preferential basis. [12]   Currently, only half of OPEC production is thus available. [13]

Such a shift would not necessarily cause increased instability in the world oil market, were it not for the fact that preferential access and long-term contracts have been replaced by much less secure arrangements — short-term contracts, either with other state governments or with major oil companies. The most volatile kind of short-term contract, of course, is the spot market for crude oil. When OPEC countries nationalized oil operations in the 1970s, and as long-term contracts were terminated, oil supplies became unstable or, in the case of the 1973 embargo, nonexistent. This situation helped trigger the phenomenal growth of the spot market: oil companies were forced to rely on it to satisfy their supply needs; OPEC producers also used it when tightening supplies and high and rising spot prices enabled them to earn larger profits than had been possible under long-term contracts. Whereas the spot market is estimated to have accounted for no more than 5 to 10 percent of internationally traded oil in the 1970s, it now takes in 40 to 50 percent, the largest share of which is OPEC oil. [14]

Not only has the spot market made short-term prices more volatile, it has also influenced prices elsewhere, including long-term contracts: when spot market prices are high, high prices tend to prevail in other markets. During the 1970s, this led many OPEC governments to abandon or simply ignore official OPEC prices in favor of a pricing system with monthly or even weekly adjustments based on spot prices. This, of course, increased OPEC's profits. But after the 1979-80 price increase, when excess supplies began to develop, the tables turned. Consumer governments and oil companies increasingly chose to terminate or not renew existing long-term supply agreements, turning instead to the spot market, where they could take advantage of continuously falling oil prices. By now, an estimated 80 percent of world oil is sold at prices that reflect the free market. [15]   Thus every price fluctuation has a much more disruptive ripple effect than it used to. Responsibility for stabilizing the situation — by shoring up the spot price during times of excess supply, and by relieving pressure on the spot price in times of excess demand — has moved from the oil companies, which negotiated long-term contracts, to the oil producers, primarily OPEC.

Similar shifts have occurred in other areas. Over the past decade, oil companies themselves have turned more inward and market-oriented, which has had the effect of placing more of the burden for market regulation on OPEC. Before the 1970s, for example, the major oil companies invested and explored for oil in a variety of locations. But more recently they have restricted themselves to areas of the world under the control of the oil-consuming countries, unwilling to take the risks involved in doing business in much of the developing world. Between 1975 and 1982, 57 percent of exploration was invested in the industrial countries and 90 percent of exploratory wells were drilled there. [16] (Certain non-OPEC developing countries — those not considered to be politically risky — also were the focus of exploration.) At the same time, as the costs of exploring for oil in such places as Alaska, Canada, and the North Sea rose, many oil companies concluded that it was cheaper to secure their access to crude supplies by buying existing reserves through takeovers of other oil companies.

The net result has been a decline in external investment for exploration in OPEC countries holding the world's largest proven reserves. The burden has thus fallen on the OPEC governments themselves. But as oil prices have fallen through the 1980s, these governments have had less and less capital available for such projects. The irony, then, is that the pressure on them to increase their role in the world oil market has increased just as their ability to do so has decreased.

This situation has been exacerbated by the oil companies' tendency to draw down the oil inventories they hold worldwide. When those companies controlled the oil market, they held crude oil inventories in order to have an additional buffer against short-run fluctuation in demand and supply and thereby to increase their control over the market. In times of falling oil prices, oil companies would add to their inventories, taking oil off the market and thus helping to firm up prices; conversely, when prices were rising, the companies would draw oil from their stocks and place it on the market, thus relieving pressure on prices.

After the 1979-80 price rise, however, oil companies began to slowly draw from their oil inventories to the point that they are no longer viable against short-run shocks to the market. This tendency was encouraged by recent government policies in a number of countries that emphasized creating national oil reserves for use in times of emergency — programs that were well intentioned but that tended to keep surplus stocks from being used to help counteract market swings. More and more of the burden of regulating the market has thus fallen on OPEC. In fact, far from stabilizing the market, oil companies tend to exacerbate its cyclical movements: when a glut seems about to occur, they tend to shy away from buying crude oil, instead drawing down their inventories, in the process adding to the downward pressure on spot prices and accentuating the glut.

A new pricing arrangement has further weakened OPEC's position. In late 1985, Saudi Arabia announced that it had concluded "netback" agreements with the four Aramco partners — Exxon, Mobil, Chevron, and Texaco. These netback agreements link the price of crude oil to the prices of the products that can be refined from it. In other words, the price of crude oil is pegged to the prices that the various products derived from it will later fetch on the spot market. This reflects the fact that oil is, for now at least, a buyer's market: the seller, rather than the buyer, absorbs any adverse price movements that may occur between the time of the sale of crude oil and the time of the sale of its products. OPEC has thereby become even more vulnerable to price fluctuations. Accordingly, the 1985-86 price collapse was steeper than warranted: a mere 5 percent in the global oil supply resulted in a 60 percent drop in prices, all within a few months. [17]

In late 1986 Saudi Arabia coordinated a new OPEC agreement designed to fix the price of crude oil at $18 per barrel. OPEC reduced its output accordingly, and at first oil prices did rise, to the $18-$19 per barrel range. But by the end of January 1987 prices once again began to weaken because of continued excess oil supplies in the world market — evidence that certain OPEC members are persisting in overproduction and that oil companies are drawing down the inventories they built up when oil prices fell lower than $10 per barrel in 1986. Despite a firming of prices in late February, the market is still far from long-term stability. The spring of 1987 is likely to witness a showdown in the world oil market, as Saudi Arabia leads OPEC in direct confrontation with the international oil companies that are resisting signing binding long-term agreements at official OPEC prices.

Another important recent development has been the movement of OPEC producers into downstream operations. In the late 1970s, many

OPEC nations launched ambitious plans to make such a move into various activities, including the refining of oil, the production of petrochemicals, the transportation of oil and oil products, and in some cases the actual retailing of final products to consumers. This represented a change in OPEC's position in the oil market: traditionally, it had been a supplier of crude, while the rest of the industry was left to the oil companies. With their expanded activities, OPEC producers will have to become more responsible for the workings of the overall market, taking into account product prices and refinery margins when they set crude prices. In the short run, this has added one more complicating factor to OPEC's role as price regulator, and consequently will further accentuate oil market instability (although, as we shall see, it could in the long-run strengthen OPEC's position). Moreover, OPEC is likely at first to have trouble breaking into new markets and capturing any significant share of them.

All these smaller changes in the oil market have added up to a structural shift: the burden of regulating the world oil market has moved from the international oil companies to OPEC. Paradoxically, this has happened at a time when the increase in non-OPEC production and the decline in world oil consumption have made it difficult for OPEC to assume that burden, as the world oil market has slipped beyond its control. Consequently, we face in the short term a period of greater volatility and instability in the world oil market, with prices more likely to remain relatively low than to rise sharply. The long term, however, is another question.

A MORE DOMINANT OPEC

Paradoxically, the changes in the structure of the oil market that have weakened OPEC's market control may also, in the future, help bring OPEC back into a position of greater power. It is important to remember that OPEC's inability to control the oil market during the 1980s has been largely a result of the fall in world demand and the increase in non-OPEC production — factors that are beyond OPEC's control and are not permanent changes in the world oil equation. But oil demand and supply could shift in the early 1990s just as dramatically as they did in the early 1980s, thus putting OPEC in a position at least as strong as the one it occupied during the 1970s. To ignore these trends is both shortsighted and unwise.

One obvious factor to consider is world demand for energy. This demand is expected to grow at an annual rate of 2.9 percent between 1985 and 1990 and 1.68 percent from 1990 to 2000. Oil will continue to be the world's major energy source, with its share declining only marginally from 35 percent in 1985 to 32 percent in 2000. [18] Thus world demand for oil, which bottomed out and then began to grow in 1983, is predicted to increase at moderate rates in future.

This means that at best there will be only a modest amount of interfuel substitution. Although world natural gas use increased from 21.3 million barrels per day of oil equivalent (mmbdoe) in 1973 to 28.3 mmbdoe in 1984, [19] the share of world energy supplied by natural gas is likely to remain constant at about 18 percent [20] — despite the fact that gas is the one fossil fuel for which reserve estimates have risen significantly (34 percent in a decade). [21]

World coal use also increased between 1973 and 1984, from 33.4 mmbdoe to 43.8 mmbdoe. [22] Nevertheless, even though coal is by far the world's most abundant fossil fuel, and even though unprecedented investments have been made in mining, transportation, and burning coal, its share of world energy is predicted to remain constant, at around 27 percent. [23] Thus the two fuels often seen as prime candidates for oil substitutes are not expected to do better than hold their own in world energy.

Nuclear power is also unlikely to make a major contribution to the energy picture. Between 1973 and 1984, nuclear power use grew from 1 mmbdoe to 5.7 mmbdoe, [24] and during the next several years it will be the fastest growing energy source. Yet even if, as predicted, energy supplied by nuclear power doubles by 2000, it will still provide only 6 percent of world energy use. [25] Little additional capacity is likely to be added once plants now under construction are completed, since high capital costs, low prices for alternative fuels, and safety concerns — heightened by the Chernobyl accident — will discourage increased resort to nuclear power.

Hydroelectric and other renewable energy sources, such as wood fuels, wind, geothermal, biomass and solar power, supplied 28.7 mmbdoe in 1984 — up from 23.5 mmbdoe in 1973. [26] Yet in the absence of government support, these sources — except for hydropower and wood fuels — will play relatively insignificant roles in the world energy supply through 2000.

Oil will therefore remain the foremost source of world energy well into the twenty-first century, even as it becomes more scarce. Despite recent conservation measures, the rate of oil consumption worldwide still exceeds new discoveries — and is likely to continue to do so. Thus despite the current oil glut, it is a mistake to write off OPEC, for a number of reasons. For one thing, OPEC nations still control more than three-quarters of the world's proven oil reserves, [27] estimated at 707 billion barrels; [28] more than 56 percent is held by Middle East OPEC countries alone. [29] More importantly, OPEC's dominance of trade in world oil is likely to increase. Though many countries in the world produce oil, most of them consume a great deal of it. The Soviet Union and the United States, for instance, are the world's two largest oil producers; but of the 12.4 million barrels a day the Soviet Union produced in 1985, it consumed 9 million barrels itself, and although the United States produced 10.4 million barrels a day in 1984 it had to import over 5 million barrels a day to meet its needs. What indicates a nation's impact on the international economy, then, is not simply its crude oil production, but rather its trade in oil. In this connection, it is important to note that even though OPEC's net exports of oil fell from 29.6 million barrels a day in 1973 to 16 million barrels per day in 1984, OPEC still accounts for 70 to 75 percent of world oil trade. [30]

Also contributing to OPEC's long-term resurgence is the fact that non-OPEC production will have reached its peak by the end of the 1980s. Even if output does not then fall precipitously, there will be few if any non-OPEC countries or, for that matter, non-Persian Gulf OPEC countries that will have any export capability by the mid-1990s. Alaska's North Slope product, for example, is projected to begin falling in 1990. The exploration and development costs of oil fields in the North Sea are among the highest in the world: further declines in world oil prices could make a number of North Sea projects uneconomical, and in any case North Sea production is predicted to peak before 1990 and to decline steadily thereafter. Mexican production is not likely to peak before the mid-1990s, but given the country's rapidly growing domestic needs it will probably never export much more than the present 1.5 million barrels per day — in fact, Mexico could become a net importer by the year 2000. [31] Although there has been rising production in other non-

OPEC countries, which has contributed to the oil glut, the ultimate significance of these new sources is still dwarfed when considered in the context of OPEC's considerable reserves.

Furthermore, because non-OPEC oil reserves are considerably smaller than OPEC's, the current downward spiral in oil prices is causing non-OPEC oil to be depleted much more quickly than new oil discoveries are being made. Thus, ironically, falling oil prices are actually helping to conserve OPEC oil: the depletion of the world's most abundant reserves has slowed, while depletion of some of the scarcest and most strategically important reserves has accelerated. For example, at the 1984 extraction rate, the oil reserves of the United States, the Soviet Union, and Great Britain will last only 9 years, 14 years and 24 years respectively, while those of Saudi Arabia, Kuwait, and Iraq will last 99 years, 250 years, and 104 years. [32]

From all indications, then, world oil demand will continue to grow through the 1990s, and OPEC will be the major supplier of that incremental demand, making it the world's "supplier of last resort." In other words, oil importers will try to exhaust all other possible sources of oil before turning to OPEC, especially during periods when OPEC oil prices are on the rise. This will tend to amplify the cyclical movements in the demand for OPEC oil. The effects will be double-edged. In times of slowing economic growth and declining demand overall, there will be a more than proportional drop in demand for OPEC oil, since consumers will exhaust other sources of energy, including non-OPEC oil, before they turn to the OPEC supply. Likewise, as economic growth increases, raising demand for energy and oil, the demand for OPEC oil will grow more than proportionally, since the supply of non-OPEC oil is relatively fixed. Thus even though, as we have seen, the overall relationship between energy and GNP has been declining, the relationship of OPEC oil to oil-importing nations' GNPs will actually be far stronger than in the past. At crucial points, oil-importing nations will be much more vulnerable to OPEC than they were in the 1970s.

OPEC's expansion into downstream operations will be another factor in increasing its control over the world oil market. For example, as OPEC moves farther into the oil industry, adding to its own refining and transportation capacity, the oil companies will be less and less able to use their current dominance of refineries and transportation networks to counter OPEC's moves. And because OPEC will be a supplier of both crude oil and an assortment of refined petrochemical products, it will be able to price oil products so as to better achieve its overall pricing strategy. Of course, since not all OPEC members are moving into downstream operations, and since some are moving there faster than others, there will most likely be a certain amount of friction between those that remain primarily exporters of crude and those that increase their vertical integration within the world oil market.

In the long run, in fact, not all OPEC nations will fare well. Rather, the market will be dominated by a few key exporters: Iran, Iraq, Kuwait, Libya, Saudi Arabia, and the United Arab Emirates, which together have estimated reserves of 405 billion barrels — 56 percent of the world's proven oil reserves. [33] Several other OPEC countries with more limited reserves are already producing at nearly maximum capacity in an effort to generate the funds they need for internal development. In contrast, Persian Gulf countries with the largest reserves are restricting production in order to support OPEC prices. The impact of these current patterns will be strongly felt by the turn of the century, when OPEC exporters outside the Persian Gulf, such as Indonesia, Nigeria, Algeria, Ecuador, and Gabon, whose estimated reserves are one-fifth those of the Persian Gulf countries, will face resource constraints due either to declining oil production capabilities or to increasing domestic demand. As a result, they will export only a inconsequentially small amount of oil — or may be out of the oil export business altogether. The key Persian Gulf oil exporters mentioned above will then dominate the world oil market. In fact, recent studies conclude that, given current levels of demand and expected additional discoveries of oil, these states can continue to supply oil to the world into the second half of the twenty-first century. [34]

Finally, when thinking about the world oil market, it is important to remember that the current glut tends to mask OPEC's real power. OPEC still dominates the international oil market: as recently as 1984, its share of net world exports was 88 percent. [35] All available evidence indicates that this share will increase over time. Thus if any independence from OPEC — specifically, from Middle East oil producers — has developed in the 1980s, it has served only to provide a false sense of security: to the extent that Western industrialized nations have failed to develop alternative energy sources and have rapidly depleted their strategically secure reserves, they have only increased their long-term dependence on OPEC oil. The lower OPEC's current share of the world market, the greater its share will be at the end of the century, when many other countries will be running out of oil. OPEC may then become a more powerful organization — smaller, more geographically concentrated in the Middle East, and more cohesive, being Islamic and predominantly Arab. At the same time, the world's reserves will be more limited than at any time in recent history.

In such a situation, America's position would be even weaker than it was during the 1970s, when OPEC was considered to be at the peak of its power. Between 1985 and 2000, U.S. demand for oil will grow by more than 1 percent per year, rising by 3 million barrels per day over that period. On the other hand, because of drastically reduced drilling, U.S. crude production will fall by 2.5 percent per year between 1984 and 2000, resulting in a decline of 3 million barrels per day. Natural gas output will also fall. [36] Consequently, net oil imports will rise from 5 million barrels per day in 1985 to nearly 12 million barrels per day in 2000. [37] Just as OPEC's control is strongest, then, the United States will become more dependent on imported oil.

FUTURE ENERGY PROSPECTS

What we are now witnessing is the start of a transition to a more concentrated, more cohesive, and more powerful OPEC. Certainly such a regime will have costs to the United States and other nations, as indicated above. But the real problem is not high oil prices or (if one regards the situation from an OPEC perspective) low oil prices; it is, rather, the oil market's overall instability. That instability has been severe under the current oil regime, and it could become even more so in the transition period ahead, causing dramatic swings in prices that, in the final analysis, will benefit neither producers nor consumers.

The consequences of oil market instability are numerous. For one thing, it creates serious international adjustment problems — disequilibriums in capital and trade flows that cannot be managed without government intervention and that can disrupt both national and world economic growth. It can also cause shock effects, which may be either inflationary or deflationary. This has caused some economists to worry about the possibility of a new deflationary era analogous to the 1930s.

Furthermore, oil market instability distorts investment, both in energy development and in industry in general. On the one hand, investments in oil production that are made during periods of skyrocketing prices have to be given up as unprofitable when prices fall. On the other hand, dramatic oil price drops tend to postpone those investment decisions needed to secure energy supplies in the future.

Thus America's current complacency over the weakening of OPEC is causing it to neglect what it needs to do to manage its energy needs in the 1990s. This is especially serious because the current regime of low oil prices is setting the stage for declining oil supplies in the future. First, as suggested above, it has led to a significant decline in world oil industry investment, since new exploration and field development is too expensive to be attractive. If prices remain around current levels, or sink even further, the funds oil companies have for exploration will be billions of dollars a year lower than in earlier years. As a result, companies will be able to undertake fewer projects and production will suffer. According to an American Petroleum Institute survey, if prices remain roughly at current levels, U.S. expenditures on oil exploration and production could drop from $75 billion in 1985 to $32.1 billion in 1991 — a cut of more than one-half. Over the same period, the number of wells drilled could decrease by nearly 60 percent, from 75,000 to 30,000; total U.S. oil production could fall by 2.7 million barrels per day; and there could be a loss of some 300,000 jobs — almost 20 percent of all U.S. petroleum jobs. [38]

Furthermore, low oil prices make high-cost oil production, especially offshore oil and enhanced extraction processes, unprofitable. It is difficult to estimate how much world production will become uneconomical if prices remain at or below current levels, since, in the short run, owners of high-cost wells may continue to keep them operating in the hope that prices will recover. Even so, U.S. production in 1986 was more than 120,000 barrels per day lower than in 1985, as companies began shutting down high-cost oil wells and thousands of stripper wells (those producing fewer than 10 barrels per day). Once shut in, many of these wells may never be reopened, even when prices do rise. [39]

Current low oil prices also make certain deposits uneconomical to develop. This would cause already proven and recoverable reserves to be revised downward. Thus U.S. proven reserves — 28.4 billion barrels as of 1985 — are likely to fall over the next several years, just as U.S. crude oil reserves fell rapidly during the early 1970s. America's free-market ideology exacerbates this problem. Because U.S. laws encourage debt rather than equity, it is easier for U.S. oil companies to add to their reserve stocks through corporate takeovers than to use their resources to explore for new deposits. Consequently, the 1980s have seen a wave of oil company acquisitions that has reduced the number of independents by more than 25 percent.

Not only will the recent collapse of oil prices most likely reduce the future availability of oil, it will also slow down if not halt the fuel diversification process, since oil has once more become attractive relative to other energy sources. Accordingly, there have been severe declines in investment in coal and natural gas. Renewable and alternative energy industries, such as solar, biomass, and synthetic fuels, have suffered even more drastically. The Synfuel Corporation established under the Carter Administration has been disbanded — a casualty of the Reagan White House's "hands-off" approach. More importantly, falling oil prices reduce or even eliminate major conservation efforts. With no contingency plans to tax the gains that consumers are realizing from falling oil prices, current policies can only foster America's traditional energy-guzzling mentality.

If a future energy crisis is to be avoided, steps will have to be taken to improve our ability to manage tighter oil supplies in the 1990s. Unfortunately, current U.S. policy, more than that of any other nation, is encouraging the developments that will bring on the next energy crisis. Tax incentives for conservation and solar energy have been dropped. The oil industry has been left to the vagaries of the free market. And not only is less and less investment going toward exploring and developing new reserves, but those reserves that are being tapped are being depleted too quickly, as oil prices have been allowed to fall dramatically. A more logical policy would be to conserve domestic oil reserves while consuming relatively inexpensive foreign oil. This could be combined with an oil tax, which would take effect when oil prices fell below a certain predetermined level — $20 per barrel, for example. Such a consumption tax would counter-act any benefits to consumers from falling oil prices, thus encouraging conservation and discouraging the return to wasteful energy habits. The resulting tax revenue could be directed toward research and development of alternative and renewable energy sources, which in recent years have been virtually abandoned by both the private and public sectors.

The United States needs an overall national energy policy. Maintaining a steady energy supply cannot be left to the private sector alone, since the time frame required to take the necessary actions is beyond the private sector's quarter-to-quarter profit-and-loss planning mentality. What is needed is a long-range, three-pronged national energy plan aimed at adding to the U.S. energy supply, increasing energy diversification, and maximizing energy efficiency.

Unilateral U.S. actions will not be enough, however, to ensure a stable world oil regime. Development of new energy sources needs to increase throughout the world. Unfortunately, the fall in oil prices has wreaked havoc with the infant energy industries of many Third World countries. In Brazil, for example, imported oil has once again become as cheap as domestically produced energy, which has made offshore oil exploration prohibitively costly and has halted investment in the country's fuel alcohol program. The United States could use its influence in international agencies, such as the World Bank, to counteract these negative effects of the oil price slump and to encourage the development of a broader range of energy sources. America could also work to set up a compensating fund, similar to the existing Compensatory Financing Facility, which helps countries cover export shortfalls beyond their control, in order to assist oil-producing countries to make up for severe declines in revenues. This sort of scheme, though much more limited than the comprehensive exporter-consumer arrangement that is needed, would be a step in the right direction — especially considering the effects oil instability has on international banking and the Third World debt crisis.

Yet even if progress is made in energy diversification and efficiency and in helping oil-producing nations cope with revenue drops, there will be limits to what can be accomplished in the next few years. Eventually there must be a dialogue between the major oil-producing and oil-consuming countries, probably within existing multinational institutions such as OPEC and the OECD (Organization of Economic Cooperation and Development — the association of Western industrialized nations). Such a dialogue would require all involved parties to make concessions. Consumers would have to agree to pay oil prices higher than those dictated by the market during times of surplus;

producers would have to accept prices lower than those dictated by the market during times of shortage; and oil companies would have to refrain from abusing the power they gain from their involvement in the spot market and their role as major oil traders.

Realistically, this kind of willingness to compromise does not seem forthcoming. The differences among the various parties would appear to make a comprehensive oil dialogue difficult — even one limited to OPEC and the OECD. But given the current structure of the oil market and the underlying trends that will affect its movements in the future, it is only a matter of time before producers and consumers realize that, because price instability is the essence of the energy crisis, cooperation is in the long run more beneficial than confrontation. Thus a long-term agreement on oil pricing and output is in everyone's best interest.

For example, because the oil-producing nations are still, in essence, less developed countries, they desperately need the steady income that stable oil prices would ensure them. In recent years, they have committed huge sums of money to long-term development programs. Many or most of these investments are either just beginning to generate a positive rate of return or have not done so at all. With billions of dollars already invested, and with much greater resources needed in the future if these investments are to bear fruit, it is imperative that oil-producing countries be able to count on a steady stream of oil revenue so that they can continue to finance long-term development. This would eventually enable them to diversify their economies, in anticipation of the day their oil reserves run out. Furthermore, a general oil-price agreement would reduce the threat of cutthroat competition from non-OPEC producers, which could result in a free-for-all world oil market.

The oil-consuming countries would also benefit from oil price stability. The price fluctuations of recent years have adversely affected the world economy, contributing to the world inflation of the 1970s and the slowdown in world economic growth and development in the 1980s. Overall, the ups and downs of the world business cycle seem to have been accentuated by oil price swings, and to have become much less responsive to the traditional barrage of discretionary economic policies governments can resort to. A steady supply of oil at stable prices would help counteract these negative trends.

But we must not lose sight of the global energy picture, of which oil is only one part. Worldwide fossil reserves are limited — that is the stark reality. The presence or absence of an international agreement on oil prices could not alter the fact that proven reserves are dwindling. It could, however, carry us beyond the year 2000, providing the medium-term stability necessary for us to develop alternative, more secure energy sources. Without such an agreement, which would bridge the limited fossil fuel supplies of the present with the alternative supplies of the future, the world might find itself facing a very cold and dark twenty-first century.

Notes

1   Dermot Gately, "Lessons from the 1986 Oil Price Collapse," Brookings Papers on Economic Activity (Washington, DC: 1986), pp. 238-239.
2   Christopher Flavin, World Oil; "Coping with the Dangers of Success," Worldwatch Paper 66 (Washington, DC: July 1985), pp. 6-7.
3   Ibid., pp. 42-43.
4   International Energy Agency, Energy Policies and Programs of IEA Countries, 1984 Review.
5   BP Statistical Review of World Energy (London: June 1986).
6   Flavin (fn. 2), p. 14.
7   Gately (fn. 1), p. 239
8   Michael G. Renner, "Stabilizing the World Oil Market," unpublished monograph, New York, January 1987, p. 10.
9   BP (fn. 5).
10 Flavin (fn. 2), p. 15.
11 Gately (fn. 1), pp. 241-242.
12 Fereidun Fesharaki, "International Oil Market: The Future Relations Between Producers and Consumers," unpublished manuscript for inclusion in a book (Honolulu, HI: The East-West Center, June 1984), pp. 10-12.
13 Youssef Ibrahim and Allanna Sullivan, "Strength in Oil Prices Isn't Likely to Last," Wall Street Journal, April 23, 1985.
14 The Economist, October 20-26, 1984, p. 69, and Wall Street Journal, October 30, 1984.
15 Wall Street Journal, June 28, 1985.
16 Renner (fn. 8), p. 8.
17 Johangir Amuzegar, "Cheap Oil: Whose Trojan Horse?" OPEC Bulletin, July-August 1986, p. 15.
18 Conoco, World Energy Outlook Through 2000 (Wilmington, DE: September 1986).
19 BP (fn. 5).
20 Conoco (fn. 18).

21   Flavin (fn. 2), p. 37.
22   BP fn. 5).
23   Flavin (fn. 2), pp. 34-35.
24   BP fn. 5).
25   Flavin (fn. 2), p. 41
26   BP fn. 5).
27   Conoco (fn. 18).
28   BP(fn. 5).
29   United States Geological Survey, 1983.
30   IMF, World Economic Outlook, 1985.
31   Flavin (fn. 2), p. 29
32   BP (fn. 5).
33   Ibid.
34   Fesharaki (fn. 12), p. 19. See also R. Nehring, Giant Oilfields and World Oil Resources (Santa Monica, CA: Rand Corporation, June 1978), pp. V-X, and F. Fesharaki and S. Hoffman, "Determinants of OPEC Oil Supplies: Physical, Economic and Political Factors," paper presented to the International Association of Energy Economists, November 17-19, 1983.
35   IMF, World Economic Outlook, 1984.
36   Conoco (fn. 18).
37   American Petroleum Institute, Two Energy Futures: National Choices Today for the 1990s, July 1986, p. 28.
38   Ibid., pp. 11-12.
39   Ibid., p.11

VII

INTERNATIONAL MONETARY REFORM: IS THE CURRENT SYSTEM WORKING?

Since the collapse of Bretton Woods in 1971, the major currencies in the world, the U.S. dollar, the Japanese yen, the German mark, and the British pound have all been allowed to float against one another in a relatively free market. For the first ten years the system worked reasonably well, but during the eighties exchange rates have been extremely unstable. In particular, the U.S. dollar increased dramatically in value in the early eighties only to lose roughly 40% of its value between 1985 and 1988. One of the most disturbing aspects of the rise of the dollar was that it continued to rise in the early eighties despite mounting trade deficits in the U.S. and despite a general agreement among economists, government officials and financiers that the dollar was overvalued.

The instability in exchange rates during the eighties has led to closer scrutiny of the current system. Many economists call for an overhaul of the world's monetary system and a return to a system which more closely resembles the Bretton Woods arrangement. Others argue that the instability of the eighties cannot be blamed on the world's monetary system, but rather is the result of inconsistent and uncoordinated monetary policies among the world's major economies as well as the decline in the U.S. as an economic power.

The articles below present the major sides of the debate. The first article, "The case for flexible exchange rates," is a classic statement of the virtues of a laissez-faire approach to international monetary policy. Although the article is now over thirty years old, Friedman's arguments for a flexible exchange rate system are still relevant today. Friedman argues that attempting to fix exchange rates will in fact lead to more instability than a floating-rate system because financiers will speculate on differences between the equilibrium exchange rate and the official exchange rate supported by the government. Friedman contends that this type of speculation is destabilizing and that ultimately the market will thwart any attempt by governments to set an unrealistic exchange rate. In contrast, under a free market approach to international exchange, speculation can only lead to more stability since speculators who bet incorrectly on the future direction of an exchange rate will lose.

After presenting a brief description of different types of monetary systems employed over the centuries, Mundell focuses on our current dilemma. He argues, in contrast to Friedman's position, that the floating rate system has lead to a great deal of instability, particularly with respect to the balance of payments accounts. Since the decline of Bretton Woods, this instability has become worse and worse. Mundell proposes the creation of a fixed rate system coupled to some market basket of major currencies, whose value in turn would be tied to the value of gold.

Fred Bergsten proposes a solution somewhere between that of Friedman and Mundell (though closer to Mundell). He believes that a system of target zones similar to the European Monetary system would provide the appropriate amount of stability while allowing market forces to work in a limited way. Under a system of target zones, currencies are allowed to fluctuate within a certain range (e.g., 5 or 10% above and below a certain set exchange rate); once the exchange rates move outside of this range the governments and their central banks are required to intervene just as they would under a fixed rate system. Bergsten argues that this type of system would have enough flexibility yet would give countries some discipline. Under the current system, according to Bergsten, countries do not have sufficient incentive to coordinate their macroeconomic policies with each other.

In the final article, Frenkel argues that given the instability inherent in the world's economic system during the past 20 years, any exchange rate system would have had difficulty. He concludes that until this underlying instability subsides, one can not expect much from any exchange rate regime.

16

The Case for Flexible Exchange Rates*

Milton Friedman

The Western nations seem committed to a system of international payments based on exchange rates between their national currencies fixed by governments and maintained rigid except for occasional changes to new levels. This system is embodied in the statutes of the International Monetary Fund, which provides for changes in exchange rates of less than 10 per cent by individual governments without approval of the Fund and for larger changes only with approval; it is implicit in the European Payments Union; and it is taken for granted in almost all discussions of international economic policy.

Whatever may have been the merits of this system for another day, it is ill suited to current economic and political conditions. These conditions make a system of flexible or floating exchange rates — exchange rates freely determined in an open market primarily by private dealings and, like other market prices, varying from day to day — absolutely essential for the fulfillment of our basic economic objective: the achievement and maintenance of a free and prosperous world community engaging in unrestricted multilateral trade. There is scarcely a facet of international economic policy for which the implicit acceptance of a system of rigid exchange rates does not create serious and unnecessary difficulties. Promotion of rearmament, liberalization of trade, avoidance of allocations and other direct controls both internal and external, harmonization of internal monetary and fiscal policies —all these problems take on a different cast and become far easier to solve in a world of flexible exchange rates and its corollary, free convertibility of currencies. The sooner a system of flexible exchange rates is established, the sooner unrestricted multilateral trade will become a real possibility. And it will become one without in any way interfering with the pursuit by each nation of domestic economic stability according to its own lights.[1]

Before proceeding to defend this thesis in detail, I should perhaps emphasize two points to avoid misunderstanding. First, advocacy of flexible exchange rates is *not* equivalent to advocacy of unstable exchange rates. The ultimate objective is a world in which exchange rates, while *free* to vary, are in fact highly stable. Instability of exchange rates is a symptom of instability in the underlying economic structure. Elimination of this symptom by administrative freezing of exchange rates cures none of the underlying difficulties and only makes adjustment to them more painful. Second, by unrestricted multilateral trade, I shall mean a system in which there are no direct quantitative controls over imports or exports, in which any tariffs or export bounties are reasonably stable and nondiscriminatory and are not subject to manipulation to affect the balance of payments, and in which a substantial fraction of international trade is in private (nongovernmental) hands. Though admittedly vague and subject to considerable ambiguity, this definition will do for our purposes. I shall take for granted without detailed examination that unrestricted multilateral trade in this sense [2] is a desirable objective of economic policy. [3] However, many of the arguments for flexible exchange rates remain valid even if this premise is not accepted.

ALTERNATIVE METHODS OF ADJUSTING TO CHANGES AFFECTING INTERNATIONAL PAYMENTS

Changes affecting the international trade and the balance of payments of various countries are always occurring. Some are in the "real" conditions determining international trade, such as the weather, technical conditions of production-consumer tastes, and the like. Some are in monetary conditions, such as divergent degrees of inflation or deflation in various countries.

These changes affect some commodities more than others and so tend to produce changes in the structure of relative prices — for example, rearmament by the United States impinges particularly on selected raw materials and tends to raise their prices relatively to other prices. Such effects on the relative price structure are likely to be much the same whether exchange rates are rigid or flexible and to raise much the same problem of adjustment in either case and so will receive little attention in what follows.

But, over and above these effects on particular commodities and prices, the changes in question affect each country's balance of payments, taken as a whole. Holders of foreign currencies want to exchange them for the currency of a particular country in order to purchase commodities produced in that country, or to purchase securities or other capital assets in that country, or to pay interest on or repay debts to that country, or to make gifts to citizens of that country, or simply to hold for one of these uses or for resale. The amount of currency of a particular country that is demanded per unit of time for each of these purposes will, of course, depend in the first instance on the exchange rate — the number of units of a foreign currency that must be paid to acquire one unit of the domestic currency. Other things the same, the more expensive a given currency, that is, the higher the exchange rate, the less of that currency will in general be demanded for each of these purposes. Similarly, holders of the currency of the country in question want to exchange that currency for foreign currencies for the corresponding purposes; and, again, the amount they want to exchange depends, in the first instance, on the price which they can get. The changes continuously taking place in the conditions of international trade alter the "other things" and so the desirability of using the currencies of various countries for each of the purposes listed. The aggregate effect is at one time to increase, at another to decrease, the amount of a country's currency demanded at any given rate of exchange relative to the amount offered for sale at that rate. Of course, after the event, the amount of a particular currency purchased must equal the amount sold — this is a question simply of double-entry bookkeeping. But, in advance, the amount people want to buy need not equal the amount people want to sell. The *ex post* equality involves a reconciliation of these divergent desires, either through changes in the desires themselves or through their frustration.

There is no way of avoiding this reconciliation; inconsistent desires cannot simultaneously be satisfied. The crucial question of policy is the mechanism whereby this reconciliation is brought about. Suppose the aggregate effect of changes in the conditions affecting international payments has been to increase the amount of a country's currency people want to buy with foreign currency relative to the amount other people want to sell for that foreign currency at the pre-existing exchange rate — to create an incipient surplus in the balance of payments. How can these inconsistent desires be reconciled? (1) The country's currency may be bid up, or put up, in price. This increase in the exchange rate will tend to make the currency less desirable relative to the currency of other countries and so eliminate the excess demand at the pre-existing rate. [4] (2) Prices within the country may rise, thus making its goods less desirable relative to goods in other countries; or incomes within the country may rise, thus increasing the demand for foreign currencies. (3) Direct controls over transactions involving foreign exchange may prevent holders of foreign balances from acquiring as much domestic exchange as they would otherwise like to; for example, they may be prevented from buying domestic goods by the inability to get a required export license. (4) The excess amount of domestic currency desired may be provided out of monetary reserves, the foreign currency acquired being added to reserves of foreign currencies. The monetary authorities (or exchange equalization fund or the like) may step in with a "desire" to buy or sell the difference between the amounts demanded and supplied by others.

Each of these four methods has its obvious counterpart if the effect of the changes is to create an incipient deficit. Aside from purely frictional frustrations of desires (the inability of a buyer to find a seller because of imperfections of the market), these are fundamentally the only four ways in which an *ex ante* divergence between the amount of a country's currency demanded and the amount supplied can be converted into the *ex post* equality that necessarily prevails. Let us consider each in turn.

CHANGES IN EXCHANGE RATES

Two different mechanisms whereby exchange-rate changes may be used to maintain equilibrium in the balance of payments must be sharply distinguished: (1) flexible exchange rates as defined above and (2) official changes in temporarily rigid rates.

1. *Flexible exchange rates.* — Under flexible exchange rates freely determined in open markets, the first impact of any tendency toward a surplus or deficit in the balance of payments is on the exchange rate. If a country has an incipient surplus of receipts over payments — an excess demand for its currency — the exchange rate will tend to rise. If it has an incipient deficit, the exchange rate will tend to fall. If the conditions responsible for the rise or the fall in the exchange rate are generally

regarded as temporary, actual or potential holders of the country's currency will tend to change their holdings in such a way as to moderate the movement in the exchange rate. If a rise in the exchange rate, for example, is expected to be temporary, there is an incentive for holders of the country's currency to sell some of their holdings for foreign currency in order to buy the currency back later on at a lower price. By doing so, they provide the additional domestic currency to meet part of the excess demand responsible for the initial rise in the exchange rate; that is, they absorb some of what would have been surplus receipts of foreign currency at the former exchange rate. Conversely, if a decline is expected to be temporary, there is an incentive to buy domestic currency for resale at a higher price. Such purchases of domestic currency provide the foreign currency to meet some of what would have been a deficit of foreign currency at the former exchange rate. In this way, such "speculative" transactions in effect provide the country with reserves to absorb temporary surpluses or to meet temporary deficits. On the other hand, if the change in the exchange rate is generally regarded as produced by fundamental factors that are likely to be permanent, the incentives are the reverse of those listed above, and speculative transactions will speed up the rise or decline in the exchange rate and thus hasten its approach to its final position.

This final position depends on the effect that changes in exchange rates have on the demand for and supply of a country's currency, not to hold as balances, but for other purposes. A rise in the exchange rate produced by a tendency toward a surplus makes foreign goods cheaper in terms of domestic currency, even though their prices are unchanged in terms of their own currency, and domestic goods more expensive in terms of foreign currency, even though their prices are unchanged in terms of domestic currency. This tends to increase imports, reduce exports, and so offset the incipient surplus. Conversely, a decline in the exchange rate produced by a tendency toward a deficit makes imports more expensive to home consumers, and exports less expensive to foreigners, and so tends to offset the incipient deficit.

Because money imparts general purchasing power and is used for such a wide variety of purposes abroad as well as at home, the demand for and supply of any one country's currency is widely spread and comes from many sources. In consequence, broad, active, and nearly perfect markets have developed in foreign exchange whenever they have been permitted — and usually even when they have not been. The exchange rate is therefore potentially an extremely sensitive price. Changes in it occur rapidly, automatically, and continuously and so tend to produce corrective movements before tensions can accumulate and a crisis develop. For example, if Germany had had a flexible exchange rate in 1950, the crisis in the fall of that year would never have followed the course it did. The exchange rate would have been affected not later than July and would have started to produce corrective adaptations at once. The whole affair would never have assumed large proportions and would have shown up as a relatively minor ripple in exchange rates. As it was, with a rigid exchange rate, the warning of impending trouble was indirect and delayed, and the government took no action until three months later, by which time the disequilibrium had grown to crisis dimensions, requiring drastic action at home, international consultation, and help from abroad.

The recurrent foreign-exchange crises of the United Kingdom in the postwar period are perhaps an even more dramatic example of the kind of crises that could not develop under a system of flexible exchange rates. In each case no significant corrective action was taken until large disequilibriums and been allowed to cumulate, and then the action had to be drastic. The rigidities and discontinuities introduced by substituting administrative action for automatic market forces have seldom been demonstrated so clearly or more impressively.

2. *Official changes in exchange rates.* — These examples suggest the sharp difference between flexible exchange rates and exchange rates held temporarily rigid but subject to change by government action to meet substantial difficulties. While these exchange-rate changes have the same kind of effect on commodity trade and the like as those produced automatically under a system of flexible exchange rates, they have very different effects on speculative transactions. Partly for this reason, partly because of their innate discontinuity, each exchange-rate change tends to become the occasion for a crisis. There is no mechanism for producing changes in exchange rates of the required magnitude or for correcting mistakes, and some other mechanism must be used to maintain equilibrium during the period between exchange-rate changes — either internal price or income changes, direct controls, or monetary reserves.

Even though an exchange-rate change would not otherwise be the occasion for a crisis, speculative movements are highly likely to convert it into one, for this system practically insures a maximum of destabilizing speculation. Because the exchange rate is changed infrequently and only to meet substantial difficulties, a change tends to come well after the onset of difficulty, to be postponed as long as possible, and to be made only after substantial pressure on the exchange rate has accumulated. In consequence, there is seldom any doubt about the direction in which an exchange rate will be changed, if it is changed. In the interim between the suspicion of a possible change in the rate and the actual change, there is every incentive to sell the country's currency if devaluation is expected (to export "capital" from the country) or to buy it if an appreciation is expected (to bring in "capital"); either can be done without an exchange loss and will mean an exchange gain when and if the rate is changed. This is in sharp contrast with the situation under flexible exchange rates when the decline in the exchange rate takes place along with, and as a consequence of, the sales of a currency and so discourages or penalizes sales, and conversely for purchases. With rigid rates, if the exchange rate is not changed, the only cost to the speculators is a possible loss of interest earnings form an interest-rate differential. It is no answer to this argument to say that capital flows can be restricted by direct controls, since our ultimate objective in using this method is precisely to avoid such restrictions.

In short, the system of occasional changes in temporarily rigid exchange rates seems to me the worst of two worlds: it provides neither the stability of expectations that a genuinely rigid and stable exchange rate could provide in a world of unrestricted trade and willingness and the ability to adjust the internal price structure to external conditions nor the continuous sensitivity of a flexible exchange rate.

CHANGES IN INTERNAL PRICES OR INCOME

In principle, changes in internal prices could produce the same effects on trade as changes in the exchange rate. For example, a decline of 10 per cent in every internal price in Germany (including wages, rents, etc.) with an unchanged dollar price of the mark would clearly have identically the same effects on the relative costs of domestic and foreign goods as a decline of 10 per cent in the dollar price of the mark, with all internal prices unchanged. Similarly, such price changes could have the same effects on speculative transactions. If expected to be temporary, a decline in prices would stimulate speculative purchases of goods to avoid future higher prices, thus moderating the price movement.

If internal prices were as flexible as exchange rates, it would make little economic difference whether adjustments were brought about by changes in exchange rates or by equivalent changes in internal prices. But this condition is clearly not fulfilled. The exchange rate is potentially flexible in the absence of administrative action to freeze it. At least in the modern world, internal prices are highly inflexible. They are more flexible upward than downward, but even on the upswing all prices are not equally flexible. The inflexibility of prices, or different degrees of flexibility, means a distortion of adjustments in response to changes in external conditions. The adjustment takes the form primarily of price changes in some sectors, primarily of output changes in others.

Wage rates tend to be among the less flexible prices. In consequence, an incipient deficit that is countered by a policy of permitting or forcing prices to decline is likely to produce unemployment rather than, or in addition to, wage decreases. The consequent decline in real income reduces the domestic demand for foreign goods and thus the demand for foreign currency with which to purchase these goods. In this way, it offsets the incipient deficit. But this is clearly a highly inefficient method of adjusting to external changes. If the external changes are deep-seated and persistent, the unemployment produces steady downward pressure on prices and wages, and the adjustment will not have been completed until the deflation has run its sorry course.

Despite these difficulties, the use of changes in internal prices might not be undesirable if they were called for only rarely and only as a result of changes in the real underlying conditions of trade. Such changes in underlying conditions are likely in any event to require considerable changes in relative prices of particular goods and services and only changes of a much smaller order of magnitude in the general level of internal prices. But neither condition is likely to be satisfied in the modern world. Adjustments are required continuously, and many are called for by essentially monetary phenomena, which, if promptly offset by a movement in the exchange-rate, would require no change in the actual allocation of resources.

Changes in interest rates are perhaps best classified under this heading of changes in internal prices. Interest-rate changes have in the past played a particularly important role in adjustment to external changes, partly because they have been susceptible to direct influence by the monetary authorities, and partly because, under a gold standard, the initial impact of a tendency toward a deficit or surplus was a loss or gain of gold and a consequent tightening or ease in the money market. The rise in the interest rate produced in this way by an incipient deficit increased the demand for the currency for capital purposes and so offset part or all of the deficit. This reduced the rate at which the deficit had to be met by a decline in internal prices, which was itself set in motion by the loss of gold and associated decrease in the stock of money responsible for the rise in interest rates. Conversely, an incipient surplus increased the stock of gold and eased the money market. The resulting decline in the interest rate reduced the demand for the currency for capital purposes and so offset part of all of the surplus, reducing the rate at which the surplus had to be met by the rise in internal prices set in motion by the gain of gold and associated rise in the stock of money.

These interest-induced capital movements are a desirable part of a system relying primarily on changes in internal prices, since they tend to smooth out the adjustment process. They cannot, however, be relied on alone, since they come into operation only incidentally to the adjustment of internal prices.

Primary reliance on changes in internal prices and incomes was tolerable in the nineteenth century partly because the key countries of the Western world placed much heavier emphasis on freedom from government interference at home and unrestricted multilateral trade abroad than on domestic stability; thus they were willing to allow domestic economic policy to be dominated by the requirements of fixed exchange rates and free convertibility of currencies. But, equally important, this very emphasis gave holders of balances confidence in the maintenance of the system and so make them willing to let small differences in interest rates determine the currency in which they held their balances. Furthermore, the emphasis on freedom from government interference at home gave less scope to internal monetary management and so meant that most changes affecting international trade reflected real changes in underlying conditions, or else monetary changes, such as gold discoveries, more or less common to the major nations. Modern conditions, with the widespread emphasis on full employment at home and the extensive intervention of government into economic affairs, are clearly very different and much less favorable to this method of adjustment.

DIRECT CONTROLS

In principle, direct controls on imports, exports, and capital movements could bring about the same effects on trade and the balance of payments as changes in exchange rates or in internal prices and incomes. The final adjustment will, after all, involve a change in the composition of imports and exports, along with specifiable capital transactions. If these could be predicted in advance, and if it were technically possible to control selectively each category of imports, exports, and capital transactions, direct controls could be used to produce the required adjustment.

It is clear, however, that the changes in imports and exports and the required capital transactions cannot be predicted; the fact that each new foreign-exchange crisis in a country like Britain is officially regarded as a bolt from the blue is ample evidence for this proposition. Even if they could be predicted, direct control of imports, exports, and capital transactions by techniques other than the price system [5] necessarily means extending such control to many internal matters and interfering with the efficiency of the distribution and production of goods — some means must be found for rationing imports that are being held down in amount or disposing of increased imports and for allocating reduced exports or getting increased exports.

Aside from the many unfortunate results of such a process which are by now abundantly clear, it has a perverse effect on the foreign-payments problem itself, particularly when direct controls are used, as they have been primarily, to counter an actual or incipient deficit. The apparent deficit that has to be closed by direct controls is larger than the deficit that would emerge at the same exchange rate without the direct control and, indeed, might be eliminated entirely or converted into a surplus if the direct controls on imports and exports and their inevitable domestic accompaniments were removed. The mere existence of the direct controls makes the currency less desirable for many purposes because of the limitations it places on what holders of the currency may do with it, and this is likely to reduce the demand for the currency more than it would be reduced by the fluctuations in exchange rates or other adaptive mechanisms substituted for the direct controls. In addition, permitted imports are generally distributed at prices lower than those that would clear the market and so are used wastefully and in the wrong places, increasing apparent import "requirements"; similarly, the composition of imports is determined by administrative decisions that tend to have the same effect. Both of these are particularly important in hindering exports, because export industries are not likely to get so large a fraction of the imports as they would bid away in a free market, even if the government supposedly favors export industries, and cannot make their influence fully felt in determining the composition of imports; and the direct controls have a tendency to make the incentive to export lower than it would otherwise be. [6]

The considerations mentioned in the preceding paragraph may help to reconcile — and, indeed, their elaboration was stimulated by my own need to reconcile — the impression of casual visitors to England, and the conclusions of some careful students of the subject, that the pound is currently (1952) undervalued in purchasing power terms with the recurrent pressures on the pound and the restrictive measures that seem to be required to maintain the pound at its present rate. They show that there is no necessary inconsistency between the following two assertions: (1) the market value of the pound would be higher than $2.80 if all exchange restrictions and associated controls were removed and the exchange rate were allowed to be determined by primarily private dealings in a free market; (2) given the retention of an official exchange rate and of the existing *system* of exchange restrictions and associated internal controls, an *easing* of restrictions would produce pressure on the exchange rate and require a rate lower than $2.80 to keep exchange reserves from being depleted. Both statements may not, in fact, be correct; but there is no such obvious contradiction between them as there appears to be at first sight.

Finally, whatever the desirability of direct controls, there are political and administrative limits to the extent to which it is possible to impose and enforce such controls. These limits are narrower in some countries than in others, but they are present in all. Given sufficient incentive to do so, ways will be found to evade or avoid the controls. A race develops between officials seeking to plug legal loopholes and to discover and punish illegal evasions of the controls and the ever-numerous individuals whose inventive talents are directed toward discovering or opening up new loopholes by the opportunities for large returns or whose respect for law and fear of punishment are overcome by the same opportunities. And the race is by no means always to the officials, even when they are honest and able. In particular, it has proved extremely difficult in all countries to prevent capital movements by direct controls.

USE OF MONETARY RESERVES

Given adequate reserves, tendencies toward a surplus or a deficit can be allowed to produce an actual surplus or deficit in transactions other than those of the monetary authority (or exchange equalization fund, or whatever the name may be) without a change in exchange rates, internal prices or incomes, or direct controls, the additional domestic or foreign currency demanded being supplied by the monetary authority. This device is feasible and not undesirable for movements that are small and temporary, though, if it is clear that the movements are small and temporary, it is largely unnecessary, since, with flexible exchange rates, private speculative transactions will provide the additional domestic or foreign currency demanded with only minor movements in exchange rates.

The exclusive use of reserves is much less desirable, if possible at all, for movements of large magnitude and long duration. If the problem is a deficit, the ability of the monetary authorities to meet the deficit is immediately limited by the size of their reserves of foreign currency or the equivalent plus whatever additional sums they can or are willing to borrow or acquire in other ways from holders of foreign currency. Moreover, if the internal price level (or level of employment) is to be kept stable, the proceeds from the sales of foreign-exchange reserves must not be impounded or used in other deflationary ways. This assumes, of course, that the deficit is not itself produced by internal inflationary policies but occurs despite a stable internal price level. The proceeds must be used to retire debt or to finance a deficit in the budget to whatever extent is necessary to prevent a price decline.

If the problem is a surplus, the monetary authorities must be prepared to accumulate foreign exchange indefinitely, providing all the domestic currency that is demanded. Moreover, if the internal price level is to be maintained constant, it must obtain the domestic currency it sells for foreign currency in noninflationary ways. It can print or create the currency only to the extent that is consistent with stable prices. For the rest it must get the amount required by borrowing at whatever interest rates are necessary to keep domestic prices stable or from a surplus of the appropriate amount in the government budget. Entirely aside from the technical problems of monetary management involved, the community is unlikely to be willing to exchange indefinitely part of its product for unproductive currency hoards, particularly if the source of the surplus is monetary inflation abroad, and thus the foreign currency is decreasing in real value.

Traditionally, of course, monetary reserves have not been used as the primary method of adjusting to changes in external conditions but as a shock absorber pending changes in internal prices and incomes. A deficit has been met out of monetary reserves in the first instance, but the proceeds or even a multiple of the proceeds have been, as it were, impounded; that is, the stock of money has been allowed or made to decrease as a result of the decline of monetary reserves, with a consequent rise in interest rates and downward pressure on internal prices. Similarly, the domestic currency exchanged for a surplus of foreign currency has, as it were, been created and allowed to or made to increase the stock of money by the same amount or a multiple of that amount, with a consequent decline in interest rates and upward pressure on internal prices. [7]

Since the end of the first World War, nations have become increasingly unwilling to use reserves in this way and to allow the effect to be transmitted directly and immediately to internal monetary conditions and prices. Already during the 1920s, the United States, to cite one outstanding and critical example, refused to allow its surplus, which took the form of gold imports, to raise domestic prices in the way the supposed rules of the gold standard demanded; instead, it "sterilized" gold imports. Especially after the Great Depression completed the elevation of full employment to the primary goal of economic policy, nations have been unwilling to allow deficits to exert any deflationary effect.

The use of monetary reserves as the sole reliance to meet small and temporary strains on balances of payments and of other devices to meet larger and more extended or more basic strains is an understandable objective of economic policy and comes close to summarizing the philosophy underlying the International Monetary Fund. Unfortunately, it is not a realistic, feasible, or desirable policy. It is seldom possible to know in advance or even soon after the event whether any given strain in the balance of payments is likely to be reversed rapidly or not; that is, whether it is a result of temporary or permanent factors. Reserves must be very large indeed if they are to be the sole reliance in meeting changes in external conditions until the magnitude and probably duration of the changes can be diagnosed with confidence and more fundamental correctives undertaken in light of the diagnosis, far larger than if they serve the function they did under the classical gold standard. Except perhaps for the United States, and even for the United States only so long as gold is freely acceptable as an international currency, reserves are nothing like this large. Under the circumstances there is a strong tendency to rely on reserves too long for comfort yet not long enough for confident diagnosis and reasoned action. Corrective steps are postponed in the hope that things will right themselves until the state of the reserves forces drastic and frequently ill-advised action.

A COMPARISON

One or another of the methods of adjustment just described must in fact be used to meet changes in conditions affecting external trade; there is no avoiding this necessity short of the complete elimination of external trade, and even this would be an extreme form of direct controls over imports and exports. On the basis of the analysis so far, flexible exchange rates seem clearly the technique of adjustment best suited to current conditions: the use of reserves is not by itself a feasible device; direct controls are cumbrous and inefficient and, I venture to predict, will ultimately prove ineffective in a free society; changes in internal prices and incomes are undesirable because of rigidities in internal prices, especially wages, and the emergence of full employment — or independence of internal monetary policy — as a major goal of policy.

The argument for flexible exchange rates is, strange to say, very nearly identical with the argument for daylight saving time. Isn't it absurd to change the clock in summer when exactly the same result could be achieved by having each individual change his habits? All that is required is that everyone decide to come to his office an hour earlier, have lunch an hour earlier, etc. But obviously it is much simpler to change the clock that guides all than to have each individual separately change his pattern of reaction to the clock, even though all want to do so. The situation is exactly the same in the exchange market. It is far simpler to allow one price to change, namely, the price of foreign exchange, than to rely upon changes in the multitude of prices that together constitute the internal price structure.

OBJECTIONS TO FLEXIBLE EXCHANGE RATES

Three major criticisms have been made of the proposal to establish a system of flexible exchange rates: first, that flexible exchange rates may increase the degree of uncertainty in the economic scene; second, that flexible exchange rates will not work because they will produce offsetting changes in domestic prices; and, third, that flexible exchange rates will not produce the best attainable timing or pace of adjustment. The first objection takes many different forms, and it will promote clarity to deal with some of these separately, even though this means considerable overlapping.

FLEXIBLE EXCHANGE RATES AND UNCERTAINTY

1. *Flexible exchange rates mean instability rather than stability.* — On the naïve level on which this objection is frequently made, it involves the already-mentioned mistake of confusing the symptom of difficulties with the difficulties themselves. A flexible exchange rate need not be an unstable exchange rate. If it is, it is primarily because there is underlying instability in the economic conditions governing international trade. And a rigid exchange rate may, while itself nominally stable, perpetuate and accentuate other elements of instability in the economy. The mere fact that a rigid official exchange rate does not change while a flexible rate does is no evidence that the former means greater stability in any more fundamental sense. If is does, it is for one or more of the reasons considered in the points that follow.

2.   it impossible for exporters and importers to be certain about the price they will have to pay or receive for foreign exchange. — Under flexible exchange rates traders can almost always protect themselves against changes in the rate by hedging in a futures market. Such futures

markets in foreign currency readily develop when exchange rates are flexible. Any uncertainty about returns will then be borne by speculators. The most that can be said for this argument, therefore, is that flexible exchange rates impose a cost of hedging on traders, namely, the price that must be paid to speculators for assuming the risk of future changes in exchange rates. But this is saying too much. The substitution of flexible for rigid exchange rates changes the form in which uncertainty in the foreign-exchange market is manifested; it may not change the extent of uncertainty at all and, indeed, may even decrease uncertainty. For example, conditions that would tend to produce a decline in a flexible exchange rate will produce a shortage of exchange with a rigid exchange rate. This in turn will produce either internal adjustments of uncertain character or administrative allocation of exchange. Traders will then be certain about the rate but uncertain about either internal conditions or the availability of exchange. The uncertainty can be removed for some transactions by advance commitments by the authorities dispensing exchange; it clearly cannot be removed for all transactions in view of the uncertainty about the total amount of exchange available; the reduction in uncertainty for some transactions therefore involves increased uncertainty for others, since all the risk is now concentrated on them. Further, such administrative allocation of exchange is always surrounded by uncertainty about the policy that will be followed. It is by no means clear whether the uncertainty associated with a flexible rate or the uncertainty associated with a rigid rate is likely to be more disruptive to trade.

3. *Speculation in foreign-exchange markets tends to be destabilizing.* — This point is, of course, closely related to the preceding one. It is said that speculators will take a decline in the exchange rate as a signal for a further decline and will thus tend to make the movements in the exchange rate sharper than they would be in the absence of speculation. The special fear in this connection is of capital flight in response to political uncertainty or simply to movements in the exchange rate. Despite the prevailing opinion to the contrary, I am very dubious that in fact speculation in foreign exchange would be destabilizing. Evidence from some earlier experiences and from current free markets in currency in Switzerland, Tangiers, and elsewhere seems to me to suggest that, in general, speculation is stabilizing rather than the reverse, though the evidence has not yet been analyzed in sufficient detail to establish this

conclusion with any confidence. People who argue that speculation is generally destabilizing seldom realize that this is largely equivalent to saying that speculators lose money, since speculation can be destabilizing in general only if speculators on the average sell when the currency is low in price and buy when it is high. [8] It does not, of course, follow that speculation is not destabilizing; professional speculators might on the average make money while a changing body of amateurs regularly lost larger sums. But, while this may happen, it is hard to see why there is any presumption that it will; the presumption is rather the opposite.   To put the same point differently, if speculation were persistently destabilizing, a government body like the Exchange Equalization Fund in England in the 1930s could make a good deal of money by speculating in exchange and in the process almost certainly eliminate the destabilizing speculation. But to suppose that speculation by governments would generally be profitable is in most cases equivalent to supposing that government officials risking funds that they do not themselves own are better judges of the likely movements in foreign-exchange markets that private individuals risking their own funds.

The widespread belief that speculation is likely to be destabilizing is doubtless a major factor accounting for the cavalier rejection of a system of flexible exchange rates in the immediate postwar period. Yet this belief does not seem to be founded on any systematic analysis of the available empirical evidence. [9] It rests rather, I believe, primarily on an oversimplified interpretation of the movements of so-called "hot" money during the 1930s. At the time, any speculative movements which threatened a depreciation of a currency (i.e., which threatened a *change* in an exchange rate) were regarded as destabilizing, and hence these movements were so considered. In retrospect, it is clear that the speculators were "right"; that forces were at work making for depreciation in the value of most European currencies relative to the dollar independently of speculative activity; that the speculative movements were anticipating this change; and, hence, that there is at least as much reason to call them "stabilizing" as to call them "destabilizing."

In addition, the interpretation of this evidence has been marred by a failure to distinguish between a system of exchange rates held temporarily rigid but subject to change from time to time by government action and a system of flexible exchange rates. Many of the capital movements regarded as demonstrating that foreign-exchange speculation is destabilizing were stimulated by the existence of rigid rates subject to change by government action and are to be attributed primarily to the absence of flexibility of rates and hence of any incentive to avoid the capital movements. This is equally true of post-World War II experience with wide swings in foreign-payments positions. For reasons noted earlier, this experience has little direct bearing on the character of the speculative movements to be expected under a regime of genuinely flexible exchange rates.

4. *Flexible exchange rates involve increased uncertainty in the internal economy.* — It is argued that in many countries there is a great fear of inflation and that people have come to regard the exchange rate as an indicator of inflation and are highly sensitive to variations in it. Exchange crises, such as would tend to occur under rigid exchange rates, will pass unnoticed, it is argued, except by people directly connected with international trade, whereas a decline in the exchange rate would attract much attention, be taken as a signal of a future inflation, and produce anticipatory movements by the public at large. In this way a flexible exchange rate might produce additional uncertainty rather than merely change the form in which uncertainty is manifested. There is some merit to this argument, but it does not seem to me to be a substantial reason for avoiding a flexible exchange rate. Its implication is rather that it would be desirable, if possible, to make the transition to a flexible rate at a time when exchange rates of European countries relative to the dollar would be likely to move moderately and some to rise. It further would be desirable to accompany the transition by willingness to take prompt monetary action to counter any internal reactions. A fear of inflation has little or no chance of producing inflation, except in a favorable monetary environment. A demonstration that fears of inflation are groundless, and some experience with the absence of any direct and immediate connection between the day-to-day movements in the exchange rate and internal prices would very shortly reduce to negligible proportions any increase in uncertainty on purely domestic markets, as a result of flexible yet not highly unstable exchange rates. Further, public recognition that a substantial decline in the exchange rate is a symptom of or portends internal inflation is by no means an unmixed evil. It

means that a flexible exchange rate would provide something of a barrier to a highly inflationary domestic policy.

Very nearly the opposite of this argument is also sometimes made against flexible exchange rates. It is said that, with a flexible exchange rate, governments will have less incentive and be in a less strong position to take firm internal action to prevent inflation. A rigid exchange rate, it is said, gives the government a symbol to fight for — it can nail its flag to the mast of a specified exchange rate and resist political pressure to take action that would be inflationary in the name of defending the exchange rate. Dramatic foreign-exchange crises establish an atmosphere in which drastic if unpopular action is possible. On the other hand, it is said, with a flexible exchange rate, there is no definite sticking point; inflationary action will simply mean a decline in the exchange rate but no dramatic crisis, and people are little affected by a change in a price, the exchange rate, in a market in which relatively few have direct dealings.

Of course, it is not impossible for both these arguments to be valid — the first in countries like Germany, which have recently experienced hyperinflations and violently fluctuating exchange rates, the second in countries like Great Britain, which have not. But, even in countries like Britain, it is far from clear that a rigid exchange rate is more conducive under present conditions to noninflationary internal economic policy than a flexible exchange rate. A rigid exchange rate thwarts any immediate manifestation of a deterioration in the foreign-payments position as a result of inflationary internal policy. With an independent monetary standard, the loss of exchange reserves does not automatically reduce the stock of money or prevent its continued increase; yet it does temporarily reduce domestic inflationary pressure by providing goods in return for the foreign-exchange reserves without any simultaneous creation of domestic income. The deterioration shows up only sometime later, in the dull tables of statistics summarizing the state of foreign-exchange reserves. Even then, the authorities in the modern world have the alternative — or think they have — of suppressing a deficit by more stringent direct controls and thus postponing still longer the necessity for taking the appropriate internal measures; and they can always find any number of special reasons for the particular deterioration other than their internal policy. While the possibilities of using direct controls and of finding plausible excuses are present equally with flexible exchange rates, at least the deterioration in the foreign-payments position shows up promptly in the more readily understandable and simpler form of a decline in the exchange rates, and there is no emergency, no suddenly discovered decline in monetary reserves to dangerous levels, to force the imposition of supposedly unavoidable direct controls.

These arguments are modern versions of an argument that no longer has much merit but was at one time a valid and potent objection to flexible exchange rates, namely, the greater scope they give for government "tampering" with the currency. When rigid exchange rates were taken seriously, and when the armory of direct controls over international trade had not yet been resurrected, the maintenance of rigid rates left little scope for independent domestic monetary policy. This was the great virtue of the gold standard and the basic, albeit hidden, source of its emotional appeal; it provided an effective defense against hyperinflation, against government intervention of a kind that had time and again led to the debasement and depreciation of once-proud currencies. This argument may still be a source of emotional resistance to flexible exchange rates; it is clear that it does not deserve to be. Governments of "advanced" nations are no longer willing to submit themselves to the harsh discipline of the gold standard or any other standard involving rigid exchange rates. They will evade its discipline by direct controls over trade if that will suffice and will change exchange rates before they will surrender control over domestic monetary policy. Perhaps a few modern inflations will establish a climate in which such behavior does not qualify as "advanced"; in the meantime we had best recognize the necessity of allowing exchange rates to adjust to internal policies rather than the reverse.

CONCLUSION

The nations of the world cannot prevent changes from occurring in the circumstances affecting international transactions. And they would not if they could. For many changes reflect natural changes in weather conditions and the like; others arise from the freedom of countless individuals to order their lives as they will, which it is our ultimate goal to preserve and widen; and yet others contain the seeds of progress and development. The prison and the graveyard alone provide even a close approximation to certainty.

The major aim of policy is not to prevent such changes from occurring but to develop an efficient system of adapting to them — of using their potentialities for good while minimizing their disruptive effects. There is widespread agreement, at least in the Western world, that relatively free and unrestricted multilateral trade is a major component of such a system, besides having political advantages of a rather different kind. Yet resounding failure has so far marked repeated attempts to eliminate or reduce the extensive and complex restrictions on international trade that proliferated during and immediately after World War II. Failure will continue to mark such attempts so long as we allow implicit acceptance of an essentially minor goal — rigid exchange rates — to prevent simultaneous attainment of two major goals: unrestricted multilateral trade and freedom of each country to pursue internal stability after its own lights.

There are, after all, only four ways in which the pressures on balances of payments produced by changes in the circumstances affecting international transactions can be met: (1) by counterbalancing changes in currency reserves; (2) by adjustments in the general level of internal prices and incomes; (3) by adjustments in exchange rates; and (4) by direct controls over transactions involving foreign exchange.

The paucity of existing currency reserves makes the first impractical for all but very minor changes unless some means can be found to increase the currency reserves of the world enormously. The failure of several noble experiments in this direction is testimony to the difficulty of this solution.

The primacy everywhere attached to internal stability makes the second method one that would not be permitted to operate; the institutional rigidities in internal price structures make it undesirable that it should be the major means of adjustment.

The third — at least in the form of a thoroughgoing system of flexible rates — has been ruled out in recent years without extensive explicit consideration, partly because of a questionable interpretation of limited historical evidence; partly, I believe, because it was condemned alike by traditionalists, whose ideal was a gold standard that either ran itself or was run by international central bankers but in either case determined internal policy, and by the dominant strain of reformers, who distrusted the price system in all its manifestations — a curious coalition of the most unreconstructed believers in the price system, in all its other roles, and its most extreme opponents.

The fourth method — direct controls over transactions involving foreign exchange — has in this way, by default rather than intention, been left the only avenue whereby pressures on balances of payments can be met. Little wonder that these controls have so stubbornly resisted elimination despite the repeated protestations that they would be eliminated. Yet this method is, in my view, by all odds the least desirable of the four.

There are no major economic difficulties to prevent the prompt establishment by countries separately or jointly of a system of exchange rates freely determined in open markets, primarily by private transactions, and the simultaneous abandonment of direct controls over exchange transactions. A move in this direction is the fundamental prerequisite for the economic integration of the free world through multilateral trade.

Notes

*   This paper had its origin in a memorandum written in the fall of 1950 when I was a consultant to the Finance and Trade Division of the Office of Special Representative for Europe, United States Economic Cooperation Administration. Needless to say, the views it expresses are entirely my own. I am grateful to Joel Bernstein and Maxwell Obst for criticism of the original memorandum, and to Earl J. Hamilton and Lloyd A. Metzler for criticism of a subsequent draft. The paper owes much, also, to extensive discussion of the general problem with a number of friends, particularly Aaron Director, James Meade, Lloyd Mints, and Lionel Robbins. Unfortunately, these discussions failed to produce sufficient agreement to make a disclaimer of their responsibility unnecessary.

1   Indeed, I have elsewhere argued that flexible exchange rates are the logical international counterpart of the monetary and fiscal framework for economic stability that seems to me the most promising. See "A Monetary and Fiscal Framework for Economic Stability," supra, pp. 133-56.

2   And indeed in the even more extreme sense of trade free from all barriers, including tariffs and export bounties.

3   In brief, it is desirable in its own right as one of the basic freedoms we cherish; it promotes the efficient use of resources through an appropriate international division of labor and increases consumer welfare by maximizing the range of alternatives on which consumers can spend their incomes; it facilitates international political amity by removing potent sources of conflict between governments.

4   It is conceivable that, under some conditions and for some range of exchange rates, a rise in exchange rates would increase the excess demand. Though this possibility has received considerable attention, it will be neglected in what follows as of little practical relevance. As a purely theoretical matter, there will always be some set or sets of rates that will clear the market, and, in the neighborhood of at least one of these sets of rates a rise in the rate will mean a decline in excess demand (i.e., a negative excess demand); a fall, a rise in excess demand. Exchange rates can remain in a region in which this is not true only if they are not free to move and if some non-price mechanism is used to ration domestic or foreign currency. As a practical matter, the conditions necessary for any relevant range of rates to have the property that a rise increases excess demand seem to me highly unlikely to occur. But, if they should occur, it would merely mean that there might be two possible positions of equilibrium, one above, the other below, the existing controlled rate.   If the higher is regarded as preferable, the implication for policy would be first to appreciate the controlled rate and then to set it free.

5   Note that a tariff of a uniform percentage on all imports used to pay a subsidy of a uniform percentage on all exports is equivalent to a depreciation in the exchange rate by the corresponding percentage; and , similarly, a subsidy of a uniform percentage on all imports financed by a tax of a uniform percentage on all exports is equivalent to an appreciation in the exchange rate by the corresponding percentage. Thus devices such as these should be classified under exchange-rate change rather than direct controls.

6   Selling import licenses at a price that would clear the market would eliminate the first effect; it would not eliminate the second and third unless the permits were not for specific commodities but for foreign exchange to be used in any way desired. Even this would not eliminate the fourth unless the proceeds were used to pay a percentage subsidy to exports and other transactions leading to the acquisition of foreign exchange. This final system is, as indicated in the preceding note, identical with a change in the exchange rate. If the price of permits to use foreign exchange and the subsidy for acquiring it were determined in a free market so as to make total receipts equal total payments, the result is equivalent to or identical with a system of flexible exchange rates.

7   Under a pure gold standard, these effects follow automatically, since any international claims not settled otherwise are settled by gold, which, in case of a deficit, is bodily extracted from the monetary stock and, in case of a surplus, bodily added to it.

8   A warning is perhaps in order that this is a simplified generalization on a complex problem. A full analysis encounters difficulties in separating "speculative" from other transactions, defining precisely and satisfactorily "destabilizing speculation," and taking account of the effects of the mere existence of a system of flexible rates as contrasted with the effects of actual speculative transactions under such a system.

9   Perhaps the most ambitious attempt to summarize the evidence is that by Ragnar Nurkse, International Currency Experience (Geneva: League of Nations, 1944), pp. 117-22. Nurkse concludes from interwar experience that speculation can be expected in general to be destabilizing. However, the evidence he cites is by itself inadequate to justify any conclusion. Nurkse examines only one episode in anything approaching the required detail, the depreciation of the French franc from 1922 to 1926. For the rest, he simply

lists episodes during which exchange rates were flexible and asserts that in each case speculation was destabilizing. These episodes may or may not support his conclusion; it is impossible to tell from his discussion of them; and the list is clearly highly selective, excluding some cases that seem prima facie to point in the opposite direction.

Even for the French episode, the evidence given by Nurkse does not justify any firm conclusion. Indeed, so far as it goes, it seems to me clearly less favorable to the conclusion Nurkse draws, that speculation was destabilizing, than to the opposite conclusion, that speculation was stabilizing.

In general, Nurkse's discussion of the effects of speculation is thoroughly unsatisfactory. At times, he seems to regard any transactions which threaten the existing value of a currency as destabilizing even if underlying forces would produce a changed value in the absence of speculation. At another point, he asserts that destabilizing transactions may occur on both capital and current account simultaneously, in a context in which these two accounts exhaust the balance of payments, so that basic statement is an arithmetical impossibility (pp. 210-11). It is a sorry reflection on the scientific basis for generally held economic beliefs that Nurkse's analysis is so often cited as "the" basis or "proof" of the belief in destabilizing speculation.

17

International Monetary Reform: the Optimal Mix in Big Countries

Robert A. Mundell

Economic theory is studied from the standpoint of a closed economy, but economic policy must deal with open economies.

If the world economy were organized within the political framework of a world government, the theoretical treatises of the early masters of economic science would have direct policy relevance. Our planet, however, is organized around the political framework of interacting nation-states. The economic interaction is manifested in the imports and exports of goods, services, factors, claims, and money, the major categories of the balance of payments.

The balance-of-payments accounts of a country summarize its economic dependence on the rest of the world. This is as obvious in monetary and fiscal policy analysis as it is in problems of tariffs and quotas, foreign aid lending and investment, and international currency relations. The international monetary framework must therefore be the starting point for applicable monetary analysis for every economy.

The need to focus on the international monetary environment was well known in the early days of economic theorizing when ideal monetary standards were first debated. Plato, for example, favored national monetary standards, a token currency for each state convertible into hard money (gold and silver) at arbitrary prices fixed by the government under a disciplined exchange-control arrangement. His pupil, Aristotle, favored a convertible hard money like gold or silver, as valuable inside a country as it was outside. Aeschines, the founder of the School of Rhodes, favored something in between, like the ambiguous lottery money of Carthage, with either a precious stone or a piece of gravel (known only to the maker) sealed in leather. The different solutions were inspired by the life experiences of the three philosophers, one as monetary adviser to the kings of Syracuse, one as a teacher of Alexander in the era of Philip II, and the third as monetary historian of the Mediterranean.

In the twentieth century monetary proposals have also developed out of the peculiarities of time and place. Fisher in 1912, envisioning the problems of an emerging monetary superpower, favored cutting loose from the gold standard and gearing monetary policy to a stable price level, achieving a compensated dollar. Keynes, from the perspective of a declining monetary superpower in post-World War I Britain, rejected the deflationary solutions of a restoration of the centuries-old traditional gold price in 1925 and eventually, in the wake of the collapse of sterling in 1931 and the Great Depression, favored in 1935 a wage standard. Cassel and von Mises, economists brought up in small countries, favored (like Aristotle) an international standard based on gold, as did Rueff. Friedman, from the vantage of a mature superpower, advocated stable monetary aggregates with floating rates and, more recently, fixed exchange rates (currencies pegged to one or another of the monetary leaders) for the less-developed countries. What these alternatives have in common, and what links the solutions to the different monetary schemes of Plato, Aristotle, and Aeschines, is the parochialism of the designers. Economists have a tendency to generalize from their own experience or knowledge of a particular time and place to situations to which the experience is not relevant.

A similar problem emerges at the global level. The world economy has experienced many different forms of international monetary systems in the past. The monetary systems of the ancient world changed with political solutions. The currencies of the great empires of antiquity "overflowed" to neighboring countries and frequently provided the base of the international currency system of the time. At one time or another the daric, stater, solidus-besant, drachma, dinar, maravedi, florin, ducat, sequin, écu, carlino, lira, livre, franc, pound, rupee, dirham, daler, thaler, peso, mark, ruble, sovereign, yen, and dollar are outcomes of the process by which the dominant currencies of the time reflect the historic importance of the international power structure and the role of trade within and between the great empires. The connecting link of these currencies is the substance of which it is made: at the international level the precious metals provided the common material out of which international money was made before the invention of paper, telegraphic transfers, and electronic money. Monometallism, bimetallism, and even trimetallism formed the basis of monetary theory in great treatises on money in the past, of which one of the examples that still retains relevance is De Moneta of Nicole Oresme, the discoverer in the middle ages of Gresham's law.

The bimetallic standard established by Napoleon in 1803 gave the world a monetary unity until the pivot country dropped silver after 1870-71, leaving in its wake a deflationary gold bloc organized around the city of London, and an inflationary silver standard in much of the nonmetropolitan world. The heyday of gold from 1870 to 1914 gave a monetary unity to a comparatively tranquil and innovative European civilization ordered around imperialism and colonialism when Europe was "mistress of the world." When European unity became unhinged between 1914 and 1945, the vast subcontinents on the wings of European culture flapped into their superpower preeminence and the dollar era began in earnest. Neither emulation of nor nostalgia for a past tranquillity could restore the monetary system that assisted in its creation. The decentralized European gold standard provided the cement for great power economic interaction, but there is no way now that the circumstances of the past can be revived to fulfill the characteristics of the political environment needed to perpetuate that destiny. The old gold standard is as dead as a doornail. The rise of America killed it.

The Bretton Woods system was based on the U.S. dollar at a time when the U.S. economy was the manufactory of the world. But we cannot, and would not, restore the temporary conditions of that time. From 1945 to 1982 more than one hundred newly independent nations were born while only a few were aborted (chiefly in the Baltic region). The gross national product of the United States is only one-fifth of world GNP. The other four-fifths of the world economy does not want a world monetary system based solely on the U.S. dollar, subject to the vicissitudes of U.S. politics and arbitrary mismanagement. A global dollar standard would work only under an American imperium not wanted by the rest of the world or the overwhelming majority of U.S. citizens.

A combination of the attributes of a gold standard and a dollar standard would be more appealing than either a pure gold standard or a pure dollar standard. In the first amendment to the International

Monetary Fund Articles of Agreement promulgated in 1968, which established a gold-backed special drawing right (SDR) worth, like the dollar, 1/35 of an ounce, the concept of "paper gold" became popular. But the solid foundation of the SDR collapsed with the convertibility of the dollar on August 15, 1971. The SDR proved to be a close substitute neither for the dollar nor for gold. From a reserve asset that was a "ghost" of both gold and the dollar, it degenerated into a basket of sixteen currencies, which was not satisfactory to the less developed countries (because it lacked universality and its allocation was not linked to foreign aid), nor was it satisfactory as a unit of account; to predict its value one had to predict the monetary policies of the sixteen countries. The latest version of the SDR is a basket of five currencies, which makes it less universal but more operational; it is still complicated as a unit of account by the need to forecast the monetary policies of five countries, the United States, Japan, Germany, Britain, and France. In 1976 at Jamaica the nations agreed to endorse the already existing "managed flexible exchange rate system," to reduce the role of gold, and to enhance the role of the SDR. This second amendment to the IMF Articles revealed the gap in international theorizing on matters of monetary reform. The lessons of the 1970's were negative, showing how not to create an international substitute for gold or the dollar. The regional solutions attempted in various parts of the world — the Gulf of Mexico, Arabia-Persia, and Eastern and Western Europe — have not fared much better. The failures to create effective collective new currents do not make one optimistic about the future.

Both history and the political condition of the world have combined to make a special role in international finance for gold and the dollar, the two "perennial" assets that have continued to dominate international reserves. The misconceptions that have become explicit in the failure of the experiments with international reserve creation in the 1970's should alert us to the possibility that, far back in the past, serious mistakes were made in the field of international currency theory. To err is human; to err twice is forgiveable; but to err again and again makes a mockery of belief in the progress of man's collective intelligence.

The gold standard broke down in 1914 when all major nations withdrew gold from circulation and centralized it in treasuries to form the basis for wartime inflationary finance. After the war the value of gold had fallen precipitously, even in U.S. dollars, and the supply was insufficient for the world's needs despite greatly increased production by South Africa. When Germany, Britain, and France spearheaded the return to gold in the 1920's, the scarcity of gold became obvious. When Churchill in 1925 abolished the use of gold coins in circulation, he said that such a use of gold "would be an unwarranted extravagance which our present financial stringency by no means allows us to indulge in." This policy set a bad precedent for President Roosevelt, who did the same thing in 1934, when the United States restored gold at the new parity of 13 5/7 grains, equivalent to $35 an ounce. The entrance of France into the system in June 1928 at a value of 3.92 cents instead of the prewar parity of 19.30 cents undervalued the franc relative to its purchasing power and enabled France to draw gold away from the United States and Britain. From the end of 1925 to the end of 1929 U.S. gold reserves not only failed to rise but fell (from $4 billion to $3.9 billion), which certainly helped create the monetary stringency that caused the crash on Wall Street. French gold reserves, on the other hand, went from $0.7 billion in December 1926 to $2.3 billion in August 1931. Britain dropped gold in the following month, but the United States hung on to its overvalued dollar for almost two years of a sickening slide into the slough of stagnation. Even today people have trouble understanding the crash of 1929 and its link to the undervaluation of gold thoughout the 1920's.

With the new price of gold after 1934, gold was still considered scarce enough to prohibit Americans from holding it or using it as coinage. The U.S. reserve ratio was 40 percent behind notes and 35 percent behind deposits. With the inflationary expansion of World War II the Treasury, as early as 1945, considered it prudent to reduce the reserve cover to 25 percent behind both notes and deposits. By 1965 the backing for deposits was reduced to zero, and in 1968 the cover behind the notes was also eliminated. Thus all formal semblance of the national gold standard discipline had broken down by 1968.

The shortage of gold in the world monetary system had become apparent early in the 1920's, and in retrospect it would have been better to raise the price of gold after World War I in order to spare the world economy the painful adjustment of deflation that caught up with the system in the next decade. Instead, the palliative of the gold exchange standard propped the system up for another decade.

When the system broke down in 1931 with the fall of sterling and 1933 with the fall of the dollar, a new price of gold was set up, but the increase in price was not sufficient to restore a full gold standard. In the Great Depression each country was hungry, but the excess of surpluses over deficits in the world as a whole has to equal the increase in the value of gold stocks, which in 1938, for example, constituted 93 percent of world reserves. A higher gold price than actually took place would have raised the excess of surpluses over deficits and had multiplier effects, spurring recovery from the depression.

The world economy did repeat after World War II some of the mistakes authorities had made after World War I. The symptoms of gold shortage appeared early, not only in the prohibition on gold in the United States or the high-dollar black market price, but by the need felt by the United States to increase "free " reserves by lowering Federal Reserve gold cover requirements to 25 percent while continuing to prohibit gold for American citizens. When the London gold market opened in 1954, the drain of gold started, dollar interest rates began to climb, and by 1960, during the U.S. election campaign, gold had climbed in the free market to $40 an ounce. Gold losses imposed a constraint on expansionary monetary policies, a fact that many considered a serious defect of the gold standard. Perhaps we should admit with the hindsight of the present that Sir Roy Harrod and Professor Rueff, who eloquently advocated a higher gold price in the 1950's, were closer to the mark than those who in the 1950's and 1960's objected to it. By then, however, the infectious enthusiasm for international monetary reform and a world central bank along the lines of a Keynes-Triffin plan had caught on, and this hope for an alternative to gold stood in the way of the retrospectively attractive option of raising the price of gold. The better argument for floating exchange rates had been that the U.S. balance-of - payments deficit would disappear, so that monetary and fiscal policies would be freed to preserve internal balance, with full employment and a stable price level. The monetary disequilibrium of the 1970's showed how wrongly conceived or badly implemented this solution was.

No theory can be further from the facts. The balance-of-payments deficits of the reserve countries have not been eliminated; they have multiplied ten times since floating rates came into existence. From 1952 to 1969 foreign exchange reserves, mainly dollars and sterling, rose from $16 billion to $33 billion, a little more than doubling over seventeen years. Then from 1969 to 1981 they rose by $272 billion, to $305 billion, almost a tenfold increase in only twelve years, feeding the inflation of the 1970's and the steady depreciation of the dollar in terms of goods. It was not just the explosion of official holdings of foreign exchange, however, that led to the inflation. The expansion of international liquidity held by the international deposit money banks (Eurodollars, and so forth), which amounted to $30 billion in 1963 and $117 billion in 1969, rose to $2,098 billion at the end of 1981, a figure indicative of an enormous inflation, even if it does involve double counting. To this phenomenal expansion must be added the increase in the dollar value of gold reserves from $35 billion in 1971 to over ten times that amount in 1981. With the liquidity onslaught of the combined forces of foreign exchange, Eurodollars, and gold, it is suprising that world inflation and the commodity depreciation of the dollar have not been greater than they have.

It is important for economists, bankers, and officials to realize how grossly erroneous were the calculations of those who advocated the breakdown of both the gold reserve standard and the system of fixed exchange-rate parities. The discipline of a currency system convertible at fixed exchange rates into one or a few major currencies that are in turn convertible directly into gold or an internationally stable world asset (such as a gold-backed SDR) offers far better prospects for a stable world economy in the future.

The IMF was actually set up to provide the framework to avoid fluctuations in exchange rates, which were believed to have smashed the international lending mechanisms, driven countries into economic nationalism, exchange controls, and protection, and deepened the depression, leaving the road open to the work of totalitarian forces that spread across the continent of Europe in the 1930's. The IMF system, however, was weakened from its birth by an inadequate level of gold liquidity and soon came to rely on the U.S. dollar. This inadequacy was concealed by the magnificent growth of the United States as a superpower of colossal dimensions, generously spreading technological bounty to the rest of the world on a scale never before offered so freely. The miracles of growth on the continent of Europe, in Japan, and in the Soviet Union were based on the catch-up possibilites inherent in the new technology of American corporate capitalism, laying a basis for a new epoch in computers, electronics, communications, and outer space. The breakdown in the gold exchange standard and the monetary instability of the 1970s were dismal but should not conceal the improvements that continued despite rather than because of flexible rates. The errors were forgiveable: undervaluing gold in the Bretton Woods arrangements, failing to specify the meaning of "fundamental disequilibrium," lacking a coherent theory of "currencies in need," and not elaborating a suffiently accurate analysis of the adjustment process or understanding the theory of key or dominant currencies. The basic concept of a workable framework for a kind of humanized gold standard based on the dollar and a revolving bag of other currencies was not in error. Today the IMF and the World Bank Group are a durable reminder of the idealistic intentions of the time to forswear the relapse into the chaotic jungle of fluctuating currencies.

It is for that reason that progress in the future, I believe, lies in the development of a monetary standard combining the virtues of gold and the amalgam of currencies making up a possibly revised SDR, defined in a third amendment of the IMF Articles of Agreement. A genuine convertible world reserve currency unit composed, say, of half gold and half SDRs would provide a more stable compromise that could last for several decades. This unit should be acceptable everywhere and accorded the status of legal tender in every member country. Some other suggestions follow.

First, countries should stabilize currencies (within margins) to gold, a major currency, or the new composite basket, allowing changes in reserve positions to affect monetary policies and give the new system features of an adjustment process for correcting the balance of payments along the theoretical lines of the monetary approach to the balance of payments.

Second, allocation of the new composite basket should increase at a definable target rate announced in advance after being agreed upon by the Committee of Twenty and endorsed by the Executive Board under the instructions of the Board of Governors.

Third, the price of gold in terms of the dollar and perhaps a few other currencies should be kept as stable as possible. Federal Reserve policy can make it consistent with the needs of internal balance. In an interim transitional period a crawling peg around gold established by a reform gold pool would be a desirable transitional feature.

Fourth, budgetary policy in the United States should be geared to the preservation of internal balance to the extent that it is consistent with optimal public debt policies and interest rate objectives.

This approach envisages a new constitutional convention of the IMF governors, prepared in advance by committees of the IMF, member governments, and the interested community of bankers, academics, officials, and other relevant parties in the private sector.

Reform of the IMF is only a starting point generating the new international monetary system needed to replace the one currently damaging prosperity and threatening the fabric of the international society that played so useful a role in the institutions created after World War II. Because of the new demands on the system arising from international debt problems, prompt action is needed.

International monetary reform is not the only answer, however. In the interim the immediate problems facing the world economy must be tackled, particularly the high unemployment of the current recession, and a noninflationary way found to increase the supply of jobs in the world economy. The approach I favor is to alter the fiscal policy mix toward supply-and-demand-promoting reduction in key tax rates and an accommodating monetary policy to accompany employment-enhancing growth without accelerating inflation.

The mistakes of "Reaganomics" were in failing to press forward with international monetary reform, a necessary prerequisite for efficient long-run reduction in the interest rates, and in tightening monetary policy before the tax stimulus had been allowed to take effect. Tight money is the best solution to inflation only if it is accompanied by employment-fostering reducton in tax rates and adaptive fiscal policy. Budgetary and monetary policies have differential effects on the inflation-unemployment target mix.

The mistakes of the recent past are correctable. When planned saving exceeds planned investment at full employment, it is desirable for the budget deficit to take up the slack. When this lesson, attributable to Keynes, is recalled, new policies can rise out of the ashes of sole reliance on balanced budgets and monetary aggregates. Budget deficits alone are not the cause of high interest rates. In the long run, international monetary reform must be accomplished to provide rational prediction of future monetary policy. It would be better to produce that reform in a climate of world prosperity than in the exigencies of global depression.

18

Louvre's Lesson — the World Needs a New Monetary System.

C. Fred Bergsten

One unmistakable lesson from the global turbulence of the past few years is the need for a new international monetary system.

The near-universal dissatisfaction with unmanaged floating led the Common Market countries to create the European Monetary System a decade ago; more recently, it has prompted the Group of Seven to launch a two-track reform effort — the "indicators" approach to coordination of national macroeconomic policies, and the use of "reference ranges" to limit exchange-rate fluctuations. The failures of both the floating-rate system and its predecessor, the Bretton Woods system of adjustable pegs — combined with the shortcomings of the reform efforts so far — underscore the need for new arrangements.

Unmanaged floating has failed on three crucial counts: First, it permitted the dollar, the monetary system's key currency, to become overvalued by more than 40% at its peak in early 1985 — double the overvaluation that finally destroyed the Bretton Woods system in 1973. The huge trade and financial imbalances triggered by the latest dollar misalignment were the primary cause of the bond market's plunge last spring and the stock market crashes last autumn. They continue to threaten the entire world economy.

Second, floating has failed in its primary job of preserving open markets for world trade. Protectionism has grown steadily throughout the 1980s, mainly in the U.S., but also in Europe and the developing world. There's a double asymmetry here: the overvaluation of currencies breeds import controls, which often remain intact even after overvaluation is corrected; at the same time, undervaluation breeds protectionism because it generates artificial levels of exports that inevitably spawn demands for protection later after the undervaluation disappears. The endemic overshooting and undershooting under unmanaged floating can thus intensify protectionist pressures at an alarming pace, threatening the open world trade system.

One paradox of the 1980s is that trade flows have become increasingly circumscribed while capital flows have been increasingly liberalized. There's a direct relationship between the two: In the absence of any systemic counterweights, the vastly greater volume of capital movements can push exchange rates far from their equilibrium levels in terms of trade flows and heighten protectionist pressures. The only way to maintain relative freedom for both trade and capital flows is to improve the monetary system so as to avoid large misalignments.

Third, floating has had no meaningful effect on the way governments conduct their own economic policies. Countries no longer have any serious international monetary obligations, even on paper. The International Monetary Fund has been rendered irrelevant for the industrial countries. Small, open economies instinctively take into account the international consequences of their actions, but the larger and more self-contained economies needn't do so. As a result, unbridled floating has permitted the three largest countries — the United States, Japan, and West Germany — to pursue diametrically opposite economic policies during the 1980s, leading to huge currency misalignments that have brought about today's massive external imbalances.

Some observers absolve the floating-rate system, instead blaming the misguided economic policies that countries are following. But this misses the point. No system is truly a system unless it has a serious effect on the policies in its member countries, at least to the point of forcing governments to consider the compatibility of their trading partners. The main purpose of any international regime is to push national policies toward sustainable global norms — for the longer-run interests of the countries involved if not necessarily for the benefit of incumbent governments that have very short time horizons. No system can prevent governments from adopting inconsistent or irresponsible policies. But it's surely better to try to engineer more stable trade and capital patterns than to leave the process untended.

Countries cherish the "autonomy illusion" of nominal sovereignty over their economic policies. But growing interdependence has made real sovereignty more difficult to maintain. Yet the largest countries, particularly the United States, seem to need constant reminders that unilateral excursions, while successful for a while, always fail in the end — as Presidents Nixon, Carter and now Reagan have all learned.   In light of the US's proclivity to exploit the absence of international rules to pursue disruptive policies, it's a mystery that the other major countries don't leap at offers by American officials — most recently by U.S. Treasury Secretary James Baker — to adopt international mechanisms that might restrain America's own temptations in the future.

The exchange-rate obligations of Bretton Woods and the EMS have worked well in warning countries about the international repercussions of their actions. So have the GATT rules on trade. The systemic flaw of unmanaged floating is that it lacks any such obligations.

In recognition of these problems, the Europeans began to create their own "zone of stability" in the late 1970s. The EMS has worked reasonably well in practice. It demonstrates that international rules can have a meaningful impact under economic conditions of the 1980s, which have changed dramatically from the 1950s and early 1960s, when the similar (but more rigid) Bretton Woods regime enjoyed its biggest success.

Moreover, the EMS has worked in the face of intra-EMS inflation rates and other key economic variables that have differed much more sharply than those of the U.S., Japan and West Germany. So the success of the EMS provides considerable encouragement that such an arrangement could work at the global level as well. To be sure, the EMS won't be subjected to sizable capital flows until the United Kingdom decides to join. But some Europeans, particularly the West Germans, seem to reject the notion of broadening the EMS's concepts to encompass a wider group of countries. Perhaps while Bonn and Frankfurt are confident that they can dominate the EMS, their policymakers fear West Germany couldn't continue to follow the domestic policies it wants as freely if it had to take account of global obligations.

The quest for a better monetary system began when the ideological floaters left the U.S. Treasury in early 1985. At the famous Plaza meeting that September, the Group of Five finance ministers acknowledged that — contrary to the assurances of the ideologues during the previous four years — policy convergence among the major industrial countries had not resulted in international monetary stability, and that direct governmental intervention was required. This reversal opened the door for constructive reform efforts. Beginning with the Tokyo Summit in May 1986, the Group of Seven created a set of economic indicators to provide benchmarks against which to measure the results of their efforts at policy coordination. Their goal was to enhance the prospects that countries' internal and external policy targets would be consistent with each other, and hopefully that the sum of the targets would both be consistent internationally and would promote stable growth for the world as a whole. Within the overall list of indicators, Secretary Baker noted on several occasions that the United States regarded the current account balance and the exchange rate as the most important.

The second reform track — the use of reference ranges for each of the major currencies — was far more important in actual operation, beginning with the Baker-Miyazawa accord on the yen-dollar rate in October 1986 and later the Louvre Accord in February 1987. The idea was to stabilize the currencies within fairly narrow ranges around the rates which existed at that time and then to adopt policy changes needed to support that objective. The U.S. would cut its budget deficit while Japan and West Germany would stimulate their domestic demand. Market pressures forced an upward "rebasing" in April of the yen's range in relation to the dollar, but the enforcement effort continued until even heavier market attacks in the fall rendered the Louvre Accord unsustainable. It was clear by then that the reference ranges alone never would have brought the American current account deficit below $100 billion, if that far, without implementation of the promised policy changes.

For 1988, the issue is not whether to reform the international monetary system. The shortcomings of unmanaged floating and the efforts of the recent past provide stark testimony to the need and desire for change. The issue is how to fashion a system that will work.

There's been extensive debate on whether such reform should focus initially on exchange rates themselves or on coordination of national economic policies. But the debate essentially is over tactics; in truth, exchange-rate equilibrium can be preserved only through effective policy coordination, while effective policy coordination will normally produce equilibrium exchange rates. The postwar record both globally and in Europe suggests that success would be more likely if policymakers begin by trying to set appropriate exchange rates. In essence, countries would examine the interaction of national policies through the lens of the exchange rate — viewing the exchange-rate system as a means to the end of more effective coordination of overall national policies.

Source: The International Economy, January / February 1988

   That doesn't mean policymakers should rule out an eventual return to fixed rates — possibly along the lines of the EMS, which has a reasonably effective procedure for requiring countries to move quickly to adjust parities by small amounts when imbalances begin to show up. However, such narrow margins could prove harder to maintain between the United States and Japan with their much larger volumes of capital flows. And it isn't clear that the Big Three powers would be as ready as some EMS members to change parities promptly. If they weren't, then the new system, too, could prove too rigid. The present imbalances also make it very hard to choose precise parities any time soon that would offer great hope of remaining in place for very long. But it isn't necessary to return to fixed rates now; the primary objective of the exercise should be to avoid the substantial misalignment that characterized the first half of the 1980s. This could be achieved with a less-sweeping approach.

The most promising strategy for now may be to find a compromise, built on the indicators and reference-range efforts of the past two years, that would avoid the excessive rigidity of the Bretton Woods system and the endemic misalignments of floating. It's interesting to recall that when the Bretton Woods system was breaking down, in the late 1960s and early 1970s, many proponents of monetary reform similarly called for intermediate solutions — then labeled "crawling pegs" and "wider bands." The leading contender today would be target zones, which would permit rates to fluctuate on a day-to-day basis but would limit the extent of such movements and thus prevent misalignments sufficient to damage the international system.

Under target zones, the participating countries would first agree on what the proper current positions of each of the major countries should be — such as a modest surplus for Japan and deficits for most developing countries — and then decide what exchange rates are needed to bring this about. Then they would establish initial zones that would range from 5% to 10% above and below some optimum exchange rate (adjusted continuously for inflation). The zones would be announced publicly to help stabilize capital flows. They would be revised regularly to make sure that they continued to reflect underlying competitive positions and take account of significant shocks, such as significant changes in worldwide oil prices.

Once the zones were set, rates would be free to fluctuate within them without intervention by the authorities. Most short-term disturbances, such as modest changes in interest rate differentials, would continue to be reconciled through fluctuations in exchange rates. National policies would be no more constrained under unmanaged floating. But when rates approached the edges of the zones, there would be strong pressure on countries to alter their policies. In some cases, direct intervention in the exchange markets and jawboning might be enough. If that didn't work, countries could then alter their monetary policies — the quickest way to make an impact on the markets. Fiscal policy could then be adjusted to provide an offset, producing a similar macroeconomic outcome but altering the country's external position through a change in the policy mix. To enable this element of the scheme to work properly, several of the major countries (notably the United States and Germany) would have to devise internal reforms to make their budget policies more flexible. Institution of a new international system requiring such changes might help to provide the needed spur politically for governments to act at home.

A major operational question would be whether interest rates should be raised in the country whose currency was weakening or reduced in the country whose currency was rising. The answer would depend largely on the outlook for the world economy. If global inflation threatened, the weak-currency country should tighten; if recession loomed instead, the strong-currency country would loosen. If the situation were less clear-cut, both might make adjustments.

In the last issue of The International Economy, Bundesbank President Karl Otto Poehl denounced proposals for the "robotization" of policymaking and "those who wish to replace persons and ad hoc decisions by regulatory mechanisms and indicators." While correctly noting that "the willingness of each individual country to take into account the implications of its own economic policy for the rest of the world...cannot be decreed from outside," he goes on to say that "no system — no matter how sophisticated it may be — can help when this political willingness is lacking."

But Mr. Poehl is attacking a straw-man: No one, except perhaps the unreconstructed gold standard bugs, is proposing "automatic" or "robotized" rules in a world of sovereign nation-states.

What's more, elsewhere the Bundesbank president has ardently defended the EMS because it has "influenced national decisionmaking processes in economic and monetary policy" and it is "subjecting the participating countries to an exchange-rate discipline...." And it has. France's mid-1980s decision to reverse the early socialist policies of the Mitterand administration was largely to avoid violating its obligations to maintain the EMS. And many countries, including the U.S., frequently altered their policies to stay within the confines of the old Bretton Woods regime.

The Bundesbank itself pays considerable attention to its own "target zone" for growth of the money supply, viewing it quite properly as a useful (but not "automatic") guideline which helps fend off critics who favor tighter or more expansionary policies. Why, then, must all international "conflicts of aims only be resolved ad hoc, by the persons involved," as Mr. Poehl has argued?

The target zone approach would in fact effectively meet concerns expressed most frequently by German officials. The nominal exchange rate targets would change automatically if inflation accelerated in some countries, permitting appreciation in the more stable countries (and thus warding off inflationary pressure). The exchange rate could appreciate within the wide zone, further relieving the risk of importing inflationary pressure. Also in light of the wide zone, monetary policy could be targeted to a considerable degree to counter inflationary pressures. And all of the policy adjustments would take global demand conditions fully into account, to avoid giving any push to global inflation (or recession).

Mr. Poehl is correct that individual judgment must be applied in specific cases. The issue is whether to develop and install norms to help guide such decisions, or leave them all to ad hockery. The experience of 1987 with the Louvre Accord should clinch the case for the former: The Louvre Accord sought to stabilize exchange rates at levels that were clearly unsustainable. It defined exchange rates in nominal rather than real terms, setting up a further inherent instability in light of lower inflation in Germany and Japan than in the United States. It apparently sought to maintain existing rates within very narrow margins, providing inadequate scope for short-term fluctuations and thus triggering premature (and ultimately unsuccessful) intervention in both April and October. And the unwillingness of the Big Three countries to carry out major policy changes when exchange rates threatened to pierce the boundaries only encouraged speculators to challenge these targets.

Fortunately, all of these shortcomings of the Louvre Accord can be remedied once the major countries decide that the time has come to improve the international monetary system. Indeed, the structure of reference ranges embodied at the Louvre provides a promising foundation for launching the more far-reaching effort that is needed, as indicated above.

But caution is in order. It would be a mistake to revive the unrealistic expectations of the Louvre effort by trying to install a target-zone system before the present currency disequilibrium is eliminated. We should wait until a new set of exchange rates and policies produces an acceptable correction of today's massive current account imbalances that is ratified by the markets. The new system would then aim to stabilize the situation, and prevent yet another cycle of costly and disruptive misalignments.

The basic issue isn't whether countries will adjust to the realities of global interdependence. They will, as even the largest learn periodically to their dismay. Nor are countries being asked to conform to international norms or presumptions "to pursue global interests" rather than their own interests. The object is to minimize the costs to a country's own economy by providing early warning that it can't escape adverse international consequences from its own actions, and that it should behave accordingly.

The issue is whether countries will adjust constructively and preemptively, or belatedly and reactively. The former course may on occasion mean foregoing some short-term economic benefits. The latter will almost always mean accepting very heavy, lasting costs.

The goal of restructuring the international monetary system is to help push countries toward earlier, less costly changes in their economic policies so that those policies will be more internationally compatible — and thus more sustainable. No system can assure an outcome on all occasions, or prevent countries from the unhappy results of their own policy failures. But a well-conceived system that is implemented with good faith, based on enlightened definitions of self-interest, could tilt policies in a constructive direction and make a significant difference. Creation of such a system should rank high on the policy agenda for 1988 and beyond.

19

The International Monetary System: Should it be Reformed?

Jacob A. Frenkel

A casual glance through the *Proceedings* of past annual meetings of the American Economic Association reveals that in almost every year during the past twenty years, president-elects of the AEA have devoted at least one session to an examination of issues concerning the international monetary system. Prominent on the agenda has been the question of reform. How should the international monetary system be reformed so as to function more effectively? The premise underlying this question is that the international monetary system has failed and that it must be reformed by an institutional change. In what follows I present some skeptical notes on both the verdict on the failure of the system and on some proposals for reform, especially the target-zones proposal.

To set the stage, it is worth noting that one of the main sources of disenchantments with the present monetary system has been the unpredictability of exchange rates. There has been nothing more confusing than reading through the *ex post* journalistic explanations offered for the day-to-day changes in the U.S. dollar. For example, over the past few years we were told that "The dollar *fell* since the budget deficit exceeded previous forecasts — thereby generating inflationary expectations on the belief that the Fed will have to monetize the deficit," but, on another occasion we were told that "The dollar *rose* since the budget deficit exceeded previous forecasts — thereby generating expectations that government borrowing needs will drive up interest rates since the Fed is unlikely to give up its firm stance." On yet another day we were told that "The dollar *fell* since oil prices fell — thereby hurting Mexico and other debt-ridden oil-producing countries whose bad fortune may bring about the collapse of important U.S. banks," but, on another occasion we were told that "The dollar *rose* since oil prices fell

— thereby helping the debt-ridden oil-consuming countries whose improved fortune will help the vulnerable position of important U.S. banks." More recently the dollar changed again, and this time the explanation was a bit more sophisticated: "The dollar changed because the extent of the revision of the estimated GNP growth rate was smaller than the expected revision of previous forecasts of these estimates." One cannot but sympathize with the difficulties shared by newspaper reporters and financial analysts who feel obligated to come up with daily explanations for daily fluctuations of exchange rates, and one can only imagine the deep frustration that yielded the recent headline in the *International Herald Tribune* according to which "The dollar rose on no news."

The dismal performance of short-term forecasting does not reflect a lack of effort. Rather, it is an intrinsic characteristic of efficient asset markets. Difficulties in forecasting short-term indices of stock markets (like the Dow-Jones index) do not call however, for a reform of the way stock markets operate. For similar reasons one should not assess the performance of the international monetary system on the basis of short-term forecastability of exchange rates. This does not imply of course that the present monetary system is without faults or that it should not be reformed. It implies, however, that if a reform is warranted, then it had better be justified on different grounds.

A second noteworthy observation is that over the years, both academics and policy-makers have made numerous proposals for reform while, at the same time, the monetary system itself has been in a constant state of change. It evolved from the gold standard to paper money, from the Bretton Woods system to managed float. We also had the Gold Commission but stayed with floating rates, and now attention is focused on target zones, with soft or hard margins.

In spite of the ongoing debate there seems to be little convergence of views about the characteristics of the desired system. This lack of convergence in my view does not reflect lack of effort. Rather, it reflects more fundamental factors that are unlikely to vanish over time. Several are noteworthy. First, participants in the debate have not shared the presumption concerning the relevant alternative to the system they promote. Thus, extreme promoters of fixed rates believe that the relevant choice is between a "good fix" and a "bad flex"; on the other hand, extreme promoters of flexible rates believe that the relevant choice is between a "bad fix" and a "good flex." As is obvious, if these are the alternative choices the outcomes are self-evident, for who would not prefer a "good fix" over a "bad flex"? And, by the same token, who would not prefer a "good flex" over a "bad fix"? In reality, however, the choices are much more complex and much less trivial since they may involve comparisons between a good fix and a good flex, or, even more frequently, between a bad fix and a bad flex. When these are the choices, one may expect lack of unanimity. Reasonable people may also differ in their assessments of which "good" system is more likely to gravitate toward its "bad" counterpart. Furthermore, the likelihood that a given good system would deteriorate and be transformed into its bad counterpart depends on the circumstances and, therefore, it is likely that some countries would be wise to choose greater fixity of rates, while other countries would be equally wise to choose greater flexibility.

Second, there are different concepts of the "equilibrium" exchange rate and not all participants in the debate share the same concept. A trivial definition would identify the equilibrium rate as the one that is generated by the free operation of the market place. A more subtle definition emphasizes the *sustainability* of policies as the criterion for equilibrium. Accordingly, if, for example, the current exchange rate reflects unsustainable budget deficits, then this rate is not viewed as an equilibrium rate even though it reflects equality between demand and supply in the market place. An even more subjective view emphasizes the *consequences* of the exchange rate as the ultimate criterion. Accordingly, if the exchange rate yields undesirable results in terms of growth, export, resource allocation, unemployment, and the like, then this rate is not viewed as an equilibrium rate even though it emerges from the market place and reflects sustainable policies.

Third, different countries face different shocks. On purely theoretical grounds, it is clear that the appropriate exchange rate regime depends on the nature and origin of shocks. Are the shocks real or monetary? Are they induced by the private sector or by the public sector? Is their origin domestic or foreign? Are they permanent or transitory? The list of questions is long and circumstances vary across countries and over time.

Fourth, the cost of mistaken policies and the ability to correct errors differ across countries. They depend on the exchange rate regime and on the structural characteristics of the economy. Countries differ from each other in the flexibility of their economic system (for example, the degree of wage indexation, labor mobility, external and internal debt position) as well as in the flexibility of the policy making process (for example, the speed by which fiscal and monetary policies can be assessed and modified).

Fifth, countries differ from each other according to the various criteria governing the choice of optimal currency areas. These criteria include the degree of openness of the economy, the size of the economy, the degree of commodity diversification, the degree of inflation rates among prospective members, the degree of capital mobility, the degree of other prevailing forms of integration (like custom unions), the degree of similarities of tax structures and other fiscal characteristics, and the degree of similarities of external and domestic monetary and real shocks.

Sixth, views differ about the functions of exchange rates in general and of market mechanisms in particular. On the one hand, there are those who believe that exchange rates are just a nuisance, especially if they move, and anything that moves had better be stopped. (One only wonders whether proponents of this view would also like to see greater fixity of stock market indices?) There are also those who, in spite of the meager evidence, advocate the bubble theory according to which exchange rates have "life of their own" unrelated to "fundamentals." On the other hand, there are those who view exchange rates as an important gauge which provides valuable information about current as well as prospective policies. According to this view, manipulating the exchange rate by intervention and blaming the volatility, unpredictability, and misalignment on the monetary system makes as much sense as blaming the messenger for conveying bad news.

Finally, there are also different views about the advisability and effectiveness of foreign exchange intervention. In spite of growing evidence that the effectiveness of sterilized intervention in exchange rate management is very limited (at least as it operates through the portfolio-balance mechanism), there are those who are still ready to rely on such intervention. In principle, sterilized intervention can be defective by signalling to the market the intent of policymakers. Since the credibility, and thereby the effectiveness, of such signals depend on the track record of past policies, circumstances differ across countries.

The foregoing arguments explain why views about the need for and the desired characteristics of a reform are likely to differ across countries, and may not converge even with the passage of time.

Has the system failed? It is clear that during the past decade foreign-exchange markets have gone through great difficulties. In addition to the volatility and the unpredictability of exchange rates, there is the perception that real exchange rates have been misaligned, and that this misalignment has been costly in terms of resource allocation and general economic performance. The relevant question is whether these faults reflect deficiencies of the *international monetary system* or of macroeconomic policies? I believe that faulty policies, especially the lack of synchronization of fiscal policies in the United States, West Germany, and Japan, are the root cause of the misalignments. Reforming the monetary system without reforming the policies will not do any good and may in fact do harm by diverting attention from the root cause of the problem to the monetary system.

There is also the view that the system has failed since it did not yield current-account balance among the major trading partners. Taken by itself, however, this can be viewed as one of the achievements of the monetary system. The ability to rely on international capital markets to smooth out consumption in spite of real shocks may be highly desirable.

We may also wish to ask whether the United States could have carried out its highly successful disinflation policy of the early 1980's while committed to fixed exchange rates? I believe not! The key point that needs emphasis is that the volatility and the misalignment of exchange rates may not be the source of the difficulties, but rather a manifestation of the prevailing package of macroeconomic policies. Fixing or manipulating the rates without introducing a significant change into the conduct of policies may not improve matters at all. It may amount to breaking the thermometer of a patient suffering from high fever instead of providing him with proper medication. The absence of the thermometer will only confuse matters and will reduce the information essential for policymaking. If volatile events and macropolicies are not allowed to be reflected in the foreign-exchange market, they are likely to be transferred to, and reflected in, other markets (such as labor markets) where they cannot be dealt with in as efficient a manner.

The preceding argument ignores, however, one of the important characteristics of the gold-dollar system — the imposition of discipline. Accordingly, it could be argued that, the obligation to peg the rate or to follow a predetermined intervention rule would alter fundamentally the conduct of policy by introducing discipline. This view, however, can also be challenged. First, it could equally be argued that by being highly visible, flexible exchange rates also impose discipline, since current and (expected) future policies are immediately made transparent to both private and public sectors at home and abroad. Indeed, the G-5 Plaza Agreement of September 1985 and the subsequent Paris agreements reached in February 1987 may be viewed as a manifestation of the disciplinary capabilities of flexible exchange rates. Furthermore, it may be argued that national governments are unlikely to adjust the conduct of domestic policies so as to be disciplined by the exchange rate regime. Rather, it is more reasonable to assume that the exchange rate regime is likely to adjust to whatever discipline national governments choose to have. It may be noted in passing that this is indeed one of the more potent arguments against the restoration of the gold standard. If governments were willing to follow policies consistent with the maintenance of a gold standard, then the gold standard itself would not be necessary; if, however, governments were not willing to follow such policies, then the introduction of the gold standard per se would not restore stability since, before long, the standard would have to be abandoned.

Webster's dictionary defines reform as an improvement and a removal of faults. How can anyone be against reform? The key questions, however, are what should be reformed, what are the *costs of* the reform, and *when* should such reform be adopted. A prerequisite for target zones is that there be agreement on the approximate value of the equilibrium exchange rate, on the boundaries of zones, and on the actions that must take place once the boundaries are reached. At the present such agreement is not in hand. Even if there was agreement on the "equilibrium" exchange rates, one would need to specify in detail what happens if the boundaries are exceeded. It is not enough to say "push them back." We must decide which country should bear the burden of adjustment and which policy will effect that move — monetary, fiscal, government spending, tax? Once this is recognized, it becomes clear that the key difficulties may not lie in the formal structure of the present international monetary system, but rather in the overall mix of macroeconomic policies.

Some say that it is just a matter of tactics whether one examines the system by looking through the exchange rate lens or through the global lens, and that they prefer to focus on the exchange rate lens. I disagree. I believe that the difference between the two lenses is fundamental. It is not a matter of tactics, but is the difference between having a general framework and having a particular framework. It is the difference between patching up a hole here and forgetting that the dam is going to collapse there versus having a consistent set of policies. In principle the adoption of target zones could be acceptable if they encompassed the entire *array* of macroeconomic policies, including in particular fiscal policies. At present the diverging international positions of fiscal policies suggest that it is entirely unlikely that international agreement on such a sweeping reform is feasible. Most of the burden, therefore, is likely to fall on the instruments of monetary policy. As long as fiscal policies are misaligned, a "successful" targeting of the exchange rate by using monetary policies may exacerbate the departures from the optimal mix of fiscal and monetary policies and may be very costly in terms of the overall economic system.

An argument favoring target zones is that the very process of negotiations is likely to enhance the degree of international policy coordination. It must be noted, however, that some successful coordination efforts have also occurred during the past decade (for example, the U.S. dollar support package of November 1978, the Bonn economic summit of 1978, and more recently the G-5 agreement of September 1985). Further, it might be argued that coordination should not be complete, because the perception of independent monetary policy may be necessary for sustaining confidence that monetary policy will not be inflationary in the long run. In addition, there is the danger that the process of negotiating target zones could produce serious frictions among the negotiating parties and could lead ultimately to a reduced level of coordination in this and other areas.

Every system must have a safety valve which allows some flexibility and prevents a crisis and collapse with every conflict. With misaligned fiscal policies and with monetary policies geared towards exchange rate targeting, it would be unfortunate if governments were to exercise their sovereignty by resorting to protectionistic trade policies —

to an even greater extent than has been the case under the present system of floating rates with independent monetary policy. The growing frustration with the efforts to reduce the U.S. fiscal deficit by conventional measures has brought about new desperate arguments for the adoption of protectionist measures like import surcharges. The danger with such recommendations is that they might receive the political support of two otherwise unrelated groups. They are likely to gain the support of the traditional advocates of protectionism who claim to defend local industry and workers from what they believe is unfair foreign competition. But, more dangerously, they may gain the support of those whose exclusive concern with the budget deficit leads them to support almost any policy that raises fiscal revenue. Import surcharges, once in place (even those surcharges that are adopted as "temporary measures") are hard to remove since, as George Stigler once remarked, "a sustained policy that has real effects has many good friends." At the present there are very few measures whose long-term costs to the interdependent world economy may be as high as protectionist measures. Taxes on trade will hurt exports, and will restore inward-looking economic isolationism instead of outward-looking economic coordination. Protectionist measures will transmit the wrong signals to those developing countries that are still attempting to resist domestically popular pressures to default on their debt, and, further, they may ignite a trade war. This argument should be considered against the claim that by preventing misalignments of exchange rates target zones reduce the protectionist pressures. With misaligned fiscal policies, the net effect of target zones for exchange rates, implemented through monetary policy, are not clear cut.

The key point made by proponents of target zones is that such a system encompasses the *best* of both worlds — it possess the flexibility of the flexible exchange rate regime as well as the stability of the fixed exchange rate regime. The same logic could be used, however, to argue that this hybrid system encompasses the *worst* of both worlds — it possess the instability of flexible rates and the unsustainability of fixed rates. For in contrast with fixed parties, the target zones are moving. As they move, how do we escape from the inherent difficulty of having the private sector speculate against governments? In the absence of an anchor, what ensures credibility? How exactly are conflicts resolved?

What ensures that the moving target zones do not increase turbulence in the foreign exchange market rather than reduce it?

A central feature of any operational monetary system must be a formal resolution of the so-called n-1 problem. We have n currencies and only n-1 independent exchange rates. We thus have one degree of freedom and its disposal must be explicitly specified. It takes two to tango and it takes one for intervention. The original Bretton Woods system allocated the degree of freedom to the United States which obliged itself to peg the price of gold at \$35 an ounce; the other n -1 countries then committed themselves to peg their currencies to the U.S. dollar. A design of the international monetary system is not complete unless it provides an explicit resolution to this n -1 problem. Therefore, it is essential to ask how the various proposals, including those for target zones, deal with the extra degree of freedom.

As a general rule, a reform of the system should not be viewed as an instrument for crisis management. The considerations appropriate for crisis management focus on *short-term* effectiveness. In contrast the considerations appropriate for designing the optimal monetary system should be governed by a *long-term* perspective. The two need not coincide and it is sensible to separate them. In the present context, the short-term crisis concerns the fiscal imbalances in the world economy rather than the monetary system. To be sure, the existing international monetary system is not perfect and it might benefit from a face lift or even from a more drastic reform. A target-zones system is clearly one of the options. But such a reform should perhaps wait until nations restore a more sustainable course of fiscal management.

A reform of the international monetary system should be viewed as a constitutional change that should not be taken lightly. The success of a new monetary arrangement depends on the adoption of a consistent set of policy tools and on a reasonable understanding of the implications of each course of action. In these matters, the cost of delaying the adoption of a new international monetary arrangement until its full implications are understood is likely to be small relative to the cost of a premature implementation. The various proposals for reform of the present international monetary system have many attractions. But since they are novel, prudence is clearly called for. More discussions and critical evaluations can be highly desirable. In view of this it may be a good place to conclude with a quote from John Maynard Keynes' remarks in his closing speech at the original Bretton Woods Conference held over forty years ago. Speaking on the desirability of critical evaluations of the proposed system, Keynes said: "I am greatly encouraged, I confess, by the critical, sceptical and even carping spirit in which our proceedings have been watched and welcomed in the outside world. How much better that our projects should *begin* in disillusion than that they should *end* in it!"

VIII

THE IMF: PRO AND CON

The International Monetary Fund (IMF) was established after World War II with the idea that it would support the Bretton Woods fixed exchange rate system and provide temporary financing to countries facing short term balance of payments problems. Over the past few decades, the role of the IMF has increased substantially; today, few people would dispute the fact that the IMF is one of the most important and most powerful financial institutions in the world, particularly for developing countries. The key role that the IMF plays in the world economy is not so much due to its lending, which is on the same order of magnitude as many other financial institutions, but rather it is due to the fact that most private banks and many development agencies require the IMF's seal of approval before they will lend to a country.

As a result of its position as lender of last resort and as the chief evaluator of a country's economic policies, the IMF has been heavily criticized, particularly by the left. Critics of the IMF argue that in order to meet IMF approval, a country is required to follow very restrictive macroeconomic policies (e.g., reducing budget deficits dramatically, cutting the money supply, etc.) which lead to high unemployment and to a restriction of social programs. Much of the burden of these policies falls on the poor. In response to IMF policies it is not uncommon to see rioting in urban centers of the third world. Critics also argue that IMF policies can only be enforced by coercive, authoritarian governments and thus the IMF thwarts attempts at democracy in the third world.

In the first article below, "Back to Keynesianism: Reforming the IMF," Frances Stewart contends that the current policies of the IMF are in sharp contrast to the ideas that Keynes envisioned when he first proposed the IMF. Stewart argues that the IMF has been taken over by monetarists and that the contractionary policies that they recommend have not encouraged the type of self-sustaining growth necessary for economic development. She believes that the IMF should follow a more explicitly Keynesian, expansionary approach in its recommendations to developing countries.

In contrast, the second article, "The IMF under fire" defends the IMF. Amuzegar argues that the IMF's policies are a necessary response to the past excesses of many third world governments living beyond their means. The IMF has been given the unfortunate role of telling countries when they have reached their credit limit.

20

Back to Keynesianism: Reforming the IMF

Frances Stewart

The 1944 Bretton Woods conference may be seen as an attempt to institutionalize at an international level the revolution in economic ideas brought about by John Maynard Keynes. Keynes believed that the prosperity of nations — in particular, their levels of production and employment — did not need to be the unplanned outcome of an uncoordinated and erratic system, but could be controlled by government. At a national level, this revolution in theory did not require new mechanisms and institutions, but rather new approaches to existing ones: adjustments had to be made in government spending and taxation and in central banks' money creation and interest rate determination. But no mechanisms existed at the international level to perform these functions; there were no international counterparts to central banks or national budgets. In 1941, then, Keynes developed the idea of an International Clearing Union — a sort of world-level central bank. His plan provided the main basis for the Bretton Woods discussions.

The 44 nations represented there had set out to create international institutions throughout the world that would prevent the recurrence of a 1930s-style depression, with its massive unemployment, escalating tariffs, and collapsing commodity prices. After considerable negotiation, the International Monetary Fund (IMF) and World Bank were established. Although in structure and functioning the IMF differs quite radically from Keynes' own plan, [1] its fundamental objective was decidedly Keynesian. According to the first of its Articles of Agreement, one of the IMF's basic purposes was

> To facilitate the expansion of balanced growth in international trade, and to contribute thereby to the promotion and maintenance of high levels of employment and real income and to the development of the productive resources of all members as primary objectives of economic policy.

The Bretton Woods Agreement charged the IMF with prime responsibility for short-term macroeconomic developments — specifically, with maintaining stable exchange rates, except in situations of fundamental disequilibrium, and with providing finance to assist countries whose balance of payments were in short-term equilibrium. The World Bank was oriented more toward development. As indicated by its official name — the Bank for International Reconstruction and Development — it initially had two main functions. The first was temporary: to help finance the reconstruction of the war-devastated economies of Europe. The second primary duty, as described by Keynes, was "to develop the resources and productive capacity of the world with special attention to the less developed countries, to raise the standard of life and the conditions of labor everywhere, and so to promote and maintain equilibrium in the international balance of payments of all member countries." [2]

During the 40 years that have elapsed since Bretton Woods, there have been many changes in the international economy. New centers of economic power, notably Japan, have developed; and the positions of old centers such as Great Britain have sharply eroded. International capital markets have grown enormously, and have changed in nature. Of major significance, both politically and economically, has been the displacement of colonialism and the subsequent emergence of 100 or so independent Third World governments.

Such shifts have contributed to changes in the Bretton Woods institutions. The World Bank has become a major development institution — a significant source of finance and advice for projects, sectoral development, and development policy — but it contributes little to the making of world macroeconomic policy. This has been the responsibility of the IMF. At regular intervals, the Fund makes assessments of the world economy. Although it has made some moves toward generalized interventions, it has for the most part — especially in recent years — focused most closely and vigorously on influencing the policies and finance of deficit countries seeking access to its resources. Accordingly, any attempt to analyze the IMF's effects on Third World countries and on the world economy as a whole must concentrate on IMF country programs.

The IMF's influence on the policies of individual countries has grown over the decades. The 1950s saw the development of the practice of "conditionality," which makes access to IMF finance conditional on a country's adopting certain macroeconomic policies. Initially, conditionality requirements were imposed only on a minority of countries receiving loans (about one out of four in the 1970s, for example); but by the 1980s conditionality had become more pervasive, applying to over three-quarters of IMF loans. At the same time, as more countries have experienced economic difficulties, more have turned to the Fund for finance. In the 1970s, an average of 10 countries initiated programs each year. In the 1980s, this number has never fallen below 20, and throughout the first half of the decade over 40 countries had IMF programs in effect for at least one month each year.

The Fund itself generally only provides a small proportion of most countries' financial needs. Yet its influence extends well beyond its strictly financial significance, since other institutions have come to demand that countries have IMF agreements before they will agree to supply additional finance. The private banking sector almost universally makes such a requirement before rescheduling Third World countries' loans, as does the Paris Club, which deals with official loans from bilateral borrowers. This type of "cross-conditionality," whereby conditions imposed by one institution (the IMF) serve as requirements for other institutions as well, has also extended to the Structural Adjustment Loans of the World Bank. Consequently, for countries in financial difficulty, obtaining finance from nearly any source — the private banking sector, bilateral donors, the World Bank — has become contingent on the country's agreeing to IMF conditionality.

While the Fund's influence has grown over the decades, the condition of the world economy has declined. Unemployment in developed nations has risen in every decade since the 1940s. Output growth has slowed. The 1980s has so far proved the worst decade for all countries — especially the poorer ones — since the Great Depression. Indeed, in many respects they seem to be a repeat of that time: as in the 1930s, the markets of the developed countries have been stagnant and protectionism has risen, while the terms of trade of primary producers have been worsening and commodity prices have fallen lower than they have been for 50 years. To make matters worse, voluntary private lending to developing countries through the banking system, which became a dominant source of finance in the 1970s, has more or less stopped.

This widespread economic deterioration has caused acute problems for many developing countries. The stagnancy of world markets, the growth of protectionism, and the fall in commodity prices have made it increasingly difficult for them to earn their way out of their economic troubles. In 1985, their export earnings were 15 percent below the 1980 level. At the same time, trade deficits have become less and less easy to finance. The bank lending that flowed freely in the 1970s has dried up in the 1980s, yet debt service obligations have continued to mount, pushed upward by high interest rates. Some countries have had to set aside more than half of their export earnings for debt servicing, which leaves a small portion of a declining total available to pay for imports. From this situation emerged an acute foreign exchange crisis, which led more and more Third World countries to turn to the IMF.

Indeed, the first half of this decade could be described as years of IMF conditionality in Africa and Latin America. Two-thirds of the countries in those regions undertook IMF programs; the overall shift in economic climate caused many others to adopt policies similar to IMF programs in order to satisfy their hungry creditors. Thus, in effect, the IMF became the major policymaker in most African and Latin American countries. These years therefore provide an opportunity to assess the impact the Fund's advice has had on individual countries. Moreover, because of the IMF's central role in the world financial system, and because its advice has been taken by so many countries, its impact has extended well beyond developments in individual countries to the world economy as a whole.

There is a paradox in the events of the first half of the1980s. These were years when Keynesian policies were most needed, and when the IMF had more influence than at any time in its history. Yet they were also years when the world economy, and particularly developing countries, veered away from the path envisioned by the IMF's founders — that of high income and employment and development of productive resources. Faced with this seeming contradiction, one has to ask what effect IMF conditionality programs have had on the world economy.

CONDITIONALITY PROGRAMS IN THE 1980s

It would be impossible to provide a through and fair assessment of IMF programs in the 1980s. Not all the facts are in; moreover, because the international economic environment was deteriorating so sharply, it is difficult to determine how countries would have fared if Fund programs had *not* been in place. Nevertheless, a general examination of the IMF's impact during this period does lead me to some broad conclusions, and suggests that all concerned parties would most likely benefit from a search for improved alternatives to current IMF conditionality.

At present, the Fund programs applied to different countries have a great many characteristics in common. They are usually negotiated in secret on a bilateral basis — in other words, independent parties, other countries, and international institutions besides the IMF are not involved. Instead, the details of the conditionality agreement are typically worked out between the IMF representatives and officials from the country's finance ministry and central bank. It is partly because of these individuals' orientation that IMF programs rely heavily on macroeconomic policy instruments and tend to neglect the social and political aspects of a country's situation.

Fund programs are usually introduced when a country's economy is in severe imbalance — externally, with large current account deficits in the balance of payments, and internally, with high rates of inflation and deficits in the domestic budget. In order to correct these imbalances, IMF programs use three types of policy. One is to restrain demand, through cuts in government spending, limits on credit creation, increases in taxation, and restraints on wages and public sector employment. Another is to encourage the channeling of resources into tradable goods, through devaluations in the country's currency and through price reforms. The third is to implement such measures as financial reform and import liberalization intended to raise the medium- and long-term efficiency of the economy.

In actuality, the second and third types of policy, which are supply- oriented, tend to receive less emphasis than the first. This heavy reliance on demand restraint is due partly to the short time horizon of most programs — typically 12 to 18 months. Such a period is long enough to make short-term improvements in the balance of trade by curtailing incomes, expenditure, and demand and thereby almost immediately reducing imports. Measures to expand supply, on the other hand, nearly always take much longer. For example, Brazil's highly successful import substitution strategy in the 1980s was based on massive investments it had made during the 1970s in energy and machinery production. Sri Lanka's tremendous surge in rice production after 1977, which allowed it to eliminate rice imports, was the result of a decade-long investment in irrigation. Without such substantial, long-term investment, it is extremely difficult to significantly increase output of products that can be exported or can serve as substitutes for imports. Accordingly, any program requiring short-term improvements in the balance of trade will inevitably stress reduction of demand. (It should be noted that in the IMF's 1952 decision to endorse conditionality, the adjustment period was defined as 3 to 5 years — far longer than today's normal standby. [3] The IMF's Extended Fund Facility introduced during the late 1970s, is usually for three-year periods; but it has been used relatively infrequently in recent years.)

Perhaps more than any other factor, it is the IMF's philosophy — its beliefs about political economy and economic causality — that most influences the specific content of Fund programs. In general, this philosophy, largely shared by the World Bank, is monetarist; for a long period, the Fund explicitly adopted a monetary approach to balance-of-payments problems and also (somewhat inconsistently, since one instrument cannot normally be used to achieve two objectives) to inflation. The Fund's philosophy is also laissez-faire, with emphasis on price rather than controls, the private rather than the public sector, and free trade rather than protectionism. Because of its strong and pervasive philosophy, the IMF is not only concerned with policy objectives but also takes a firm view about which policy instruments are preferable. Thus even though the intentions of the Bretton Woods fathers were Keynesian, the institutions they created have turned out to be anti-Keynesian.

It is not surprising, then, that the original Keynesian objectives have not been achieved. The record of the 1980s shows just how far short of achieving those objectives IMF programs have fallen. Many countries with Fund programs experienced severe economic difficulties:

- Per capita income tended to contract. This was true of more than 70 percent of IMF-assisted countries in Africa and Latin America; by contrast, 83 percent of Asian countries had rising per capita incomes.
- Unemployment rose. In more Latin American countries, urban unemployment increased dramatically: in Chile, from 10.4 percent

in 1981 to 15.9 percent in 1984; in Bolivia, from 7.5 percent in 1980 to 13.3 percent in 1984; in Mexico, from 11.7 percent in 1980 to 18.5 percent in 1984.

- Urban poverty increased, as both employment and real incomes decreased. For example, between 1981 and 1984 real wages fell by 28 percent in Brazil, 13 percent in Peru, and 30 percent in Mexico. In Ghana, the real urban wage in 1985 was less than one-quarter of what it had been in 1974; in Zambia, real wages have been cut by half. In general, there has been less change in the situation of the rural poor.

- Per capita government spending, including expenditure on social services and food subsidies, was reduced. As a result, between 1980 and 1984 real government expenditure per head fell in over 50 percent of African countries and 70 percent of Latin American countries.

- There was a rise in malnutrition among children in a large number of African countries, many of which also suffered from acute drought, and in several Latin American countries — Bolivia, Jamaica, Brazil, Chile, Guyana, and Uruguay, all of which had Fund programs at some time in the 1980s.

- Between 1980 and 1983, levels of real investment were stagnant or falling in 60 percent of African countries with IMF programs and 58 percent of Latin American countries.

- Between 1980 and 1984, there was no improvement in the current account of the balance of payments in 40 percent of African IMF-assisted countries and 52 percent of Latin American countries. In some cases the payments balance actually deteriorated.

- Current levels of output and income have fallen; and the combination of stagnant real investment, rising malnutrition, and falling health and educational standards has adversely affected physical and human capital. As a result, the prospects for medium- and long-term economic growth are being undermined. Thus, after undergoing tough IMF programs, many countries have found themselves with reduced real incomes, increased poverty, deteriorating social conditions, reduced growth potential — and, often, no significant improvement in their external accounts balance. In this last respect, the IMF programs failed even to meet their most narrowly defined goal — to improve the imbalance on the external account.

It must be emphasized that these negative developments have not been confined to countries with Fund programs and therefore cannot be wholly attributed to Fund conditionality as such, especially because the external economic environment worsened significantly over this period. The facts do not prove that the situation would have been better without IMF conditionality; indeed, it might have been worse. But the facts do show — unambiguously — that the developments associated with Fund programs in the 1980s have been highly unsatisfactory.

This is particularly evident in the experience of sub-Saharan Africa. [4] At one time or another, most countries in this region had IMF programs. Many had a succession of them, each broken off as performance criteria were violated. From 1980 to 1985, the Fund's cumulative lending to sub- Saharan Africa was approximately $4.6 billion. But despite this substantial inflow of funds, and despite the fact that over this period African countries made a nearly 20 percent cut in imports, the region's current account deficit did not improve; it was minus $7 billion both in 1980 and in 1985, and worse during the intervening years. And the $4.6 billion lent by the IMF is due to be repaid, with interest, in the second half of the decade.

This repayment will be made more difficult by the deterioration in the domestic economies of most sub-Saharan countries from 1980 to 1985. Per capita incomes fell. Progress toward improving health, education, and nutrition was brought to an abrupt halt, and in many countries was reversed. Newly established clinics could not operate effectively because of lack of medicine.. Schools had no money for books or paper; low salaries led to high teacher absenteeism; and children dropped out in increasing numbers, since household survival depended on their working. Malnutrition rates of 50 percent and over among children under five were recorded in many countries in addition to those affected by drought. Even those countries that fared better than average in economic terms — such as Zimbabwe, the Ivory Coast, and recently Ghana — remain in precarious positions, with large deficits and foreign exchange shortages that threaten to undermine their growth potential.

AGGREGATE EFFECTS OF IMF ACTIVITIES

The inadequacy of Fund programs at a world level becomes clearer if one examines the impact they have had not only on individual countries but on the world economy as a whole. In general, the IMF's approach to correcting payments imbalances has created a worldwide tendency toward deflation. Adjustment programs require deficit countries to attempt to eliminate their deficits by cutting expenditure and employment so that their imports fall. Such a strategy might, under the right conditions, help reduce deficits in Third World countries' current account balances. But when applied to many of these countries simultaneously, it also causes a significant drop in Third World demand for both Third World and Western products. A significant part of the U.S. trade deficit, for example, can be traced to decreased demand in the Third World; 70 percent of the $23 billion drop in U.S. exports during the 1980s resulted from lower demand for U.S. products in Latin America alone. Thus IMF-mandated cutbacks in Third World spending and employment have caused world-wide decreases in demand and therefore output.

Deflation is not the only way to correct imbalances in external accounts. The alternative would be to correct surpluses through reflation; surplus countries would try to eliminate their surpluses by increasing their spending so that their imports rise. The net effect on external accounts would be the same — because exports, output, and incomes of deficit countries would be raised, their deficits would be lowered. The IMF's original charter did include a "scarce currency" clause designed to encourage symmetry of adjustment by placing pressure on chronically surplused countries to bring their surpluses down. But the clause has never been invoked, and the Fund's approach has remained highly asymmetrical; the major burden of policy change and adjustment is imposed on deficit countries.

Other aspects of IMF conditionality have had similarly negative effects when the same program is imposed on many countries at once. At the same time that the Fund's overall impact has been deflationary, so that basic demand for developing products has not been sustained, Fund programs have also tended to increase the supply of these products. IMF country programs have been tailored to expand production of primary commodities — in some cases, the same product in more than one country. For example, both Ghana and the Ivory Coast have had programs to increase cocoa production. This upward shift in cocoa output, because it did not result from or cause an upward shift in demand, had the result that could have been predicted by anyone with rudimentary knowledge of the laws of supply and demand: prices were driven down. In fact, for commodities with low demand elasticities — commodities for which a price cut does not induce a substantial rise in demand, since consumption is not much affected by price — an increase in production may lower prices so much that a country's total earnings from those commodities actually fall. Past experience has shown that this is the case for many commodities, especially those in which some very poor countries specialize, such as cocoa, tea, and coffee. [5]

Thus when the IMF encourages production increases from a number of major producers of particular commodities without simultaneously taking action to increase demand for those commodities, the net result may be to decrease deficit countries' foreign exchange earnings from commodity production while increasing the resources they devote to that production. Fund programs have thereby contributed to primary producers' worsening terms of trade, which were in turn partly responsible for the limited improvements many Third World countries were able to make in their current account balances. Once again, IMF policy worked at cross-purposes to its stated goals.

Currency devaluations have often had a similarly damaging effect on the terms of trade of exporters of manufactured goods, since such devaluations lower the relative price that producers receive for their manufactured exports. But in this case, as opposed to that of primary commodities, there is more potential for the Third World as a whole to increase its share of the world market. As a result, reduced prices may be more than offset by an increase in the quantity sold — provided, of course, that developed countries do not impose trade restrictions.

When assessing the aggregate effect of Fund financing in the 1980s, one must consider the economic environment in which deficit countries operated. This environment was one of sharp decline, not only in world output and trade, but also in financial flows to the Third World. In 1977-78, there was a positive net transfer of $8.6 billion to Africa; by 1984-85, that had become a negative flow of $5.4 billion. The change was even more dramatic for Latin America, where a positive balance of $4.9 billion had become a negative transfer of $39 billion by 1984-85. To make matters worse, in 1986 real commodity prices, measured in dollars, were 24 percent below their 1980 level. Measured against this background of great need, the IMF's own contribution to developing countries was small. From 1980 to 1985, the cumulative net transfer of Fund credit to capital- importing countries was $31.5 billion; their cumulative current account deficit was $464.3 billion. By 1985, the net transfer from the IMF had actually become negative, as money borrowed earlier came due for repayment. This negative transfer is expected to persist for the rest of the decade, so that if it continues present policy, the IMF will make no net financing contribution in the difficult years ahead. In fact, the real net transfer that was effected through the Fund is even smaller than the above figures suggest, since deficit countries have often been required to channel IMF finance toward repayment of arrears to other debtors.

Another way in which the Fund has had an impact on deficit countries is through its role in the debt crisis. Because debt servicing accounts for such a large proportion of countries' external payments — $24 billion among capital-importing countries in 1985 — the IMF's approach to the debt situation greatly influences countries' financial situations. As the crisis unfolded after 1982, the commercial banks turned to the IMF to provide coordination and leadership. The IMF's general approach has been to deal with each country in turn, "case by case." First, the country must accept an IMF program. At that point, the debt is rescheduled. This delays the immediate burden of amortization, but it increases the amount ultimately owed, since interest accumulates on the unpaid debt and since banks charge a servicing fee for the rescheduling exercise. Throughout this process, the debtor country is required to maintain interest payments.

This approach has placed heavy financial demands on debtor countries — so much so that the IMF can almost be viewed as the major commercial banks' debt collector. Recently, a few countries have rebelled, arguing that payments demanded are far too large for them to stick to the IMF agreements while also trying to maintain investment, economic growth, and basic social services. Peru, for example, announced last year that it would limit debt service payments to 10 percent of export earnings. Since then, economic growth in Peru has exceeded 8 percent.

That countries are taking such measures is an indication of how hostile the world economic climate has become. According to its originally stated goals, the IMF should be responsible for ensuring that the international environment be compatible with increasing world output, employment, and development. Yet the IMF has not made its own programs — much less the world economy — consistent with these goals. The basic hopes and intentions of the Bretton Woods founders have not been realized, as the IMF has not evolved in such a way as to discharge its original responsibilities. The problem is not technical but political: the dominant governments, which set the major limits on Fund functioning, have imposed their own vision on the IMF.

There are two different ways to interpret the role of international financial institutions. As originally stated at Bretton Woods, the IMF's and World Bank's objectives were to promote world employment, incomes, and growth, and to work to eliminate world poverty. But these institutions have also been seen as having the primary function of preserving world financial stability and an open trading environment — one in which multinational companies can invest freely with confidence. Put more crudely, this means ensuring that debtors do not renege but rather repay the commercial banks, and the developing countries maintain open markets for Western products, imposing no troublesome restrictions on multinational investment. In this view, international financial institutions are meant primarily to support the interests of Western banks and companies.

The history of the IMF and World Bank, especially the policies they have followed in the 1980s, suggests that the second function has been given absolute supremacy and that the first has been sacrificed to it. Some observers would argue that there is no real conflict between the two, and that achieving the second — making the world economy safe for Western banks and companies — is a prerequisite for achieving the first. It is true that there are some positive interrelationships, which work both ways, and that a certain amount of stability in finance and trade is necessary for international economic prosperity, including that of the Third World. But financial stability maintained at the *expense* of Third World prosperity actually threatens the long-term profitability of Western interests. Third World markets for Western producers will not grow if the Third World incomes do not grow, or if all available resources are preempted for debt servicing. Moreover, as the case of

Peru has made clear, countries that are forced to pursue deflationary policies in order to service their debts may eventually refuse to continue playing the bankers' game — much to the banking community's loss. By giving so much priority to international financial interests and so little to Third World well-being, the international financial institutions have secured a financial stability that is temporary and fragile. Rather than forcing deficit countries to bear the entire burden of adjustment, the IMF would be better advised to work toward Third World prosperity, which would provide a much more secure basis for world economic growth and vitality.

ALTERNATIVES

Changes in the world's economic and financial arrangements are needed at two levels — the international and the country-specific. At present, it seems more feasible to take action on the second level, that of individual countries' policy-making, in order to prevent the further impoverishment of those who are most deprived. But unless alterations are also made at the international level, other changes can only be a kind of mopping-up operation. Thus it is important to work toward a consensus on the long-term adjustments that need to be made in the international economy, especially as it affects the Third World.

Particularly crucial is the need to expand world demand and trade. If countries are to continue to grow at the same time that they work to improve their trade imbalances, they must be able to expand their export earnings rather than simply cutting their imports, which results in decreased output and investment. Export expansion, however, does not automatically occur when countries increase their supplies — there must also be increased demand, so that those exports can be absorbed. So if the Third World as a whole is to pursue a path of growth-oriented adjustment by increasing its exports, there must be a sustained rise in world demand.

Such growth in demand for Third World products depends largely on the major industrialized countries' domestic policies — specifically, those regarding growth in their domestic demand and access to their markets by developing nations. Such growth in demand and free market access do not come about simply through the operations of an unregulated world economy; international intervention is needed.

Of the institutions currently in existence, the IMF is the most appropriate one to undertake such intervention. In addition to monitoring world economic developments, which to some extent it already does, the Fund should be empowered to take actions that would ensure a world environment conducive to balanced growth.

Two sorts of actions are appropriate. First, pressure should be put on countries that chronically run surpluses. The pressure should be backed by sanctions, such as trade and exchange rate discrimination to force surplus countries to expand their domestic demand, thereby increasing their imports and reducing their surpluses. In the past, the Fund has not taken this kind of symmetrical approach to adjustment — requiring policy changes in surplus countries as well as deficit countries. But today there may be more support for adjustment steps aimed at surplus countries, given that the United States has become the world's largest debtor. Indeed, Washington has already moved in that direction, initiating sanctions against surplus companies both multilaterally, through the Group of Five, and bilaterally, by restricting imports. These efforts are bearing some fruit because of America's strong position in the world. What is needed is to systematize and institutionalize sanctions so that all deficit countries benefit, as was intended at Bretton Woods. The object would not be to prevent any and all sustained surpluses, but rather to ensure that at a minimum they are balanced by long-term capital outflows on reasonable terms, so as to prevent deflationary impact on their countries.

Second, if adequate adjustment does not occur among surplus countries, the IMF should be empowered to issue additional Special Drawing Rights to deficit countries in order to grant them the liquidity needed to finance their deficits. Under Keynes's original plan prepared for Bretton Woods, an international central bank would have been in a position — indeed, would have had the duty — to sustain world output by issuing new money (bancors, to use Keynes's term) if the policies of national governments seemed likely to lead to world depression. The IMF has never had that authority as such. But the creation in 1969 of the Special Drawing Right, which was designed to cope with a shortage of liquidity, has given the Fund potentially the same power — if, that is, member governments authorize the SDR issue. Currently, however, the IMF must seek explicit approval from donor governments before issuing SDRs, a requirement that has prevented it from playing a more substantial role in maintaining world growth and output. The IMF charter should be altered to give the Fund itself discretionary power to make special SDR issues.

Beyond these two adjustment mechanisms, consideration must also be given to stabilizing the prices of commodities, upon which many developing countries remain dependent, and to ensuring adequate long-term development financing. Expanded world output and trade would help sustain commodity prices and could make commodity price agreements unnecessary. But given the presently uncertain prospects for world commodity demand — compounded by IMF policies that mandate increased commodity production — commodity prices are likely to continue their disastrous 10-year slide unless commodity price agreements are reached. Such agreements should stipulate floor prices, limitations on supply, and the creation of buffer stocks. Again, additional SDRs could be issued to support commodity prices when they fall below a certain level. This would help stabilize both prices and world demand.

By boosting prices of Third World products and improving markets for them, the changes described above would reduce the extent of adjustment that deficit countries needed to make. But it would be necessary not just to reduce deficits in the short term, but also to improve the prospects for long-term growth and development. This means that developing countries must have access to adequate development financing. Expansionary and growth-oriented adjustment typically requires a significant amount of foreign exchange to finance the investment and imports that are needed for constructing a productive base. Currently, growth prospects in many countries are being undermined by a lack of finance, which forces cuts in investment, maintenance, and spending on education and health — the crucial element of "human capital." In Zambia, for instance, copper exports are falling because of the scarcity of foreign exchange for essential equipment and parts; in Tanzania, shortage of import finance has led to deterioration of the transport system and extreme shortages of incentive consumer goods, with the result of continuing stagnation in the production of export crops. A downward spiral of disequilibrium can occur in cases like these; a shortage of foreign exchange causes a drop in export production, which in turn exacerbates the foreign exchange crisis.

Substantially more finance — particularly more medium term finance — is essential for growth-oriented adjustment. The World Bank, making unrealistically optimistic calculations for sub-Saharan Africa based on a hypothesized 10 percent annual increase in export earnings for the rest of the decade, estimated a foreign exchange gap of $2.5 billion for low-income countries. The true gap is much greater, its exact extent depending on how developments in the World economy affect African exports. The gap is great in Latin America as well: substantial additional finance is essential if countries are to be able to meet the objectives of adjustment and growth and fulfill their debt-servicing obligations.

What is needed is substantial additional net transfer of funds — inflows of new money beyond what flows out for amortization and interest. In this sense, much existing finance is not additional, as it simply finances repayment of old debts. Moreover, banks today are making virtually no additional voluntary loans; since other funding is also relatively scarce, perhaps the most effective way to gain additional net transfer is to slow down or limit outflows for debt servicing. Peru has done so, its policy of limiting debt-servicing payments has prevented many new inflows, the amount Peru has saved on reduced outflows exceeds the amount of finance it might otherwise have been able to bring in. In general, the smaller the new inflows from aid or commercial sources, the more likely it is that additional net transfer will have to come about as a result either of renegotiation of payments on existing debt or unilateral moratoria on debt servicing. This means major, across-the-board reductions in debt servicing, instead of the current case-by-case approach.

If these proposed changes in the international environment — increased finance for development, support for commodity prices, expansion of world demand and trade — are to have necessary beneficial impact, they must be considered in relation to each other. In other words, they must be considered as a whole, not one by one. On the one hand, the extent of a change needed in one area depends on what happens elsewhere; for example, less finance would be necessary if countries could earn more commodity sales. On the other hand, changes in one area can actually be quite ineffective unless changes are made elsewhere — more aid can simply mean more debt servicing. Such a wholistic approach would be quite alien to the international financial institutions; they treat each issue separately, discussing different ones in different arenas and dealing with countries' problems on an individual basis. These procedures need to be substantially revised.

If these revisions were made, and major changes were effected in the world economy, there would be less need for adjustment by individual developing countries (although some adjustments would still be necessary to permit countries to take full advantage of the improved external conditions). But since, in the near future, radical changes in the international economy are unlikely, substantial country adjustment will continue to be necessary.

At present, the IMF affects the Third World primarily through country conditionality programs. These programs have been accompanied in recent years by negative effects on output and social welfare, as described earlier. For long-term development to occur, present trends must be reversed: imbalances in external and domestic accounts need to be reduced, yet at the same time there should be efforts to maintain the incomes of the poorest, protect social welfare, and promote the conditions for medium-term growth. What is needed is adjustment with a human face. [6]

To begin with, the IMF and Third World countries need to reach agreement about the legitimate boundaries of conditionality. Some conditionality is legitimate and may be necessary. Lenders, including the IMF (which is not an aid institution but has to revolve the funds at its disposal), do require some assurance that they will be repaid. When there is no suitable collateral, policy conditionality provides some assurance of repayment for international loans intended to support balance of payments adjustment. Some Third World governments have rejected this notion, however, and in their confrontations with the IMF have denied any role for conditonality. This is one reason they have been so unsuccessful in gaining access to finance or in improving the terms under which they receive it. The cases of Jamaica under Michael Manley, and Tanzania in the late 1970s and early 1980s, are obvious examples.

At the same time, conditionality has, in practice, far exceeded admissable and legitimate limits. Conditionality has been applied to nearly any country seeking IMF finance, regardless of the country's repayment record or prospects. Furthermore, as we have seen, the policies prescribed go well beyond those strictly related to repayment.

In attempting to reformulate conditionality along more appropriate lines, one should keep in mind that it must be country-specific, geared toward each individual country's economic, social, and political situation and prospects. One cannot, therefore, lay out a detailed conditionality program that could be universally applied. But it is possible to point to the kinds of changes that in most cases are needed:

- The IMF and World Bank need to take a more open and less dogmatic view both of the underlying works of the world economy and of the desirability of particular policy instruments and institutions. The prevalent philosophy in the international financial institutions — broadly neo-classical and monetarist, laissez-faire and antistate — is not proven theoretically or empirically. Certainly, as we have seen, its recent achievements have not been spectacular. Unless a more open, flexible, and empirical view is adopted by all parties, the search for a better alternative will be impeded; and progress toward programs that are jointly initiated and developed, rather than imposed, will be limited.

- Conditionality programs need to take fuller account of social and political realities. Economists' "first-best" solutions, such as large currency devaluations or eliminations of consumer subsidies, may need to be discarded in order to avoid political unrest and disruption of the program. In Zambia and the Sudan, for instance, tough "first-best" programs led to civil unrest, political upheaval, and the abandonment of a series of IMF agreements.

- Macroeconomic policies need to be more expansionary (or less deflationary). How far this is possible depends partly on the availability of external finance. But even within financial constraints, more expansion can be achieved if greater stress is placed on import substitution and sectors with low imports.

- Short-term policy changes should be designed to be consistent with the requirements of medium-size development. In sub-Saharan Africa, for instance, the present conditionality is focused mostly on agriculture and is having deindustrializing effects. Yet for the medium to long term, a country's industrial sector must play an important role in providing simple consumption and investment goods for the domestic economy, for export to the region, and eventually for world markets.

- Within any given macroeconomic policy framework, mesopolicies must be used to channel resources toward economic growth and to meet the needs of the vulnerable. Mesopolicies are those that take into account the impact of all policy instruments — including taxation, government expenditure, tariffs, foreign exchange allocations, and credit policies — on the distribution of resources and income. Priorities need to be established for the way goods and services will be distributed to different economic groups, and all mesopolicies should be used consistently to ensure that economic growth and alleviation of poverty are given precedence. Current conditionality programs often do not allow for this setting of priorities for resources and spending.

- Sectoral policies should be introduced that would restructure the productive sector in order to strengthen employment and income generation and to raise productivity in low-income activities. Particular attention should be paid to small farmers and informal sector producers in industries and services.

- Policies should also aim to restructure the social sector, in order to increase its equity and efficiency, and to redirect public spending toward low-cost basic services and growth promotion.

- There should be compensatory policies to protect basic health and nutrition during adjustment, until resumption of growth permits low-income households to meet their basic needs independently. Such programs would include employment creation schemes and nutrition support for the most deprived.

- IMF monitoring should be broadened, so that it covers not just monetary targets but also indications of growth performance, such as output growth and investment levels, and of social development, such as nutrition levels and the incomes of the poorest 40 percent.

- There need to be changes in the system by which IMF agreements are negotiated. At both national and international levels, discussions should be broadened to include those parties concerned with economic growth and the social sectors, as well as those responsible for financial matters. Developing countries need technical support to help them fashion and negotiate workable alternatives.

These changes are not just theoretical possibilities; each has been successfully adopted in some country or countries in recent years. For example, South Korea, Botswana, and Zimbabwe have all achieved significant adjustments, while restoring growth and protecting the vulnerable in society, at times of considerable economic or climatic adversity. In each case, many of the policies suggested above were used. [7]

A RETURN TO BRETTON WOODS?

Beyond doubt, the present international institutions are not fulfilling the objectives laid down for them at Bretton Woods. Apart from recent moves to coordinate policies on, for example, exchange rates among the major industrialized countries, these institutions have more or less abandoned any attempts to exert broad influence on the international economic system in such a way as to maintain balanced growth throughout the world. Their impact has been mainly at the level of individual countries, through IMF conditionality programs. As we have seen, the results of these programs have often been cutbacks in expenditure and employment, which have weakened growth prospects and threatened the living standards of many who are already just barely subsisting.

It is sometimes suggested that the world needs to hold a new Bretton Woods, but the agenda is rarely defined with any precision. The analysis outlined here suggests a very clear agenda: restructuring the institutions so they do fulfill their original aim of maintaining output, employment, and development. The necessary policies must cause short-term losses among particular interests, such as bankers and industrialists in developed countries, who may therefore oppose such changes. But in the long run, these parties would gain by a return to high growth throughout the world. The challenge is to generate political alliances that respond to long-term creative vision — the type that was displayed at the original Bretton Woods and in America's Marshall Plan — rather than to the currently predominant short-term considerations of financial interests.

Notes

1   R.F. Kahn, "Historical Origins of the International Monetary Fund," in A.P. Thirlwall, ed., Keynes and International Monetary Relations (London: Macmillan, 1976).

2   Keynes' opening remarks at the first meeting of the Second Commission on the Bank for Reconstruction and Development, in The Collected Writings of John Maynard Keynes, Vol. XXVI: Activities 1941-1946, Shaping the Post War World (London: Macmillan, 1980).

3   J.K. Horsefield, ed., The International Monetary Fund 1945-1965 (Washington D.C.: International Monetary Fund, 1969).

4   See, for example, R.H. Green, "The IMF and Stabilization in Sub-Saharan Africa: A Critical Review," IDS Discussion Paper 216 (IDS: Sussex, 1986); and G.K. Helleiner, "The IMF and Africa in the 1980s," Essays in International Finance 152 (Princeton, NJ: Princeton University, 1983).

5   M. Godfrey, "Trade and Exchange Rate Policy: A Further Contribution to the Debate," in T. Rose, ed., Crisis and Recovery in Sub-Saharan Africa (Paris: OECD), pp. 168-179.

6   See A.C. Cornia, R. Jolly, and F. Stewart, eds., Adjustment with a Human Face: Protecting the Vulnerable and Promoting Growth (Oxford: Oxford University Press, 1987).

7   For detail and further examples, see Cornia, Jolly, and Stewart (fn.6).

21

The IMF Under Fire

Jahangir Amuzegar

The global economic challenges of the 1980s — the colossal debt overhang, wild swings in exchange rates, and continued imbalances in external payments — have presented the International Monetary Fund (IMF) with the immense task of devising orderly and effective solutions. And they have focused unprecedented attention on the organization. Thrown suddenly and inadvertently into the epicenter of the world economic crises after the 1973-1974 oil price shocks, the IMF has gradually, and erroneously, come to be seen as the world's master economic trouble-shooter. A limited-purpose organization, conceived in 1944 to deal with 1930s-style exchange and payments problems, the Fund has recently been pushed by circumstances into becoming a superagency in charge of the global debt and development problems of the 1970s and 1980s — tasks for which it has neither adequate expertise nor sufficient resources.

The IMF still enjoys the support and respect of many multinational economic organizations; bankers, business leaders, government officials, and academics in both industrialized and developing countries. But misconceptions and unrealistic expectations have prompted harsh and often distorted criticisms from other quarters, especially the media.

Initially confined to some left-leaning fringe elements in the Third World, recent attacks on the Fund have been echoed by a curious coalition — including some U.N. agencies — that defies both North-South and Left-Right divides.

Critics from the less developed countries (LDCs) and their supporters paint the IMF as a highly rigid, single-minded, biased institution dominated by a cabal of industrial countries. These critics accuse the Fund of following a narrow, free-market approach to external imbalances and contend that the Fund shows little or no concern that its adjustment policies often cripple economic growth and further skew income distribution in Third World countries. They also think that the

IMF is cruelly indifferent to the social and political consequences of its stabilization programs.

Fund detractors in industrialized countries criticize the IMF for being insufficiently market-oriented; for helping noncapitalist and anti-Western countries; and for progressively evolving into a softheaded foreign-aid agency.

Some observers from both sides of the North-South divide claim that Fund-supported adjustment programs, by checking demand in many countries simultaneously, give a deflationary bias to the world economy as a whole.

Some skeptics see no useful role for the IMF under the present world economic order. A few believe that the Fund's existence blocks the Third World's economic interests; others argue that, in a world of floating exchange rates, the IMF — which was devised to ensure currency stability — has no part left to play. A hodgepodge of consumerists, religious activists, and neoliberals oppose the Fund because the IMF allegedly bails out big multinational banks, favors the rich, helps big business, and supports dictorial regimes. Some old-line conservatives and free-market ideologues disapprove of the IMF because they generally oppose public intervention of any kind in the economy. And monetarist critics of the U.S. Federal Reserve Bank would like to dismantle anything that seems like an international central bank.

There are Western analysts who believe that Fund programs and facilities — increasingly tailored for and used by the LDCs — no longer benefit industrialized countries. Other radical critics, such as the political economist Cheryl Payer, believe that only a radical restructuring of the international economic system will solve today's international economic problems. They believe that Fund assistance frustrates the very type of economic discipline and financial autonomy LDCs need to break out of "imperialism's grip." [1]

Many analysts, by contrast, urge major reforms of the Fund. Some conservatives want the IMF to be stricter with borrowing countries. Their liberal counterparts emphasize creating a more Third World-oriented Fund.

Five aspects of the relationship between the IMF and its LDC clients dominate the debate over the organization: the Fund's philosophy and principal objectives; its approach to economic stabilization in deficit countries; the conditions attached to the use of

Fund resources; the costs of domestic economic adjustment; and the IMF's alleged biases in the application of its policies and programs.

Critics accuse the IMF of deviating from its principles and objectives as contained in its Articles of Agreement. They include a call for "the promotion and maintenance of high levels of employment and real income." The Fund, they argue, favors internal and external stability in deficit member countries at the expense of economic growth and full employment. Most LDC-oriented critics would like to see the IMF facilitate capital flows and encourage stabilization and expansion of trade in the primary commodities that many Third World countries depend on for export earnings. Many also would like to see more IMF control over the creation, distribution, and management of global liquidity, and more Fund authority over worldwide capital flows, the domestic policies of reserve-currency countries, and external debt issues. The positions taken by the Third World blocs in the United Nations Conference on Trade and Development, the U.N. General Assembly, and the Fund's Interim Committee and its annual meetings point in the same direction.

These critics argue that at its birth, the Fund was expected to deal with problems of the developed countries. Since no major industrial country currently used Fund resources or is expected to tap them in the near future, the Fund should now cater to its new, Third World, clientele.

The Fund staff rejects allegations of a vested interest in restoring external balances at the expense of other objectives such as employment and growth. The IMF maintains that its stabilization programs are designed to ensure domestic prices stability and a sustainable external balance, and are, in fact, the very ingredients of increased domestic production, more jobs, and larger incomes. By improving the allocation and use of internal resources like capital and labor, Fund programs help a country increase its productive capacity over the long term.

Additionally, the Fund has adapted its role and its policies to the perceived needs of its LDC membership by developing special facilities such as the buffer stock financing facility, the extended fund facility, the subsidy account, the supplementary financing facility, the cereal imports facility, the Trust Fund, and the latest structural adjustment facility.

DEFINING RESPONSIBILITIES

The debate here seems largely a matter of nuance and emphasis rather than basic philosophy. The Fund's argument is that, within the Bretton Woods framework for postwar stability and development, its global task has been to serve as a monetary and financial agency, dealing with short-term gaps in external payments, exchange fluctuations, and capital flows. Its added responsibility for economic expansion and larger productive capacity in the Third World, the IMF emphasizes, must be achieved by encouraging balanced growth in international trade and by evening out short-term capital movements, not by dispensing aid.

Economic stabilization under the IMF's standard "monetarist" model sees short-term external balance as a precondition for long-term growth. But many liberal critics insists that IMF programs must speed up economic growth and thereby achieve a viable balance of payments by stimulating supply instead of reducing demand. They believe that growth is a condition for adjustment.

According to these critics, the Fund's model subverts LDCs' development strategy in many ways. Essentially, they claim the the IMF view blames inflation on excess aggregate demand while the real culprits are structural bottlenecks in the agricultural, foreign trade, and public sectors; supply due to unused capacity; and other nonmonetary problems common in developing countries. Thus combating inflation and external imbalances by choking off demand — by devaluing currency, reducing credit subsidies and imports, and raising taxes — results in depressing the economy instead. Economic stability requires removing supply bottlenecks by reallocating investment, cutting taxes, and somehow restraining prices and wages.

But the record of the IMF shows that as the nature and causes of the initial problems differ widely in different countries, so do the Fund's policy recommendations. A 1986 Fund staff study, *Fund-Supported Adjustment Programs and Economic Growth* by Mohsin S. Kahn and Malcolm D. Knight, reiterates that Fund-supported adjustment programs comprise three distinct features: demand-side policies aimed at cooling and overheated economy, supply-side measures designed to expand domestic output, and exchange-rate incentives to improve a country's external competitiveness. For example, IMF programs in Gabon, Panama, Peru, and South Korea during the late 1970s and early 1980s did emphasize demand restraint. But similar programs in Burma and Sri

Lanka encouraged an increase in the rate of public investment and the liberalization of imports. In Gabon, Panama, Peru, South Korea, and Sri Lanka, the objective was to increase supply by using excess capacity, improving external competitiveness, or boosting private or public investment.

According to a 1985 Fund report, *Adjustment Programs in Africa*, IMF staff members Justin B. Zulu and Saleh M. Nsouli show that IMF programs in 21 African countries strove to tailor each country's adjustment policies to that country's specific circumstances. While most programs aimed at increasing growth, reducing inflation, and improving balance of payments, considerable flexibility was shown with regard to budgetary deficits, credit expansion, inflation rates, and import volume. According to the same study, all stabilization programs in recent years have emphasized both supply- and demand-oriented policies. The former, addressing exchange rates, prices, interest rates, investment incentives, and efficiency of public enterprises, have all been conducive to growth.

A review of some 94 Fund-supported programs in 64 countries during the 1980-1984 period, prepared by Charles A. Sisson and published in the March 1986 issue of *Finance and Development*, shows a distinct variety of approaches to the adjustment problem and a wide range of policy measures. Although nearly all programs contained limits on credit expansion and government current expenditures, only 55 per cent included measures related to currency values and external trade liberalization; 41 per cent required a cap on or reduction in consumer subsidies; and a mere 28 per cent dealt with budgetary transfers to nonfinancial public enterprises. Even some of the Fund's more knowledgeable critics, such as the economist Graham Bird, clearly admit that "it is far too simplistic and inaccurate to claim that the Fund is a doctrinaire monetarist institution." [2]

Critics who concede that the Fund's primary objective is restoring short-term external balance still assail its approach to adjustment. They maintain that the Fund perceives LDC balance-of-payments deficits, foreign-exchange shortages, budgetary gaps, supply crunches, declining rates of productivity, inflation, and black markets to be largely of domestic origin — the result of economic mismanagement, overspending, exorbitant social welfare programs, and price controls. Domestic inflation and balance-of-payments deficits, in turn, are allegedly traced by the Fund to excessive consumption, insufficient investment, excessive import levels reflecting increased aggregate demand and caused by large budget gaps and loose credit, and anemic export earnings due to domestic inflation and overvalued currencies.

These critics maintain that LDC external imbalances are in fact frequently caused by a host of other external factors beyond LDC control that have nothing to do with domestic waste or inflation: oil prices, artificially stimulated rapid growth through easy credit, world-wide inflation, declining demand for commodities, deteriorating terms of trade and protectionism, rising real rates of interest on foreign debt, and poor harvests. The Fund is thus blamed for believing that deficits — no matter how they are caused — call for adjustment, and that adjustment must focus on the deficits, whether temporary or persistent.

The Fund is also often accused of identifying the adjustment's success with improvements in the trade or current account balance — an interpretation that the critics see not only as tautological but also as harmfully misleading. For improvements in the trade balance, they argue, result overwhelmingly from cuts in imports, not necessarily in bit increases in exports. Such drastic and unsustainable cuts in foreign purchases not only limit LDCs' current and future output levels, they also hurt LDC trading partners, who end up losing markets. The real adjustment, say the critics, must be structural, involving such permanent changes as a shift in the composition of production and demand to boost export earnings and reduce dependence on imports.

The Fund's critics are right in claiming that it always insists on adjustment regardless of the nature or origin of the external balance. But the Fund also has an equally valid position in arguing that the need for adjustment is a pragmatic necessity, not the reflection of any dogma. In the March 1986 issue of *Finance and Development*, IMF Management Director Jacques de Larosière observes that countries with soaring inflation, enormous fiscal deficits, huge and wasteful public sectors, money-losing public enterprises, distorted exchange rates, and low interest rates are unlikely to mobilize domestic savings or attract foreign investment, and are bound to crowd out domestic resources in a way that will hurt growth. Without adjustment, writes Fund staff member Wanda Tseng, external and internal imbalances eventually will deplete the country's international reserves, erode its international credit worthiness, dry up access to foreign funds, and result in the stoppage of needed imports. [3]

With regard to the origin of external deficits, Fund critics seem bent on constructing a general thesis out of isolated cases. Some, but not all, balance-of-payments gaps are clearly caused by factors outside a country's control. In the case of Jamaica, for example, even one of the Fund's most astute critics admits that during the 1972-1980 period domestic policies and structural factors were the prime culprits behind the excess demand and the worsening payments position. Nor was imported inflation found to be a "major cause" of the island's deteriorating economy. In general, the authorities declined to adopt unpopular adjustment measures necessitated by their own profligate fiscal and monetary policies. Another IMF critic attributed Indonesia's 1965-1966 crises mainly to hyperinflation between 1962 and 1966 resulting from government deficit financing. Even in Kenya between 1974 and 1981, where major external factors — mainly the two oil shocks — were at work, domestic monetary forces and the mismanagement of the coffee and tea boom had to bear their share of responsibility. [4]

The critics, however, seem to have a strong point in arguing that, for most of the deficit-ridden LDCs, the external shocks of the 1970s and the early 1980s almost totally altered the fundamental assumptions on which their medium-term economic planning was based. A completely different type and direction of adjustment was required for many of these countries, such as a much bigger shot of capital and much more stimulation of supply, instead of routine belt tightening.

IMF BIASES

A much stronger and more vituperative attack is aimed at the Fund's conditions for making its resources available. The main condition — a "viable" payments position — is defined as a current account deficit that can be sustained by capital inflows on terms compatible with a country's development prospects without resorting to restrictions on trade and payments, which add to rather than correct the existing distortions.

Almost all critics agree on the need for some conditionality. The quarrel, then, is about the types of conditions needed. At the macroeconomic level, the IMF's "draconian" approach and "shock treatment" are blamed for hindering economic growth, raising unemployment, lowering the already low Third World standards of living, ravaging the poorest of the poor, and seriously undermining the country's capacity for realistic adjustment. [5]   Even in countries committed to adjustment and stabilization, the critics point out, formidable constraints — internal political friction, inadequate central financial control mechanisms, pressure groups or broader public resistance, and bureaucratic inefficiencies — make Fund measures hard to swallow.

Fund-prescribed microeconomic remedies are considered by the critics particularly ill-conceived, if not downright harmful. Devaluation is regarded as inherently regressive because it raises the costs of essential imports, leaves untouched exports subject to extremely low supply elasticities, and adds to domestic inflation. Higher interest rates are judged irrelevant in the context of Third world economies because so much credit goes to the public sector, because private savers are usually few and insignificant, and because capital flight has little to do with interest-rate differentials. Reduced real wages, lower subsidies for the poor, and cutbacks on other social welfare programs are regarded as the nemeses of sociopolitical stability. Credit restrictions are thought to reduce employment rather than inflation.

The IMF responds by arguing that conditions are neither rigid nor inflexible and that they are designed jointly with the member country. IMF conditions are applied flexibly as well, with varying socioeconomic circumstances taken into account. The periodic review of Fund programs confirms the agency's interest in ensuring sufficient flexibility. Further, the IMF's approach to balance of payments does not work only through demand deflation and real-income reduction. The relationship between monetary factors and external imbalances is important, but the IMF approach embraces all aspects of economic policies, bearing on both demand and supply conditions. Finally, although restoring the external balance is admittedly a Fund objective, it is not the sole purpose of adjustment. The IMF believes that adjustment ultimately encourages high employment and long-term growth by balancing aggregate demand and supply better.

Fund programs are also often blamed for their allegedly high social and economic costs. The critics argue that, despite its best efforts, the IMF can hardly avoid politics. National strikes, riots, political upheavals, and social unrest in Argentina, Bolivia, Brazil, the Dominican

Republic, Ecuador, Egypt, Haiti, Liberia, Peru, Sudan, and elsewhere have been attributed directly or indirectly to the implementation of austerity measures advocated by the IMF.

The companion charge of undermining national sovereignty and political democracy in Third World countries follows from the social frictions and imbalances that austerity allegedly brings. LDC governments add that the Fund does not quite appreciate the political risks involved in applying the IMF recipe.

Conditionality is also thought to undermine fair income redistribution. The argument maintains that the Fund's adjustment programs almost always require a cut in both public and private consumption, in order to transfer resources to investment and the export sector. Critics frequently argue that the heaviest and most immediate burdens of adjustment are likely to be passed by the upper and middle classes to the poor. The Fund's alleged insistence on reducing or eliminating food and other consumer subsidies is further attacked on the ground that these policies are in fact a rational means of internal income redistribution in countries lacking an effectively progressive tax system or adequate social security schemes.

Fund supporters argue that blaming the IMF for fomenting political unrest merely confuses cause and effect. Many countries do not come to the IMF until the seeds of political turmoil are firmly rooted in their soil. Indeed, economics-related civil disturbances are hardly unknown in countries without Fund programs — witness Iran, Nigeria, South Africa, and Tunisia. And scores of countries adjusting with the IMF's assistance have been remarkably stable. Of the 67 countries that carried a stabilization program at some period between 1980 and 1983, critics can single out only the 10 mentioned previously as having experienced serious turmoil — not all of it fund-related. Nevertheless, the unrest that can be blamed on the IMF must be considered a minus for adjustment policies.

Finally, the Fund is charged with harboring biases toward capitalism and against government planning and economic intervention. Worse, it is called an agent of neocolonialization for the West. More moderate critics accuse the Fund of an ideological slant the results in the scrapping of public enterprises, the abandonment of price controls, the reduction of food subsidies and free medical and educational facilitates, and the elimination of social services from already deprived populations.

The Fund is also alleged to discriminate in its treatment of poor and rich members. LDC supporters claim that the Fund opposes as distortions of the free market such policies as exchange restrictions, wage-price controls, rationing, and subsidies when pursued by the developing countries. Yet the IMF is virtually impotent in the fight against similar practices by its industrial members. Critics additionally see a perceived asymmetry in treatment between reserve-currency centers (and surplus countries) on the one hand and the rest of the world on the other. This asymmetry is considered not only inconsistent in itself, but also crucial in shifting the onus of adjusting external imbalances to deficit LDCs. Reserve-currency countries like the United States, it is alleged, cannot be pressured by the IMF to adjust, and can continue their profligate ways year after year.

Finally, critics see an IMF political bias that is reflected in sympathy and leniency toward regimes pivotal to the economic, military, strategic, or geopolitical interests of the United States or other major Fund shareholders, and toward countries with international economic clout because of enormous debts that threaten the global monetary system. [6] To prove this political bias, critics such as staff members of the Center for International Policy claim that proposed IMF loans to "countries from the wrong side of the track," including Grenada before the U.S. invasion, Nicaragua, and Vietnam, have been vetoed by major shareholders for "technical reasons." Credit for others, such as El Salvador and South Africa, is routinely approved.

Yet Fund members today include countries with distinctly nonmarket philosophies. Any penchant toward the market simply reflects the belief that market allocations are more efficient. On the question of discriminatory treatment of the poor, the dividing line is not poverty but the balance-of-payments situation. Surplus or reserve countries may indeed escape the Fund's strict discipline. After all, they have no need for Fund resources. But this is a choice open also to poor countries, which can decide not to approach the IMF. Further, some of the rich deficit countries that have drawn on the Fund in the past, such as Great Britain, France, and Italy, have been similarly treated.

It is no secret that the IMF statutes and covenants expect the Fund to promote a world of free markets, free trade, and unitary exchange rates under a multilateral payments system. To allow any different course of action would place the IMF in violation of its legal mandate.

Yet not only do such centrally planned economies as China, Hungary, Romania, and Yugoslavia enjoy full IMF membership and make ample use of its resources without any encumbrances or impositions, but some left-of-center governments, in fact, have in the past benefited more from Fund assistance than supposedly favored regimes. By one key measure, Jamaica, under then Prime Minister Michael Manley's democratic socialist regime in 1979, was the world's largest recipient of Fund resources, receiving 360 per cent of its quota compared with only 64 percent for other developing countries. [7]

The Fund adamantly maintains that its Articles of Agreement specifically prohibit political considerations for the use of its resources. Yet the charges of political bias deserve closer scrutiny. The Fund's ability to maintain absolute neutrality is, to be sure, affected by the interests of influential member governments, by the decisions of the executive board to grant or deny loans to a given country, and by the evaluation reports and recommendations of staff missions on a country's underlying economic conditions.

Major shareholding governments obviously have political, strategic, and economic interests in their own zones of influence or involvement and do not wish to separate economic from political and other considerations. The U.S. Congress, for example, explicitly requires that the American executive director at the Fund vote in a prescribed manner in regard to certain countries and regimes. Other major governments may have similar predilections, but are not quite prepared to legislate them.

The executive board has a mixed position. Its members are appointed or elected by developed or developing member governments, to whom they are beholden. They, too, cannot be purely apolitical robots. They lobby for their views among their colleagues; they try to win over management and staff; and they endeavor to protect the political and other interests of their constituencies. At the same time, board members are required and expected to uphold the Fund's basic objectives and to ensure the proper functioning of the international monetary system. In neither of these two capacities can the executive directors as a whole be found to be practicing a distinct, or immutable, political bias. The burden of proof is still on the critics to show that many IMF decisions are make deliberately according to political considerations. Significantly, the IMF staff has never been accused of partisan political bias.

The issue of inherent bias against the poor is more intractable. In general, allegations that the Fund's reluctance to suggest specific national redistributive priorities is of no help to the poor and the powerless may have a certain moral validity. It is also true that the objective of better income distribution, or at least of proportionate sacrifices, is not explicitly included in a country's letter of intent as a condition for Fund assistance. But claims that the IMF is indifferent to such factors are grossly unfair.

More important, the critics' ardent contention that the cost of adjustment is always borne disproportionately by the poor has seldom been supported by any statistical evidence. Rather, there is usually an a priori presumption that Fund programs aggravate income inequities because the rich and the strong see to it that they avoid the effects of the stabilization measures. The arguments have been at best theoretical, and usually anecdotal. The countless books, articles, speeches, and statements critical of the Fund contain not a single piece of empirical information or statistical data showing that Fund-supported programs have, in a clear and convincing manner, aggravated internal income-distribution patterns.

Moreover, the impact of IMF programs on income distribution essentially depends on how the program is implemented by national authorities. In the Fund's view, any other approach would entangle the IMF directly in microeconomic policy measures closely related to a country's social and political choices. Such involvement probably would be vehemently resisted by most countries, and would also violate the Fund's own mandate and guidelines.

In addition, the Fund believes that changes in income distribution as such cannot be performance criteria in adjustment programs because this area is so difficult to quantify. The numbers can be affected by methods of classifying income recipients. Further, few programs last long enough to allow a comprehensive study of their distributional implications, particularly where necessary information on consumption, government transfers, nonmonetary sources of incomes, and personal income levels is inadequate or unreliable — as is generally the case in developing countries. Finally, the Fund maintains that any given domestic distributional system is the product of deep-rooted economic, social, political, and cultural phenomena going back decades, if not centuries. Fund programs, being of relatively limited scope and duration, cannot be expected to make much of a dent in the system.

In the absence of clear-cut evidence and good data, theoretical arguments do assume importance. In the short run, stabilization programs can worsen income distribution. But the story scarcely ends there. The distributional outcome of a cut in government outlays, for example, depends on where the specific reductions are make. A reduction of food subsidies to urban workers could help the rural poor by raising farm prices. A tax on urban services and amenities could likewise redistribute income from workers in modern industries — a minority in the labor force — to the rural poor. Moreover, a reduction in inflation itself tends to favor poorer groups because they can rarely adjust their incomes to rising prices.

A forthcoming IMF study, *Fund-Supported Programs, Fiscal Policy, and Income Distribution*, concludes, after presenting some case studies, that Fund programs have not been directed against the poor; often, in fact, policies have been designed to protect low-income groups as much as possible. Even when total consumption has been reduced through prudent demand-management policies, high-income groups probably have been hit hardest. The elimination of large general subsidy programs has inflicted some hardships on the population as a whole, including the poor. But the study calls such programs "inefficient and ineffective" mechanisms for redistributing incomes.

SOME SUCCESS STORIES

Some Fund detractors are quick to denigrate the IMF's achievements in the Third World and cite Mexico's current crisis in particular as a blatant example of the failure of the adjustment formula. More moderate critics admit that Fund programs have succeeded in improving the balance of payments in several countries. But they contend that other significant benefits have not followed.

Yet the overall track record of IMF programs shows some noteworthy accomplishments. An independent 1984 study by the German Federal parliament, *The Conditionality Policy of the IMF*, shows that although the current account deficits of all non-oil-developing countries (NODCs) tended to expand between 1970 and 1980, most Fund-assisted countries managed to close those gaps perceptibly. The inflation rate for all NODCs increased during that period, while the tempo in countries with adjustment programs was slower. Countries undergoing adjustment experienced sharper decreases in short-term growth than the group as a whole, but their long-term expansion rates were above average. Finally, the report noted, the increase in real consumption in program countries was only slightly less on average — 4.3 per cent as opposed to 4.7 per cent annually — than in the whole group.

According to the aforementioned 1985 IMF study of the 21 African countries where the IMF had an ongoing program from 1981 to 1983, economic growth targets were achieved in about one-fifth of the countries, inflation targets were reached in roughly one-half of the cases, and the balance-of-payments goals were reached in about two-fifths of these states.

At first glance, improvements under Fund-supported programs may show that the IMF's advice is often better suited to containing inflation and rectifying external imbalances than to fostering growth. But some short-term consolidation in the growth tempo may in fact be necessary for longer-term expansion. And although the success stories may not be numerous or seem spectacular or even truly impressive to the hostile critics, they nonetheless tend to contradict the allegations that Fund programs bring few, if any, benefits to LDCs. Moreover, these detractors frequently fail to ask where these countries would be without the IMF.

Still, it is disturbing that, despite its valiant rescue efforts across the Third World, the IMF is hard pressed to show more than a few clearly viable programs out of the roughly three dozen under its wing. Why haven't the programs done better?

One answer is that the IMF's latest perennial clients have been among either the poorest LDCs with large balance-of-payments disequilibriums, or the newly industrializing countries with gargantuan external debts. Adjustment has been make more difficult by outside factors such as high energy costs, high interest rates, world recessions, and protectionism.

Second, IMF programs often bring some concealed problems into the open, making partial success look like a setback and partial recovery like a retrogression. In a country living beyond its means, the real causes of payments difficulties — such as overvalued currencies, artificially low prices, and virtual rationing, as evidenced by shortages and black markets — are rarely acknowledged. When Fund programs begin to remove some of the existing distortions and dislocations through cost-price adjustments, the economic weaknesses that these policies hid or suppressed begin to emerge for all to see.

Third, the worse a country's problems, the harder it will be for IMF programs to succeed. The host government's cooperations is crucial as well. A 1984 Fund study showed a "striking" correlation between the success of IMF programs and the observance of policy measures by the governments concerned. [8]

Fourth, most of the Fund-assisted countries that have been less than successful are those that had long postponed adjustment efforts. As stabilization is delayed, distortions become solidified, and rectification becomes correspondingly costlier and more painful. It literally pays economically, socially, and politically to go to the IMF early.

In no other North-South debate has the so-called dialogue of the deaf been so evident as in that over the IMF. The biggest reason for the critics' persistence is surely the Fund's patchy track record. The increasing number of cases where disbursement of standby credits has been suspended because of noncompliance with Fund criteria, and the growing number of members declared ineligible for further assistance because of long overdue financial obligations, show that the path of the Fund-Supported programs has been neither short nor smooth.

Indeed, in spite of prolonged sue of Fund programs by certain members, economic imbalances persist for many internal and external reasons. Fund successes in other countries also have often been temporary.

But if the IMF cannot or will not influence domestic priorities, such as the size of military budgets or the pattern of income distribution, that have a major impact on the economy, why, the critics ask, impose and austerity program that skirts these problems? The same question is prompted by the IMF's inability to do much about external problems, such as protectionism or foreign recessions, that lie beyond the control of deficit LDCs and that can often make or break a country's prospects. If the IMF's conditional assistance produces no more than certain short-term improvements in the country's external balances and some temporary reductions in the rate of inflation at the cost of growth, full employment, social welfare, and self-reliance, is it worth the attendant sacrifices?

Convincing answers to these questions are not easy to come by because all these critical inquiries seem to miss two crucial points. First, what other choices do LDCs facing deteriorating debt and development problems have?   Second, putting aside the merits of the critics' arguments or of the Fund's defense, are there other practical and effective policies that the IMF, as presently constituted, can pursue?

Debt-strapped countries incapable of paying their external bills and unable or unwilling to adopt Fund-supported adjustment programs have three alternatives: repudiate external debt altogether and seek to start afresh; seek bilateral accommodations with bondholders; or go it alone.

An outright repudiation, or even a debt moratorium, obviously would release resources for more urgent outlays. But it might close off larger and more valuable access to foreign reserves, assets, credits, markets, and technology. For this reason, even the poorest African countries assembled for the July 12985 Organization of African Unity summit refused to endorse any suggestion of wholesale default. Nor did Cuban Premier Fidel Castro's similar proposal for Latin America attract any takers.

The second alternative is appealing, but except for a very few lucky and resourceful countries, foreign creditors usually ask LDC debtors to accept the Fund's discipline before engaging in debt renogotiations or extending new credits. The consequences of doing nothing, the third alternative, would be further economic deterioration and perhaps a need for stricter adjustment efforts. In the Fund's view, the costs of nonadjustment by any measure will probably greatly exceed those of adjustment.

The IMF, in its turn, can adapt to external realities and the critics' challenges in four ways: by increasing its resources and expanding both the scope and the number of its special LDC facilities to serve its Third World members better; by revising its rules and statutes to become more adjustment-oriented toward its developed members and comparatively more finance-directed toward LDCs; by abdicating its structural adjustment role in the LDC economies in favor of the World Bank; or by doing nothing.

A Fund with twice as much liquidity could accommodate its LDC members with less painful adjustment programs. The Fund also could revise its rules to improve more decisively its role in overseeing the exchange-rate system, its surveillance capabilities over the surplus and reserve-currency countries, and its management of international liquidity.

The Fund staff has already recommended improvements in the design of adjustment measures in favor of low-income groups. These include exchange-rate changes that provide adequate incentives for the agricultural sector dominated by small farmers, greater access to domestic credit markets, taxation of global income, expansion of tax bases, replacement of quotas by tariffs, and the provision of basic skills and vocational training for unemployables. [9]

In addition, the Fund could get out of medium-term or Extended Facility financing — and activity that may duplicate the World Bank's structural adjustment loans. This step would free the Fund to concentrate on its exchange-related functions and operations.

The fourth alternative — and perhaps the easiest — is for the Fund to do nothing. But the status quo includes the current and thorny problem of the repayment of the Fund's past loans, some of which are now technically in default. Without fresh efforts and initiatives, the number of countries in arrears will steadily rise. Further, the continued attacks on the Fund, if not properly dealt with, may further tarnish and distort the Fund's image, discourage some member governments form seeking badly needed IMF help because of domestic political opposition, and weaken and erode world public support for the Fund's surveillance, guidance, and assistance.

Meanwhile, the difficulty for the IMF in adopting any of the first three alternatives remains its members' inability to agree on either the need for fundamental revision of the current trade and exchange regime or the nature of critical procedural changes in the system's implementation. Most developed countries repeatedly have rejected such basic Third World proposals as a system of target zones for keeping major currencies in leash, a doubling of IMF quotas, larger LDC access to Fund resources, periodic issues of the special Drawing Rights (SDRs), the IMF's reserve currency, a link between SDRs and development finance, a grant to LDCs of 50 per cent of the vote on all Fund decisions, the reactivation of the Trust Fund for fresh lending to poorer countries, and the establishment of a new interest-rate facility.

And the LDCs deem unacceptable such rich country suggestions as giving greater publicity to the outcome of Fund consultations with members, extending the techniques of enhanced surveillance, assuring that commercial banks continue to play a big role in providing international reserves, and increasing World Bank — IMF collaboration in the design of conditionality.

No realistic compromise is yet in sight, except for possible elaboration of the Baker plan. Memories of the past create the uneasy feeling that, without a major new financial crisis, the Fund's principal shareholders and their bankers may not have enough incentive to accommodate poorer countries. Some concerned observers actually believe that such a crisis is already on the horizon. Averting disaster requires genuine debtor-creditor cooperations — no matter which side has a more valid position or better arguments.

Any new initiative must synthesize the positions of the two groups. The chances of reaching this consensus, in turn, would be greatly enhanced if the sparring partners could agree upon several fundamental postulates. first, LDC debtors must admit that the bulk of their credit needs must be reasonably conditioned. The debtors must also be willing, in exchange for fresh inflows of foreign credit, management, and technology, to adopt certain genuine domestic economic reforms.

The industrialized creditors must accept the fact that no matter how economically necessary adjustment conditions are, they must be politically palatable and operationally feasible and must offer a clear promise of growth in addition to economic stability. Also needed are improvements in the workings of the international exchange system, a multilateral trading regime where the handicaps of different players are properly reckoned with, and a system of resource transfers based on both country needs and global competitiveness. Such measures as multiyear reschedulings of debts, the reduction of interest rates, or some eventual debt write-offs might be part of the solution.

Serious North-South negotiations in the framework of the forthcoming meetings of the Fund's Interim Committee and the joint Bank/Fund Development Committee — or a new global monetary conference — may offer new possibilities for such an approach. Without them, the expectations of critics and the Fund's capacity to meet these expectations will remain far apart. The persistence and poignancy of the attacks on the Fund — and eventually on the World Bank, once its inevitable conditionality begins to bite — will further damage the prestige and influence of both organizations at a time when their involvement in the Third World is more necessary than ever to ensure global economic stability and growth.

Notes

1   See, for example, Cheryl Payer, *The Debt Trap* (New York: Monthly Review Press, 1975).
2   Graham Bird, "Relationship, Resource Uses, and the Conditionality Debate," in *The Quest for Economic Stabilization,* ed. Tony Killick (New York: St. Martin's Press, 1984), 179.
3   Wanda Tseng, "The Effects of Adjustment," *Finance and Development,* December 1984, 2-5.
4   Jennifer Sharpley, "Jamaica, 1972-80," Mary Sutton, "Indonesia, 1966-70," and Tony Killick, "Kenya, 1975-81," in *The IMF and Stabilization,* ed. Tony Killick (New York: St. Martin's Press, 1984).
5   See Chuck Lane, "Dunning Democracy," *The New Republic,* 4 June 1984, 9-12; and Richard E. Feinberg and Valeriana Kallab, eds., *Adjustment Crisis in the Third World* (Washington, D.C.: Overseas Development Council, 1984).
6   See, for example, Amir Jamal, "Power and the Third World Struggle for Equilibrium," in *Banking on Poverty: The Global Impact of the IMF and World Bank,* ed. Jill Torrie (Toronto: Between The Lines, 1983); and Ismaïl-Sabri Abdalla, "The Inadequacy and Loss of Legitimacy of the IMF," *Development Dialogue,* , 1980, no. 2: 25-53.
7   Sharpley, "Jamaica, 1972-80," in *IMF and Stabilization,* 160.
8   Justin B. Zulu and Saleh M. Nsouli, "Adjustment Programs in Africa," *Finance and Development,* March 1984, 7.
9   Charles A. Sisson, "Fund-Supported Programs and Income Distribution in LDCs" *Finance and Development,* March 1986, 36.

IX

MACRO AND MICRO ADJUSTMENTS AFTER THE FALL OF THE DOLLAR

In general, economic theory predicts that a country running a trade surplus should experience an increase in the value of its currency whereas a country running a trade deficit should experience a decline. Ideally, these adjustments should take place relatively quickly and bring about a trade balance without too many dislocations in an economy. The experience of the U.S. in the 80's indicates that, in practice, this ideal may be far from being realized. During the early 80's the value of the U.S. dollar continued to rise despite growing trade deficits. After 1985, when the value of the dollar fell, the U.S. continued to rise for a trade deficit longer period than most economists would have predicted.

The first article, which was written by Martin Feldstein and originally appeared in *Foreign Affairs* , presents an overview of the dramatic rise and fall of the dollar in the eighties. Feldstein points out the relationship between the budget deficit and the trade deficit. He goes on to argue that the dollar will eventually fall in the 1990's and that indeed the U.S. will probably run a trade surplus in the early 1990's.

In contrast, Krugman finds the fall of the dollar to be a rather disturbing consequence of the low U.S. savings rate. He believes that much of the fall in the dollar can be explained as the result of a loss of confidence by foreign investors in the U.S. economy.

22

Correcting the Trade Deficit

Martin Feldstein

The principal problem with which the world's economies must deal during the coming decade is the unsustainable imbalance of international trade. The United States cannot continue to have annual trade deficits of more than $100 billion, financed by an ever-increasing inflow of foreign capital. The U.S. trade deficit will therefore soon have to shrink and, as it does, the other countries of the world will experience a corresponding reduction in their trade surpluses. Indeed, within the next decade the United States will undoubtedly exchange its trade deficit for a trade surplus. The challenge is to achieve this rebalancing of world demand in a way that avoids both a decline in real economic activity and an increase in the rate of inflation.

II

The trade deficit of the United States is now so large, and its effect on the American economy so pervasive, that it is easy to lose sight of the fact that in almost every year between the end of World War II and 1981 the United States realized a significant trade surplus. In 1981 U.S. exports of goods and services exceeded imports by more than $14 billion, and the United States had a current-account surplus with which to finance net investments in other countries. But now U.S. trade in goods and services is running a deficit at the rate of about $125 billion a year.[1] The trade deficit in goods alone (i.e., the merchandise trade deficit) has reached an annual rate of more than $160 billion, or more than four percent of U.S. gross national product. The previous capital outflow has been reversed and a foreign capital inflow is financing the U.S. current-account deficit at an annual rate of about $140 billion.

The primary reason for the deteriorating trade imbalance is the 70-percent rise of the dollar that occurred between 1980 and the spring of 1985. This unprecedented increase in the exchange value of the dollar dramatically increased the price of American products relative to foreign products, causing the volume of U.S. exports to decline while merchandise imports increased by nearly 50 percent.

There were, of course, other factors that affected the U.S. trade deficit. The international debt crisis that began in 1982 caused a decline in U.S. exports to Latin America. The dramatic improvement in agricultural productivity that followed the introduction of an incentive system in China caused a decline in American agricultural exports to that country. Balanced against these changes were other special factors such as a decline in the price of oil which, by raising real incomes abroad and improving foreign trade balances, increased the demand for exports from the United States. But even taken all together, these special factors were not nearly as important as the sharp appreciation of the dollar.

The dollar's dramatic rise began when the United States shifted from the accelerating double-digit inflation of the late 1970s to a sound monetary policy. The resulting temporary rise in real interest rates and the prospects for a sustained lower rate of inflation made dollar-denominated bonds more attractive to investors throughout the world. It was the increased demand for dollars to invest in those bonds that initially raised the exchange value of the dollar.

But it was the anticipation of massive and protracted U.S. budget deficits that sustained the rise in long-term real U.S. interest rates relative to foreign rates, and that therefore caused the dollar to continue its rise after 1982. The budget deficit rose from 2.5 percent of GNP in 1980 to more than 6 percent of GNP in 1983, absorbing virtually all of the net savings generated by American households, businesses, and state and local governments. As a result of this sharp rise in government borrowing, the real rate of interest on long-term bonds rose sharply; the market interest rate on such bonds was as high in 1983 as it had been in 1980 even though the rate of inflation had fallen by 8 percentage points, from more than 12 percent in 1980 to less than 4 percent in 1983. This dramatic increase in the U.S. real long-term interest rate attracted funds from around the world to invest in dollar securities and thereby raised the exchange value of the dollar.

The changes in U.S. domestic monetary and budget policy that raised U.S. interest rates relative to interest rates abroad were not the only reasons for the rise in the real value of the dollar. The 1981 change in tax rules and the fall in inflation produced a higher real after-tax return on corporate investments in plant and equipment, which permitted corporate borrowers to pay higher real interest rates. The deterioration of the Latin American debt situation discouraged additional lending to the developing countries. And stronger economic growth in the United States compared to Europe raised the relative level of dollar interest rates, further increasing the attractiveness of investing in American securities.

But the principal reason for the substantial and sustained rise of the dollar was undoubtedly the rise in U.S. real interest rates that resulted from the massive increase in projected budget deficits in a monetary environment that aimed at preventing a return to high inflation.[2]

III

By early 1985, the dollar had reached a level that could not be sustained. With the dollar at 3.3 West German marks and 250 yen, a sharp decline in the dollar at some point in the future had become inevitable. Although dollar bonds paid a yield of about four percentage points more than German bonds, that extra interest was not enough to compensate the holders of dollar bonds for the decline of the dollar that would eventually have to occur. Ultimately, with a four-percentage-point interest differential, holders of dollar bonds would be as well off as holders of German bonds only if the dollar declined at a rate of four percent a year or less. But so slow a decline of the dollar would cause a massive rise in the U.S. trade deficit and an explosive growth of U.S. debts to the rest of the world. U.S. annual borrowing needs from the rest of the world would snowball so rapidly that they simply could not be financed.

The only way to slow the growth of the country's trade deficit and future borrowing needs was for the dollar to drop at a faster rate than four percent a year. As 1985 began, it became clear to an increasing number of investors worldwide that a very gradual and orderly reduction of the dollar was no longer possible. Although some foreign investors who held dollar bonds continued to hope that they would be able to sell before that inevitable decline began, eventually the fear of losses outweighed that unfounded optimism. Investors began to sell dollars and the dollar began to decline in value.

The attractiveness of the dollar was reduced further as interest rates fell in response to the slowing of the U.S. expansion and the easing of monetary policy. By the spring of 1985, there was also a growing understanding that the politics of the budget deficit had changed and that Congress would soon legislate significant reductions in future budget deficits.[3] When this actually happened, with the enactment of the congressional budget resolution in the summer of 1985 and of the Gramm-Rudman-Hollings legislation in the fall, realistic projections of annual budget deficits in the near future were reduced from $300 billion and six percent of GNP to less than four percent of GNP. As a result, the U.S. real interest rate and the interest differential in favor of U.S. bonds narrowed significantly, encouraging the continued decline of the dollar.

After the dollar had been falling for six months, the finance ministers and central bankers of the Group of Five major industrial countries (the United States, West Germany, Japan, Britain and France) held a highly publicized meeting at the Plaza Hotel in New York to put their weight behind the continued fall of the dollar. With the dollar already on a steady downward course, U.S. government officials could no longer continue to claim that the strong dollar was an indication of the world's approval of U.S. economic policies. Treasury Secretary James Baker therefore reversed his earlier position and acknowledged that the still-overvalued dollar was a serious problem for American industry. In an even greater departure from previous U.S. policy, Secretary Baker also agreed with the other G-5 finance ministers that the United States would join in coordinated exchange market intervention aimed at reducing the dollar further in the future.

Although much has been said and written about that G-5 meeting, I believe that its significance in reducing the dollar has been greatly exaggerated. There is no doubt that it did initiate a temporary turning point in Japanese monetary policy; the Japanese government increased domestic interest rates with the aim of raising the value of the yen in an attempt to forestall support for anti-Japanese protectionist legislation that was then heating up in the U.S. Congress. But for West Germany and the other G-5 countries, the Plaza meeting was essentially a non-event, and even the change in Japanese monetary policy was soon abandoned.

The G-5 meeting and the subsequent exchange market intervention had no sustained effect on the dollar's overall rate of decline. In the first few days after the G-5 meeting the dollar declined by about four percent against the other major industrial currencies. But then the dollar resumed its previous gradual rate of decline. More specifically, the dollar fell against a weighted average of other industrial currencies at the same rate in the year after the G-5 meeting as it had fallen in the six months before the meeting. There is simply no evidence in the dollar's behavior since early1985 to suggest that the G-5 meeting and the process of coordinated intervention had any effect on the rate of decline of the dollar's value. It was not currency intervention or coordinated jawboning that depressed the dollar but the basic fundamentals of the decline in international interest differentials, in projected U.S. budget deficits, and in the price of oil.[4]

Although the yen-dollar exchange rate did change more quickly in the period after the G-5 meeting than it had before, there is no reason to attribute this yen-dollar shift to the G-5 meeting as such, or to the exchange market intervention that followed, since those actions did not appear to affect any of the other currencies. Of more fundamental importance was the already-mentioned temporary shift by the Bank of Japan to a tighter monetary policy that raised interest rates in Japan, and the unanticipated fall in the price of oil in early 1986 that was far more important for Japan than for other countries.

Between February 1985 and December 1986 the dollar declined by more than 40 percent in real inflation-adjusted terms against a weighted average of all the major industrial currencies. The corresponding real decline against a broader group of currencies, including the currencies of virtually all the developing nations, would be between 30 percent and 35 percent. The driving force in lowering the dollar was not the pronouncements of government authorities, or government intervention in currency markets, but the actions of private portfolio investors as they responded to changes in their perception of the risks and rewards of investing in alternative currencies.

IV

Even with the substantial fall of the dollar that had occurred by the end of 1986, the level of the dollar at that time still implied a substantial, persistent U.S. trade deficit and therefore a continually rising capital inflow to the United States. Portfolio investors around the world will not be willing to go on providing dollar-denominated securities for what is now a relatively modest or nonexistent real interest rate advantage. The dollar must therefore continue to decline and the cumulative fall below its current level must be substantial. The key to this conclusion is the fact that the United States has already shifted from being a net creditor in the world capital market to a net debtor — or, more accurately, to having a substantial negative international investment position in which foreign loans to U.S. borrowers, plus foreign equity investments in the United States, exceed the sum of the U.S. loans and investments abroad. Although the level of the dollar, which as of this writing is approximately 1.85 West German marks and 155 Japanese yen, would bring a significant reduction of the trade deficit during the next two or three years, the combination of the trade deficit plus the interest and dividends that must be paid on the U.S. net "debt" to the rest of the world would soon need increasing capital inflows to finance its growing debt service requirements.

More specifically, as the International Monetary Fund has noted, the present value of the dollar implies that U.S. net obligations to the rest of the world would increase from $200 billion now to about $800 billion by the beginning of the next decade. The annual cost of interest and dividends on these obligations would be some $60 billion. Even if the merchandise trade deficit were cut in half from its current level to about $80 billion, the United States would then have an annual current-account deficit of $140 billion, i.e.,$80 billion of trade deficit plus $60 billion of net interest and dividends to foreigners. This means that the U.S. debt to the rest of the world would have to increase by an additional $140 billion in that year. And, in each successive year the amount would have to be even larger because of the ever-growing debt service costs.

Such an exploding level of debt is unsustainable. As overseas investors accumulate a larger and larger volume of dollar securities, they are exposed to increasing risks of fluctuation in the value of the dollar and in dollar interest rates. That increased exposure makes additional investments in dollar securities less attractive. Moreover, the real interest differential that originally attracted funds to the United States has now disappeared. The real net-of-inflation interest rates that will ultimately be realized on U.S. bonds is probably less today than the corresponding real rates on West Gernam bonds.

The combination of increased exposure to exchange rate risk and the vanishing real interest advantage of dollar securities will make foreign investors unwilling to finance the projected capital flow to the United States. As they seek to shift their new investments from dollar bonds to securities denominated in their own or other currencies, the value of the dollar will be driven down further. Eventually the dollar must fall far enough to cut the subsequent current-account deficit (the sum of the ordinary trade deficit and the net interest on our foreign obligations) to the level that foreign investors are willing to finance. As long as foreign investors are not willing to buy enough bonds to finance the existing current-account deficit at the prevailing exchange rates, the dollar will fall and the subsequent current-account deficit will shrink. Moreover, as financial investors become aware that the dollar's current level is unsustainably high, their fear of a currency decline will accelerate the portfolio shifts that cause the dollar to decline.

It is important to emphasize that it is the individual portfolio decisions of investors around the world that will depress the dollar and therefore the U.S. trade deficit. It is true, of course, that as long as the United States has a trade deficit, the resulting current-account deficit must be financed by a capital inflow from abroad. It is also true that foreign portfolio investors cannot now find an alternative place to invest the present massive current-account surpluses of the United States' major trading partners. But in the process of trying to shift their funds to non-dollar securities, the portfolio investors have driven down the dollar and will continue to do so, thus shrinking the subsequent trade deficit of the United States and therefore the surplus balance that its trading partners have to invest overseas. Thus each portfolio manager, responding to his own assessment of the risks and rewards of investing in dollar securities and other securities, will move the value of the dollar down, and therefore bring the U.S. trade balance closer to a sustainable level.

At some point the United States will begin to meet the cost of servicing its overseas debt by exporting more than it imports. Even reducing the capital inflow to $60 billion a year by 1990 or 1991 would require that U.S. trade be in balance because that entire $60-billion capital inflow would be needed just to finance the interest and dividends on accumulated international obligations. To reduce the capital inflow below $60 billion a year would require a trade surplus.

I expect that by the early 1990's the United States will again be running a merchandise trade surplus. The longer it takes for the United States to achieve a trade surplus — that is, the longer that the U.S. international debt continues to grow because of a combination of a trade deficit and the cost of servicing existing U.S. overseas debt — the larger the ultimate trade surplus must be. Just when the United States will return to a trade surplus is uncertain. But there can be little doubt that the United States must eventually have a trade surplus in order to finance at least part of the net interest and dividends that Americans will owe to investors abroad.

The speed and extent of future progress in reversing the U.S. budget deficit will affect the pace and character of the shift in the American trade balance, but not the inevitability of an eventual decline and reversal of the American trade deficit. A more rapid reduction of future U.S. budget deficits would speed the decline of U.S. real interest rates and of the dollar. The trade deficit would therefore shrink more rapidly. The ultimate size of U.S. overseas obligations would be smaller and the magnitude of the eventual U.S. trade surplus needed to service that international debt would also be smaller. A smaller budget deficit would also make it easier for the United States to compete in the world market for capital-intensive goods and services.

But even if the budget deficit were to remain at three or four percent of GNP, the dollar and the U.S. trade deficit would eventually decline, as foreign portfolio investors became satiated with dollar securities. The combination of persistently high government borrowing and a reduced inflow of foreign capital would raise real U.S. interest rates and thereby slow the dollar's decline. But eventually the unwillingness of foreign investors to keep increasing the shares of their portfolios that are invested in dollar securities will cause the decline of the dollar and the reversal of the U.S. trade deficit.

That this forecast of an inevitable U.S. trade surplus runs counter to the common impression — that the world does not want to purchase U.S. products and that even Americans want to buy only foreign products — only shows that the common assertions in this area are misinformed. In 1986 the United States exported $150 billion of manufactured products to the rest of the world. Moreover, more than 70 percent of the American demand for manufactured goods is being satisfied by products produced in the United States. There is little reason to doubt that U.S. exports and the country's ability to satisfy domestic markets will both increase as the declining dollar reduces the relative price of American goods.

By the 1990s, the world trade imbalance will have come full circle. The domestic policies in the United States that created a massive trade deficit for the United States in the mid-1980s are setting the stage for a major U.S. trade surplus in the 1990's.

V

My emphasis on the declining dollar as the key factor that will improve the U.S. trade balance contrasts sharply with the comments of those in the Reagan Administration who have suggested that the trade problem could be solved without any further decline of the dollar if West Germany and Japan would only increase the pace of their economic activity. Such pronouncements may be intended to stabilize the foreign exchange market, to fight protectionism, or even to establish foreign scapegoats for future U.S. economic problems. But they have no plausible basis in economic analysis.

Even if not only West Germany and Japan but all of the countries of the world (other than the United States) were to increase their real rates of economic growth from a projected average of about 2.5 percent a year for the next two years to an implausibly high 4.5 percent a year, the resulting 4-percent extra rise in the rest of the world's real GNP would, by itself, only raise demand for U.S. exports by about 6 percent, or $15 billion a year. A $15-billion increase in exports is less than one tenth of our current merchandise trade deficit.

The real reason why foreign governments should be thinking about the future expansion of demand in their own countries is not to help the United States but to pick up the slack that will result from the decline in their own net exports. If the decline in the dollar causes the U.S. merchandise trade deficit to be eliminated over the next five years, foreign producers will have lost $160 billion in markets at home and abroad. And if the dollar falls far enough to stop the flow of new capital to the United States, foreign producers will have lost nearly $250 billion a year in markets at home and abroad.

To maintain a growing level of real output and employment at home, foreign governments around the world will have to permit domestic demand to increase more rapidly than domestic production. As such, this is a pleasant assignment: permitting the standard of living of their population to rise more rapidly than the increase in production would otherwise allow. But the precise timing of the needed increase cannot be known with any assurance. The delays between a change in the exchange value of the dollar and the resulting changes in trade are long and uncertain. Similarly, the response of the domestic economies to changes in domestic monetary and fiscal policies is also uncertain. The major challenge to foreign governments will be to avoid both the excessive stimulus that could lead to a rekindling of inflation and the excessive caution that could permit their economies to drift into recession as export demand declines.

The reversal of current trade surpluses abroad will also shift the primary threat of increased protectionism from the United States to our trading partners. While it will then be tempting for them to protect their domestic demand by restricting imports, the resulting trade war would not only hurt consumers everywhere but would, by reducing exports from all countries, make the adjustment process more difficult.

VI

Although the declining dollar will expand demand for U.S. industrial products and give a desirable boost to American manufacturing firms, the combinations of the dollar's decline and the massive net U.S. obligations to foreigners will reduce the overall rate of growth of the American standard of living. A lower dollar means that Americans trade U.S. products for foreign products on less favorable terms. American firms will receive fewer Japanese yen or West German marks for their products and American consumers will have to pay more dollars to purchase foreign products.

The net foreign obligations of more than $800 billion in the 1990s will mean annual interest and dividend payments to foreigners of some $60 billion a year. This implies that more than one percent of each year's gross national product will be given to foreigners in payment for the excessive imports of the 1980s. Taken together, the deterioration in the U.S. terms of trade and the increase in overseas debt service could reduce the annual rate of increase of real income in the United States over the next five to ten years by between 0.5 percent and one percent a year. Since per capita income has grown at a rate of about two percent a year over the past few decades, this is equivalent to losing between one fourth and one half of our historical rate of real per capita income growth.

A failure of the U.S. budget deficit to shrink in parallel to the decline of the capital inflow from abroad would compound this problem. The combination of a reduced capital inflow and a persistent high level of government borrowing would mean less capital for investment in plant and equipment and in housing. The resulting decline in the growth of productivity and in the quality of the housing stock would reinforce the adverse effects on the American standard of living of the deteriorating U.S. terms of trade and the increased international debt service. The long-term importance of reducing the U.S. budget deficit thus remains undiminished.

The process of simultaneously unwinding the U.S. trade deficit and the budget deficit carries with it the risk that a mismatch of timing could push the American economy into recession. This risk is the unavoidable consequence of the imbalances that have developed during the past half decade. But a clearer view of the inevitable decline of the dollar and the future reversal of the U.S. trade deficit would help government officials and the Congress to avoid misguided policy shifts that exacerbate these risks.

Notes

1   As this paragraph indicates, there are three related but different aspects of the annual trade deficit. The "merchandise trade deficit" is the difference between the imports and exports of goods (manufactured products, raw materials, etc.). The "goods and services balance" includes the net exports of services such as transportation, banking and construction, as well as net investment income. Finally, the "current-account balance" is equal to the balance of goods and services plus unilateral transfers such as pensions and remittances.

2   See Martin Feldstein, "The Budget Deficit and the Dollar," in NBER Macro-Economics Annual 1986, Cambridge: MIT Press, 1986.

3   See Martin Feldstein, "American Economic Policy and the World Economy," Foreign Affairs, Summer 1985.

4   For the evidence summarized in this paragraph, see Martin Feldstein, "New Evidence on the Effects of Exchange Rate Intervention," National Bureau of Economic Research Working Paper No. 2052, 1986.

23

Exchange Rate Policy.
The J-Curve, the Fire Sale, and
the Hard Landing

Paul Krugman

The dollar peaked almost four years ago. The subsequent era of dollar decline, that has now lasted longer than the era of the strong dollar, has confounded the expectations of both optimists and pessimists. Optimists believed that a return of the dollar to historical levels would quickly bring about a restoration of U.S. external balance; yet although the dollar is now by any measure below its previous low point in the late 1970s, the United States continues to run current account deficits that would have been inconceivable a decade ago. Pessimists feared that a declining dollar would lead to capital flight, cutting off the supply of foreign savings on which the U.S. economy has become dependent; yet capital inflows have remained large, and there has so far been little sign of financial crisis due to a loss of foreign confidence.

The failure of a declining dollar to produce either good news about trade or bad news about financial markets has led to a recasting of the debate. There are still optimists, but their optimism no longer takes the form of cheerful predictions of a rapid decline in the trade deficit. There are still pessimists, but they no longer predict a "hard landing" in which a cutoff of capital creates a dramatic economic crisis.

The new optimists, instead of predicting fast improvement in trade, ask what is so bad about a trade deficit. They point to the fact of continuing capital inflow, and conclude that the United States will not have any problem with financing its investment for many years. Of course the budget deficit needs to be brought down, and the national savings rate increased, but there is no urgency: foreigners have been willing to cover the gap between savings and investment for the last seven years, and will surely be willing to do so for some while longer, while a "flexible freeze" slowly reduces the federal deficit and private savings spontaneously recover.

The new pessimists look at the same facts, and reach a different conclusion: that dollar depreciation has failed, and indeed been disastrous. The trade deficit remains huge; meanwhile foreigners have bought up large quantities of U.S. assets at bargain prices, thanks to the weak dollar. The problem as now seen by the pessimists, is not that the United States is on the verge of sudden crisis, but that it is selling its birthright for a mess of pottage.

The purpose of this paper is to argue that both the new optimism and the new pessimism on the dollar are off the mark. The optimists, in looking at the continuation of capital inflows, have failed to notice that this continuation results from the sluggish response of trade flows, not from continued foreign confidence. The pessismists are correct in their observation of a "fire sale" in which the United States has been able to continue to attract capital inflows only by making its assets much cheaper through dollar depreciation.   They are wrong, however, in decrying this fire sale as a great mistake; it is in fact an inevitable part of the adjustment process. And both optimists and pessimists have been too quick to dismiss the possibility of a hard landing for the U.S. economy: a financial squeeze due to a cutoff of foreign capital is not only a live possibility, it is arguably already in process.

CAPITAL INFLOWS AND THE FIRE SALE

When the dollar was at its peak, economists who warned of trouble ahead feared that once the bubble burst there would be a cutoff of the supply of foreign capital, leading to a financial hard landing. Experience has thus far belied this fear. Even though the current account deficit actually widened in nominal terms until recently, the United States has continued to finance this deficit without any obvious strain. The absence of crisis has led to a new consensus among many economists: that the external deficit is a problem only because of its long-run implications for living standards, not because of prospective problems of financing.

The combined persistence of the current account deficit and of capital inflows — which are of course, equal — has led to a reversal of opinions among many about the wisdom of allowing the dollar to decline. A few years ago, the orthodox view that the strong dollar was a key factor in the plunge of the United States into net debtor status was generally accepted. Now, however, a growing body of opinion holds that the strategy of weakening the dollar has actually worsened rather that improved the U.S. position as a debtor. In this view, which we may describe as the fire sale theory, the main effect of a cheap dollar is not to make U.S. goods more competitive, but to make U.S. assets cheap. Foreigners in general, and the Japanese in particular, therefore are more, not less, able to buy up U.S. assets.

The fire sale view is sometimes expressed in melodramatic terms, as something that will turn us all into paupers within a few years. This is an overdrawn picture. Yet there is clearly some truth here. Those who look only at the flow of foreign capital into the United States since 1985, and not at the decline in the dollar needed to attract that capital, are missing an important aspect of the situation.

Yet there is also something wrong with the fire sale view. Many of its advocates treat the dollar's decline as if it were some kind of exogenous event, foisted upon the country by James Baker. They also treat the sale of U.S. assets at bargain prices as if it represented a pure windfall to foreign investors. This cannot be right. If U.S. assets are such a good buy, then why is it that their prices do not get bid up? And if it is now so attractive to invest in the United States, should not the desire to keep investing here drive up the value of the dollar? The point is that neither asset prices not the value of the dollar (which is an asset price itself) can be regarded as givens.

In order to make sense of what has been happening to the United States in recent years, it is necessary to tell a more complete story. In this story the key element is the sluggish response of trade flows to the exchange rate.

CONFIDENCE, THE J-CURVE, AND THE EXCHANGE RATE

Suppose that international investors were suddenly to lose confidence in the United States. What it means to "lose confidence" is a slightly problematic issue; perhaps investors start to demand a risk premium on U.S. assets, perhaps, they revise downward their views about the long-run equilibrium real exhange rate, or perhaps they start to have a "peso problem," viewing a catastrophic fall in the dollar as a possibility though not a probability. Whatever the precise nature of the loss of confidence, the important point is that we suppose that investors become unwilling to hold claims on the United States at their current rates of return.

What happens next? Investors cannot simply pull their money out of the United States, since there would be nobody on the other side of the transaction. When everybody wants to sell, the result is not a lot of sales but a fall in the price. The immediate result of a loss of confidence in the United States, then, is not a sudden flight of capital but a sudden fall in the dollar.

The textbook view of what happens next is that the fall in the dollar leads to a reduction in the U.S. current account deficit. This deficit reduction has as its counterpart a decline in the rate of capital inflow, so this is the channel through which a decline in confidence leads to a cutoff of capital flows. The move toward current account balance also reduces the supply of savings domestically, driving up the interest rate; equilibrium is reached when the interest rate is driven up sufficiently to make investors willing to hold U.S. assets again.

This textbook view is consistent, and correct as a description of the medium run. As a short-run story, however, it overlooks a crucial point: the sluggishness with which the trade balance responds to the exchange rate. As recent experience has confirmed, the response of trade flows to the exchange rate takes years, both because consumers are slow to change habits and, even more important, because many changes in supply and sourcing require long-term investment decisions. As a result of this sluggishness, a fall in the dollar does not lead to any immediate reduction of the U.S. trade deficit, and indeed probably leads to a temporary rise in that deficit. Since the rate of capital inflow is by definition equal to the current account deficit, we have a paradoxical result: capital markets cannot determine the rate of capital inflow. All they can do is determine the value of the dollar, which itself can influence the rate of capital flow only with a long lag.

This may at first sight appear to leave the dollar with no bottom. As the dollar drops, however, it falls relative to its expected long-run level, and thus offers foreign investors a higher expected rate of return. At some point this will be enough to induce these investors to hold on to U.S. assets. And since the current account deficit remains, foreign investors will actually continue to put funds into the United States; indeed, thanks to the J-curve they may be putting capital in at a greater rate than before.

Only over time does a textbook answer emerge, as the weak dollar *gradually* reduces the trade deficit. Eventually the result is a smaller external deficit on one side, and a rise in interest rates on the other. But this result takes time, and meanwhile foreigners continue to finance the deficit.

In this not entirely hypothetical story, we see some aspects of the U.S. story of the past few years emerge. The loss of confidence by foreigners is initially reflected in a decline in the currencey, not in a decline in the rate of capital inflow; someone who looked only at the current account financing would conclude that foreigners were as willing to invest here as ever. What attracts the foreigners is precisely the fire sale of U.S. assets: the fall in the dollar makes the assets cheap, thus presenting foreigners with a higher expected rate of return. This fire sale is not, however, a windfall presented to foreigners by an arbitrary decline in the dollar; both the decline in the dollar and the fire sale result from the unwillingness of foreigners to keep investing in the United States, which requires that they be offered a higher expected rate of return.

Finally, notice that a hard landing — a financial squeeze brought about by the cutoff of foreign financing — does occur in this story, but not immediately. Because the loss of confidence by foreign investors cannot immediately show up in a reduced capital inflow, the hard landing takes time to develop. It would clearly be a mistake, however, to look at the absence of financial strain in the immediate aftermath of dollar decline and conclude that there will never be a financial problem.

POLICY IMPLICATIONS

The analysis presented here suggests that a loss of foreign confidence in the United States is not something that might happen in the future; it is something that has already happened. Foreign investors are continuing to finance the U.S. current account deficit only because they regard U.S. assets as cheap, due to a weak dollar. If they are right, and the dollar really is cheap, then there will eventually be serious crowding out of domestic investment as the current account deficit widens. Thus, raising national savings is a more urgent matter than optimists, who think the United States has no financing problem, have imagined.

It is of course possible that the markets are wrong; that only modest further narrowing of the trade gap will occur at the current value of the dollar. If that turns out to be the case, however, the markets will drive the dollar down still further: if they are not now getting assets at fire sale prices, they will insist on doing so in the future.

It is a mistake, however, to decry the fire sale as some kind of mistake of exchange rate policy. If foreigners are no longer willing to invest money here without a high expected rate of return, this is not something that could have been avoided if only the U.S. Treasury had supported the dollar. The only way to avoid a fire sale is not to need one — that is, to provide enough domestic saving so as to avoid reliance on foreign capital inflows.

So the policy moral of this analysis is one that has become boring through repetition, but is still as true as ever. The United States needs to restore its national savings rate to historical levels, as soon as it can. International investors have signaled that they are unwilling to continue financing massive current account deficits, not by cutting off capital flows suddenly, but by driving the dollar down to unprecedented lows. Putting aside the alarmist or conspiratorial view of some fire sale theorists, the point remains that the growing complacency about perpetual foreign borrowing will lead us to a rude awakening, sooner than most economists think.

References

Branson, William, "Causes of Appreciation and Volatility of the Dollar," in *The U.S. Dollar — Recent Developments, Outlook and Policy*, Federal Reserve Bank of Kansas City, 1985.

Dornbusch, Rudiger, "Exchange Rate Expectations and Monetary Policy," *Journal of International Economics*, August 1976, 6, 231-44.

X

THE DEBT CRISIS: DIAGNOSES AND PRESCRIPTIONS

Since 1982 when Mexico announced that it would suspend payments on its debt to American (and other) banks, there has been a great deal of talk about the international debt crisis. By now the history of the debt crisis is relatively well known; after the OPEC oil embargo of the early seventies, many developing countries faced with growing trade deficits turned to the private banking system, especially the Eurodollar market, for loans. Multinational banks, such as Citibank, lent billions of dollars to Latin America and other developing countries. The banks, ignoring the lessons of the thirties, assumed that since these loans were made to sovereign countries, the risk of default was low. The second OPEC price hike brought about another wave of lending for much the same reasons. By the early eighties, however, interest rates began to rise and the world economy went into a recession. Many developing countries found that their exports were dropping just as interest payments on these loans started to rise.

By the late eighties it became clear to nearly everyone that these loans would never be paid off in full. Various proposals for debt relief have been offered, some by the US government and some by private economists. The three articles below present different perspectives on debt relief. In the first article, Jeffrey Sachs, a professor at Harvard and a leading expert on the debt crisis, argues that most Latin American countries have already experienced severe economic dislocation from trying to pay off these debts. The austerity programs imposed by the IMF have created a climate of slow or negative growth and high unemployment to countries which are already quite poor. Sachs supports the Bush administration's recent proposal for debt relief, the Brady plan, but argues that it does not go far enough. Sachs believes that the Brady plan punishes creditors who extend debt relief first, since they will receive fewer cents on the dollar than creditors who wait. Sachs proposes rewarding banks who extend debt relief first with greater returns than current debt markets would give.

The third reading, "Punishing the profligate and rewarding the poor: some recent proposals for debt relief," Buitan and Srinivasan argue that debt relief proposals such as the Baker plan or the Brady plan are unfair because they channel funds toward the middle income Latin American countries (whose per capita incomes are in the 2000 to 3000 dollar range) and away from much poorer countries such as China, India, or most African countries (whose per capita incomes are much lower, typically only a few hundred dollars). According to Buitan and Srinivasan, the debt problems facing most Latin American countries are of their own doing; the countries borrowed the money in the seventies (although in most cases the money was borrowed under a different regime) and now refuse to pay. They contend that debt bailout plans create a bad precedent and encourage countries to borrow money in the future in hopes that they will be bailed out in the end.

The final paper, "Swapping third world debt," is enthusiastic about another proposed solution to the debt crisis: debt-equity swaps. In a debt-equity swap, a debtor country swaps an IOU representing some portion of its debt for local property or currency which will be used by a multinational corporation for investment in the country. The article suggests that debt-equity swaps create new investment which would not have existed otherwise and thus foster growth and development in the debtor country. Others (for example Sachs) have argued that debt equity swaps are just a zero sum game where one form of debt is swapped for another leaving the indebted country no better off.

24

Making the Brady Plan Work

Jeffrey Sachs

The Bush Administration has changed the direction of U.S. policies on Third World indebtedness. The new initiative, announced by Treasury Secretary Nicholas F. Brady in March 1989, calls on U.S. commercial banks to accept an orderly process of debt reduction, and calls on the international financial institutions — the International Monetary Fund (IMF) and the World Bank — to support this process through changes in their lending policies. [1] The plan implicitly recognizes that many debtor countries will be unable to repay their commercial bank debts in full, even if repayment is stretched out over time. The focus on cutting the debt burden contrasts sharply with earlier Treasury policies, under both Donald Regan and James Baker, which had held that eventually all of the commercial bank debt should be repaid on market terms.

The Brady Plan is a welcome shift, although to date the proposal's details have remained vague. The general mechanism for achieving debt reduction called for in the new plan is for creditor banks to agree voluntarily to reduce the value of their claims (either through a cut in principal or interest) in return for guarantees on the remaining portion of the debt. In the Treasury's view of the negotiations between the banks and the debtor countries, the banks are to be presented with a "menu of options" of debt reduction mechanisms. The banks will be free to choose one of these, but they may decide to hold on to the existing debt (perhaps with some commitment to make new loans) in the belief that they will be repaid eventually.

To encourage the banks to accept debt reduction rather than hold their debt, the IMF and the World Bank are called upon to help finance the guarantees, either by providing collateral on the reduced value of the debt or by giving debtor governments financial support to repurchase their debt directly for cash. These international institutions have agreed to provide up to $25 billion over three years, and Japan has committed $4.5 billion.

The Treasury has avoided precise targets for debt reduction; the details are to come out of negotiations between the banks and the debtor countries, and in the course of specific market transactions. The Treasury is informally promoting four countries — Costa Rica, Mexico, the Philippines and Venezuela — as the first for early negotiations with the banks under the Brady Plan, although the Treasury has stated that any of 39 countries engaged in commercial bank debt restructurings could eventually qualify to participate. To qualify for debt reduction, the plan stipulates that debtor countries should be undertaking sound economic policies aimed at encouraging domestic savings and foreign investment and promoting the return of flight capital.

Thus, the Treasury is relying on "market" solutions, based on the "voluntary" actions of creditors, to bring about the debt reduction. "Market-based" debt reduction techniques are not new, but the extent of reduction has been limited. The promise of guarantees is intended to encourage debt reduction, but the specific terms and amount of guarantees will be crucial in determining the extent of reductions.

The Brady Plan is a first step in focusing on debt reduction as a way out of the debt crisis. Success depends on the amount of debt reduction and the structure of the negotiations to achieve it. There are reasons to doubt that the voluntary approach of the Brady Plan can deliver an adequate amount of debt reduction. Behind this doubt is the continuing debate over who will determine the allocation of burdens among the banks, the debtors, the international institutions and national governments.

II

The new U.S. focus on debt reduction is rooted in the changing U.S. interests in the developing country debt crisis. Since the early 1980s the debt crisis has actually presented U.S. policymakers with two crises: a crisis of U.S. banks, which had lent too much to the developing countries, and a crisis of the developing countries, which had borrowed too much. Until 1988 concern over the banks took precedence; in 1989 the foreign policy concerns over the deteriorating situation in the debtor countries came to the fore.

The shift in concern can be easily explained. The emergence of the debt crisis in 1982 put the nine major U.S. banks at profound risk.

Having followed the optimistic dictum of Citicorp's former chairman, Walter Wriston, that countries never go bankrupt, the banks had lent freely. In the 1970s they had earned huge overseas profits on their foreign loans. By the end of 1982 they had lent 176.5 percent of bank capital to Latin America alone, and 287.7 percent of bank capital to all developing countries (See Table 1).

Table 1

Exposure of U.S. Banks in the Debtor Countries

	End-1982	End-1986	End-1988
Nine Major U.S. Banks			
Percentage of Bank Capital in:			
Developing Countries	287.7%	153.9%	108.0%
Latin America	176.5%	110.2%	83.6%
All Other U.S. Banks			
Percentage of Bank Capital in:			
Developing Countries	116.0%	55.0%	32.2%
Latin America	78.6	39.7	21.8
Total Bank Capital			
(in billions of dollars)			
Nine major banks	$29.0	$46.7	$55.8
All other U.S. banks	41.6	69.4	79.8

Source: Federal Financial Institutions Examination Council, "Country Exposure Lending Survey," April 25, 1983, April 24, 1987, and April 12, 1989

When the debt crisis hit in 1982, debt reduction as a response to the crisis was not considered. If even a third of the claims on developing countries went bad, many major U.S. banks would have been insolvent. Thus, Treasury policies were aimed at keeping the pressure on the debtor countries to continue servicing the debt. The developing countries squeezed their economies sharply to meet the interest bills. Latin America alone paid about $25 billion more in interest and principal each year than it received in new loans, which slowed to a trickle.

In 1985 the Baker Plan was introduced with the stated goal of reducing the net outflow from the debtor countries in order to spur growth in their economies. Secretary Baker called on the banks to relend $20 billion over three years to the debtor countries, through country-by-country negotiations. Since the countries owed around $80 billion in interest to the banks in those three years, the $20 billion in new loans would have reduced the net outflow by about one-fourth. In the end the banks even failed to deliver on the $20 billion. The Baker Plan is therefore viewed as a failure, but it benefited the banks by providing a political context to press the debtor countries to keep paying the interest.

Between 1982 and 1988, therefore, the banks received most of the interest due on the old debt, while also cutting back decisively on new lending to the debtor countries. At the same time the banks raised new capital. In this way the banks sharply reduced their risks from the developing countries' debts. By the end of 1988 the exposure of the major banks in Latin America had fallen to just 83.6 percent of capital — still high, but low enough to put the banks out of danger of insolvency. [2] This was an important precondition to any change in policy.

At least since 1985 market participants have doubted that the debts would actually be repaid in full, contrary to the official optimism of the Baker Plan. For that reason, the debts have actively traded on a secondary market at a large and growing discount. Table 2 shows the value of the larger countries' debt in this market as of February 1989, on the eve of the Brady Plan. Note that the total medium- and long-term bank debt amounted to a face value of $279.4 billion, or an average market prices of just 35 cents per dollar of debt. [3]

The stock market values of those commercial banks holding the developing countries' debts are also deeply discounted, in line with the secondary market prices of the debt. For example, the stock market seems to value Citicorp as if each $1 of its claims on Mexico were actually worth about $0.40, i.e., the price of the debt in the secondary market. This fact is very significant. It suggest that if Citicorp were to sell $1 of Mexican debt at the price of $0.40, the stock market value of the bank would remain unchanged, even though the bank would report a $0.60 book loss on the transaction. Thus, the banks can now afford to accept large losses on their portfolios without further reducing the banks' market value.

Table 2

Outstanding Debt of Selected Countries
(In billions of dollars) [1]

Country	Debt (billions $)	Market Value (billions $)	Market Price (% of face value)
Argentina	$33.6	$6.3	19%
Bolivia	.9	.1	10
Brazil	62.2	21.0	34
Chile	11.2	6.6	61
Costa Rica	1.5	.2	14
Ecuador	5.5	.8	14
Mexico	63.8	21.1	38
Nigeria	11.5	2.4	21
Philippines	10.5	4.8	46
Poland	12.3	4.9	40
Venezuela	22.6	8.2	37
Total for 39 Eligible Countries	**279.4**	**96.7**	**35**

Sources: Total debt, from World Bank Debt Tables (with adjustments made to eliminate debt already guaranteed by export credit agencies). Market price of debt, percent offer price in secondary market, Salomon Brothers, February 1989; and Merrill Lynch Capital Markets, April 1989 (for Poland).

[1] Debt and market value rounded to nearest hundred million; market price to nearest percent.

As for the debtor countries, many have fallen into the deepest economic crisis in their histories. Between 1981 and 1988 real per capita income declined in absolute terms in almost every country in South America. Many countries' living standards have fallen to levels of the 1950s and 1960s. Real wages in Mexico declined by about 50 percent between 1980 and 1988. A decade of development has been wiped out throughout the debtor world. The crisis of confidence has led to a collapse of investment, which will create a legacy of hardships in the 1990s.

Unprecedented inflation is raging in Brazil (934 percent inflation in 1988), in Argentina and Peru (annual inflation rates in both reached several thousand percent in spring 1989) and elsewhere. The region is rife with political instability, with a sharp shift toward support for populist politicians. The explosive situation in Latin America was registered most dramatically in February 1989, when Venezuelans rioted in Caracas and other major cities, in protest against austerity measures prompted by Venezuela's debt crisis. In the course of a few days an estimated 300 people died. This was particularly shocking since Venezuela had long been regarded as one of the most stable Latin American democracies.

U.S. interests are engaged throughout the debtor world. The bankers view the crisis mainly in terms of the six largest debtors — which together account for about 75 percent of the U.S. money-center banks' exposure in the developing world. But U.S. interests arising from debts are actively engaged not only in Latin America and the Philippines, but in Eastern Europe and sub-Saharan Africa as well.

III

The Brady Plan carries forward two key precepts of its predecessor, the Baker Plan. First, it calls for the debt problem to be handled on a case-by-case basis, in which each debtor country negotiates separately with its creditor. Second, it envisions that any easing of the terms of the debt must be linked to economic reforms under the supervision of the IMF and the World Bank. The Brady Plan diverges from the Baker Plan, of course, in its stress on the need for debt reduction.

The Baker Treasury had raised two objections to debt reduction. First, it maintained that debt reduction would slow the return of the debtor countries to creditworthiness, because banks would be unwilling to lend to countries that has failed to repay their debts. Second, stretching out the debt repayments was deemed sufficient to restore prosperity. Opposition to debt reduction came not only from the Treasury but from the banks, given the continuing weakness of their balance sheets.

The Brady Treasury has now rejected these arguments. It has recognized that when a debt burden is too high to be repaid, it must be reduced before creditworthiness can be regained. The Brady Treasury has also recognized that a further stretching out of the debt payments without debt reduction is unlikely to restore prosperity, because of the continuing crisis engendered by the large stock of bad debt.

As for the debt itself, the Treasury has pointed to several ways to reduce it: buybacks, conversion of debt into bonds with lower principal or interest, and exchanging debt for equity in the debtor countries.

In a buyback, the debtor country uses cash reserves (either its own, or money borrowed from the IMF or World Bank) to repurchase some of its debt from its creditor banks, but at a deeply discounted price. For example, as noted, Mexican debt now sells for about $0.40 per $1 of debt. At this price, Mexico can purchase $2.50 of debt for $1 of cash. By borrowing $1 from the World Bank for this purpose, Mexico would be able to reduce its *net debt* by $1.50 (the bank debt falls by $2.50, the World Bank debt rises by $1).

Another way to achieve debt reduction is through a debt conversion, in which some of the existing debt is converted into a new asset. For example, the banks and Mexico might agree to convert some of its existing debt, which carries a floating market interest rate (approximately 11 percent as of May 1989), into a new debt that carries a fixed below-market interest rated, say five percent, with some or all of the future interest payments guaranteed. Thus, the new asset would have a lower contractual debt service burden. It would be made safer than the original debt by backing it with guarantees or collateral.

The guarantees could be arranged in a number of ways. For example, the World Bank could lend Mexico money to purchase various assets to deposit in escrow as collateral on the new bonds. Alternatively, Mexico could create a mechanism to pledge future oil earning against the payments of interest.

The third debt reduction mechanism suggested by the Treasury is a debt-equity swap. The debtor government repurchases existing bank debt using local currency, which must then be used by the seller to make a foreign direct investment in the debtor country. The seller may be a creditor bank, or a company that purchases the debt from a bank and then sells the debt to the debtor country's central bank. Typically, the foreign investor acquires the bank debt at its secondary market price, but then sells it to the central bank at a much higher price, albeit one that is paid in local currency.

Debt-equity swaps evidently reduce the amount of outstanding bank debt, but they risk causing tremendous disruptions in the debtor countries. The problem is that the direct repurchase of debt for local currency represents an increase in the money supply, and thereby induces a rise in inflation. Typically, the debtor government will offset the monetary effects of the transaction by selling a bond in the local financial market to soak up the money supply increase. In effect, the government rids itself of its external bank debt by increasing its domestic debt. The bank debt is reduced, but the overall debt is not. And since the local debts carry much higher interest rates, the overall interest payments will tend to rise, not fall, after the debt-equity swap. For these reasons, several debtor countries have suspended their debt-equity programs, though other countries continue with them because of pressure from the banks, lobbying by local firms that benefit from the sways and misguided advocacy by the U.S. Treasury.

IV

While the Brady Plan enunciated some general suggestions for debt reduction operations, the Treasury is relying on market transaction between debtor countries and the credit banks to achieve the debt reduction. In the Treasury's view, significant debt reduction can occur without a guiding hand. This optimism is questionable in view of the slow progress in voluntary debt reduction to date. [4]

Two factors introduced by the Brady Plan were intended to tilt the balance toward rapid debt reduction. First is the financing that official institutions are to provide for some of the debt reduction transactions. Secondly, the Brady Plan asked the banks to amend the terms of their loan agreements through waivers to permit the rapid introduction of new debt reduction mechanisms. [5] The banks have balked at unilaterally amending their agreements in order to expedite debt reduction operations.

It appears that the Treasury has miscalculated the chances for significant debt reduction in the current negotiating framework. "This is not because the banks dispute the inevitability of losses on the debt — most do not — but because the negotiating framework gives too great an opening for each individual bank to hold out, hoping that somebody else (other banks, the IMF, Japan, etc.) will bear the inevitable losses. The Brady Plan does not ask the banks to do anything specific (except to agree to waivers in the loan agreement). Thus, each bank can readily endorse the Brady Plan in the abstract without conceding anything concrete.

Moreover, there is an inherent limitation to any voluntary scheme: participation in the new plan must be no worse for the banks than sticking with the original claim. But an obvious paradox arises. If the debt reduction is deep enough that creditworthiness is truly restored, then *all* of the claims on the debt, even the "holdout" debt not involved in the debt reduction plank will rise in value to face value (i.e., to close to 100 cents on the dollar in the secondary market). Therefore, if a voluntary scheme appears likely to work, banks will decide to hold out until creditworthiness is restored, and the goal of debt reduction will not be achieved after all.

This difficulty is often called the "free rider" problem; it is very real and very serious. A senior executive at a money-center bank told me recently: "Mexico will get its debt reduction. We're not going to give it, but we're sure that other banks will." Even aside from the unfairness of this view (why should one bank escape from the burden of debt reduction that is accepted by other creditors), the analysis is probably wrong. Just as the one bank will not participate, other banks will follow the same logic and fail to participate in the "voluntary" scheme. Some money-center banks are privately pressing for a comprehensive approach to the debt negotiations; they express a willingness to engage in deep debt reduction, but only if their corporate competitors do likewise.

Other banks argue that they should be allowed to make new loans while some banks accept debt reduction, but new lending is in practice just a disguised form of free-riding. The bank lending new money does not reduce the value of its original claim, and will also insist on full repayment of the new loan.

Another problem is that the major commercial banks see an advantage in waiting for further bailouts from the official creditor community. For example, they may expect to benefit if Mexico can attract new loans or grants from the official creditors that can be used to make debt service payments. In this case, the banks' optimism would not be misplaced: the IMF, the World Bank and increasingly the Japanese government have acted in recent years to supply some of the money needed by the debtor countries to meet interest payments to the banks.

The large U.S. banks are especially resistant to debt reduction operations for two basic reasons. First, even though debt reductions should raise market values of bank stock, they generally require book losses, because the banks are holding the vast proportion of the debt on their books at the original face value. [6] Since capital adequacy standards are based on book values, many banks are loath to report book losses even for the sake of market gains. [7] Second, the large banks have better access to debt-equity swaps than do the smaller banks; these swaps offer the large banks a less costly way of divesting debt, though the swaps increase debtor countries' overall debt.

In sum, sufficient debt reduction will likely be unachievable through a decentralized, "voluntary" process.

V

How then should the Brady Plan be elaborated in order to overcome these problems?

The Treasury must emphasize the need for concerted participation of the banks in debt reduction, with no free riders. All banks should accept an equivalent reduction of their debt, although they may choose among methods of participation, e.g., buybacks or debt conversion. But perhaps the simplest mechanism would be to cut the interest charged on the debt to a fixed level below market rates, combined with official guarantees on part or all of the payments. This mechanism is ideal for achieving a comprehensive settlement: it is administratively straightforward, is equitable in its impact across banks, and avoids the adverse consequences of debt-equity swaps. It may even obviate the need for large, immediate writedowns of capital, because under U.S. banking regulations a debt restructuring that preserves principal but reduces interest rates does not in general require a capital writedown.

Achieving a comprehensive cut in interest rates to sub-market levels would require several steps on the part of the official creditor community (especially the IMF and World Bank) to shift the negotiating framework. All of the needed steps are within the mandate of the international institutions. All could be carried out in a case-by-case manner, conditioned on prior economic reforms in the participating country.

The first step would be an explicit recognition by the IMF and the World Bank that the debt burden of a particular country should be reduced. IMF and World Bank programs would then be designed with the necessary amounts of debt reduction in mind. The extent of austerity called for by the IMF, for example, would be lessened as the IMF explicitly recognized that some of the debt service burden of the country would be reduced rather than paid.

The targeted amounts of debt reduction would be based on a professional assessment of the country's budgetary and balance-of-payments prospects, and would take into account the price of the debt on the secondary market, the extent of economic decline or collapse in the country in recent years, and so on. The IMF and World Bank would provide guarantees for the banks that participate in the debt reduction process.

The key step would come next: gaining sufficient participation by the banks. The IMF and the World Bank would have to establish as a matter of official policy that the banks should share equally in the debt reduction. They would insist that a "critical mass" of banks holding, say, 80 percent of the debt participate in the debt reduction package before IMF and World Bank funds would be made available to provide guarantees to the participating banks.

Furthermore, the IMF and World Bank should enter into other lending programs to the debtors without tieing them to completion of the debtor-bank negotiations. To date, debtors have generally been unable to obtain new IMF programs until they agreed with the banks on a future schedule of debt service payments. With the banks insisting on full payments, the country would either have to pay or find itself without access to official lending. This is the precise sense in which the IMF has acted as a "bill collector" for the commercial banks: IMF lending has been conditioned on meeting the banks' demands for full repayment. If the country dared to sacrifice its IMF program, it generally lost access to financial support from the Paris Club, official export credits, World Bank loans and so forth.

In an important shift, the Brady Treasury recently recognized the stranglehold that the banks have held over the IMF. In his March speech, Secretary Brady called for greater IMF flexibility in making disbursements to countries even before final agreements are reached between the banks and the debtor country. But he was ambiguous about how the IMF should respond to arrearages (nonpayment of debt service due) by the debtor countries should the commercial banks balk at providing debt reduction.

It may be necessary for the IMF and World Bank to take the extra step of tolerating debtors' arrearages to the commercial banks at two crucial points in the negotiating process. Tolerating arrearages means that the official creditor community (the IMF, the World Bank, the multilateral development banks, the Paris Club, the official export credit agencies) would continue normal relations with debtors despite their arrears to the commercial banks. The official creditors would tolerate the arrears of cash-strapped debtors, first, if it proved difficult to assemble the critical mass of banks to participate in the needed debt reduction. Second, official creditors should continue to tolerate debtors' arrearages to any recalcitrant banks which refuse to join in the agreed package once the critical mass has been reached. Such a policy would isolate the holdout banks, and undermine free riding: banks that fail to participate in debt reduction would not get paid.

VI

How much debt reduction is needed, and what will it cost: This depends on (1) the terms on which the debts will be reduced and (2) which debtor countries participated.

The general goal is that debt reduction be sufficient to enable the debtor to pay the remaining debt service routinely and to resume growth. Some Bush Administration officials have suggested an average reduction of 20 percent for eligible debtors, but this amount would not come close to meeting the above goal.

As the Brady Plan suggests, the targets for specific countries should be set by a case-by-case approach after a detailed analysis of the medium-term economic and political prospects of the eligible country. The professional staffs of the IMF and the World Bank are qualified to give guidance on this question, though they should pay much more attention than they have to the simple truth that debt servicing capacity depends on political stability as well as economic factors.

As a starting point, they should use evidence of the secondary market value of the debt to judge how much the debt should be reduced. Roughly speaking, the market expects that a country with a debt selling at 40 percent of face value will be able to repay only 40 percent of the outstanding debt. If the debt burden were to be reduced in line with the current secondary market price, the country would have good prospects of full debt servicing thereafter. In fact, the debt need not be reduced this much: the secondary market value of the debt likely *understates* the long-term debt servicing capacity of the country, since it reflects all of the uncertainties and costs of the debt strategy that have been followed until now. For this reason the banks should receive something more than the secondary market price in return for their full participation.

I would propose as a basic guideline that the banks receive (in the present value of repayment) a 20-percent premium over the secondary market price as of some reference date, e.g., February 1989. [8] This number could then be adjusted upward or downward based on the medium-term economic scenario elaborated by the IMF and the World Bank, operating in consultation with economists in the debtor countries and the creditor banks. On this basis, Mexico's debt burden would be reduced to around 45 percent of the current face value.

What debtor countries should participate in debt reduction? There are 39 countries that have been identified as candidates by the Brady Plan; their foreign commercial bank debt totals $279.4 billion, with a secondary market price (as of February 1989) of $96.7 billion. But only a small fraction of these 39 countries would qualify immediately for a debt reduction program, namely, those countries that have undertaken sound, internationally supervised adjustment programs. As of mid-1989 this list would include, among others: Bolivia, Chile, Costa Rica, Ecuador, Mexico, the Philippines and Venezuela. It would not include Argentina or Brazil, which have both failed to make significant progress on economic reform programs.

Therefore, debt reduction should be first undertaken for the handful of qualifying countries. It is important that adequate reductions be made in these countries' debt. The funding already pledged by the IMF, the World Bank and Japan, totaling $29.5 billion, should be targeted to finance adequate reductions and guarantees for the currently eligible countries. Only if these test cases receive sufficient reduction of this debt burden will the plan succeed, and thereby gain the political support necessary for creditor governments to pledge additional resources for the reduction of other countries' debt as they qualify for it.

VII

What is the cost of financing debt reduction? Even though debt reduction will proceed on a country-by-country basis, it is useful to look at the overall cost of financing the program.

After a critical mass of the banks accept the package and after the debtor country is certified to be undertaking a comprehensive program of economic reform under the supervision of the IMF and the World Bank, the reduced interest rates would then be guaranteed. These guarantees would be provided by a special guarantee fund set up in the IMF and the World Bank. The principal would not be reduced, but would be rescheduled for 30 years and also guaranteed by the fund.

The key operation of the guarantee fund is to pay the reduced interest to the banks in the event that the debtor country cannot or does not meet even the reduced amount of debt servicing. Thus, the ultimate backers of the guarantee (e.g., the creditor governments) assume only a partial and contingent burden; they bear some of the cost only if the country does not meet its reduced debt repayment schedule.

Fortunately, even if the official community provides comprehensive debt reduction for all the eligible debtor countries, only very modest new budgetary outlays will be required from the creditor governments. This is because numerous other sources of financing are available.

Let us assume that the present value of the debt service of the 39 eligible countries is reduced to market value ($96.7 billion) plus a 20-percent premium. The total required to guarantee the interest and principal would be $116 billion. One way of funding this is illustrated below.

The first tranche could be provided by the banks out of the 20-percent premium that they earn over the market price. About half of the premium, $9.67 billion, would be deposited into an insurance fund at the IMF and World Bank to provide a portion of the guarantees. The banks would receive their pro-rated share of any funds remaining in the insurance fund after ten or 15 years. The other half of the premium would be kept as current income by the banks.

The proposed guarantee fund would then have to cover the remaining $106 billion. A formula for a full funding of the guarantee fund would result from detailed negotiations. Of the $106 billion required, about 60 per cent could come from funding sources already in existence and other sources that would not require appropriations by the creditor governments. Furthermore, $106 billion is the maximal cost if all 39 countries participate and then completely default. A breakdown of this magnitude is extraordinarily unlikely. Also, as interest is repaid over time, the amounts needed in the fund would decline.

Among the possible sources for the $106 billion are:

- World Bank and IMF resources ($41 billion, including the $25 billion already suggested under the Brady Plan);
- Contributions from the debtor countries themselves, including: gold reserves, or the pledge of future export earnings as collateral for future interest payments ($25 billion);
- Paid-in and callable capital from the creditor governments ($40 billion).

One key source of guarantees should be pledges by the debtor countries of future export earnings as collateral for future interest payments. Ecuador already has extensive experience with collateralizing interest payments with future oil earnings, in the form of a special "oil facility" with the commercial banks that was operative in 1986-87. Mexico and Venezuela could also pledge future oil earnings, and other countries could pledge earnings of other major exports. A reasonable estimate of the funding available from these sources is approximately $2.5 billion a year, or $25 billion in present value.

Only one-third of the guarantee fund ($40 billion) would require new authorizations by creditor governments, and only a fraction of that would require new appropriations. I propose that the paid-in capital from the Group of Seven industrialized countries be ten percent, or $4 billion, with the rest callable, and that the U.S. share of the paid-in capital be $1 billion. The total U.S. guarantee, therefore, would be $10 billion. The paid-in proportion ($1 billion) could be appropriated over several years, and so would amount to a tiny fraction of any one year's foreign aid budget. Of course, the actual U.S. contribution would rise in the event of massive defaults by the debtor countries on their reduced payments. But even an extraordinary 30-percent loss would mean a U.S. liability of $3 billion, a trivial sum assuming that the losses are distributed over many years. For comparison, this is a tiny fraction of the taxpayer obligations under the current crisis of domestic savings and loan institutions.

The Brady proposal has been attacked for recommending any use of taxpayer dollars to support debt reduction operations. As just seen, the amounts likely to be involved are in fact very small. But, in addition, this criticism ignores the fact that the taxpayer was up at much greater risk under the Baker Plan strategy. Under that plan the debtor countries were obliged to meet their full interest payments. Since such payments were beyond the capacity of the countries, and since the banks were unwilling to ease the cash-flow burden through much new lending, it fell on the official (institutional or governmental) creditors to lend the countries the money they needed to pay their interest bill.

Analyzed in this way, the tax payer stands to benefit significantly if the commercial banks recognize some losses on the debts. Using IMF and World Bank money to support debt reduction will be much safer than simply using the same money to lend to debtors so they can pay the banks' current interest bill. The guarantees will be safer the deeper the debt reduction; the smaller the remaining debt, the more likely it is that the debtor will be able to service it without drawing on the guarantees.

VII

Debt reduction is a necessary condition for renewed economic growth in the debtor world, but it is surely not a sufficient condition. Without appropriate economic reform measures, most debtor economies would remain in difficulty even after a substantial reduction of debt. Thus, it is essential for the debtor countries to use the opportunity of debt reduction to make fundamental adjustments. Also, the protection of official funds requires that guarantees be conditioned on sound economic policies.

It is sometimes suggested that debt reduction would remove the pressure for economic reforms. This argument is dubious. The economic instability caused by the debt crisis itself is a much greater barrier to economic reform. In Latin America reformers are finding themselves vulnerable to sharp political attacks by populists, who charge that economic reforms are simply a way to squeeze the domestic population in order to transfer funds to the foreign banks. In the absence of debt reduction, that charge is both accurate and politically potent. [9]

Seen in this way, the failure in recent years of IMF conditionality to "enforce" good policies is a reflection of the debt management strategy. Noncompliance with IMF programs has grown in recent years, largely because the programs have sought to impose austerity measures aimed at enabling the country to make politically unacceptable levels of debt service payments. If IMF conditionality were to be based on realistic amounts of debt servicing, IMF reform programs would be honored with much greater frequency.

There are many important and complex issues regarding the contents of "economic reform" programs. The basic orientation of IMF and World Bank programs appears to have considerable merit, based on the record of comparative economic performance in the developing world. [10] The IMF properly stresses the need for fiscal discipline, which is the *sine qua non* of overall macroeconomic stability. The World Bank properly stresses the need for an outward-oriented trade regime, the importance of which is most vividly illustrated by the success of the exporters in East Asia, compared with the inward-looking regimes in Latin America. But both institutions have found that their message gets lost in the political firestorm that breaks out when excessive debt payments overwhelm the domestic economy.

One underemphasized area for reform is the striking inequalities in Latin American societies, in which the top 20 percent of the population in some countries earn as much as 30 times the incomes of the bottom 20 percent. The vast inequalities have played a large role in the onset of the crisis, and help to explain the attractiveness of populism, the wide-spread unpopularity of private enterprise, and resentment at the wealthy elite's avoidance of their share of taxation. Future IMF and World Bank programs should give greater care that the spending, tax and trade measures that they represent help to narrow the profound income gaps in the region.

IX

The Brady Plan will soon arrive at a crossroads. The Treasury will have to choose between the easy path of overseeing a small amount of debt reduction, and the much harder path of active engagement to achieve the deep debt reduction needed to solve the crisis. The market alone will not achieve the necessary extent of debt reduction. The official creditor community must now be prepared to help design meaningful and comprehensive deals between the banks and the debtor countries.

The cost of half-measures will be very high, not only for the taxpayers who will pick up a greater bill in the end, but for the 800 million people now living in economic turmoil in debt-distressed economies. Under the Baker Plan, the Reagan Administration temporized for four years while the banks escaped from the crisis. The Brady Plan has now reawakened the hopes of the debtor nations around the world. More years of temporizing would burst those hopes, with sorrowful and harrowing consequences.

Notes

1   The Brady Plan was unveiled in a speech by Secretary Brady to the Conference on Third World Debt of the Brookings Institution and the Bretton Woods Committee, March 10, 1989, in Washington, D.C.

2   The chairman of the Federal Deposit Insurance Corporation, William Seidman, make this point clearly in testimony to the U.S. House of Representatives Committee on Banking, Finance and Urban Affairs in January 1989: "Even in what surely could be considered a worst-case scenario, each of the nine money-center banks could write off 100 percent of their outstanding loans to these six [largest debtor] countries and, on an after-tax basis, each of these banks would remain solvent."

3   The focus of the Brady Plan, and the focus of this article, is on the middle and long-term debt owed by *sovereign borrowers* (i.e., by the public sectors of the debtor countries) to the commercial banks. Debt owed to the banks that is already guaranteed by creditor governments (e.g., U.S. bank loans guaranteed by the Exim Bank) is excluded.

4   The banks assert that extensive voluntary debt reduction is already under way, and point to "more than $26 billion" of voluntary debt reduction in a recent report of the Institute for International Finance. The vast bulk of this amount is private-sector debt, where the real debt crisis lies.

5   In particular, various technical clauses in the contracts (e.g., the sharing clause) prevent the debtor country from making unequal payments to particular creditor banks. This clause rules out a buyback of debt form a particular bank, for example, because that bank would be receiving a prepayment of debt that is not received by the other banks. The Treasury has asked the banks to waive these clauses voluntary in order to expedite the debt reducing proceeds.

6   Consider a bank that holds Mexican debt on the book t full face value, with the market value at \$0.40 per dollar of debt. If the bank sells the debt for \$0.45, it makes a profit in market values of \$0.05, but might have to report a book loss at \$0.55

7   This could easily be handled, however, through appropriate regulatory policies, such as requiring the banks to hold the debt on their books at true market value.

8   To the extent that the secondary market is used as one guideline to set the target for debt reduction, a post reference date for the prices should be chosen to eliminate the incentive for a debtor country to drive down its market price artificially.

9   To date, the better a country performs, the less it needs emergency loans and the more resource transfers it must make to the rest of the world. "Good behavior" thereby results in larger net debt servicing. The result is that economic reform has come to be viewed within the debtor countries as something that is done for the sake of foreign creditors, rather than for the sake of the debtor country itself. This adverse incentive effect can be overcome only by reducing the debt that is due, so that more of the benefits of economic reform accrue to the country itself.

10   For a cross-country comparison of economic performance, see Jeffrey D. Sachs, ed., *Developing Country Debt and the World Economy*, Chicago: University of Chicago Press, 1989.

25

Rewarding the Profligate and Punishing the Prudent and Poor: Some Recent Proposals for Debt Relief

Willem H. Buiter and T. N. Srinivasan

INTRODUCTION

At a conference organized in June 1986 by the Overseas Development Council on the future of the World Bank, former West German Chancellor Helmut Schmidt, investment banker Felix Rohatyn and the Chairman of the Federal Reserve Board Paul Volcker all suggested that the massive ($60 billion) trade surplus of Japan be mobilized to solve what they termed as the debt problem of the Third World. Mr. Barber Conable, the new president of the World Bank, is quoted by the *New York Times* (3 July 1986) as saying "Clearly, there is the expectation that Japan, in view of the light defense burden it carries will participate fully in (solving) collective debt problems of the world." He characterized the Japanese surpluses as "a considerable world asset" and suggested that establishing a special facility (such as the one established by the IMF in the 1970s to tap Saudi Arabia's surplus petro dollars) to recycle them "would be one way of dealing with it."

Nearly a year ago in October 1985 at the annual meetings of the World Bank and IMF at Seoul U.S. Treasury Secretary James Baker signaled a shift in the U.S. approach to the debt crisis. The Baker Plan aimed to help highly indebted, middle-income countries (15 were mentioned by Baker, 10 of them in Latin America) resume growth and achieve adjustment towards a sustainable debt position through the adoption of the following course of action by lenders, debtors and multilateral agencies: within the context of the (then) prevailing IMF-supervised case-by-case approach, commercial banks, the World Bank and other multilateral development banks were to increase lending to these countries. Baker suggested that the commercial banks commit a total of $20 billion in net new lending over 1986-88 and the multilateral development banks an additional $9 billion during the same period. The increased net lending was to be in support of the adoption of market-oriented policies by indebted nations. Growth was to be promoted, inflation reduced and external balance restored by expanding the role of the private sector and of markets, both domestically and internationally.

The first offspring of the Baker Plan is the recent "growth-oriented" adjustment plan for Mexico, which was foisted upon a reluctant IMF (perhaps the world's last unreconstructed bastion of adjustment through austerity) by the combined pressure of the U.S. Treasury and Federal Reserve Board and the Mexican threat of repudiation. (The IMF's reservations concerned the budgetary features of the package, not the novel real growth and oil price contingency clauses, which it supported.) The 18-month standby agreement with the IMF provides Mexico with SDR 1.4 billion (about $1.7 billion) in support of what is described as a comprehensive program of adjustment and structural reform. The total financing package amounts to $12 billion of which $6 billion is to come from the commercial banks. Mexico's economic problems had of course been intensified dramatically as a result of the drop in the price of oil.

Policies aimed at bringing Mexico's real GDP growth to 3.5% by 1987 (from recent negative growth rates of 4% to 5%) involve a variety of growth-oriented, market-friendly adjustment measures (increasing public investment, current expenditure cuts, tax reform measures, market-based adjustments in tariffs and prices charged by public sector enterprises, liberalizing trade measures (Mexico is about to join the GATT) and only very mild (by traditional IMF standards) budgetary restraint (a reduction in the deficit-GDP ratio by three percentage points over 1986-87).

The aspect of the Mexican program of most interest for this discussion is the actions taken by the multilateral organizations. In addition to the standby credit of SDR 1.4 billion, there is to be a $500 million contingency fund to supplement investment if the economic recovery fails to materialize despite the implementation of appropriate policies. In addition there are provisions for additional financing in the event oil prices fall below nine dollars a barrel. The World Bank also increased its commitments to Mexico by $2 billion in 1986.

The Baker Plan was soon followed by the more radical Bradley Plan for debt relief for the same group of middle-income, highly indebted countries. The exact nature and magnitude of the relief to be provided was left open. An initial suggestion involved three successive annual reductions of one percentage point in the interest rate charged on the debt. Partial write-downs (or write-offs) of debt principal could also feature. As in the Baker Plan, the debtor countries are required to liberalize their international trading arrangements and generally to adopt market-oriented reforms. In September a study commissioned by the Americas Society (Balassa *et al.*, 1986) called for the adoption of a larger-scale version of the Baker Plan, involving $20 billion annually in capital commitments from the U.S. and other industrial nations over the next several years. The study is skeptical about the willingness of the commercial banks to provide even the $20 billion over three years called for under the Baker Plan and proposes a much larger role for the multilateral institutions such as the World Bank in the early years of the Plan.

Any approach to alleviating the debt problem that is likely to revive economic growth in the indebted countries and to improve their ability to service their debt in the long run is to be welcomed. Yet the Baker proposal, the suggested use of Japanese surpluses, and the Bradley proposal all raise some disturbing questions both as to their feasibility and as to their desirability.

After briefly considering whether there is a global debt crisis (answer in the negative), we turn to the troubling fairness and efficiency aspects of the proposals. Fairness as between a few relatively rich (or less poor) major debtor countries with debt servicing problems, and other heavily indebted countries without debt servicing problems. Fairness as between the relatively rich troubled debtors and the large number of less indebted and very much poorer countries. Fairness as between troubled debtors whose plight is due to bad luck and those whose plight is due to bad policies.

Fairness, and incentive or moral hazard problems arise in the case of the Baker proposal, because while it provides no long-run relief to the debtors it has become a program for passing part of the tab for the U.S. commercial banks' developing-country bad-loan portfolio from these banks' shareholders, creditors, and managers to the multilateral agencies. In the Conable or Japanese variant, it is the Japanese saver or taxpayer who is requested to sustain part of the loss incurred by the commercial banks.

The Bradley proposal is also subject to incentive and moral hazard problems (in addition to the already mentioned fairness problems). First, because the magnitude of the relief given to a country is in practice going to be independent of its debt-servicing efforts and of the quality of its economic management, whatever the rhetoric concerning the strictly limited and highly selective and conditional nature of the relief. Second, because potential new private lenders, witnessing *de facto* if not *de jure* "equitization" of bank debt under this proposal, will think twice before once more increasing their financial exposure in these countries.

In a nutshell these proposals, while varying in important respects, all appear to address the debt "overhang" or the problem of the existing *stock* of debt in a way that is both inequitable and likely to affect adversely the future *flow* of resources to the developing countries, particularly the poorest among them.

IS THERE A GLOBAL DEBT CRISIS?

To begin with there is no "collective debt problem of the world." It is primarily a problem of a *few Latin American countries, that are relatively rich by the standards of developing countries.* Of the 17 countries deemed heavily indebted by the World Bank, countries that owed $446 billion out of a total of $950 billion in outstanding external liabilities of all developing countries at the end of 1985, 11 are in Central and South America. Just five countries, Argentina, Brazil, Chile, Mexico and Venezuela together owed $311.7 billion. Nearly three-quarters of the debt of the five countries is owed to banks. Of the amount owed to banks, a little less than a half came from U.S. banks.

FAIRNESS AND INCENTIVE EFFECTS

Undesirable features of the Baker and Bradley proposals include likely adverse effects on the future flow of private capital to the capital-hungry developing countries and lack of fairness. Any debt relief provided under these proposals (and there is of course little if any relief other than short-term cash flow relief for the debtor countries under the Baker Plan) will benefit primarily those heavily indebted developing countries that are in serious financial trouble (e.g., Brazil, Mexico, and Argentina). No such relief will be given to those equally heavily indebted countries that have stayed out of trouble (e.g., Korea). No relief either will be given to those developing countries that, while equally or more adversely affected by external or internal shocks as the debtor countries, borrowed much less or hardly at all, whether by choice or necessity (e.g. Sub-Saharan Africa). The heavily indebted countries that are experiencing serious debt financing problems and account for most of the debt, while being poor relative to the industrial countries, are typically no poorer than the heavily indebted countries that are not experiencing debt servicing difficulties. The 1984 per capita GNP of Chile is estimated at $1,700, that of Brazil at $1,720, and that of Mexico at $2,040, that of Argentina at $2,230 and that of Venezuela at $3,410. The figure for South Korea was $2,110. The troubled major debtors are very much richer (or rather less poor) than the large number of developing countries, accounting for the vast majority of the world's population, who stand to gain little or nothing from either the Bradley or the Baker plan and may indeed end up the losers if these plans divert resources to the middle-income debtor countries that would otherwise have gone to them. They include China with a 1984 per capita GNP estimated at $310, India with $260, Bangladesh with $130, Ethiopia with $110, and Indonesia with $540. The 36 lowest income countries in Asia and Africa had an average per capita GNP in 1984 of $260. While per capita GNP figures are known to understate true standards of living more the poorer the country, there is no doubt that large numbers of countries that are very much poorer than the major beneficiaries, will not benefit and may indeed suffer as a result of these proposals.

To the extent that these proposals contain aid or relief, the question therefore rises: why choose these beneficiaries when there are so many whose claim for relief, based on poverty and need, are so much stronger?

Countries get into debt-servicing problems for two kinds of reasons: bad luck and bad management or bad policies. (Among the latter we include those that get into trouble by design.) Bad luck includes such external (to the borrowing countries) shocks as the rise in world-wide real interest rates (largely made in the U.S.A.), adverse shifts in the terms of trade (the decline in the price of tin for Malaysia and of bauxite for Jamaica), and declining future remittances due to the world recession (Greece, Turkey) or the decline in the price of oil (Nigeria). Bad luck also includes internal unfriendly "acts of God" such as the Mexican earthquake, the drought in Sub-Saharan Africa, and the recent plague of locusts there.

The proposals are unfair also between different troubled (as well as inefficient) debtor countries, in that they do not make the magnitude or the terms on which the relief is provided contingent on whether the country's problems are due to bad luck or bad management. Past policy performance is not taken into account. Future policy reform and performance is of course put at the center of the stage, but it is doubtful whether this can be taken too seriously, precisely because past policies (or how a country got into the current mess) are not taken into account. By treating the existing debt as a bygone and focusing exclusively on (promises of) future policies for trade liberalization, privatization, fiscal probity, etc., these proposals contribute to an environment in which countries are more likely to deliberately build up their debt once more to unsustainable levels in the expectation of a Bradley Plan Vintage II when the next crisis hits. There are few credible ways in which debtor governments can pre-commit to pursuing a politically unrewarding policy long enough to turn the situation around. When the way in which the issue of existing ("bygone") debt is settled influences both lenders' and borrowers' expectations of the terms on which future new borrowing will be serviced, bygones are not bygones.

MACROECONOMIC MISMANAGEMENT AND ACCENTUATION OF DEBT CRISIS

A major source of the debt accumulation in the Southern Cone countries according to Professor Dornbusch of MIT "is the extraordinarily poor performance of domestic macroeconomic policy in virtually every Latin American country" (Dornbusch, 1985). One indicator of this is the inflation rate. Compared to a modest average *annual* rate of 6% during 1973-84 in low-income countries, Argentina's inflation rate was a whopping 181%, Brazil, 71%, Chile's 75%, and Mexico's 32%. Only Venezuela had a relatively low 12% rate. The indexation policies intended to soften the impact of raging inflation in some cases worsened the problem. Except in Mexico where the average national savings rate, 24% in 1979-84, it *fell* significantly in the other countries: from 26 to 17% in Argentina, 24 to 17% in Brazil, 12 to 7% in Chile, and from 36 to 26% in Venezuela. In low-income Asia, the national savings rate remained virtually constant at about 24% of their *considerably lower* incomes. Other indicators of macro-mismanagement in Latin American according to Dornbusch, are excessive budget deficits, (often the primary cause of the low national savings rate), exchange rate overvaluation, and failure to adjust to world prices. These policies induced capital flight and flight into importables.

It is true that the external shocks of 1980-82 such as dollar appreciation, real interest rate increases, fall in commodity prices, and the reduced demand for exports due to the recession in the OECD played a role in Latin debt accumulation. But those shocks affected *all developing countries* though perhaps not to the same degree. For instance, the real interest shock may have affected to a greater extent those debtors such as the Latin ones, a large proportion of whose debt was owed to private creditors at variable interest rates. But this need not have created a crisis. For instance, the Republic of China whose external liabilities at $43.1 billion at the end of 1984 are about the same as Argentina's and of which a greater proportion (43.5%) is at floating rates than Argentina's (36.5%), has not experienced debt-servicing problems and is considered, by lenders, unlikely to experience them. This is because of its better macroeconomic as well as microeconomic policies. Thus, one is led to conclude that perhaps *domestic mismanagement rather than external shocks explains the lion's share of the Latin debt accumulation.*

RECYCLING JAPANESE SURPLUSES. A SOLUTION?

The contrast between *prima facie* "profligacy" of many Latin governments and the "prudence" of governments of low-income Asian countries has its counterpart in the contrast between the "profligate" U.S. with its low savings, large budgetary and trade deficits and "prudent" Japan with its high savings and trade surpluses. But in suggesting that Japanese surpluses be "recycled" to solve the "collective debt problem" of the world, one should not forget an elementary arithmetical identity, that the world as a whole cannot run a deficit or a surplus. This means that

Japan's surplus equals the rest of the world's deficit, including that of the U.S.. Put another way, corresponding to Japan's surplus is her accumulation of claims against the rest of the world, that is, her investment in real and financial assets abroad including U.S. government obligations. Part of the Japanese surplus is financing the U.S. budgetary deficit. The U.S. was not making such an enormous demand on the rest of the world's savings in the 1970s when the Saudi surpluses were recycled. The U.S. was not even a net borrower then.

If the Japanese current account surpluses are no longer available to finance unchanged U.S. budgetary deficits to the same extent as at present, these deficits will exert pressure on world capital markets. The repercussions may well be adverse to the Latin debtors. *Ex-post,* a larger current account surplus or lower deficit would have to be squeezed out of the world outside of Japan. That process is likely to be painful to the developing countries.

If the invitation to the Japanese to solve the "debt overhang" is an invitation to them to exchange the stock of performing assets in their portfolio for the non-performing loans of American and other banks to Latin America, it is unlikely to be accepted. Recycling through greater borrowing by the World Bank in the Japanese capital markets depends on agreement being reached on a general capital increase for the Bank. Even that by itself will not permit an increased net transfer of resources to the debtor countries, unless the fundamental precondition for such an increased transfer is satisfied and an increased current account surplus of the combined creditor countries is generated.

BENEFITS AND COSTS OF FULLY MEETING DEBT SERVICE OBLIGATIONS

It is often suggested that making the Latin debtor service their debt fully now by running current account surpluses rather than by fresh borrowing involves an inappropriate and (on efficiency grounds) premature transfer of resources from the capital poor to the capital rich. Besides, their attempt to run trade surpluses at high levels of activity will succeed only if the industrialized countries including the U.S. are willing to open their markets to their exports. Such a transfer is "inappropriate" on efficiency grounds only if there will be no reversal of it in the reasonably near future. On the contrary, the transfer by debtors can be

viewed simply as an investment in re-establishing the lost confidence of
the foreign private creditors (and their own citizens exporting capital) in
their ability to service their debt and to pursue sensible policies. But
once confidence is re-established, private creditors would presumably
resume their lending and capital flight would be reversed. If not, a
stronger multilateral agency with a much enhanced lending role may be
required to overcome the sovereign risk problem and enforce
conditIonality. If this too is not possible, a number of debtor countries
would be rational in repudiating their debt, as they are unlikely to enjoy
the benefits of future access to international finance in any case. The
threat of protectionism in the industrialized world is real and has to be
fought tooth and nail anyway.

It is possible that the austerity necessarily involved in generating
the surpluses will adversely affect the relatively worse off in the debtor
countries. Whether it does or not is in part a matter of domestic policy
choice in these countries. After all, in many countries substantial cuts
can be made in subsidies to inefficient public-sector enterprises,,
expenditures on the military establishment and, unproductive activities
without affecting the poor significantly. Internal redistribution, through
land reform and other measures, is a means to help the poor whose
potential has by no means been exhausted in many of the debtor
countries. In any case some Latin governments have not been
particularly noted (at least in the past) for any excessive concern about
the welfare of their poor. It is regrettable that much of the debt of two
Latin American countries where democracy was restored only recently
(Brazil and Argentina) was incurred under the old military regimes.
Having a democratic government has, however, never been necessary or
sufficient for receiving aid. There would have been very few recipients,
had it been necessary.

THE FLOW OF EXTERNAL RESOURCES TO POOR DEVELOPING COUNTRIES

The United States was responsible for preventing a substantial expansion
of the resources of the International Development Association (IDA), the
soft-loan window of the World Bank that lends to poor countries on
concessional terms. Nor has it looked favorably upon a general capital
increase for the World Bank that will enable it to borrow from the

world's capital markets and augment its lending. Further, the U.S. has often suggested that a poor country like India, which has not borrowed significantly from private capital markets on non-concessional terms, should indeed do so. It is not obvious that the Baker and Conable proposals will substantially expand the volume of World Bank lending to the poor countries. It will be grossly unfair to the poor countries if the proposals end up merely diverting to the heavily indebted countries World Bank resources that might otherwise have gone to them without at the same time expanding the resource flow from IDA and thus pushing them into the private (non-concessional) market.

CONCLUSION

On both equity and efficiency grounds there is a strong, indeed an overwhelming case for a significant net transfer of resources from the industrial countries to the developing countries as a group.

The aid or concessionary component of this transfer, which should go to the poorest, is urgent and cannot wait. It must be kept in mind as regards aid that transferring resources to the poorest countries is not the same as transferring it to the poorest in these countries. This legitimate concern should be a spur to more effective design of aid programs rather than an excuse for canceling the entire effort. Because many potential recipients first have to re-establish the credibility of their future debt service, the non-concessionary part of the transfer towards the developing countries may not take place immediately but instead will be medium-term in nature. It is here that international institutional reform may conceivably speed up the reconstruction of debtor credibility. A stronger, reformed IMF-cum-World Bank (a "World Fund"?) with the expertise to design or evaluate stabilization and structural adjustment programs and the authority to enforce financial and real conditionality might help overcome, or at any rate reduce, the problems of sovereign risk and borrower credibility. However, the first problem with such a proposal is that an institution with the required degree of expertise and authority may be impossible to create. The second is that even if it were possible, the problems of national sovereignty of debtor nations in their relations with this "World Fund" would make its survival very dodgy.

The Baker and Bradley proposals fail where they involve, in different ways, undesirable distributions of the concessionary component of transfers at both ends (among the industrial "transferring" countries and among the receiving developing countries). In addition to the fairness issues, these proposals are problematic because the way in which the aid, concessionary, non-commercial or non-market part of the transfer is arranged interferes with and generally reduces the commercial or market part of the transfer.

The Baker proposal involves no long-run concessionary transfer to the developing countries and mainly concerns concessionary transfers within the industrial world: a transfer toward the shareholders, creditors and managements of the industrial countries' exposed commercial banking sector and, through the multilateral agencies' acquisition of bad bank debt, away from the industrial countries' taxpayers in general or, in the "Japan variant," from the Japanese saver or taxpayer. It will encourage a repeat of the often careless and incompetent sovereign lending policies pursued by the commercial banking system. Since debtors at most get temporary cash-flow relief, this incentive to "over lend" created by the Baker proposal may not be translated into a significant increase in net bank lending because of the reluctance of potential borrowers who have lived through the early and mid 1980s.

The Bradley proposal involves a significant net transfer toward the developing countries, but as the amount of relief given is likely to vary only with the magnitude of the debt and the magnitude of the debt problems, both equity and efficiency appear ill-served by it.

Where will the resources come from under the Bradley proposal, or under any proposal involving a net flow of resources towards the developing countries? Not by "tapping" the Japanese surplus, as the ODC recommends (Feinberg, 1986, p. 10). That, and more, is already fully tapped by the U.S. current account deficit (a "considerable world liability"?), itself a reflection of the U.S. budget deficit. Do we want the Japanese to run even a larger current account surplus to allow *ceteris paribus* the developing countries to lower their surpluses or increase their deficits? Whatever the academic merits of the case, one can imagine the howls of outrage in Europe and the U.S.A. if the Japanese were in fact to pursue policies aimed at increasing their surplus. That leaves Europe and the U.S.A. No prizes will be awarded for guessing the correct answer. A turnaround of the U.S. current account deficit, which requires a significant reduction of the U.S. budget deficit, is the *sine qua non* of a healthy net transfer of resources towards the developing countries. It is essential that this fiscal correction be achieved without a U.S. and world recession. The required U.S. current account surplus is a *full employment* surplus, not a recession-induced surplus. Here Europe and Japan can help, through coordinated fiscal and monetary policy measures aimed at keeping demand in line with potential supply.

It is apparent that the driving forces behind the Baker proposal are the exposure of the U.S. banking system in Latin America and the geographical proximity and/or geo-political significance to the U.S. of the major debtor countries. The Bradley proposal does not share this concern for U.S. commercial bank profits, but is even more emphatic on the need to provide relief to an area that is of great political and economic importance to the United States. As regards the U.S. banking system, it is clearly essential to prevent a financial panic, a "run on the banks" if the banks are forced to value their foreign loans as true market loans rather than at book value. This, however, is what the Federal Reserve Board's lender of last resort function is all about. It need not involve a "socialization" of the banks' losses, the form of socialism for the rich favored by much of the banking community. It is not beyond the combined wits of Paul Volcker and James A. Baker III to safeguard the integrity of the U.S. payments and credit mechanism while letting the shareholders, creditors and managers of the commercial banks with the bad loans take the full measure of the losses caused by bad luck and/or bad bank management. Continental Illinois, where the shareholders lost everything and the management was fired but the bank survived, is one example of what can be done.

Should the Southern debtor countries get aid and relief from the industrialized countries? If the U.S. government wishes to provide relief because this serves its perception of the U.S. national interest in Latin America, it should do so using its own resources. Multilateral agencies, which are not supposed to serve any individual country's national interest, should base their policies on criteria of global equity and efficiency. On those grounds, the major beneficiaries under the Baker and Bradley proposals should not in fact be given relief in preference to countries that are poorer and/or have pursued superior policies. It is not obvious why, as in the Mexican program, one country should be compensated for a deterioration in terms of trade or for real growth disappointments due to reasons beyond its control, without the arrangement being extended to every developing country.

On efficiency grounds, resources should flow to the country whose investment projects offer the highest rate of return. Unless there are clearly diagnosed reasons for international capital failure, such resource transfers can take place efficiently on commercial, market terms. Sovereign risk and the inability of borrowers to make credible commitment to commercial lenders concerning future economic and debt-servicing policies, are one such crucial cause of capital market failure. We have already argued that a more powerful multilateral organization (the "World Fund") might be able to overcome the problem of sovereign risk on its loans to developing countries. This would call for a large expansion of its lending activities, "crowding out," but less than one-for-one, commercial bank lending. This supranational lending, however, would still be lending on non-concessional terms. It would not be aid or relief. If such an arrangement (or any other one achieving the same objective) were to be in effect, of course, the spread over the Libor currently charged to rescheduling countries by the commercial banks would be much reduced or even eliminated, and the fat rescheduling fees would disappear. This is observationally equivalent to aid or relief, and the Southern Cone debtor countries, like all other debtors, are entitled to it. Neither proposal tries to address the issue of how to overcome sovereign risk and to restore borrower credibility. It is time to think twice before the human and financial resources of the multilateral agencies are concentrated excessively on one relatively small problem area and before scarce aid is diverted away from those most in need of it.

References

Balassa, Bela *et al.*, *Toward Economic Growth in Latin America*. A study commissioned by the Americas Society (1986).

Dornbusch, Rudiger, "Dealing with debt in the 1980's," *Third World Quarterly*, Vol. 7, No. 3 (1985), pp. 532-551.

Feinberg, Richard E. *et al.*, *Between Two Worlds: The World Bank's Next Decade*, U.S.-Third World Policy Perspectives No. 7, Overseas Development Council (New Brunswick: Transaction Books, 1986).

26

Swapping Third World Debt

Richard S. Weinert

Markets work. So President Ronald Reagan and his backers have taught legions of skeptics, and examples keep popping up in unlikely places. One is Third World debt. When the debt crisis arrived in 1982, many analysts — including this writer — foretold dire consequences if forceful action was not taken to write down the value of the debt and give relief to debtor countries. This did not happen. To date no public entity — creditor-country governments, debtor-country governments, the International Bank for Reconstruction and Development (World Bank), or the International Monetary Fund (IMF) — has taken any specific initiative to reduce debt-service burdens.

Yet markets have not been idle. Despite, or because of, the public policy vacuum, capital markets have begun to adjust. A new secondary market in discounted Latin American and other Third World debt has developed, with big discounts regularly applied to the debt's face value. In fall 1986, for example, Brazilian government debt could be bought for about 75 per cent of its face value; Mexican government debt for about 57 per cent; Philippines, 60 per cent; Argentine, 65 per cent; Chilean, 67 per cent; and Peruvian, 22 per cent. Bolivian and Nicaraguan debt, by contrast, each sold for less than 10 per cent of their face values. These steep discounts belie the claim that the loans are still good, that the debtor countries are merely experiencing some temporary illiquidity. The claim may be true, but the market does not believe it.

Understanding how and why this debt swapping developed and how it works will help reveal whether the practice should be encouraged or restrained. Even more important, it can show how swapping can serve as a model for a lasting and politically acceptable solution to the debt crisis that will help debtors and creditors alike.

The secondary market in debt serves three purposes that feed off each other. first, it enables private banks to readjust their portfolios by shuffling loans around, much as children trade baseball cards. Second, debtor countries encourage investors to use discounted debt to make investments. Third, debtors use the market to retire debt. Shuffling loans reduces risks to the international financial system by permitting individual banks to strengthen their balance sheets. Debtors have benefited by encouraging investment flows and by starting to lighten their debt burdens.

No one knows exactly how big the market for debt swaps has become. No transactions are publicized, and most banks are very secretive about them. It is clear, however, that the market is still small but growing quite rapidly. It may have totaled about $1 billion in 1984, $3 billion in 1985, and $6 billion in 1986. This trend is likely to continue and presents some challenges and opportunities to the world economy.

Initially, swapping was stimulated by some banks' desires to modify their exposure to troubled debtors. this could be done in several ways. The simplest would be for a bank to sell off its loans to a given country at a discount and register the loss suffered against its earnings. This tack was eventually taken by smaller banks to the extent that they had sufficient profits to absorb the loss or had already written the loans down to the market's discounted values. At first, however, such transactions were modest simply because there were no buyers, even at discounted prices.

Major creditors could not sell loans for two additional reasons. Financially, they could not afford to take the implicit losses. For example, large private banks typically held Latin American debt equal to two to three times their capital. to register a loss of even 25 per cent of that portfolio would imply wiping out one-half to three-fourths of their capital. This was clearly impossible. Moreover, the political consequences would have been unbearable. The world's big banks had painstakingly forged cooperative links on the debt issue that served all of their interests. For one bank to break ranks and try to dump its debt would have threatened those links and shaken international banking and capital markets.

Accounting gimmickry came to the rescue. By exchanging, or swapping, the debt of one country for that of another, banks could reduce or even eliminate their exposure in some countries without registering any loss. The key to this sleight of hand was what banks call "historical cost accounting." That is, some debt was on their books at its historical cost, or par, although its secondary-market value was far less.

Through intricate swaps involving higher-value debt for lower-value debt, the latter could be made to disappear with no loss registered. In this way, some large banks eliminated such countries as Nicaragua and Bolivia from their portfolios while taking on larger amounts of Mexican and Brazilian debts.

Some banks swapped debt not to reduce or eliminate loans to weak countries but to balance their portfolios. A bank with too much Mexican exposure could exchange it for some other comparable risk, such as Brazil or the Philippines, where its loans were relatively modest. Or a bank might wish to reduce the number of countries in its portfolio to simplify its administration — for example, by exchanging Chilean for Argentine debt. such transactions could also be structured to avoid any losses — or gains — even though the secondary-market valuations of the loans being exchanged differed.

In addition, debtor countries swapped loans to alter the foreign-debt exposure of their overseas branches. During the heyday of expanded international lending in the 1970s, many Third World countries entered global capital markets not only as borrowers, but also as lenders. Today this seems absurd, but at the time it was quite fashionable for public and private Latin banks to set up branches in the Bahamas, London, New York, and elsewhere, and to participate in the lending boom side by side with the major multinational banks. Predictably, banks from the larger countries such as Brazil and Mexico were the most numerous and the most active. But Argentine, Colombian, and Venezuelan banks played a significant role, and even Chilean and Peruvian banks dabbled in the Eurodollar market.

When the music stopped in 1982, these Latin banks found themselves in the awkward, not to say farcical, role of holding one another's debts. They were obliged to participate in each other's rescheduling efforts even while claiming hardships of their own. The situation cried out for a remedy.

The remedy was provided by the secondary market. Through swapping, banks of one country could exchange debts of other counties for their own country's debt. Thus Latin banks could shed their foreign loans and end up with what for them were domestic loans. From the debtor countries' point of view, even when carried out by private banks, this process in effect nationalized some of their debt. Although the debt was not retired, it no longer represented the same claim on foreign exchange. All the overseas Latin bank branches have swapped debts this way, and by the end of 1986 most of them will have reduced sharply, if not eliminated, their loans to other countries.

DEBT CAPITALIZATION

But a market limited to these kinds of swaps would have stagnated at very low levels. Real growth was stimulated when cash buyers appeared. Where did this money come from? It did not come from nontraditional lenders, such as insurance companies or pension funds, which some thought could be lured into the Third World. Having avoided these countries during the boom, these institutions not surprisingly maintained their distance during the bust. Nor did the cash come from private speculators, who have yet to join this drama to any significant degree.

Enter the debtors. For countries, retiring debt through direct purchases at discounted prices was problematical. How could a government plead with banks for lower interest rates and extended maturities while simultaneously prepaying debt through secondary-market purchases? Yet ways were found through imaginative programs of "debt capitalization." In December 1982, Brazil became the first country to adopt a debt capitalization scheme. Chile followed in June 1985 and Mexico announced its own version in mid-1986. Argentina, Bolivia, Costa Rica, and Ecuador are thought to be working on plans. Outside Latin America, the Philippines permitted three deals on an experimental basis and then formulated its program. Nigeria reportedly has also expressed interest. But Latin America is the source of most Third World debt and where most of the debt capitalization remains.

Debt capitalization schemes served two quite different purposes. One was to stimulate new investment by converting debt to equity. The second was to retire debt. For either purpose, a buyer would purchase foreign debt at a discount and obtain local currency. the debtor country thereby succeeded in retiring some of its foreign debt without using up any scarce foreign exchange.

The basic concept of converting debt to equity is quite simple. It borrows from the process of reorganizing bankrupt corporations with a view to revitalizing them. In corporate reorganizations, a common technique is to convert part of the debt owed to capital stock of the corporation. The result: lower corporate debt and thus lower interest burdens. Lenders receive some stock in the corporation in lieu of their loans, and if the company survives and prospers, they may see some return. The well-publicized Chrysler corporation bailout scheme employed this technique, and lenders eventually benefited.

Countries, of course, are not corporations, and this concept could not be applied directly. However, debt capitalization was conveniently married to another notion that became commonplace as bankers pondered with hindsight the origins of the debt crisis. Countries had acquired too much debt and not enough direct investment, they solemnly intoned. Debt, they observed, saddled countries with very high interest payments that had to be paid irrespective of changes in the world economy, such as plunging commodity prices, which rendered unprofitable some of the uses to which the borrowed funds had been put. In addition, borrowing countries were deprived of the discipline of the marketplace, which might have reined in some of the public investments made with borrowed funds.

Converting some of the existing debt to equity — capitalizing it — met this criticism. Governments devised schemes under which debt could be used to make an investment. This practice led to two types of transactions. First, banks might convert some of their own debt into local investment. Bankers Trust did this in Chile, converting some of its Chilean loans to shares in a pension management company. In Brazil, its loans were turned into shares in an investment bank. The National Commercial Bank of Saudi Arabia converted some of its Chilean loans into shares in industrial companies, and the American Express Company converted some Philippine debt into shares in a commercial bank.

The more common type of transaction, however, involved multinationals and used the secondary market. Fiat, for example, used Brazil's capitalization scheme to expand its plant there. It bought Brazilian debt at a discount and delivered it to the central bank. The central bank registered the debt as if it were a new investment and gave Fiat the cruzado equivalent of the face value of the debt. Nissan Corporation has arranged a similar deal in Mexico, and the Dow Chemical Company has entered one in Chile. Nissan and Dow shared the discount with the Mexican and Chilean central banks, respectively, receiving less than the peso equivalent of the face value of the debt. Whether used by banks or by multinationals, however, these schemes retired debt and transformed it into an equity investment. Moreover, debt capitalization stimulates new investment. The secondary market is an essential element in making this possible.

A second type of capitalization scheme aims directly at retiring debt. The idea is to permit someone to purchase foreign debt at a discount and to obtain payment in local currency. Chile has instituted the most ambitious and most successful program of this type to date. An enterprising investor, or a firm with a local operation, can purchase Chilean dollar debt at a discount and receive payment in pesos, which it can then use as it wishes. The central bank shares the benefit of the discount and succeeds in retiring foreign debt with local currency. Although anyone can use this scheme, it is designed for wealthy Chilean nationals. They may use some of their assets to buy Chilean debt and obtain pesos, which they might then use either to pay off local debts or to make new investments. By the end of 1986, Chile will have retired about $1 billion — about 5 per cent of its foreign debt — this way.

This form of capitalization scheme might induce Latin Americans who have transferred their holdings abroad to bring them back home, or at least prevent some of this flight capital from leaving. The sums involved are widely believed to represent a substantial percentage of Latin debt, and their return — even in part — would both alleviate the burden of debt service and stimulate growth through local investment.

Such schemes created a steady demand for cash purchases of Brazilian and Chilean foreign debt by companies that could use them locally. Because of these programs' technical complexities, they also generated a steady demand for more swapping. Generally, only certain types of Brazilian or Chilean debt are eligible. Often the holder of the eligible type is not willing to sell because of accounting or other considerations. The holder might, however, swap for some other similar debt or for debt of another country. Hence market dealers often have to construct a daisy chain of several swaps to produce a single purchase. For instance, a dealer might purchase Philippine debt, swap it for Brazilian, swap that for ineligible Chilean, and swap that for the eligible Chilean debt, which the dealer can sell. Some transactions have involved up to 20 steps. These cash purchases keep the secondary market expanding, and, through swapping, create cash purchases of the debt of countries lacking such schemes. For instance, Argentine debt might be sold by swapping it for Chilean debt, which could then be sold for cash.

Debtor countries benefit from these activities since they reduce their debt. But these countries have another option in the secondary market — to purchase their own debt directly. Direct, open purchases by debtor countries were not officially acknowledged as of late 1986, but several have come close. One large Argentine private bank, for instance, purchased substantial amounts of Argentine government debt at discounts and then used that debt to settle its own obligations with multinational banks. This step could only have been taken with Buenos Aires' knowledge and approval. A Venezuelan government bank has been active in purchasing at discounts debt of other Venezuelan government entities. There have been substantial purchases of Peruvian debt under circumstances that suggest governmental involvement, though officially they have been private transactions. This last case is especially interesting, since Peru has been behind on interest payments since October 1984 and since its debt commands only about 22 cents on the dollar. Peru may well have concluded that using, say, $22 million to retire $100 million in debt makes more sense than using this sum at face value to make a small dent in overdue interest, which now exceeds $600 million. It is only a matter of time before this use of the secondary market spreads.

Debt swapping is not a panacea for the debt crisis. Capitalization schemes and direct purchases can chip away at the debt mountain, but these transactions can substantially reduce debt overhang only over a very long period. To begin with, the market is relatively small. The few billion dollars' worth of swaps in 1986 is dwarfed by the several hundred billion dollars or so in total debt of the countries whose debt is traded in the secondary market. Moreover, structural limitations inhibit the use of the secondary market to retire debt. First, direct foreign investment in Latin America never exceeded more than a few billion dollars annually during the lending boom. Total foreign investment in Mexico, for example, is estimated at only $15 billion, compared with a total debt of some $100 billion. Even if capitalization schemes were to restore the investment flow to earlier levels, these would amount to only a small fraction of the debt service. Second, many of the largest creditors could not bear the financial or the political cost of liquidating their loans at substantial discounts. Therefore, much of the debt probably will not become available on the secondary market.

Retiring debt through capitalization schemes will be helpful at the margin, but will probably never amount to more than a few per cent per year of a country's debt, if that. Some flight capital may be seduced back (or inhibited from leaving), but political and economic uncertainties will continue to crimp that flow. Direct purchases will also help, but will be constrained by the very foreign-exchange limitations that produced the discounts in the first place.

IMPLICATIONS OF DEBT SWAPPING

The market has a significance beyond its size. As debt swapping expands and develops further, it will profoundly influence debtor-creditor negotiations. Bank creditors simply cannot continue solemnly to negotiate full-interest payments and multiyear reschedulings with other governments while dealing in the secondary market for the same debt at substantial discounts. Debtors will point to the market valuations of their loans to legitimate larger concessions, and banks will find it hard to insist on full market terms of rescheduling when the secondary market provides such different signals.

Thus far, only the market's benefits are apparent, but swapping poses a serious dilemma for U.S. bank regulators and accountants. Loans traded at deep discounts in the secondary market are carried at substantially higher values on banks' balance sheets. American banks still carry most of them at par. Canadian, Japanese, and West European banks have taken write-downs against many of these loans, but rarely to the levels applicable in the secondary market. How should banks account for loans traded at deep discounts? Should more write-downs be required? Does debt swapping require special accounting treatment?

There are good reasons to avoid wholesale write-downs. First, they could cause heavy losses at some banks and thus shake confidence in the financial system. Second, forcing banks to write down the debt to secondary-market values would undercut the prevailing strategy of dealing with the debt crisis. Since 1982, banks have been rescheduling and lending new money. At the 1985 IMF meetings, Secretary of the Treasury James Baker unveiled a plan that essentially called for more of the same — more rescheduling and more new lending in exchange for economic policy reforms by debtor countries. Cajoling banks to lend new money is difficult enough in today's circumstances; it would be impossible if combined with forced debt write-downs. No lender would willingly make new loans knowing that those loans would be immediately marked down below face value.

Yet the concern for conservative, prudent balance sheets argues for sharp write-downs in light of the economic deterioration of the borrowers, as signaled by secondary-market valuation. The accounting profession, backed by the Securities and Exchange Commission, has a strong institutional interest in large write-downs and disclosures, since accountants can be sued by disgruntled shareholders. Accountants therefore favor the largest write-downs and disclosures possible. Bank regulators, however, are more concerned with maintaining confidence in the financial system and facilitating banks' ability to raise capital. Consequently, they are torn between their support for conservative balance sheets and their fear of weakening banks and jeopardizing the rescheduling of Third World debt. The accounting profession examined debt swaps in 1985 and produced a set of accounting guidelines vague enough to permit significantly differing interpretations. Bank regulators have been looking hard at the secondary market but have yet to take a firm stand.

No one has suggested that banks immediately write down all or most of their debt to secondary market values, but many accountants feel that any secondary-market trade should trigger a write-down of the traded debt to its discounted value. These write-downs, however, can cause banks to record losses they would otherwise not have to record. Thus some banks are wary of the secondary market. Others are not participating at all for fear of accounting or regulatory disapproval. Banks that do swap battle continually to persuade their auditors and regulators to approve completed or proposed transactions.

But the secondary market helps everyone and should be encouraged by regulatory authorities. Creditors benefit because they can reduce or adjust their portfolios as they see fit. Debtors benefit because they reduce their foreign debt, gaining either an investment or the return of flight capital in the bargain. the financial system is strengthened as banks adjust and as debt burdens are lowered. Banks must continue to build their loan loss reserves but should not be required to register specific losses as a result of swapping debt.

Although swapping per se is no panacea for the debt crisis, the secondary market does contain the seeds of a more profound solution. As numerous analysts have suggested, the most promising approach to easing the crisis involves a partial assumption of the debt by public-sector entities in exchange for substantial interest-rate relief. The secondary market both suggests the basis for doing this and provides a mechanism. The basis would be to use the secondary-market valuation to determine the amount of interest-rate relief provided. the mechanism would be a swap: government bonds for Third World debt.

Suppose some public entity — the World Bank, developed-country governments, or some combination of the two — offered to swap its bonds for debts of troubled debtors. The swap would be voluntary and would be conditioned on a range of economic and political reforms. Obviously, the interest rate on these bonds would be lower than the rates on the debt, and the savings could be passed on to the debtor countries.

The main problems would involve determining the savings and avoiding offering relief to stronger countries. A solution could be based on the market valuation of a given country's debt. For example, Brazil's debt is currently offered at around 75 per cent of face value. In today's market, a government-entity 15-year dollar bond with an interest rate of 4.9 per cent would have a similar price. Mexico's debt goes for roughly 57 per cent of face value — approximately equivalent to a government-entity 15-year bond with an interest rate of 2.75 per cent. Hence, the government entity could issue bonds with those interest rates and offer to swap them on a one-for-one basis with banks. It would offer the 4.9 per cent bonds for Brazilian debt and the 2.75 per cent bonds for Mexican debt.

The rate on the government bonds, then, would depend on the value of the specific country debt for which they are swapped. This policy preserves differences among countries and concentrates assistance where it is needed most. Relatively well-off countries whose debt sells for relatively higher prices in the secondary market would receive bonds with correspondingly higher interest rates. A country whose debt commanded a very low market price would receive bonds with lower interest rates, and possibly longer maturities, to equalize their value with the value of that country's debts in the secondary market.

Debt swapping on this grand scale would not be a substitute for the economic and political reforms needed in debtor countries. On the contrary, only reforming debtor countries would be eligible to participate. Thus large-scale debt swapping would overcome a fatal weakness of the Baker plan — its insufficient incentives to carry out economic change that could be painful in the short run.

Moreover, this approach provides incentives in the right proportions. The least solvent countries probably need the most thoroughgoing reforms, and will have the greatest difficulty adopting them. They therefore need the strongest incentives. This form of debt swapping provides them through lower interest rates on bonds. Economically healthier countries would qualify for and receive less interest-rate relief through the bond swap.

Banks that accepted this swap would suffer reduced interest income in future years, but they would also strengthen their balance sheets by replacing uncertain assets with riskless ones. Regulators should facilitate the swap by not requiring any write-down, permitting banks to swap if they wished with no immediate effect on their balance sheets. Passing on the interest savings to debtors would strengthen the banks' financial situation and make repayment more likely. And because repayment would be more likely, there should be no cost to the bond-issuing government entity, which would be able to collect enough from Brazil and Mexico to make the necessary payments on the bonds it had issued.

The broader political and economic gains would probably exceed the financial gains. Such swapping could defuse a smoldering crisis. It could avert a political confrontation that threatens to sour relations between the United States and many countries. In fact, it would enable the United States to exercise leadership to alleviate severe financial strains in a way that would benefit all concerned. The resulting improvements for both debtors and creditors would facilitate economic growth worldwide and would increase trade — which would mean greater purchases of U.S. goods. Therefore, swapping would contribute to raising living standards in both debtor and creditor countries. Finally, this approach is consistent with free markets, whose emergence and valuation provide its very framework.

XI

RECENT DEVELOPMENTS IN THE EURODOLLAR MARKET

The final article of this reader examines the increasing integration and globalization of financial markets. Today the dollar value of financial flows between countries is 50 times greater than that of goods flows. The most important financial markets are the Eurodollar and Eurobond markets, sometimes also simply referred to as Eurocurrency markets since loans are no longer always determined in dollars. In these Eurocurrency markets banks buy and sell financial instruments outside of the jurisdiction of their home country; as a result they are not subject to local banking laws. For example, if Citibank, an American bank, operates in London and loans dollars to Nigeria, this transaction cannot be regulated by the Federal Reserve or any other US government agency.

Some economists have argued that this lack of regulation may lead to a global financial panic similar to what happened in the 1930's. Indeed most of the US banking regulations were passed after the 30's with the intention of increasing financial stability; the Eurodollar market allows banks to escape these laws. In the article below, "Guiding Global Finance," Joan Spero examines recent attempts to regulate international financial markets, particularly after the stock market crash of 1987.

27

Guiding Global Finance

Joan E. Spero

The globalization of financial markets is one of the most critical, though least understood, developments in the international economy in recent years. World financial flows now dwarf goods flows by a factor of 50 to 1. Integrated global markets such as the Eurobond and Euroequity markets have developed; national markets now welcome foreign international participation; and, increasingly, national markets are joined electronically.

It took the stock market crash of October 1987, however, to demonstrate just how closely linked international financial stability and world economic prosperity now are. The crash was fundamentally a result of a persistent disequilibrium in the international economy, which was then reflected through the various national financial markets. But the October crisis also revealed new risks created by the global markets themselves and exposed the danger of great instability in the new, closely integrated world system.

Little attention has been given to the fact that the crash of 1987 was a global phenomenon influenced by the new international characteristics of the markets. Although the various studies that analyzed the October crash did note the importance of globalization, none examined in depth the practical implications: the significance of swift flows of information and panic around the globe made possible by new global information systems; the availability of large pools of funds that could and did move around the world at the push of a button in response to troubling economic information; and the integration of formerly isolated national economies into one increasingly seamless global market.

Three central developments in the 1980's have driven the globalization of financial markets. First, deregulation ended many controls around the world on foreign investment in financial services and on international capital flows. Second, advanced technology enabled financial institutions to use computers to create new products unimagined only a few years ago and to apply sophisticated communications technology to link markets and offer financial products globaly, often on a 24-hour basis. Finally, volatility of prices, exchange rates, and interest rates led to a demand for innovative ways to hedge against or take advantage of new risks.

The consequence was a dramatic increase in international market activity. Between 1980 and 1986 new international bond issues — Eurobonds and bonds issued by foreigners in various domestic markets — rose from $38.3 billion to $225.4 billion. Trading in Eurobonds issued shot from $240 billion to $3,570.1 billion. Euroequity offerings of common and preferred stock jumped from $200 million in 1983 to $11.8 billion in 1986. And in 1986 U.S. investors bought and sold a record $277.6 billion worth of U.S. domestic corporate stock.

In such a world, purely domestic financial markets are a thing of the past, as the chain-reaction effects of the October crash made clear. Before deregulation, national markets were deliberately shielded from international influences by capital controls and regulations on interest rates and lending policies. But in the 1980's, countries decided to modernize national financial markets to spur national growth. They began to remove exchange controls, eliminate regulations on interest rates, dismantle barriers among different types of financial institutions, and open domestic markets to foreigners.

Great Britain's "Big Bang" — so called because most of the changes were implemented simultaneously in October 1986 — was the first major national reform. It replaced fixed commissions with negotiated rates, removed barriers among different types of financial institutions, opened domestic securities markets to foreigners, and set up a new system of financial regulation and supervision. This bold reform of the British financial system set off a competitive chain reaction. Canada's "Little Bang," launched in 1987, is removing barriers between the "four pillars" of commercial banking, investment banking, trust banking, and insurance; ending limits on foreign participation in Canadian markets; and establishing new regulatory responsibilities. Other smaller "bangs" are going off in France, the Netherlands, Sweden, and West Germany. By 1992 the European Economic Community (EEC) plans to remove barriers among its member states and to lower barriers among different types of financial institutions. Even Japan has progressively deregulated interest rates, allowed foreign firms into the Tokyo Stock Exchange and the Securities and trust banking businesses, opened the Tokyo Offshore Banking Market, and allowed greater international use of the yen. In the United States, institutions have found cracks in the regulations that enable them to broaden their activities.

As deregulation progresses, securities firms are moving into areas once dominated by banks. Banks in turn are taking on characteristics of securities firms and investment banks. Institutions diversify their overseas activities to seize new opportunities and escape domestic regulatory restrictions. For example, U.S. and Japanese commercial banks, barred from engaging in securities activities at home, have set up investment banking operations abroad.

As banks did before them, securities firms are establishing branches in all the world's major financial centers. Foreign firms may now join the London Stock Exchange, and 76 have done so. Foreigners received 16 of the 22 new seats in 1987 on the Tokyo Stock Exchange.

To compete with a broader array of products, firms are also developing international alliances, many across traditional institutional lines. Credit Suisse, a Swiss commercial bank, owns 44.5 per cent of what is now Credit Suisse-First Boston. Sumitomo Bank Ltd. of Japan has invested in US-based Goldman, Sachs and Company, and Nippon Life Insurance Company has purchased a share of Shearson Lehman Hutton. In Europe, Banque Nationale de Paris of France has bought Ark Securities of Britain, and Barclays de Zoete Wedd, a British bank, now owns 70 per cent of Puget, a French brokerage house.

Meanwhile, borrowers are approaching international markets to raise funds. In 1986 U.S. issuers raised a record $43.7 billion through international bond issues while foreign issuers raised $6.1 billion in the U.S. bond market. Increasingly companies list and trade stocks outside their home countries. At the end of 1986, 512 foreign corporations had listed their securities on the London Stock Exchange, 59 foreign companies had been listed in the New York Stock Exchange, and 52 had been listed on the Tokyo Stock Exchange.

Trading volume in these foreign shares is mounting steadily. Turnover volume for foreign equity issues on all West German exchanges was 11.6 per cent in 1986. On the New York Stock Exchange, trading in foreign equity issues increased from 3.7 per cent of total volume in 1986 to 4.5 per cent in 1987. By early 1988, trading in foreign equities for customers accounted of nearly 30 per cent of total equity trading on the London Stock Exchange.

Closely related to the global nature of the financial markets today is their dependence on technology. The widespread application of new technologies in communications and computers has reduced transaction costs and stimulated the creation of new, complex financial instruments. Information is cheaper and easier to obtain. Even with markets in different time zones, investors and borrowers worldwide are in competitive equality and react instantaneously. They trade around the clock and around the world. Because technology enables financial transactions to take place more frequently and more rapidly, there has been a sharp increase in recent years in the velocity of money, in the liquidity of markets, and in the magnitude of international capital flows. Various trading exchanges are now linked across national boundaries. Trading linkages have been established between the American Stock Exchange and the European Options Exchange; between the London Stock Exchange and the National Association of Securities Dealers Automated Quotations, better known as NASDAQ, in the United States; and between the Chicago Mercantile Exchange and the Singapore Monetary Exchange.

More and more, large institutional investors such as pension funds, money market and equity funds, and insurance companies are dominating today's markets. From 1980 to 1987, large block transactions conducted by institutions grew from 29.2 per cent of total reported volume on the New York Stock Exchange to 51.2 per cent of total reported volume. Institutions are also playing a greater role in Japan, where individual stock transactions fell from 40.7 per cent of total transactions in 1982 to 29.2 per cent in 1986.

The concentration of financial assets has encouraged the managers of these funds to develop sophisticated global management techniques to control these large pools of capital. Professional fund managers now move money regularly across international boundaries to diversify risk and to take advantage of market differentials. As home governments have eased controls on purchases of foreign securities, foreign investment by private-sector pension funds has shown a dramatic jump. Foreign investment by British pension funds soared from $9.7 billion in 1980 to $56.6 billion in 1986, or from 9 per cent to 20 per cent of total assets. And foreign investment by Japanese private pension funds rose from $400 million in 1980 to $14.5 billion in 1986, or from 1 per cent to 10 per cent of total assets.

In placing this flow of capital, financial innovations are running rampant. They appear in a greater variety of currencies than ever before. For example, one of the most rapidly growing markets involves currency and interest-rate swaps. Swaps are agreements to exchange streams of payments over time. Currency swaps were devised to take advantage of the better access to certain currencies of different parties; exchanging those currencies, therefore, can lower their risks or reduce their costs. Similarly, interest-rate swaps are based on the different interest-rate terms available to different borrowers. Parties to interest-rate swaps, for example, may exchange fixed-rate securities for floating rates of fixed-rate flows in one currency with floating-rate flows in another currency. The global market for interest-rate swaps outstanding in 1986 was estimated at $341 billion, up from $170 billion in 1985 and just $3 billion in 1982. The estimated combined size of the outstanding interest-rate and currency swaps may have reached as much as $400 billion in 1987.

Another characteristic of today's markets is securitization — that is, the growing practice of raising and investing money through securities such as bonds and equities rather than through bank lending and borrowing. Securities firms have prospered by offering better rates and more flexible and innovative terms than the banks. In 1983, for the first time, new bond issues in the Euromarkets surpassed the volume of syndicated commercial bank loans there. Securitized financings accounted for only 44 per cent of funds raised on the international financial markets in 1982. By the end of 1986 this figure was 87 per cent.,

SYSTEM SAFEGUARDS

The new global markets accentuate the dangers of financial crises. Thanks to technology, huge amounts of capital move rapidly across national boundaries. Further, greater information may actually contribute to more, rather than less, market volatility as traders and investors overreact or panic. During the October crash such responses were in alarming evidence. Consequently, globalizing financial markets also increases the speed and force with which market shocks are transmitted around the world, increasing the volatility in and the vulnerability of the total system.

Moreover, foreign capital tends to be more unstable than domestic capital. Foreign investors generally have less information available to them, are more concerned about currency risk, and are also less confident that their interests will be taken care of in the event of a crisis. When a crisis does occur — for instance, when the Franklin National Bank collapsed in 1974, when Continental Illinois faced financial problems in 1984, or when the stock market crashed in October 1987 — foreign capital is the first to flee. Its actions cause trouble for those institutions that rely heavily on foreign funds. In October 1987 the London and Frankfurt markets, which rely more heavily on foreign investors, declined more than those in New York and Tokyo. In Tokyo the foreign investors were selling Japanese shares while Japanese investors were buying. According to Brady, now the U.S. treasury secretary, Japanese investors' heavy selling of U.S. government bonds precipitated the October crash.

At the national level, countries have developed a variety of mechanisms to safeguard the financial system from shocks caused by the collapse of financial institutions. Deposit insurance, for example, is intended to prevent a crisis of confidence among bank customers. In addition, central banks in practice do act as lenders of last resort to the financial system. In the event of a real or threatened crisis, they provide liquidity to the system either by lending to individual institutions through the discount window in the United States or by injecting liquidity into the system overall through open market operations and changes in reserve requirements. In the even of a global crisis, however, there is no well-understood concept of international lender of last resort.

In recent years some international cooperation has emerged among central banks and regulators to improve the safety and soundness of the international banking system. The Cooke committee and the Basel Concordat set guidelines for worldwide supervisory activities and , by implication, for arrangements approximating lender-of-last-resort responsibility for offshore banking. However, those agreements, as well as historical experience, assume a financial system dominated by banks and threatened by banking crises. That world no longer exists.

Understandably, there is no tradition of lender of last resort for nonbank financial institutions such as securities firms. Traditionally banks have been considered special, both as holders of consumer deposits and as tools of national economic policy. For this reason, banks have had access to various forms of public insurance and to central bank lending. Although individual institutions were not to be protected against loss, the depositor was; and the system was shielded from collapse. Securities firms, however, were considered risk takers, especially in the United States, with no special need for access to central bank lending.

But in a world where nonbank institutions constitute a growing part of the international financial markets, attention must be paid to the impact that these firms have on the international system's financial safety and soundness. In the recent crash, the West's central banks did, in fact, act as lenders of last resort to the new, global securities markets. When markets began to collapse around the world, the first reaction of many banks that had lent to institutions in those markets was to reduce lines of credit. Such a policy would have had disastrous contracting effects on international markets. The world's central banks recognized this reality and strongly encouraged banks to continue lending to securities firms by providing greater liquidity to the system through open market operations. At the same time, central banks and other supervisory authorities sent examiners into banks and kept in close contact with their officials and with each other to assure that bank lending to securities firms was based on adequate credit and thus did not threaten the banking system. Fortunately, this informal central bank intervention was sufficient. Because the crisis did not reach a point of requiring central bank lending to trouble financial institutions, authorities did not have to come to grips with whether and how they would have make funds available.

Financial officials also took other steps. The Bank of England helped to provide market support for the public sale of shares of the British Petroleum Company, calming the markets and setting a floor on underwriter losses. Japan's Ministry of Finance kept in close touch with the "Big Four" Japanese securities firms, including discussing with them the government's plans to issue Nippon Telegraph and Telephone stock to the public according to a November 1987 schedule.

Quick and creative action worked — this time. Before there is a next time, authorities need to explore the new demands on the lenders of last resort created by the global securitized markets.

As the October 1987 crash demonstrated, the globalization of financial markets has brought not only benefits but also risks. Regrettably, the Brady commission report and other studies of the events of October provide no analysis of those risks, nor do they advance guidelines for developing public policies to address them. Yet given the global nature of financial markets, governments cannot adequately improve the safety and soundness of national markets without considering their new international dimension. In the post-October era, as policymakers try to modify the rules of financial markets, they must also act on international issues.

First, national regulatory reform must take into account international reality. In the United States, the Glass-Steagall separation of commercial banking from securities and investment banking should be overhauled to reflect the blurring lines among institutions both at home and abroad. Glass-Steagall has become not a first line of defense against risky activities, but a Maginot line that cannot be defended and needs to be redefined. The degree of change at home plus the freedom of activity abroad make it impossible to put the genie back in the bottle. Regulation is needed that takes into account the new diversification in activities of financial institutions but that also provides adequate regulation of those activities. Several proposals presented in the 100th Congress would have authorized various degrees of diversification and provide regulation by function. The Depository Institutions Affiliation Act would have created a new federal charter alternative to allow financial and nonfinancial activities to be conducted in separately capitalized subsidiaries of a holding company regulated along functional lines; to provide safeguards, or fire walls, to insulate and protect insured entities; to provide regulators with more flexible powers over affiliated transactions; and to allow any company that wished to continue functioning under its current regulatory scheme and existing legal restrictions to do so. Legislation of this type should be enacted.

Second, regulatory and supervisory reform cannot stop at the water's edge. the international community needs to begin now to develop compatible and effective standards for international securities regulation along the lines of the common banking standards developed over the last decade. Many countries are re-examining national regulatory policy as a result of evolving market reality and of the October 1987 crash. The EEC is developing its own market for securities.

This would be a good time to inject international realities into the development of national and regional policies. To do that, cooperation among international securities regulators must be expanded.

Forums for international dialogue such as IOSCO should be energized through a mandate to achieve similar standards and practices. Perhaps the Group of Seven, the leading democratic industrial countries, should set up an international body similar to the Brady commission. Such a commission could examine jointly the new international nature of financial markets, the regulatory gaps, and the need to modernize regulation, clearance, and settlement. Such a study could provide not only analysis but also an agenda for change. It could suggest guidelines for improving operational efficiency and financial strength of clearing and settlement systems. It could also develop an agenda for regulatory modernization.

The chairman of the SEC, David Ruder, has suggested a set of principles that could serve as a model for evolving global regulatory standards. They are based on American law and include minimum disclosure, auditing, and accounting standards; minimum market fairness and antifraud and manipulation principles; widespread availability of current market information; safe and efficient international clearance and settlement systems; adequate registration, qualification, and conduct requirements for broker-dealers; steps to ensure the financial integrity of multinational financial firms; and international market surveillance and mutual assistance in conducting enforcement investigations. This list, or some other, could be the basis for international discussion and study. Early agreement is unlikely. But because the issues are so important, the process must begin now.

Finally, central bankers must act to protect the global financial system. Modernization of financial regulation at the national level and cooperation among securities regulators at the international level are necessary but not sufficient. the system also needs lenders of last resort. Central banks have the responsibility and the financial means for preserving the safety and soundness of the system. They must consider broadening the lender-of-last-resort policy to cover, directly or indirectly, securities firms, investment banks, and other financial intermediaries that now play key roles in the system. As with banking, this does not mean bailing out individual institutions or their managers.

It does mean protecting the financial system and the economy from unacceptable and unforeseen shocks.

Central bankers already have a framework for expanding the lender of last resort. Through their cooperation in the Cooke committee they have now redefined the national lender-of-last-resort concept and coped with various shocks to international banking markets during the 1970's. Their history of past efforts should make it possible for them to work together to expand the concept yet again. It should also make it possible for them jointly to review problems in bank settlement systems.

The October 1987 crash has brought to the forefront a number of important issues that regulators and market players alike need to address. Now is the time to recognize the global character of financial markets. The common goal is a prosperous global economy. But the world's advanced economies may experience several serious shocks in pursuit of that goal if they do not act now to ensure the continuing safety and soundness of the global financial system.

Acknowledgments

I

The Cost of Trade Restraints: Charles Collyns and Steven Dunaway, from *IMF Staff Papers*, March 1987; pp. 150-175. Reprinted with permission.

Voluntary Export Restraints:: Clemens F. J. Boonekamp, from *Finance and Development*, December 1987; pp. 2-5. Reprinted with permission.

The Evolution of Protection in Textiles and Apparel: William R. Cline. Institute for International Economics. Reprinted with permission.

Japan's Intangible Barriers to Trade in Manufacturers: Dorothy Christelow from *Federal Reserve of New York Quarterly Review*, Winter '85-'86; pp. 11-18. Reprinted with permission.

Countertrade, Offsets, Barter and Buybacks: Stephen S. Cohen with John Zysman, © [1986] by the Regents of the University of California. Reprinted /Condensed from the *California Management Review*, Vol. 28, No. 2. By permission of The Regents.

II

Creating Comparative Advantage: Bruce Scott, from *U.S. Competitiveness in the World Economy*; pp. 75-102. Reprinted with permission.

Is Free Trade Passé?: Paul R. Krugman from *Economic Perspectives*, Fall 1987; pp. 131-144. Reprinted with permission.

U.S. Competitiveness: Beyond the Trade Deficit: George N. Hatsopoulos, Paul R. Krugman, Lawrence H. Summers, from *Science* , July 15, 1988; 1 Report, Vol. 241 ; pp. 299-307. © 1988 by the AAAS. Reprinted with permission.

III

Trade Conflicts of the 1980s: Robert Henriques Girling, from *Multinational Institutions in the Third World Management, Debt, and Trade Conflicts in the*

The International Monetary System: Should it be Reformed?: Jacob Frenkel , from *American Economic Review*, May 1987; pp. 205-210.

VIII

Back to Keynesianism: Reforming the IMF: Frances Stewart, from *World Policy* journal, Summer 1987; pp. 465-484. Reprinted with permission.

The IMF Under Fire: Jahangir Amuzegar from *Foreign Policy*, Fall 1986; pp. 98-119 Reprinted with permission.

IX

Correcting the Trade Deficit: Martin Feldstein; pp. 795-806. Reprinted with permission of *Foreign Affairs*, Spring 1987. Copyright 1987 by the Council on Foreign Relations, Inc.

Exchange Rate Policy. The J-Curve, the Fire Sale, and the Hard Landing: Paul Krugman from *American Economic Review*, May 1989; pp. 31-35. Reprinted with permission.

X

Making the Brady Plan Work: Jeffrey Sachs; *Foreign Affairs*, Summer '89. Reprinted with permission.

Rewarding the Profligate and Punishing the Prudent and Poor: Some Recent Proposals for Debt Relief: Willem H. Buiter and T. N. Srinivasan from *World Development*; March 1987; pp. 411-8. Reprinted with permission.

Swapping Third World Debt: Richard S. Weinert. Reprinted with permission from *Foreign Policy* '65 (Winter 1986-87). Copyright 1986 by the *Carnegie Endowment for International Peace*.

IX

Guiding Global Finance: Joan E. Spero; Reprinted with permission from *Foreign Policy* '73 (Winter 1988-89). Copyright 1988 by the *Carnegie Endowment for International Peace*.